NIGHTWALKING

NIGHTWALKING

A Nocturnal History of London
Chaucer to Dickens

Yvonne, with best wishes,

MATTHEW BEAUMONT

Matthew Beaumont

VERSO
London • New York

This book is dedicated to my sons
Jordan and Aleem Beaumont

First published by Verso 2015

Some sections of Chapters 13 and 14 were first published in different form as 'The Mystery of Master Humphrey: Dickens, Nightwalking and *The Old Curiosity Shop*', in the *Review of English Studies* 65 (2013), pp. 118–36.

p. 1: From *London Night* by John Morrison and Harold Burkedin, 1934

p. 73: 'A Most Wicked Work of a Wretched Witch', printed by Richard Burt, c. 1592 (woodcut), English School (sixteenth century) / © Lambeth Palace Library, London, UK / Bridgeman Images

p. 109: 'Times of the Day: Night', from *The Works of William Hogarth*, 1833 (litho), William Hogarth (1697–1764) / Private Collection / Ken Welsh / Bridgeman Images

p. 261: 'Colinet's Fond Desire to Know Strange Lands', illustration from Dr Thorton's *The Pastorals of Virgil* (woodcut), William Blake (1757–1827) / Southampton City Art Gallery, Hampshire, UK / Bridgeman Images

1 3 5 7 9 10 8 6 4 2

Verso
UK: 6 Meard Street, London W1F 0EG
US: 20 Jay Street, Suite 1010, Brooklyn, NY 11201
www.versobooks.com

Verso is the imprint of New Left Books

ISBN-13: 978-1-78168-795-6 (HB)
eISBN-13: 978-1-78168-796-3 (US)
eISBN-13: 978-1-78168-797-0 (UK)

British Library Cataloguing in Publication Data
A catalogue record for this book is available from the British Library

Library of Congress Cataloging-in-Publication Data
A catalog record for this book is available from the Library of Congress

Typeset in Electra by MJ & N Gavan, Truro, Cornwall
Printed and bound by CPI Group (UK) Ltd, Croydon, CR0 4YY

Contents

Acknowledgments

The Leverhulme Trust funded the research on which this book is based and, first and foremost, I'd like to thank this institution for its generosity in awarding me a Research Fellowship in 2012–13. At a time when scholarly activity is more and more instrumentalized, more and more closely monitored, the Leverhulme Trust is exemplary for the freedom and independence it affords the academics whose scholarship it sponsors. I owe a deep debt of gratitude to those who supported my application: Rachel Bowlby, Terry Eagleton, Kate Flint, Colin Jones and Jo McDonagh.

My thanks go to the following for making reading suggestions, inviting me to present my ideas in the form of papers and lectures, or, more generally, providing me with encouragement and support in this project: Tariq Ali, Rosemary Ashton, Jo Barratt, Tim Beasley-Murray, Amelia Beaumont, Joanna Beaumont, Michael Beaumont, Sebastian Budgen, Ardis Butterfield, Stephen Cadywold, Ben Campkin, Warren Carter, Gregory Claeys, Holly Clayson, Oskar Cox Jensen, Greg Dart, Paul Davis, Joseph Drury, Ger Duijzings, Geoff Dyer, Gavin Everall, Mark Ford, Anita Garfoot, Helen Hackett, Andrew Hemingway, Clive Holtham, Philip Horne,

Ludo Hunter-Tilney, Colin Jones, Natalie Jones, Tom Keymer, Roland-François Lack, Eric Langley, Andy Leask, Rob Maslen, Jo McDonagh, China Miéville, John Mullan, Andrew Murray, Lynda Nead, Katherine Osborne, Francesca Panetta, William Raban, Neil Rennie, Jo Robinson, Will Self, Jane Shallice, Natasha Shallice, Bill Sharpe, Alison Shell, Nick Shepley, Nick Shrimpton, Chris Stamatakis, Gabriel Stebbing, Hugh Stevens, Matthew Sweet, Jeremy Tambling, John Timberlake, Sara Thornton, Susan Watkins, Abigail Williams and Henry Woudhuysen. Those friends, colleagues and acquaintances who made reading recommendations relating to nightwalking in the later nineteenth or twentieth centuries will, I'm afraid, have to be thanked in the sequel to this book.

For reading chapters in draft form and offering perceptive and constructive criticism, I am especially grateful to Michael Beaumont, Greg Dart, Paul Davis, Helen Hackett, Ludo Hunter-Tilney, Jo McDonagh, Nick Papadimitriou and Chris Stamatakis. Above all, I am grateful to Will Self, who read the entire book in draft form and whose support throughout its composition has been of incalculable importance to me.

Tom Penn commissioned this book, though he has since moved to Penguin, and I'd like to record my heartfelt gratitude to him. Leo Hollis inherited the project, but his commitment to it has been unstinting and in his reading of the manuscript he has been as encouraging as he has been penetrating – I could not have hoped for a better editor. My sincere thanks, too, to Mark Martin, in Verso's New York offices, for overseeing the book's production so efficiently; and to Charles Peyton for his judicious copyediting.

Finally, for accompanying me on nightwalks in London and its fringes on various occasions over the last couple of years, I owe special thanks to Ludo Hunter-Tilney, Nick Papadimitriou, Will Self and David Young. These walks, and the meandering conversations that accompanied them, have influenced this book in ways that, though perhaps not immediately apparent, have nonetheless been of crucial importance. 'This page too', as the poet Octavio Paz wrote in his 'Nocturno de San Ildefonso', is a ramble through the night.

The book is dedicated, with all my love, and in admiration, to my sons Jordan and Aleem Beaumont.

Foreword

By Will Self

In the 'Oxen of the Sun' episode of *Ulysses*, having encountered each other *en passant* earlier in the day, the novel's two protagonists are finally thrown together. Seated with a bunch of rowdy medical students and their assorted hangers-on in the hall of Dublin's Holles Street maternity hospital, Leopold Bloom's paternal feelings are aroused by the spectacle of Stephen Dedalus who, while surpassing eloquent, is nonetheless sinking deep into his cups. As Mrs Purefoy struggles through the endgame of her three-day labour in the ward above, so the novel's narrative struggles through chronologically successive English prose styles, from alliterative Anglo-Saxon to the rambunctious discursiveness of Dickens. The familiar analysis of these parodies is that they are a conflation of ontogeny and phylogeny: just as the Purefoy baby's gestation is assumed (by Joyce, in line with the scientific thinking of the day) to have recapitulated the stages of human evolution. So the text itself undergoes mutagenesis: its physiology and morphology altering to adapt to changed environments.

But if Mrs Purefoy gives birth to an infant, what precisely is it that the contractions and dilations of Joyce's prose give birth to? In part, it is to an actualization of the paternal feeling that Bloom has towards Stephen. But this sentiment finds its fuller expression in what they do together, which is to walk – specifically, to nightwalk. First, *seriatim*, they proceed to Mrs Bella Cohen's brothel at 82 Lower Tyrone Street; then, entwined, they progress to the cabman's shelter by Butt Bridge; finally, in concert, they head to Bloom's house at 7 Eccles Street.

Here, Bloom, after a long and eventful day, is able to think himself – and then actually be – at home; but for Stephen the situation is more problematic. The complacently cuckolded Bloom has absented himself from Eccles Street so his wife may keep an assignation. He is also, as a canvasser of newspaper advertisements, a peripatetic worker; moreover he partakes – in virtue of his ancestry – of the Wandering Jew's mythos, just as his diurnal divagations resonate with the decade the Homeric Odysseus took to return home to Ithaca after the Trojan War.

Yet return Bloom has: he is, in this sense, what Matthew Beaumont characterizes as a 'noctambulant': one who walks by night perhaps with some pleasure-seeking or voyeuristic purpose, although this may well be ulterior to the sheer enjoyment of the act itself.

Stephen, by contrast, is what Dickens terms in his celebrated essay 'Night Walks', 'houseless': having determined he will no longer sleep at the Martello tower in Sandymount he has nowhere to lay his head – yet he refuses Bloom's offer of a bed, preferring to assume the role of what Beaumont calls a 'noctivagant', namely one who walks by night either because he is impoverished, or possibly because he has criminal intent (although, of course, the two motivations are highly congruent).

The city that Bloom and Stephen traverse by night is Dublin rather than the London that Beaumont concentrates his night-vision on; and *Ulysses* itself is beyond the time period of the texts this study explicates. But for Beaumont, 'pedestrianism is not some primal, pre-social activity … It is a highly mediated, heavily freighted social activity.' He evokes Mikhail Bakhtin's notion of the 'chronotope' (meaning: 'the intrinsic connectedness of temporal and spatial relationships that are artistically expressed in literature') in order to explain how it is that the nightwalker's peregrinations have, throughout the centuries, been choreographed by successive English writers.

Here, the nightwalker emerges as a half-formed thing out of the Stygian darkness of the medieval period: these passages of the book, concerned as they are with a society in which movement by night was *ipso facto* delinquency, naturally concern themselves as much with the evolution of common law as with the ontogeny of the nightwalker; the texts surveyed may be unfamiliar to the non-specialist reader, and the density of factual detail can seem forbidding. Nonetheless, this substantive grounding is essential if we are to read Beaumont rightly. For what emerges from his careful synthesis is nothing less than a grand unifying theory of the counter-Enlightenment.

In his close readings of Shakespeare, Johnson, Blake, Wordsworth, De Quincey et al., Beaumont establishes a methodology that is itself a form of circumambulation: he moves around his material as an eighteenth-century promenader might revolve a landscaped garden, each circuit affording new parallaxes and perspectives – political, exegetical, philosophic – until a complete chronotope of nightwalking is achieved. Beaumont tells us that 'the literary genre of the nocturnal picaresque emerges at the end of the seventeenth century', and that, as we wander on into the eighteenth century, 'the trajectories of the poet and the vagrant in the landscape became closely entangled'.

But it is in the context of the urban – with special reference to London – that nightwalking becomes a sort of crux, joining together the personally poetic with the politically polemical; Beaumont reminds us that by the 1740s London had become, despite its superficial order, 'a city perpetually shaped and reshaped by the processes of capital accumulation, including property speculation and the dispossession of the poor'.

It is this real, social foundation for nightwalking – if you like, the ground beneath their feet – that fans the flames of Beaumont's indignation. This anger has been latent from the outset, but repressed in keeping with the necessary silence of the anonymous and the unrecorded. However, his analysis of the ambulatory Romantics leads

Beaumont to posit a dialectical relationship between their cult of the sensitized individual and the denial of personae to the benighted urban masses they wander among; and it is this dialectic that allows us to see nightwalking as a *détournement* (in the sense expounded by the Situationists) of both the philosophic Enlightenment and the physical illumination of the city in the nineteenth century.

Nightwalking is thus a book that takes flight from what, on the face of it, is a fairly restricted zone of enquiry, to become a very broad and intensely deep evocation of the strange gearing-together of social change and the human psyche.

Beaumont quotes Blake's *The Marriage of Heaven and Hell*, 'Improvement makes strait roads, but the crooked roads without Improvement, are roads of genius', to illustrate the way that nightwalking has always implied dissent from the strophic regimentation of capital, which takes the city for its *topos* – to be worked and reworked – and the circadian to be its favoured metre. In cities that had yet to be freeze-dried into the twenty-four-hour, strip-lighting of the Spectacle, the nightwalk may have been many things, but first and foremost it was a *dérive* – a drift away from the straitened and narrow into the wild, the ludic and the untrammelled.

Beaumont quotes approvingly the Marxist social historian and sometime taxi driver Henri Lefebvre: '[Urban space has] a structure far more reminiscent of flaky *mille-feuille* pastry than of the homogeneous and isotropic space of classical (Euclidean/Cartesian) mathematics.' Thus the nightwalk through the city is a sublation – in the Hegelian sense – of the city's own false consciousness, lifting it up and exalting it in purifying darkness. Also quoted in *Nightwalking* is a letter from Charles Lamb to William Wordsworth: 'The wonder of these sights impels me into nightwalks about her crowded streets, and I often shed tears in the motley Strand from fullness of joy at so much Life.'

Life being the *mot juste*, because just as Dickens, with his relentless cerebration and equally relentless pacing, comes to epitomize for Beaumont the rise of manufacturing industry in the nineteenth century, so Joyce's mind-birth of the twinned and entwined nightwalkers of *Ulysses* marks the moment when Western cities became fully gravid with the clanking, groaning phantom of modernity.

Introduction

Midnight Streets

In the dead of night, in spite of the electric lights and the remnants of nightlife, London is an alien city, especially if you are strolling through its lanes and thoroughfares alone.

In the more sequestered streets, once the pubs are closed, and at a distance from the twenty-four-hour convenience stores, the sodium gleam of the street lamps, or the flickering strip-light from a soporific minicab stand, offers little consolation. There are alleys and street corners and shop entrances where the darkness appears to collect in a solid, faintly palpitating mass. There are secluded squares where, to appropriate a haunting line from a poem by

Shelley, night makes 'a weird sound of its own stillness'.[1] There are buildings, monuments and statues that, at a distance, and in the absence of people, pulsate mysteriously in the sepulchral light. There are foxes that slope and trot across the road, in a single motion, as you interrupt their half-shameful, half-defiant attempts to pillage scraps from upended bins. And, from time to time, there are the faintly sinister silhouettes of other solitary, perhaps homeless, individuals – as threatened by your presence, no doubt, as you are by theirs. 'However efficiently artificial light annihilates the difference between night and day', Al Alvarez has commented, 'it never wholly eliminates the primitive suspicion that night people are up to no good.'[2]

It is easy to feel disorientated in the city at the dead of night, especially if you are tired from roaming its at times unremitting distances, dreamily or desperately somnambulant. For in the darkness, above all perhaps in familiar or routine places, everything acquires a subtly different form or volume. Even the ground beneath one's feet feels slightly different. Ford Madox Ford lamented in *The Soul of London* (1905) that, 'little by little, the Londoner comes to forget that his London is built upon real earth: he forgets that under the pavements there are hills, forgotten water courses, springs, and marshlands'.[3] It is not the same in the dead of night. At 2 a.m., in the empty streets, no longer fighting against the traffic of cars and commuters, the solitary pedestrian's feet begin to recall the 'real earth'. In the abstracted, monochromatic conditions of the night-time, which partially obliterate the teeming, multicoloured visual details that characterize everyday life, it momentarily becomes apparent that a sloping road, for example, secretly curves over the sleeping form of a hill and tracks the course of an underground stream. The city is at its most earthly and unearthly at night.

A prehistoric landscape, then, comes to seem palpable beneath the pavements of the city at night. And in this half-familiar environment it is difficult to eliminate entirely the archaic conviction that, as for our ancestors, the night itself remains in some innate sense ominous, threatening. Residues of a primal fear of the dark almost imperceptibly interrupt your bloodstream as you move through the streets at night. They infiltrate more comprehensible anxieties relating to the sense of threat provoked by the presence of other people in the streets or the sudden flickering movement of a rat limping into a dirty pool of darkness glimpsed from the corner of your eye. In the dead of night, in London, some of the comforting assumptions that make everyday life in the metropolitan city seem predictable or even viable are undone. Walking at night involves displacements both of the city and of consciousness – like the ones Guy Debord alluded to when, in Paris in the mid-1950s, he celebrated a relationship to the spaces of the metropolis that undermines or upsets habitual influences and is '*insubordinate* to usual attractions'.[4]

The nighttime city is another city. Rhapsodizing about the public parks of the French metropolis in *Paris Peasant* (1926), the Surrealist Louis Aragon commented that 'night gives these absurd places a sense of not knowing their own identity'.[5] It is a point that applies to all aspects of the city's architecture or terrain. The nighttime self, moreover, is another self. In 'Street Haunting' (1930), Virginia Woolf quietly celebrated 'the irresponsibility which darkness and lamplight bestow'. 'We are no longer quite ourselves', she observed.[6] If 'to haunt' a place, a verb derived from the French, originally meant to visit a place habitually, perhaps obsessively, then those who walk at night inhabit the city both in this older sense and in the more persistent, colloquial sense of disturbing it like a spectre.

Wandering Steps

Who walks alone in the streets at night? The sad, the mad, the bad. The lost, the lonely. The hypomanic, the catatonic. The sleepless, the homeless. All the city's internal exiles. 'The night has always been the time for daylight's dispossessed', writes Bryan Palmer, '– the deviant, the dissident, the different.'[7] Solitary strolling at night in the city by both men and women has, from time immemorial, been interpreted as a sign of moral, social or spiritual dereliction.

Solitary women, because of a long history of discrimination and patriarchal oppression, have been especially susceptible to this sort of suspicion. If women appear on the streets of the city at night alone they are commonly portrayed in terms of two roles, both defined in relation to men: they are either predators, in the form of prostitutes; or the predated, the potential victims of sexual assault. In both cases, they are denied a right to the city at night. The historian Joachim Schlör has pointed out that, in terms of the freedom to inhabit the nocturnal city, 'women's needs and wishes are not fundamentally different from men's', since for both it is a case of entering it and circulating inside it freely and independently – 'through the *whole* city, during the *whole* night, and not just in certain spatial and temporal reserves'. But he has rightly insisted that, historically, 'men's freedom of movement has [had] a real restrictive effect on that of women'.[8]

If solitary men on the streets at night have exercised a right to the city denied to solitary women, however, then they too have often been identified or represented as pariahs. People who walk about at night and have no ready or implicitly respectable reason for doing so, both male and female, have attracted suspicion, opprobrium and legal recrimination from patriarchs, politicians, priests and others in authority, including the police, for thousands of years. In St John's Gospel, Jesus observes that 'if any man walk in the day, he stumbleth not, because he seeth the light of this world'. It is different after dark: '[I]f a man walk in the night, he stumbleth, because there is no light in him' (John 11: 9–10).

The relationship between cause and effect in the second of these verses is far from simple. The man who walks in the night stumbles because there is no light in him ... This makes sense. The man falls in the night because, in Christian terms, he is fallen. But does he also walk in the night, in the first place, because there is no light in him? Or, instead, does he have no light in him because he walks at night? Both, perhaps. A man who walks in the night might stumble because there is no light in him; but, conversely, or so it has often been assumed by the authorities, he has no light in him because he stumbles about in the night. A late sixteenth-century edition of the early fifteenth-century Chester Mystery Plays preserves this ambiguity in its reference to walking at night. For there Jesus declares that 'whosoever walketh abowte in night, / hee tresspasseth all agaynst the right, / and light in him is non'.[9] Nightwalking has for thousands of years been seen as both the consequence and cause of a benighted spiritual condition.

Nightwalking is, in both the physical and the moral meanings of the term, deviant. At night, in other words, the idea of wandering cannot be dissociated from the idea of erring – wanderring. This elision or semantic slurring is present in the final lines of John Milton's *Paradise Lost* (1667), where the poet offers a glimpse, for perpetuity, of Adam and Eve, after their expulsion from Paradise, entering the post-lapsarian world on foot: 'They, hand in hand, with wandering steps and slow, / Through Eden took their solitary way.' Wandering steps. In a double sense, Adam and Eve are errant: at once itinerant and aberrant. They are condemned to a life of ceaseless, restless sinfulness.

This is prefigured earlier in the poem. In Book IX, when the serpent tempts her, Eve is implicitly compared to an 'amazed night-wanderer'. In Book V, she describes a dream, insinuated into her consciousness by Satan, in which she has a premonition of the Fall. Eve tells Adam that, as she slept, a 'gentle voice' close to her ear seduced her into taking a walk beneath the 'full-orbed' moon and led her on to 'the tree / Of interdicted knowledge'.[10] Eve, according to Milton's epic narrative, rehearses the Fall with a nightwalk.

Objectless, Loitering

Solitary walking at night in the streets of the city does not necessarily entail wandering. It does not automatically involve deviant movement. It might of course be perfectly legitimate, purposeful.

Contemporary capitalist society requires what Jonathan Crary has identified as the despoliation of sleep in the interests of maximizing the individual's potential – as both a producer and a consumer – for generating profit.[11] The political economy of the night, in this dispensation, means that plenty of working-class people have to commute after dark, sometimes on foot, sometimes across considerable distances. This is the daily, or nightly, reality of post-circadian capitalism, as it might be called. For the city's army of nocturnal workers, many of whom are recent immigrants forced to perform the least popular forms of labour, travelling at night is in effect travailing at night. Prostitutes and the police (or its precursors) have, for their part, always had to patrol pavements at night for professional reasons. So have street-cleaners and others employed to collect and dispose of the city's waste products.

Not all walking at night, then, is nightwalking. But most forms of solitary walking at night are nonetheless tainted, sometimes faintly, sometimes more intensely, with dubious moral or social associations. Indeed, even apparently purposeful walking in the city at night is not exempt from the assumption that it is motivated by something suspicious. To be alone in the streets at night, even if one walks rapidly, determinedly, is to invite the impression that one is on the run, either from oneself or from another.

The late Chilean novelist Roberto Bolaño alludes to these conditions of being in the night – those of the haunted and the hunted – in a reference to the life, or half-life, of the city 'at an hour when the only people out walking [are] two opposite types: those running out of time and those with time to burn'.[12] In fact, these types are not really opposite: many people who are running out of time, paradoxically, have time to burn; conversely, many people who appear to have time to burn are actually running out of time. This contradictory state, of idling and hastening at once – a state of permanent restlessness – is a comparatively common experience of being in the city. It is even more potent on the streets at night. A kind of purposive purposelessness characterizes solitary walking in the nocturnal city.

To use a Dickensian phrase, nightwalking is a matter of 'going astray' in the streets of the city after dark. Dickens is the great heroic and neurotic nightwalker of the nineteenth century. In 1860, in the guise of the Uncommercial Traveller, he made a crucial distinction in an article printed in *All the Year Round*. There he discriminated between two kinds of walking: one that is 'straight on end to a definite goal at a round pace', another that is 'objectless, loitering, and purely vagabond'.[13] If the point of the first kind of walking is to travel from one point to another, from A to B, the point of the second is that there is no point at all; its purpose is its purposelessness. Nightwalking, according to this logic, is pointless, illogical. In Dickens's formulation, it is uncommercial. In an economy in which time, including nighttime, is money, wandering the streets after dark is, in symbolic terms, incendiary.

In the aberrant and deviant form celebrated by Dickens in the mid nineteenth century, and practised by innumerable others before and since, nightwalking is quintessentially objectless, loitering and vagabond.

A Vagabond, Wandering, Unsettled Condition

So how should a nightwalker be defined, in historical perspective, for heuristic purposes? Vaguely, is perhaps the most appropriate response. For 'vagueness' is etymologically linked to vagrancy.

In a richly researched account of the language of jurors during the late Middle Ages, Marjorie McIntosh notes that, in the context of the local courts, 'a man accused of wandering at night was usually described prior to 1500 as a *noctivagator*'. She adds that this word – derived from the Latin verb *vagare*, meaning 'to wander' – 'stressed that the offender lacked a good reason for being out, as contrasted with someone walking purposefully and legitimately from one place to another'.[14] Nightwalkers, according to this etymology, are those who wander purposelessly, illegitimately, at night. Their peregrinations are not migrant but vagrant. They are 'stragglers', to cite a word often used in the discourse of late medieval and early modern discipline and punishment; that is, they are people who 'rove without fixed direction', as the *Oxford English Dictionary* explains, or 'go up and down dispersedly'. The lexicographer Richard Huloet's English–Latin dictionary, first published in 1552, translated the phrase 'night wandrer', which it paired with 'night walker', as 'Noctivagus'.[15]

Noctivagation, then, is the activity of the homeless and indigent, of those who seek a social or spiritual refuge in the streets of the city at night. Noctambulation, by contrast, is the activity of the relatively privileged. It implies a more leisurely and at the same time more purposeful sort of movement. The rotund quality of the word – like 'circumambulation' or 'perambulation' – hints at an unhurried pace. It intimates a sense of entitlement in the streets. Noctivagation is instead furtive, defensive. As its semantic and historical associations with the roguishness and idleness of the itinerant poor imply, it was from the point of view of the authorities morally and politically aberrant. Common nightwalking, to give noctivagation its customary legal name in the medieval and early modern periods, was a constitutively antinomian activity – a more or less aimless activity that, actively or passively, resisted the imperatives of the law and the marketplace.

Its patron saint is no doubt Satan. For the Prince of Darkness, as Daniel Defoe pointed out in his *History of the Devil* (1726), 'confin'd to a vagabond, wandring, unsettl'd Condition, is without any certain Abode'.[16] And the night is his peculiar domain. More than a century before Defoe, in *King Lear* (1605), Shakespeare implied that Satan and his assistants are the most consummate nightwalkers of all. According to Edgar, who has assumed the disguise of Poor Tom on the Heath, the 'foul fiend Flibbertigibbet', whom he pretends to glimpse in the darkness, 'begins at curfew, / And walks till the first cock' – that is, he starts at 8 or 9 p.m. and finishes not at daybreak but at midnight. All this time, he causes chaos and mayhem, which includes 'hurt[ing] the poor creature of earth'.[17]

In the strict etymological sense, nightwalking is 'extravagant', meaning that it involves wandering beyond bounds, both geographical and social. It is extravagant even when it is covert or surreptitious – perhaps especially when it is covert or surreptitious. The nightwalker, to use an obsolete verb, extravages.

Cities, like Cats

'Cities, like cats, will reveal themselves at night', the poet Rupert Brooke once wrote.[18] Darkness, paradoxically, illuminates the history of the metropolis. This book is an account of nightwalking, mainly in London, from the thirteenth to the nineteenth centuries. The conviction on which it rests is that nightwalkers represent some of the most suggestive and revealing guides to the neglected and forgotten aspects of the city in its long, convoluted history. In the past, as in the present, residually, walking at night is a means of uncovering the dark side of the city.

The book traces a shift, registered in both legal and literary discourse in England, from the category of the 'common nightwalker', a criminal entity since before the thirteenth century, to that of the uncommon nightwalker, as it might be called. In archetypal terms, this describes an evolution, in the streets of the city at the dead time of night, from the figure of the vagrant to that of the Grub Street poet or, more broadly, the bohemian author. But – as the continued presence of the homeless on the nocturnal streets of London in the nineteenth century, as in our time, implies – it is an uneven, intermittent and contradictory development. Throughout London's history, the homeless and the bohemian, the socially and the spiritually disenfranchised, have coexisted in its obscurest spaces.

The book's narrative, as I have briefly outlined it, also traces a partial, incomplete shift from social to literary history. In the course of the sixteenth and seventeenth centuries, in the changing social and technological conditions of the metropolitan city, the criminal identity of the common nightwalker, which played a significant ideological role in the Middle Ages, gradually came to be eroded. Thereafter, from the eighteenth century, in the emergent era of capitalist modernity, a number of penurious authors and periodical journalists, including Goldsmith, Johnson and Savage, half-consciously adopted the outcast associations of the nightwalker and took to the streets of the city at night. The late seventeenth century, when public lighting was first introduced in London at night, represents a turning point, because the streets developed a distinct nightlife from this time. But if the nightlife of the eighteenth-century city confirmed the demise of the curfew, a kind of moral curfew prevailed, especially in relation to the nocturnal activities of the poor and dispossessed.

Later, at the turn of the nineteenth century, several of the most important Romantics and post-Romantics in England, including Blake, De Quincey and Dickens, pursued an ongoing, semi-conscious attempt to reclaim the metropolis at night. Inheriting some of the déclassé habits or tendencies of the Grub Street authors who preceded them, they searched for themselves in the nocturnal city – and tried to lose themselves. These authors and others at the same time cultivated and sought to elude their sense of alienation in the city by traversing its streets at night. In its comparatively depopulated state at night, the metropolis acquired the lineaments of a landscape both intimately familiar and strange, both ordinary and, in some incipient sense, apocalyptic. Romanticized and idealized by bohemian elements of the bourgeoisie, the identity of the nightwalker was thus gradually transformed from a criminal to a counter-cultural one. In short, it became uncommon.

This book excavates hidden or occluded aspects of the history of London, then, by exploring its life after dark during the centuries before electricity – that is, from the Middle Ages to the height of the gaslight era in the mid-nineteenth century. Too often, the night has been 'reduced to a mere parenthesis', to appropriate a phrase from André Breton, in both scholarly and popular accounts of the rise of urban culture.[19] The book attempts to redress that situation. And in the process it casts light on a number of other topics, including the history of homelessness, the development and impact of public lighting, and the secret life of the streets and their inhabitants. In addition, it narrates a story about the meanings of walking and of pedestrian culture, in London and in the countryside.

But the book is also an attempt to cast unexpected light on the history of English literature by examining its night side. Curiously, the night side of literature, like the night side of the city, has often been overlooked. Chaucer, Shakespeare, Goldsmith, Johnson, Blake, Wordsworth, De Quincey and Dickens – along with others less central to the canon of English literature, including Dekker, Fletcher, Ward, Savage and Clare – all demonstrated in their works a fascination with the tempting, troubling culture of the night, including and perhaps especially the urban night. In various forms, and in changing historical circumstances, these authors used the night as a means of creatively thinking the limits of an increasingly enlightened, rationalist culture – and, in the eighteenth and nineteenth centuries, of thinking the limits of the Enlightenment itself.

Like the common nightwalkers who preceded them in the medieval and early modern periods, these poets and novelists, in their association with or depiction of the night, achieved a precarious balance between belonging and not belonging, feeling at home and feeling homeless, in the places and spaces that get forgotten in the day. In so doing, they helped define the condition of social displacement and spiritual homelessness that is central to our understanding of the everyday experience of capitalist modernity and its representation in art and literature.

Heroes of the Big City

In stalking the nocturnal city, when the streets acquire a dreamlike character, nightwalkers consciously or unconsciously reject its diurnal logic – the ceaseless movement of its commuters and its commodities. To walk at night is to exercise what the French philosopher Maurice Blanchot – in the course of a discussion of vagrancy and the 'rigorous portioning of space' associated with the surveillance culture of the Enlightenment – called 'the right to disappear, which is still denied us today'.[20] So if the nightwalker is a fugitive from the ordinary, everyday life of the city, his half-illicit activity obscurely reclaims, redeems or transfigures it.

The nightwalk is indeed a kind of fugue, a flight at once psychological and physical. Nightwalkers experience urban life as a form of phantasmagoria, one that they are at the same time utterly immersed in and oddly detached from. The nightwalker thus dramatizes the dialectic of alienation and disalienation, oppression and emancipation, the prosaic and the poetic, at the core of metropolitan modernity. In this respect, he is a characteristic modern antihero, shaped in response to the condition of 'transcendental homelessness' identified by Georg Lukács.[21]

'Do the dregs of society supply the heroes of the big city?' Walter Benjamin once ruminated. 'Or is the hero the poet who fashions his work from such material?' Is the common or the uncommon nightwalker, it might be asked, the hero of the city at nighttime? 'The theory of the modern admits both', Benjamin responded.[22]

So too does the history of nightwalking. Its heroes are the city's antiheroes: the vagrants who have survived for centuries in the big city; and the poets and writers who, in their attempts to understand the disorienting, exhilarating or simply dreary and alienating conditions of metropolitan modernity, have identified with them.

In the 'midnight streets' of the city, in William Blake's haunting phrase, nightwalkers bring to light the hidden contradictions both of the class society in which they are condemned to live and their own divided psyches.

PART ONE

1.

Crime and the Common Nightwalker

The Middle Ages and After

Contrary to Civility

Nightwalking has been a crime for a millennium or more. It has been on the statute books in England and its former colonies since the late thirteenth century. Before then it was a common-law offence. In the medieval period, those who for one reason or another inhabited the streets of London and other cities at night had a proverbial reputation for being villainous, and were liable to be arrested and detained. 'Night-walkers' were among those whom Richard of Devizes enumerated as proof of the evils of the capital in his *Chronicle* of 1192 or 1193: 'Actors, jesters, smooth-skinned lads, Moors, flatterers, pretty-boys, effeminates, pederasts, singing- and dancing-girls, quacks, belly-dancers, sorceresses, extortioners, night-walkers, magicians, mimes, beggars, buffoons.' It is a list of those denizens of the city who can under no circumstances be trusted. 'If you do not want to live with evil-doers,' he concludes, 'do not live in London.'[1]

Vestiges of the long history of legislation against nightwalking in England are visible even today in the United States. In the state of Massachusetts, for instance, you can still technically be arrested as a nightwalker. Chapter 272, Section 53 of the General Laws of the state dictates that, among other malefactors, 'common night walkers, common street walkers, both male and female' can be punished by imprisonment for up to six months, or by a fine of up to $200, 'or by both such fine and imprisonment'.[2] A 'common night walker' in Massachusetts, as a legal case from the late 1980s indicates, is generally taken to mean 'someone who is abroad at night and solicits others to engage in illicit sexual acts'.[3] On occasion, though, the police invoke the law in order to detain women in poorer neighbourhoods who, instead of soliciting for sex, merely happen to be carrying condoms.

In a contemporary legal context, then, in part because there are more female prostitutes than male ones, the phrase has come to be more closely associated with women than men. It is effectively synonymous with 'streetwalker'. Historically speaking, however, the term 'common night walker' has not been restricted to female prostitutes – as the distinction in the Massachusetts statute book between 'common night walkers [and] common street walkers, both male and female' suggests. Indeed until at least the seventeenth century, so the *Oxford English Dictionary* indicates, the phrase 'nightwalker' was applied fairly indiscriminately to men and women; and thereafter, even if it was increasingly used as a synonym for 'streetwalker', it often retained its fuzzy, murky associations with male criminal activities. As recently as the 1960s – the decade in which William Castle's lurid thriller *The Night Walker* (1964) appropriated the term and imparted sinister, dreamlike associations to it – there was a case in Massachusetts involving a man convicted of being 'a common night walker'. He successfully petitioned against this charge precisely on the grounds that the formulation was so capacious as to be unconstitutional.[4]

Elsewhere in the United States nightwalking continues to be associated with men as well as women, as it was in medieval and early modern England. It indicates all kinds of vagrant activity at night. 'An idle or dissolute person who roams about at late or unusual hours and is unable to account for his presence' is the definition of a nightwalker offered by two legal commentators who summarized a number of relevant statutes in the 1960s.[5] The ordinance against vagrants in Jacksonville, Florida, for instance, includes a reference to nightwalkers. In its infinite leniency, the state doesn't construe a single night's wandering as criminal, necessarily. 'Only "habitual" wanderers, or "common night walkers" ', the authors of a legal textbook explain, 'are criminalized.' 'We know, however, from experience,' they rather drily add, 'that sleepless people often walk at night.'[6] The sleepless, the homeless and the hopeless, then, are all susceptible to this archaic charge.

The statute against nightwalkers in Massachusetts, where the Pilgrim Fathers first colonized North America in 1620, was first instituted in the late seventeenth century. In 1660, colonial law made provision that the state's nightwatchmen should

> examine all Night Walkers, after ten of the clock at Night (unless they be known peaceable inhabitants) to enquire whither they are going, and what their business is, and in case they give not Reasonable Satisfaction to the Watchman or constable, then the constable shall forthwith secure them till the morning, and shall carry such person or persons before the next Magistrate or Commissioner, to give satisfaction, for being abroad at that time of night.[7]

One such magistrate was Thomas Danforth, who investigated the disruptive behaviour of a group of approximately twenty young people, consisting of black people, maids and even students from Harvard University, during the winter of 1676–1677. Thirteen of them were admonished with costs for 'meeting at unseasonable times, and of night walking, and companying together contrary to civility and good nurture to vitiate one another', and two others were fined or whipped.[8] Nightwalking was indelibly identified with disruptive or subversive social activity. The all-too-familiar fear that black people, women and working-class men might corrupt middle-class youths was a persistent one, and the nightwalker statute in Massachusetts was regularly reinforced by proclamations.

In Cambridge, Massachusetts, as in urban settlements throughout North America, there was in the early modern period no right to the night – particularly for plebeians. The adjective 'common', when it appertained to nightwalkers, implied that, in addition to being repeat offenders, the culprits were of mean social station. Almost by definition, the poor could not 'give satisfaction for being abroad' after dark. In the streets at night, the itinerant were an inherent threat to society.

Black Spawn of Darkness

The specific origin of the attempt to criminalize the poor at night in late seventeenth-century Massachusetts, later rolled out to other states, lies in England in the late thirteenth century, when a rudimentary national criminal justice system was first instituted. In 1285 Edward I introduced the Statute of Winchester ('13 Edw. 1' in the legislative record).

The first of a series of so-called 'nightwalker statutes', the Statute of Winchester, or Statute of Winton, was a concerted response to rising crime levels, especially at nighttime, in England's expanding towns and cities. 'Because from day to day robberies, homicides and arsons are more often committed than they used to be …', the relevant section of the statute begins. This legislation ordained that every walled town should close its gates from sunset to sunrise and should operate a night-watch system. The city's constables or watchmen were expected to arrest strangers abroad at night – by definition suspected of being felons – and to deliver them to the sheriff. Private citizens were also authorized to raise the hue and cry in order to pursue, apprehend and detain those walking about after dark – 'and for the arrest of such strangers no one shall have legal proceedings taken against him'.[9] For the purposes of this statute, implicitly, 'strangers' were simply people who failed to carry lanterns or torches – the poor.

Among other measures implemented by the Statute of Winchester in order 'to abate the power of felons', then, it confirmed the authority of the night watch. This rudimentary police force – whose principal duty, like that of all police forces, was to protect property – had been introduced in 1253. At that date, as the topographer John Stow indicated in his *Survey of London* (1598), Henry III 'commanded watches in the cities and borough towns to be kept, for the better observing of peace and quietness amongst his people'.[10] Edward I's statute instructed these watches, as 'in Times past', to 'watch the Town continually all Night, from the Sun-setting unto the Sun-rising', and stipulated that, 'if any Stranger do pass by them', they should hold them until morning before handing them over to the sheriff.[11]

Anyone on the streets at night with no good reason was automatically liable to arrest. In the medieval and early modern periods, strangers in the night were feared like evil spirits (the more furtive or predatory of them sometimes blackened their faces so as to conceal themselves or appear more threatening). They were the agents or perpetrators of 'the works of darkness' whom St Paul, in his Epistle to the Romans, insists must be cast aside. In the popular imagination, before the diffusion of Enlightenment values in the seventeenth and eighteenth centuries, the identities of vagabonds, robbers, ghosts, demons and other imaginable or unimaginable inhabitants of the night were fluid, if not interchangeable, in the dark.[12] Nightwalkers seemed spiritually as well as socially other to respectable citizens (whom priests enjoined, in St Paul's words again, to put on 'the armour of light').

In the labyrinthine spaces of London, prior at least to the institution of street lighting from the end of the seventeenth century, and the concomitant rise of a distinctive 'nightlife', the night was intuitively frightening. It retained its ancient biblical and mythological associations with anarchy, chaos and evil – what Shakespeare's contemporary John Fletcher enumerated as 'the night, and all the evills the night covers, / The goblins, Hagges, and the blacke spawne of darknesse'.[13] In the night, ordinary sounds acquired sinister overtones. The abrupt movement of a shadow glimpsed from the comparative comfort of an interior inspired preternatural or uncanny fear. Even the air at night was thought to be particularly noxious or pestilential. In this climate of heightened tension, prior to its more systematic 'colonization' by the culture of the day from the later seventeenth century, any individual who ventured into the streets at night without a light implicitly identified themselves with what Craig Koslofsky has called 'the Devil's nocturnal anti-society'.[14] The night, in other words, was the domain of felons and demons.

'The modern city', Johan Huizinga wrote a century ago in *The Autumn of the Middle Ages*, 'hardly knows pure darkness or true silence anymore, nor does it know the effect of a single small light or that of a lonely distant shout.'[15] Popular terror of the darkness, which the authorities no doubt exploited in order to preserve social order, made even innocent nocturnal activities – the scramble of a midwife hurrying through the streets to deliver a child, for example – seem intrinsically nefarious, and potentially satanic. Those who loitered in the nocturnal streets without purpose at all, probably because they were homeless, were indefensibly alien. In legal terms, night was 'an aggravating circumstance', as the French medievalist Jean Verdon has demonstrated, and criminals therefore received heavier sentences for crimes committed after sunset: 'Malefactors were not merely infringing the rules of public order; acting under cover of darkness, they were demonstrating their evil intentions, their deep perversity, and premeditation.'[16]

It is a prejudice that had an ancient, long-established provenance. The Twelve Tables, the legislation that formalized Roman law in the mid fifth century BCE, decreed that, whereas thieves apprehended during the day had to be taken to the magistrates, 'where anyone commits a theft by night, and having been caught in the act is killed, he is legally killed'. In medieval and early modern London, as in ancient Rome, acts conducted under the cover of darkness were in legal terms stained with the ineliminable pigment of a blackness both moral and mythological.

Prison for Nightwalkers

The Statute of Winchester and its successors formalized the existing common law against male and female nightwalkers. As the great Jacobean jurist Edward Coke formulated it, the provision against nightwalkers was in affirmation of the common law.[17] Before 1285, common law had stipulated that citizens were free to detain any suspicious character if he or she proved unable to offer a satisfactory explanation for their presence in the streets after nightfall.

The first book of English common law, the *Liber Albus* (1419) or 'White Book', compiled by John Carpenter, the Town Clerk to the City of London, contained a number of references to cases involving people 'going or wandering about the streets of the City after curfew [had] rung out' at the churches in Cheapside (these cases included one chaplain committed 'for being a nightwalker'). It confirmed that, in order to maintain the peace, it had long been ordained

> that no one be so daring as to go wandering about within the said city, or in the suburbs, after the hour of curfew rung out at the church of Our Lady at Bow, unless he be a man known to be of good repute, or his servant, for some good cause, and that with a light; the which curfew shall be rung at the said church between the day and the night. And if anyone shall be found wandering about, contrary to this Ordinance, he is to be forthwith taken and sent unto the prison of Newgate, there to remain until he shall have paid a fine unto the City for such contempt, and have found good surety for his good behaviour.[18]

To go wandering about in the City of London or its suburbs to the south and west after the night-bell had been sounded was indeed to be daring. 'Of late walking cometh debate' is the father's mild but nonetheless ominous observation in 'How the Wise Man Taught

His Sonne', a conduct poem composed in Middle English in the early fifteenth century.[19]

If medieval nightwalkers were not taken to Newgate, they were confined in the Tun, which was purpose-built for their imprisonment. The Tun was a stone construction – so called because it looked like a cask of ale – founded in Cornhill in 1282 or 1283 'to be a Prison for Night-walkers, and other suspicious persons'. 'To this Prison', James Howell explained in *Londinopolis* (1657), his richly informative 'Perlustration of the City of London', 'the Night-watchers to this City, committed not only Night-walkers but also other persons, as well spiritual as temporal, whom they suspected of incontinency, and punished them according to the customs of this City.' Another ordinance stipulated that, in addition to the incontinent (those who failed to restrain their sexual appetite), bakers and millers who stole dough or flour should be taken to the Tun on a hurdle before being confined. In 1401, the year after Geoffrey Chaucer's death, a cistern channelling water from the River Tyburn was built into the Tun, and it was consequently rechristened the Conduit upon Cornhill; in addition, 'a Cage, with a pair of Stocks therein', was built on top of it – 'and this was for Night-walkers'.[20]

There are no records of the numbers of nightwalkers detained at the Tun before it burned down in the Great Fire of 1666. But in his *Customs of Old England* (1911), F. J. Snell commented that in medieval London 'a woman convicted of being a common night-walker' – that is, of being a prostitute – was typically committed to the Tun and thence 'led to Aldgate with a hood of rayed cloth on her head and a white wand in her hand'. From there musicians escorted her to the 'thewe', or pillory, where her offence was proclaimed. Finally, she was removed to 'Cokkeslane', outside the City walls, where she was forced to live. If she was prosecuted a third time for being a common nightwalker, 'her hair was cropped close, while she stood in the pillory, and she was marched to one of the gates and made to abjure the City for the remainder of her life'.[21] The common nightwalker thus performed the sacrificial role of an ancient scapegoat.

No Man Walks after Nine

In *Comus*, a masque first performed in 1634, John Milton makes a proverbial reference to the 'evil thing that walks by night', who 'breaks his magic chains at curfew time'.[22] The Statute of Winchester, like the subsequent nightwalker statutes, was in effect a mechanism for policing the curfew.

William the Conqueror had instated a national curfew in England in 1068 when he ruled, according to Stow, that 'a bell should be nightly rung at eight o'clock, and that all people should then put out their fire and candle, and take their rest'.[23] Doctors, midwives, priests and veterinarians – 'persons on missions of life or death', as the historian A. Roger Ekirch puts it in his richly informative book on the meanings of the pre-Enlightenment night – were exempt from this regime in exceptional circumstances.[24] So were those who collected and sifted the city's waste. All other citizens were to be safely confined at home. Fires were to be covered in order to prevent conflagrations – the word 'curfew' is derived from the French *couvre-feu*. But, equally important, the curfew served both to pre-empt political conspiracies, which the authorities thought were most likely to be cooked up after dark, and, above all perhaps, to preserve regular hours, in order to promote industry and piety.

The credulous carpenter in Chaucer's 'Miller's Tale' (c. 1390) is exemplary in the latter respect. For, on the night he is cuckolded by the poor scholar who rents a room from him, he falls into 'the dede sleep', as the Miller reports, 'aboute corfew-tyme, or litel moore'.[25] The dead sleep Chaucer refers to here, which generally lasted from soon after the curfew until about midnight, was the first phase of the segmented or 'biphasic' sleep characteristic of the culture of the night in the medieval and early modern periods (prior to the time when a continuous night's sleep like the one to which we are used today, or to which we aspire at least, became customary and hence, apparently, 'natural'). At midnight, an interval of wakefulness or 'watchfulness' took place, when people prayed or silently meditated or made love before the 'morning' sleep, which probably lasted until dawn.[26] At first light, for most citizens at least, the labouring day resumed.

Initially set at 8 p.m., the curfew had by the end of the Middle Ages been postponed in most places to 9 p.m. or 10 p.m., depending on the season. 'And no man walke after IX of the belle streken in the nyght without light or without cause reasonable in payne of empresonment', runs a decree from 1467.[27] Throughout Europe, the ringing of church bells signalled the beginning and end of the curfew. In London, originally, the first stroke of the bell of St Martin's-le-Grand, a church that offered sanctuary to thieves and debtors, indicated that the gates of the walled city should be closed. Later, Edward III ordained that, instead of St Martin's-le-Grand, St Mary-le-Bow should be used to signal the setting of the sun.

These prominent churches also acted as the signal for the ringing of bells in other parish churches, as the Mayor and Aldermen ordered – 'so that they begin together, and end together'.[28] While they tolled, and the city gates were shut, the wickets were opened to enable latecomers to scramble in or out, before being closed again. In this brief interval, to the no doubt deafening sound of pealing, the people retreated into their homes and barricaded themselves against the darkness. 'Each evening,' as the cultural historian Wolfgang Schivelbush evocatively writes, 'the medieval community prepared itself for dark like a ship's crew preparing to face a gathering storm.'[29]

It was not so much sunset, then, but the artificial limit of the curfew, and the restrictions on the life and labour of the city that it enforced, which defined nightfall in the Middle Ages. Verdon has usefully characterized this as the 'legal night', and argued that its commencement entailed 'a whole ceremony': 'In the thick wall surrounding the city, the gates that allow an escape into the countryside or conversely an entrance for provisions are closed, making the city an enclosed space deprived for a few hours of all relation to the external world.'[30] Inside the walls, meanwhile, chains were slung across some of the more important streets in order to arrest the passage of invading soldiers or escaping robbers. Lights of all kinds – not merely hearth fires – had to be extinguished. In the Middle Ages the city largely relied for its illumination on the inconstant light of the moon. Apprentices ceased their labours; drinkers were expelled from the taverns. A thick darkness descended on the city as people retired to their rooms to sleep, and so prepare for the next day's labour. In practice, the curfew implemented a political economy.

If the legislation against nightwalkers from the late thirteenth century was designed to regulate the lives of the city's working inhabitants, especially its apprentices and labourers, and of course to protect property, then it was also intended to circumscribe the movement of the unemployed poor. In particular, it served to police itinerants and vagrants of all kinds. 'Besides those whose demeanor, looks, or location made authorities wary,' Ekirch writes, 'several groups were enjoined from circulating at night because of the perceptible threat they posed to public order', including beggars, prostitutes and foreigners – especially Jews.[31] The popular perception that these more or less nomadic tribes inhabited the streets at night deeply troubled the city's settled community.

Roberdsmen, Wastors and Draw-Latchets

In 1331, a year after the execution of Roger Mortimer, his regent, Edward III extended his grandfather Edward I's legislation against nightwalkers. This was largely in order to enable local constables to arrest them and take them to the sheriff:

> Item, Whereas in the statute made at *Winchester* in the time of King *Edward*, grandfather to the king that now is, it is contained, That if any stranger pass by the country in the night, of whom any have suspicion, he shall presently be arrested and delivered to the sheriff, and remain in ward till he be duly delivered. And because there have been divers manslaughters, felonies, and robberies done in times past, by people that be called roberdsmen, wastors, and draw-latchets, it is accorded, That if any man have any evil suspicion of such, be it by day or by night, they shall be incontinently arrested by the constables of the towns.[32]

In England, Edward III's nightwalker statute, one of several that permitted officers of the law and private citizens to make warrantless arrests for relatively minor offences, was re-enforced on a number of subsequent occasions from the mid fourteenth century. It remained a crucial mechanism for policing the citizens of London and other cities. Indeed, it will not surprise inhabitants of the twenty-first century capital – which has more CCTV cameras per citizen than any other European metropolis – that throughout the Middle Ages Londoners 'had to put up with constant surveillance'. Anyone from the lower classes seen on the streets at night, it was assumed, was likely to be a 'wastor' or 'draw-latchet' (thieves of one description or another) or a 'roberdsman' (a marauding vagabond). 'Night-walkers, male and female, and roysterers generally had a bad time of it', as Henry Wheatley comments in his *Story of London* (1904) – though he adds, in rather schoolmasterish tones, that 'probably they were very ill-behaved, and in many cases they doubtless deserved the punishment they received'.[33]

Strangers in the streets at night continued to be constructed by the authorities as a threat to social order, so the nightwalker statute was intermittently buttressed by additional judicial procedures in response to particular social circumstances. In 1311, for example, four years after the death of Edward I, an Inquisition and Delivery was made under the auspices of Sir Richard Resham, the Mayor of London, 'as to misdoers and night-walkers'. One Elmer de Multone was singled out for particular attention. He was accused of enticing strangers to taverns, deceiving people with dice, and nightwalking, and was consequently 'indicted in Tower Ward for being a bruiser and nightwalker, against the peace, as also for being a common *rorere* [a roarer or riotous person]'.[34] The statute was fortified at a local or provincial level, too. So an 'Acte for nyghtwalkeres' passed by the authorities in Leicester in 1553 specified that 'from henceforth all nyght walkers and other ydell and evyll disposyd person[s] to the plesure of God and worshippe of the towne might be restreynyd from ther lybertyes'.[35]

Long after the introduction of public street lighting, 'idleness' and an 'evil disposition' continued to be an intense irritant to the state and its representatives at night. In his *Lectures on the Constitution and Laws of England* (1776), the eighteenth-century Irish lawyer Francis Stoughton Sullivan confirmed that 'a watchman may arrest a night-walker at unseasonable hours by the common law, however peaceably he might demean himself, for strolling at unusual hours was a just cause of suspicion, of an ill intent'.[36] Indeed, across England, the legislation against nightwalking initiated in the reign of Edward I was only finally repealed in 1827. And in the UK the offence remained on the statute books, in name at least, until the introduction of the Criminal Law Amendment Act in 1967. This Act announced the abolition of several obsolete offences, including 'eavesdropping or being a common barrator, a common scold or a common night walker' (1967 c. 58, 13.1.a).

Nuisance to the Neighbours

In the medieval and early modern periods, nightwalking was hard to disentangle from other crimes associated with socially disruptive behaviour. At times, indeed, nightwalking seems to have functioned as a sort of floating signifier used by the authorities to criminalize or ostracize any errant, irritating or undesirable activity after dark.

In 1422, to take a slightly comic example, the 'Pleas and Memoranda' for the parish of St Sepulchre in the City of London presented the Smithfield 'cachepolle' – that is, the sheriff's deputy, though the word literally meant 'chicken chaser' – 'for a nyght-walkere, and also for he anoyth the feld with his dong, gret nusaunce to the neyghbores'.[37] Nightwalking was part of an intricately knotted cluster of antisocial crimes. As late as the turn of the seventeenth century, Robert Danvers of Tenbury in Worcestershire was accused, in addition to being a usurer, of being 'a common barrator and breaker of the peace', and moreover 'a night walker, and a man of ill condition'.[38] Nightwalking, which involved keeping unseasonable, strange or 'savage' hours, was almost synonymous with being of 'ill condition'.

Other antisocial crimes associated with nightwalking, as the Criminal Law Amendment Act of 1967 retrospectively indicates, included barrating (harassment), scolding (verbal abuse) and eavesdropping; also dicing, drinking and thieving. In the Middle Ages, eavesdropping was classified alongside nightwalking especially often, largely because it too tended to happen under cover of darkness. To eavesdrop literally meant to stand within the 'eavesdrip' of a house – the strip of ground liable to receive the rainwater running from the eaves – in order to listen secretly to a private conversation; or, perhaps, to keep a neighbour's sexual activities under surveillance. 'Eavesdroppers stood outside other people's houses, often at night, listening to their conversations or sometimes observing their private acts', explains the historian Marjorie McIntosh in her research on the Sessions of the Peace records from 1351 to 1599. She adds that nightwalkers, who were generally 'suspected of having more nefarious intent', were more likely to be male, while eavesdroppers were more likely to be female.[39]

The phrase 'common nightwalker' remained a generalized term of abuse even after its legal relevance had begun to fade as a result of the gradual abolition of the curfew during the sixteenth and seventeenth centuries, when the rise of nightlife and the expansion of the metropolis beyond the walled precincts of the City rendered it all but impossible to police. In 1681, Richard Kilburne's *Choice Presidents upon All Acts of Parliament, Relating to the Office and Duty of a Justice of Peace* confirmed the place of 'night-walkers' in a compendious list of those of 'ill name and fame', which included 'alehouse-haunters', 'barterers', 'eve-droppers', 'hedge-breakers', 'rioters', 'slanderers', 'sowers of discord', 'whores', 'wood-stealers' and 'those who are Idle persons, wandring up and down'.[40]

In *The London Cuckolds* (1681), a comedy first performed in the same year, Edward Ravenscroft indicated in rather more satirical tones that the phrase 'night-walker' was by then, in colloquial discourse, an insult whose referent could not be dissociated from other nefarious identities: 'This was a night-walker, a spy, a thief, a villain, he would have murther'd thee, and eat thee', one character gleefully tells another.[41]

Evil Fame

In practice, it was quite difficult to prosecute people for walking about at night, because any accusation was premised not so much on proof of committing harm as on suspicion of intending it. Reviewing the relevant statutes in his *Treatise of the Pleas of the Crown* (1716), the distinguished barrister William Hawkins admitted that there were no 'precise Rules for the Direction of the Magistrate' regarding whether it was his duty to bind someone for good behaviour if they had not caused a breach of the peace. He therefore concluded:

> he has a discretionary Power to take such Surety of all those whom he shall have just Cause to suspect to be dangerous, quarrelsome, or scandalous, as of those who sleep in the Day, and go abroad in the Night, and of such as keep suspicious Company, and of such as are generally suspected to be Robbers, *&c.* and of Eve-Droppers, and common Drunkards, and all other Persons, whose Misbehaviour may reasonably be intended to bring them within the Meaning of the Statute, as Persons of evil Fame, who, being described by an Expression of so great Latitude, seem in a great measure to be left to the Judgment of the Magistrate.[42]

The term 'nightwalking' was itself an expression of great latitude, one that always carried the opprobrium associated with people of evil fame. And in cases where no other criminal act seemed to be forthcoming, there is something almost comically imprecise about the accusations made against nightwalkers. John Key of Brigstock in Northamptonshire, for example, was reported in 1464 for 'wandering at night through the streets of common areas, to the harm of all his neighbours and a dangerous example to others'.[43] In short, the man looked shifty.

Chaucer, who possessed an omnivorous appetite for the more unsavoury aspects of life in London at the end of the fourteenth century, offers a fleeting insight into someone criminalized as a nightwalker in the Middle Ages. Nightwalking first becomes visible in the canon of English literature with him. In *The Canterbury Tales*, one of the pilgrims, the Cook, is named 'Hogge of Ware' – that is, Roger of Ware (a town in Hertfordshire). It is probable that, alongside other characters in *The Canterbury Tales*, including the Host, Harry Bailly, Hogge was based on a real person. The Cook's historical counterpart, also called Roger de Ware, appears in records in London from the 1370s both as a debtor and, in 1373, a nightwalker: 'Roger de Ware, cook, who was presented as a common nightwalker, confessed his offence and put himself at the mercy of the Court', the court records of the time read.[44]

Nothing is known about this man's appearance or disposition, but Chaucer's Cook – a man of poor reputation who repels the other pilgrims with his gaping mouth and stinking breath – is certainly a person of evil disposition. Of course, Chaucer doesn't directly allude to Roger de Ware's criminal identity as a common nightwalker, so it isn't possible to infer specific details of his antisocial activities. But the oddly truncated 'Cook's Tale' is revealing in this respect, because it centres on a thieving, gambling apprentice in Cheapside, called Perkyn Revelour, who is eventually sacked by the victualler who employs him for proving disruptive at night. 'Now lat hym riote al the nyght or leve', his master declares.[45] To 'riot', at this time, meant to act in a dissipated and unrestrained manner. The Cook, like the incontinent central character of his tale, is one of those men 'whose demeanor, looks, or location made authorities wary', to return to Ekirch's phrasing.

The arrest of characters of suspicious appearance such as John Key or Roger de Ware – if Chaucer can be credited with encoding a personal attack on him – was for the most part pre-emptive even when it was purely vindictive. In the opening scene of Francis Manning's *The Generous Choice*, a comic drama from as late as 1700, one character tries to resist another's attempt to persuade him to take a 'ramble' in the night, in pursuit of 'some Adventure or other that is diverting', in these terms: 'No, no, I'll home, I assure you. I have no mind to be mistaken for another in the dark, and so have my Throat cut, or, if I escape that way, to be seiz'd upon by the Watch for a Night-walker, that has some ill-design on foot.'[46] All those who walked at night were thought to have some ill design 'on foot', as Manning's pun has it. The nightwalker statutes, and the suspicious attitudes they expressed and formalized, were commonly applied in order to prevent the commission of nameless, perhaps even nonexistent, crimes. If they were occasionally invoked in a spiteful spirit to punish individuals, as the case of the fifteenth-century 'cachepolle' implies, the statutes were mainly used to persecute people for the crime of simply being poor or 'idle' – that is, insufficiently employed. They criminalized 'rogues' and 'vagabonds' for being visible or audible at night as well as merely indigent.

In this sense, the nightwalker statute, which invested the watchman with a warrantless arrest authority, was a forerunner of the so-called 'Sus' law, first instigated in England by the Vagrancy Act of 1824, which criminalized people who were itinerant and unemployed as 'suspected persons', on the grounds that they might at some point in the future commit an offence. This piece of legislation, aggressively revived under Margaret Thatcher's administration in order further to marginalize youths from black and other ethnic minorities, was eventually repealed in August 1981 as a result of the race riots that took place in cities across Britain that summer. Nightwalkers, too, historically speaking, have been little more than suspected persons.

Good Reputation

The *Liber Albus* had in the early fifteenth century underlined that anyone wandering about in the streets at night would be dispatched to the Tun 'unless it be some great lord or other substantial person of good reputation'.[47] Hawkins, in the eighteenth century, observed that, in addition to the legislation that insisted on the responsibility of public officers for apprehending nightwalkers, 'it is holden by some, that any private Person may lawfully arrest a suspicious Night-walker, and detain him till he make it appear, that he is a Person of good Reputation'.[48] It all depended on one's 'reputation' (a term that entered the English language from the French in the late fourteenth century) – more precisely, on one's class position.

Respectable people, even when they didn't behave respectably, tended to be exempt from the nocturnal discipline imposed by officers of the city. Aristocrats habitually travelled or sauntered across London at night with a retinue that included servants bearing lights. Other substantial persons, such as merchants, might hire a 'linkboy' loitering on the streets – 'links' were torches made from rope stiffened with fat or pitch. But even if aristocrats or merchants were carousing, or roistering, or soliciting prostitutes, they generally circumvented the night watch, which policed the streets inefficiently and partially, if not unscrupulously or corruptly. An elevated social status, or the appearance of one, was thus the best protection against harassment by the authorities at night.

Thomas Dekker, something of an expert on the social customs of the night in the early seventeenth century, advised the readers of his *Gull's Horn-Book* (1609) that, if they happened to be apprehended on the streets after dark, they should adopt a boisterous upper-class voice and address their companions as if they were aristocrats – for then 'the watch will wink at you, only for the love they bear to arms and knighthood'.[49] Half a century later, in his posthumously published *Reports and Cases* (1656), Sir John Popham, lord chief justice at the turn of the seventeenth century, confirmed that, though 'every one may arrest a Night-walker … it is said that if he appeareth a man of good fame, the party who arrests him ought to let him go at large'. The word *noctivagus*, he added in order to make the necessary class distinction, implied in legal terms that the man apprehended is 'a common Night-walker'.[50] At night, appearances mattered, as did other superficial impressions – even, or especially, if they were to be ascertained by no more than a flickering, guttering torchlight.

Those who appeared to have money to spend but evidently lacked a title or good reputation were particularly susceptible to incrimination if they were unfortunate enough to be apprehended by the authorities at night. The 'Inquests as to Evildoers and Disturbers of the King's Peace' held on 5 July 1340 by John de Shirbourne – who on this date condemned more than one 'man who sleeps by day and wanders by night' – ruled 'that Walter Walteshelf, Gracian le Palmer and John Walssh are nightwalkers, well dressed and lavish of their money, though no one knows how they got their living, and that these people, if they had their opportunity, would sooner consort with bad characters and disturbers of the peace than with men of good report'.[51] Walteshelf or Waldeshef or Waldeskef, who seems to have been stabbed to death in Lombard Street a year after this arrest, was also condemned for being addicted to playing 'knucklebones' (or jacks) at night. If individuals could not instantly be condemned for looking like 'bad characters', then they could at least be attacked, like these social upstarts, for preferring to consort with them.

At night, in the medieval and early modern periods, gentlemen and important merchants were implicitly and unquestionably regarded as 'peaceable inhabitants' of the city, even when they engaged in drinking, roistering and whoring. Plebeians, for their part, were regarded as 'disturbers of the peace'.

Sink and Dunghill Knaves

From the end of the Middle Ages, the ascendant capitalist class developed a new morality, increasingly shored up by Calvinist theology, which enshrined labour as a religious duty. According to this regimen, as Christopher Hill puts it, poverty 'ceased to be a holy state and [became] presumptive evidence of wickedness'.[52]

The Franciscan doctrine according to which the poor, and in particular the mendicant poor, were sanctified for their state of indigence was dismissed as outdated. Instead, productive forms of labour were consecrated, and individual worldly achievements, as the Humanists proposed, were lionized. So the unemployed, especially the itinerant unemployed, became socially unacceptable in the age in which agrarian capitalism emerged. If the ideology of post-feudal society, in Raymond Williams's account, created the conditions for an organized response to poverty, evident in the compulsory poor-rate and other administrative mechanisms devised in the sixteenth century, then, 'on the other side of the coin, it linked poverty to labour in new ways, so that the harrying of what was called vagrancy, itself the result of a socially created disturbance and mobility, became, in its turn, a moral duty'.[53]

Coded by the authorities as 'idleness', unemployment was seen as the primary cause of social disorder. Indeed the word 'idle' was a neuralgic point of tension in the ideological and legal discourse of the early modern era. As the financial administrator Edmund

Dudley put it in *The Tree of Commonwealth* (1509) – written from prison in an unsuccessful attempt to persuade Henry VIII not to execute him for treason – idleness was 'the very mother of all vice', as well as 'the lyneall grandam of povertie and myserie, and the deadlie enemy to this tree of common wealth'.[54] Idleness was thus considered the cause of poverty rather than its consequence. In this ideological climate, common people who – instead of restoring their bodies with sleep – crept, sauntered or careered about the streets at night without 'reasonable cause' were deliberately interrupting and upsetting the rhythms of the working day. They were condemned as idle, assumed to be thieves, and duly punished. If 'the sixteenth century live[d] in terror of the tramp', as R. H. Tawney once commented, then the early modern period reserved particular fear for those who loitered or tramped at night.[55]

In early modern England, at a time when feudal tenants were being systematically evicted as a result of the enclosure of land for sheep farming, and other poor labourers were being forced into destitution by escalating rents and prices, there was a steep rise in vagabondage. Poor people travelled to London because wages were higher there, but the capital failed to provide enough housing or employment for them all. The Geneva Bible, the complete edition of which was first printed in English in 1576, offers a revealing sense of this development. It refers in a pointed marginal comment on Acts 17: 6 to 'vagabonds … which do nothing but walk the streets, wicked men, to be hired for every man's money to do any mischief, such as we commonly call the rascals and very sink and dunghill knaves of all towns and cities'.[56] These were urban itinerants, doing nothing but walking the streets, in the day and in the night.

Idle and Lusty Rogues

The Punishment of Vagabonds Act of 1572, which in England transferred the care of vagrants from the churches to local authorities, largely in the form of regional 'houses of correction', was a response to the rising numbers of itinerants fleeing their expropriated land for the limited employment opportunities of the city.

The poor, criminalized for being impoverished, were processed through these local 'bridewells', built from the 1560s, in order to be punished, reformed through labour, and even transported.

Bridewell itself – from the mid-sixteenth century one of London's most infamous prisons – functioned increasingly as the institution in which people 'wandering in the night' were decanted and detained, replacing Newgate and the Tun. Bridewell had originally been built as a residence for Henry VIII on the banks of the Fleet River, but in the mid-1550s it became a prison for the able-bodied poor and a hospital and workhouse for the disabled poor. It pioneered a peculiarly punitive form of charity intended to instil in the unemployed discipline and the ability and desire to labour.

In a manuscript dated 1582, which detailed London's royal hospitals, the grocer John Howes, who lamented that the metropolis had become the resort of the 'caterpillars of the commonwealth', expressed his approval of the state's solution to this problem, which involved confining vagrants to Bridewell and its satellite institutions, and so reforming their characters through a regime of labour. 'Then they did devise', he noted, 'that all the ydell & lustie roges as well men as woemen shoulde all be taken up & be convayed into some house where they shoulde have all things necessarie & be compellde to labour'.[57] In his contribution to *The Honest Whore* (1604), Dekker too praised Bridewell, on the grounds that there 'the sturdy Begger, and the lazy Lowne' (or 'loon') acquire 'hard hands', and 'the Vagabond grows stay'd, and learns to 'bey'.[58]

In the early seventeenth century the lord mayor of London directed city constables to 'walk the streets within their several precincts, and forthwith apprehend all such vagrant children, both boys and girls, as they shall find in the streets and in the markets or wandering in the night to be apprehended by the watch, and then to commit to Bridewell, there to remain until further order be given'.[59] The institution played an increasingly important role in the brutal strategy, involving both adults and children, to build and populate the emergent colonies across the Atlantic. It harvested colonial labour on the streets of London. 'Millicent Cole brought in from Cheap Ward as a common night walker is to remain at labour until she be transported (*Bridewell*)', reads one characteristically stark entry in the records of emigration from this period. 'Suzan Reynolds, a common night walker and suspected pilferer, is willing to go to a plantation and is set by', reads another dated less than two weeks later.[60] One wonders how willing she really was.

In a sermon to the Virginia Company in 1622, the poet John Donne, dean of St Paul's, praised Virginia itself as a giant reformatory prison designed to cleanse London and emancipate the idle poor: 'It shall sweep your streets, and wash your dores, from idle persons, and the children of idle persons, and imploy them: and truly, if the whole Countrey were but such a *Bridewell*, to force idle persons to work, it had a good use.'[61] But if the ideological importance of Bridewell's disciplinary regime intensified, its institutional standards, like those of the regional bridewells, had by the early seventeenth century already steeply declined. In an all-too-familiar pattern, this was largely because of the corruption and poor management abilities of the private contractors running them. Bridewell thus retained its reformatory credentials for little more than a generation. It nonetheless remained the institution in which, throughout the seventeenth and even eighteenth centuries, most nightwalkers, increasingly female ones, were incarcerated.

In a revealing piece of scholarship, the historian Paul Griffiths has sifted Bridewell's archives in order to demonstrate that, in early modern England, when the population of London was rapidly increasing because of immigration from the countryside, magistrates used the term 'nightwalker' to stigmatize all kinds of suspicious behaviour among the lower classes. Used alongside words such as 'idle', 'lewd' and 'vagrant', it indicated a 'masterless' man or woman. Emphasizing the reformation of criminals through labour, as well as their correction, Bridewell pioneered a number of new penal and policing strategies for safeguarding public morals in this period, and the word performed a significant ideological role in the institution's discursive practices. The fact that it lacked a precise statutory definition made it all the more effective as a means of manipulating semi-criminal identities.

Griffiths goes on to contend that, though today the immediate associations of the phrase are most often with prostitution, 'the feminisation of nightwalking was never inevitable'. Before the early seventeenth century, in fact, it was mainly men, and especially apprentices, seamen and servants, who were arrested on this charge. At this time it was associated with 'loitering', 'straggling' and 'rouging [or making oneself up] and ranging in the streets in the nightseason'; and it tended to be applied to prostitutes' clients quite as much as to prostitutes. According to Griffiths, though, in the records of Bridewell 'a rising tide of male offenders abruptly freezes up in 1626, when all forty-seven labelled nightwalkers were women'.[62] The early seventeenth century was a period in which increasing numbers of infants were abandoned on the streets of London, especially in populous areas like Cornhill and Fleet Street (an 'Act to Prevent the Destroying and Murthering of Bastard Children' was introduced in 1624); and this situation intensified public anxieties about women walking with no apparent purpose at night. In such a climate, women were more likely than men to be arrested as nightwalkers without also having been accused of other crimes.

The intermittent presence of nightwalkers in early modern literary works of one description or another indicates that, long after the so-called 'feminisation of nightwalking', men continued to be identified in these terms in the cultural imagination. Manning's *The Generous Choice* is evidence that, at least at the start of the eighteenth century, men were still associated with the semi-criminal identity of the nightwalker. In this play, Frederick fears that, if he rambles about the streets with Bernardo, he will be 'seiz'd upon by the Watch for a Night-walker, that has some ill-design on foot'.

Where Lie You?

It was decisively in the seventeenth century, according to Griffiths, that female vagrants were more likely to be identified as nightwalkers and male vagrants as idlers and vagabonds.[63] But it is not absolutely clear from his argument why this ideological division emerged, if indeed it did emerge.

Presumably it had something to do with the fact that productive labour was gendered as male. Idle, masterless or unproductive men were probably criminalized in relation to the day because, for obvious reasons, almost all forms of manual labour took place in the light (though by the end of the Middle Ages, in larger cities at least, more and more artisans and craftsmen were working by candlelight into the evenings in order to fulfil their contracts).[64] In contrast, disreputable women were probably criminalized in relation to the night for the same reason – that is, because the productive labour of the male working day was of preeminent economic and social importance.

Griffiths argues that in the seventeenth century 'women who remained inside at night were increasingly being separated from others who paced dark streets, entered "suspect" houses, and interfered with the order of the male working day by serving as a nocturnal temptation'.[65] But for centuries prior to this the moral identities of women at night were defined in terms of whether they reinforced or undermined the diurnal economy. Respectable women remained within the family home at nighttime. They were not free to 'roam the streets at midnight', as Virginia Woolf phrased it in a discussion of the sexual politics of the Elizabethan period in *A Room of One's Own* (1929).[66]

At home, these women were expected to restore their husbands' bodies by feeding them and providing them with the optimum conditions for rest and sleep. As documents from the Star Chamber in the late fifteenth and early sixteenth centuries demonstrate, the early modern state required that in the 'dead tyme of night' its citizens devote themselves to the 'lawful and necessary repose for recreation': 'all good subjects should be at quyet takinge theire naturall rest in theire bedds'.[67] The night, according to this moral and political economy, was for sleeping – though in the interval between 'first' and 'second' sleeps, or 'dead' and 'morning' sleeps, prayer and spiritual contemplation were also acceptable activities.

As Chaucer revealed in *The Legend of Good Women*, which he composed in the late fourteenth century, virtuous men and women were required to retreat indoors at the end of the day – like the flower that closes its petals 'for derknesse of the nyght, of which she dredde'.[68] At nighttime, women of the poorer classes were expected to reproduce labour in a double sense: on a daily basis, to repair its physical strength, by restoring the labourer's body; and, in the long term, to propagate the next generation of workers. This is what it meant in the Middle Ages to be an obedient proletarian (from the Latin *proletarius*, which in ancient Rome signified the lowest class of citizens, who served the state not by owning property but by producing offspring).

In contrast to this model of domestication, female nightwalkers were distinctly daring and undomesticated. Chaucer's 'Wife of Bath's Tale' (c. 1390) provides a characteristically ribald instance of this rather less respectable sort of reputation. In her Prologue, she boasts about the tactical skill with which, in order to divert attention from her own dubious nighttime activities, she used to accuse her numerous husbands of soliciting prostitutes and, even more audaciously, convinced them that her own nocturnal ramblings were intended to police their adulterous behaviour: 'I swoor that al my walkynge out by nyghte / Was for t'espye wenches that he dighte.'[69]

Opprobrious women, then, provided recreation of a rather different sort at nighttime, for they simultaneously undermined the strength of the labouring body, sapping it with licentious pleasure, and subverted the biological and moral function of the family. They challenged the logic of both productive and reproductive labour. Women were thus sexualized at night in a way that men were not. 'Male nightwalkers were generally accused of disorderly drinking and theft', one historian comments, 'whereas women were labelled as sexually immoral.'[70] Female nightwalkers were criminalized in relation to their bodies, their biology, in a way that male ones were not. They were thought to encourage both unproductiveness and non-reproductiveness.

An emerging regime of industriousness, enforced by new penal procedures like the ones developed at Bridewell, deepened this ideological assumption in early modern England. It rested on the ancient misogynistic prejudice that if in any sense a woman enjoyed the night she must be a prostitute, or no better than a prostitute. In Dekker's *Lanthorne and Candle-Light* (1608), a persistent constable asks one woman discovered in the street at night a series of questions that exemplify this presumption: 'Where have you bin so late?' he asks, 'Are you married?' and 'Where lye you?'[71]

Barnaby Rich, a prolific author of fictions and pamphlets on military and social matters in the early seventeenth century, who provided Shakespeare with more than one of his plots, can stand in for an ancient patriarchal tradition, one codified more fully in the early modern period. In *My Ladies Looking Glasse* (1616), a conduct manual aimed at female readers, he declared that 'the woman that is impudent, immodest, shamelesse, insolent, audacious, a night-walker, a company keeper, a gadder from place to place, a reveler, a ramper [or romper], a roister, a rioter: shee that hath these properties, hath the certaine signes, and markes of a *harlot*, as *Salomon* hath avowed'.[72] It is notable that Rich does not collapse the term 'night-walker' into the term 'harlot'. Here, nightwalking is not synonymous with prostitution, as 'street-walking' later is. It is a sign or symptom of it, like bold or boisterous behaviour of other kinds. It is not a profession so much as a temptation to which all women are susceptible if they fail to embody the cardinal feminine virtues of chastity, obedience and silence.

Night Birds

Edward III's statute of 1331 had declared that nightwalkers were 'such persons as sleep by day and walk by night, being oftentimes pilferers, or disturbers of the peace'.[73] Sleeping by day and walking by night, these idle people led inverted lives. Noctivagation was an indelible sign of ill or evil living. In interrupting sleep, it snapped what Dekker called 'the golden chain that ties health and our bodies together'.[74] The legislation against 'common night walkers' was part of the ongoing campaign to criminalize the poor that, during the *longue durée* of the collapse of feudalism and the concomitant rise of capitalism, comprised such a significant aspect of the class struggle.

Historically, nightwalking by both men and women has threatened to erode the diurnal order and its political economy of industriousness. To give a particularly clear example of this, the *Constitutions of Masonry*, published in England in about 1430, singled out the dangers presented by common nightwalking, specifying that 'bi the whiche manere of nyghtwalkyng thei may not fulfyll ther day werke'.[75] Nightwalking is a kind of seduction – a going astray – that consciously or unconsciously turns its back on the discipline of wage labour. The ridiculous Absolon in Chaucer's 'Miller's Tale' resolves that he will adopt the subversive routine of a nightwalker in order to pursue his amorous ambitions: 'Therfor I wol go slepe an houre or tweye / And al the nyghte thanne wol I wake and pleye.' Glossing these lines in the late seventeenth century, the poet Richard Braithwait revealingly misread 'wake' as 'walke', and explained, 'He will go sleep an hour or two, that he may more ably turn Night-walker, or more properly, Eave-dropper.'[76]

The barrister Michael Dalton confirmed this emphasis on what might be characterized as the anti-routine of the nightwalker in *The Country Justice* (1618), where in a short section on 'Night-walkers' he identified them as people 'of Evil Behaviour, or of Evil Fame, and more particularly all such suspected persons as shall sleep in the day time and go abroad in the nights'. 'For as one saith, Such Night-walkers (or Night-birds) are ominous', he continued. 'And such Night-walkings are unfit for honest Men, and more suiting to the Thief (the right [i.e. night] Whistler) and to Beasts of the Prey; which come forth of their Dens, when Man goes to his rest.'[77] More than a century and a half later, nightwalking was still being defined in these terms – as a male activity that inverted the working day and disrupted its rhythms. In his *New Survey of the Justice of Peace His Office* (1772), William Sheppard referred to nightwalkers as 'idle *fellows* who use to sleep by day and walk abroad by night and are suspected to live by dishonest courses'.[78]

This emphasis on dubious diurnal and nocturnal habits is preserved even in the legal discourse of the later nineteenth century in the United States. In 1871, in the course of a case in Illinois, it was declared that 'one who walks the street at night is a night walker': 'Night Walkers are of suspicious appearance and behavior', it continued; 'The term denotes persons who sleep by day and walk by night'.[79] The common nightwalker, inhabiting the streets when ordinary, respectable citizens have confined themselves to their beds, is a man or woman turned upside down. He or she represents an intrinsic challenge to the diurnal regime on which, from the end of the Middle Ages, Protestant ideology and the political economy of capitalism partly depended.

This regime long outlasted the rise of 'night-labour' in the nineteenth century, against which Karl Marx among others agitated.[80] 'Factory manufacturing', as Jonathan Crary has insisted, 'did not abruptly extinguish the long-standing diurnal rhythms and social ties of agrarian milieus.'[81] Prior to the consolidation of '24/7' capitalism at the turn of the twenty-first century, not to sleep at night for one reason or another was therefore spontaneously to interrupt and undermine the diurnal rhythms that had for centuries structured the habits and routines of productive labour. If sleep, as Maurice Blanchot proposed, is a 'negation of the world' that nonetheless 'conserves us for the world and affirms the world', then the nightwalker, like the sleepwalker Blanchot invokes, 'is suspect, for he is the man who does not find repose in sleep'.[82]

In its affirmation of aimlessness and idleness, and its associations with the nomadic activities of masterless men and women, nightwalking has functioned historically as a refusal, conscious or unconscious, active or passive, of the physical and spiritual discipline imposed by feudal and capitalist societies. In the first part of John Bunyan's allegory *The Pilgrim's Progress* (1678), the poor itinerant Christian inadvertently provides a slogan for common nightwalkers when, shortly before he is benighted on 'the Hill *Difficulty*' as a result of carelessly falling asleep in the daytime, he rather rashly boasts to the two men he has encountered, Formalist and Hypocrisy: 'I walk by the rule of my master, you walk by the rude working of your fancies.'[83] Common nightwalkers – and their uncommon descendants, bohemians and poets whose movements have been comparatively free from the constraints of the city's diurnal order – implicitly resisted the rule of the masters, and walked instead according to the rude workings of their fancies.

2.

Idle Wandering Persons

Roisterers and Rogues in the Early Modern Period

Noises in the Night

On the night of Sunday, 21 January 1543, inhabitants of the City of London were disturbed by a violent commotion. It was an hour or so after the curfew, which had been rung out from St Mary-le-Bow at 8 p.m. The city's streets around Cheapside, London's principal marketplace, were dark. This was the time of 'shutting-in', when the more diligent and prosperous householders, who had lit lanterns outside their houses at dusk, extinguished the tallow candles that guttered in these slitted metal cylinders. Even thoroughfares like Cheapside itself were no more than dimly lit by candle lanterns left burning outside the more prominent houses to provide a point of navigation. Most respectable citizens were already in the beds they shared with their spouses or even servants, their rooms still half-lit by the embers from the fireplace.

On this particular night, there was shouting in the streets, and the unsettling noise of people running and laughing; then the ominous and distinctly uncommon sound of breaking glass, an expensive commodity in the sixteenth century. This was not some ordinary nighttime disturbance. The noises were too redolent of violence. After an intemperate but largely inaudible exchange, several voices cried out for the nightwatchmen, who arrived in a panic a minute or two later, to be greeted with abuse and laughter. Presumably a gang of drunken apprentices had got into a fight.

Some of the inhabitants of the city might nervously have recalled the murder that had taken place nearby at 4 a.m. one night in November 1536, little more than six years earlier, when the prominent evangelical Robert Packington, a respectable burgess, was shot dead as he crossed Cheapside to attend early-morning mass at the Mercers' Chapel. Few would have felt inclined to leave their homes and go out onto the streets to investigate, even if there hadn't been the threat of violence. Apart from the inconvenience of the soft, stinking mud of the streets, there was the danger of the night air, which was popularly believed to contain noxious vapours. Shakespeare's contemporary Thomas Dekker referred to it as 'that thick tobacco-breath which the rheumaticke night throws abroad'.[1]

Eventually the night no doubt settled back into an uncomfortable silence, interrupted by infants' cries and the intermittent barking of dogs; and those in bed buried themselves deeper under the covers against the cold. If one had preternatural hearing, one might have been able to hear sounds from the countryside surrounding the nearby city walls. In *Beware the Cat* (1553), William Baldwin's bizarre proto-novel, the protagonist Geoffrey Streamer develops a supernatural ability to hear the manifold sounds emitted at night within a hundred-mile radius of London. Holed up in a house at the end of St Martin's Lane, close to the city wall at Aldersgate, Streamer achieves this extraordinary acoustic sensitivity to the 'many noises in the night which all men hear not' by cooking, then eating, a cat, a fox, a hare, a hedgehog and a kite, and by performing an obscure ritual with various parts of their bodies, especially the ears and tongues.

In a passage that must count as the finest exercise in onomatopoeia in the English language, Streamer enumerates the 'commixed noises' that he is able to separate and isolate:

> barking of dogs, grunting of hogs, wailing of cats, rumbling of rats, gagling of geez, humming of bees, rousing of bucks, gagling of ducks, singing of swains, ringing of panns, crowing of cockes, cackling of hens, scrapling of pens, heeping of mice, trulling of dice, curling of frogs and todes in the bogs, churking of crickets, strutting of wickets, scratching of owls, fluttering of fowls, routing of knaves, snorting of slaves, farting of churls, sisling of girls, with many things else; as ringing of bells, counting of coins, mounting of groins, whispering of lovers, springling of plovers, grouting and spinning, baking and brewing, scratching and rubbing, watching and shrugging.[2]

Baldwin's list is a rich orchestration of the barely audible susurrations of the mid-sixteenth-century city after dark, from the intimate bodily noises of animals and humans to the discreet sounds of nocturnal industry; and it offers a hypnotic, if not oneiric, sense of London's relentless restlessness at night.

Breaking of Glass Windows

On Monday, 22 January 1543, the morning after the commotion in Cheapside, everyone was talking about the night's vandalism, especially once the damage done to property had become evident. It transpired that respectable citizens had been abused; incautious apprentices who happened to encounter the mysterious culprits had themselves been shot at; and, most sensationally, the windows of a number of merchants' houses, as far away as Fenchurch Street, as well as those of some churches, had been smashed. In Milk Street, off Cheapside, glass had been shattered on the façade of the expensive house belonging to Sir Richard Gresham, a trader and usurer who had been lord mayor of London in 1537.

There were also reports that, after causing all this casual destruction in the streets of the city, those responsible had headed to the banks of the Thames and commandeered a couple of boats. From the river, they had shouted obscenities and fired stones at the prostitutes congregated on Bankside (these women were making use of a final opportunity to trade their bodies at night with impunity, before the opening of parliament on the Monday morning rendered it illegal once again for the duration of the parliamentary session). The uproarious noises, it seemed, had only completely died out at about 2 a.m.

Who were the perpetrators of these acts? It was assumed by many that they were either vagabonds or inebriated apprentices. But, to everyone's shock, a Knight of the Garter, then still in his mid twenties, admitted that he had led this riotous parade through London. Henry Howard, Earl of Surrey, was a distinguished poet. He had been the protégé of Thomas Wyatt, who had died the previous autumn, and their translations and imitations of Petrarch had introduced the Italian sonnet form to England. So he could scarcely have been a more civilized and refined product of the reign of Henry VIII. But, like other poets of his time, including Philip Sidney, he was also a distinguished soldier – and one who had a relatively violent reputation.

In 1542, Surrey had been imprisoned for starting an altercation with another courtier in response to rumours that he was disloyal to the throne. He was subsequently released from the Fleet Prison so that he could be sent north with his father, the Duke of Norfolk, to fight the pro-French and papist Scots. Then, after an unsatisfactory military campaign on the borders, at the end of 1542 he had headed back to London. As his most recent biographer writes, 'His instinctive aggression, always simmering near the surface, had been unleashed by the authorized hooliganism that was the Scottish campaign, but not sated by it.'[3] He was looking for trouble, and the arrivistes of the city constituted a tempting target for his anger.

On returning to the capital, Surrey and his companions rented rooms in St Lawrence Lane, Cheapside, from one Millicent Arundel. His retinue included several reprobates, notoriously keen on gambling and drinking, and his servant, William Pickering, who some six years later was accused 'of breaking the curfew and bearing a "light and evil demeanour" towards the city's constables'.[4] At about 9 p.m., it transpired, Surrey and four other men, among them the son of Sir Thomas Wyatt, set out from Mistress Arundel's guesthouse. They wore cloaks against the cold and carried stonebows – weapons built like crossbows that fired stones rather than bolts.

Almost immediately, they marched to Milk Street, a few minutes' walk to the west – the home to 'many fair houses for wealthy merchants', as John Stow put it half a century later.[5] There, Surrey and the others fired their stonebows at Gresham's house. A good deal of class resentment probably informed this action, as Gresham was a successful merchant and a financial agent for Henry VIII, who had profited handsomely from the Dissolution of the Monasteries. No doubt the arrogance of an aristocrat on the defensive both at court and in the city – rather than mere youthful high spirits, as another biographer has indulgently claimed – partly explains the attacks of Surrey and his friends on the apprentices and prostitutes too.[6]

When the Privy Council examined the events of this night, Mistress Arundel testified (a little inaccurately) that Surrey had 'tarried forth after midnight', and added with a certain insouciance that 'next day was great clamour of the breaking of glass windows, both of houses and churches, and shooting of men in streets, and the voice was that those hurts were done by my Lord and his company'. Henry VIII, increasingly insecure at this time, felt threatened by the rumours that Surrey had been discussing the succession to the throne, so he and the bishop of Winchester conspired to have him charged both with 'eating of flesh' during Lent, which associated him with Lutheranism, and 'a lewd and unseemly manner of walking in the night about the streets and breaking with stonebows of certain windows'.[7]

Surrey denied the first charge but confessed to the second. He was duly sent back to the Fleet Prison, where he remained for a month.

Secret Silence of the Night

It was in the Fleet that Surrey wrote his 'Satire against the Citizens of London', a poem that, though still in manuscript form, was used some three years later as evidence against him when he was tried for conspiracy and treason, and finally executed.

'London! Has thou accused me / Of breach of laws?' In these arresting, accusatory tones, the 'Satire' begins. It is an extraordinary poem, at once prophetic and ironic, which challenges both London and Londoners with unprecedented urgency and vehemence. It starts out as an attempt to exculpate the poet's destructive behaviour in the metropolis on the night of 21 January. Surrey argues angrily and energetically, though not entirely convincingly, that it was precisely his loathing of the 'dissolute life' seething inside the city's 'wicked walls' – perhaps the adjective 'dissolute' is intended to evoke the Dissolution – that led him to express his 'hidden burthen' against those that 'work unright':

> In secret silence of the night
> This made me, with a rechless breast,
> To wake thy sluggards with my bow:
> A figure of the Lord's behest;
> Whose scourge for sin the Scriptures shew.

He thus identifies himself as the agent of divine justice, visiting retribution on the envious, the gluttonous, the lecherous, and on all the city's sinners: 'To stir to God this was my mind'. He reserves particular contempt, implicitly, for the city merchants who, enriched by the dissolution of monastic property, hoped to discipline and humiliate him. 'And greedy lucre live in dread', he writes, 'To see what hate ill got goods win'.[8] In the glottal, monosyllabic aggression of these strangely congested lines one can imagine the imprisoned Surrey spitting and choking with rage.

The poem ends up as an apocalyptic denunciation of the city. In language derived from the Book of Revelation, it condemns London as a 'shameless whore', a 'member of false Babylon', and predicts that famine, plague and ruin will destroy it. The city's 'proud towers, and turrets high' will be beaten 'stone from stone', and its iniquitous idols burnt. None shall bemoan its fate. It is tempting to interpret Surrey's barely controlled outburst in terms of what Freud calls a reaction formation – that is, an excessive, even obsessive reaction that represses its private complicity with the phenomenon it publicly rejects. It is as if Surrey denounces the sins of the metropolis so intemperately, so incontinently, because he is secretly conscious that he has internalized them. So if in this poem a 'new model of prophet-poet is born', as Surrey's most authoritative biographer has announced, then he is an oddly tortured, compromised prophet-poet.[9] Perhaps all prophet-poets, though, are thus compromised and tortured.

Surrey's fulmination against the citizens of London is far too emotionally confused and full of self-hatred for him to resemble some forerunner of William Blake, the mightiest prophet–poet in the city's history. But the poem makes a significant contribution to the tradition of portraying the nocturnal city as the site of, or inspiration for, apocalyptic scenes – a tradition that runs through Oliver Goldsmith and others in the eighteenth century to Charles Dickens in the nineteenth.

Blades that Roar

It was not uncommon for aristocrats to roister around London after dark in the early modern period. James Shirley, in *The Gamester* (1633), a tragi-comedy set in contemporary London, refers to

> the blades, that roare
> In brothells, and breake windowes, fright the streets
> At mid-night worse [the] Constables, and sometimes
> Set upon innocent Bell-men ...[10]

Confronting class supremacism of this sort, Gerard Winstanley was surely right to argue, in the final Digger pamphlet in 1650, that – in a properly just society – gentlemen as opposed to the itinerant poor should be punished as 'persons who wander up and down idly'.[11]

In 'The Night-Walkers; or, The Loyal Huzza', a broadside printed in 1682, there is evidence, in the more aggressively libertine culture of the Restoration, of a sort of roisterers' manifesto:

> The Town is our own,
> when the Streets are all clear;
> We manage the humour,
> and laugh at all fear;
> Then down goes the *Bully*,
> The *Heck*, and *Night-Walker*;
> The whispering *Cully*
> and every loud Talker:
> *The Constable flies,*
> *and his Club-men withdraw;*
> *When they hear the fierce cries*
> *of the dreadful* Huzza.

These brutal, over-bred upper-class oafs – 'The Wine in our heads, / and the Sword in our Hands' – resemble the seventeenth-century equivalent of members of Oxford University's Bullingdon Club.[12]

Printed in the year of the Rye House Plot against Charles II and his brother James, in a period of violent political reaction, this broadside's slogans go on both to glorify the monarch and his heir and to defy the Whigs 'and those who'd change Kings / without Reason or Law'. Acts of reckless hedonism, especially after the Civil War, constituted a declaration of Royalist allegiance. The roisterers of 'The Night-Walkers' boast about beating up lawyers, priests and captains, as well as the plebeian types identified in the opening verse. The bullies and 'hecks' are clearly male victims, and so by implication are the nightwalkers derided alongside them.[13] But the title of the broadside hints that, in a perverse and spiteful act of appropriation, these roisterers are determined to identify themselves too as nightwalkers. They seem to constitute a band of elite nightwalkers committed to terrorizing and tormenting the city's common nightwalkers.

The militant republican John Milton, in Book 1 of *Paradise Lost* (1667), wrote with admirable contempt of the ascendant nocturnal culture of the aristocracy, which flared into life like the artificial lights of a court masque as the sun set on the English Revolution: 'And when night / Darkens the streets, then wander forth the sons / Of Belial, flown with insolence and wine.'[14] Belial, whose sons resided in courts and palaces and decadent cities, was 'the proverbial devil for aristocratic vice', as one historian puts it, 'and during the English Revolution his name was synonymous with the Cavaliers'.[15] The subjects of 'The Night-Walkers; or, The Loyal Huzza' are precisely the sons of Belial Milton has in mind.

In opposition to this broadside's Royalist, ruling-class appropriation of the night for libertine purposes, Milton sought to redeem it as a time of spiritual contemplation. 'Il Penseroso' – a nocturne composed, like its companion piece 'L'Allegro', in approximately 1631 – is the clearest expression of this. The melancholic thinker of the poem's title, ambling alone among oaks in the moonlight, his lamp dimly visible, covertly reclaims the night from the Cavalier revellers who colonized it as a time of aristocratic sociability and celebration:

> I walk unseen
> On the dry smooth-shaven green,
> To behold the wandering moon,
> Riding near her highest noon,
> Like one that had been led astray
> Through the heaven's wide pathless way;
> And oft, as if her head she bowed,
> Stooping through a fleecy cloud.
> Oft on a plat of rising ground,
> I hear the far-off curfew sound.

The apparently errant character of the moon's drifting motion is no more than superficial, for she is in fact calm and chaste. The thinker, hidden from 'day's garish eye', enjoys the intimacies and the gentle ecstasies of strolling in what the poet later describes as 'a dim religious light'.[16]

Milton also battles against this decadent culture of the night in *Comus* (1634), his masque in celebration of chastity. There he proposes that, for the spiritually enlightened, night is not a time of darkness but of inner light: 'He that has light within his own clear breast / May sit i' the centre, and enjoy bright day.' The obverse is also the case. For the spiritually unenlightened, night is an internal condition, and hence one from which they cannot escape: 'But he that hides a dark soul and foul thoughts / Benighted walks under the mid-day sun; / Himself is his own dungeon.'[17] Hell is within. Nightwalking is in this sense a state of the soul, as well as merely a symptom of spiritual corruption. To paraphrase *Paradise Lost* (1667), the mind is its own place, and in itself can make a night of day, a day of night.

The seventeenth century, in spite of the interruption represented by the Revolution, was the era in which the social life of the monarch and his court increasingly centred on baroque spectacles that were dependent for their dazzling effects on the ostentatious illumination of the night. The architects of Stuart masques orchestrated fireworks, flaming torches and thousands of flickering candles, in order to stage the monarchy's brilliant authority against a background of darkness and ignorance. If there was husbandry in heaven on these nights of courtly celebration, to use Shakespeare's phrase, there was profligacy on the sets designed by Inigo Jones and others. 'This nocturnalization of political symbolism and everyday life at court', as Craig Koslofsky argues, 'arose to strengthen and supplement established symbols of spiritual and political sovereignty undermined by the confessional fragmentation of Western Christendom.'[18]

Only from the end of the seventeenth century, when London, like other European cities, became more systematically illuminated at night, did nightlife filter onto the streets and into the emergent culture of the bourgeoisie. In the first instance, it was about the spectacular representation of power as much as about forms of aristocratic recreation – gaming, whoring and roaring in the streets.

Witty Extravagants

Surrey's rampant appropriation of the metropolitan night in the mid sixteenth century might be interpreted as an incipient sign of this culture of nightlife, whose official expression at this time was the nocturnal entertainments staged at the court of Henry VIII. But his conviction for 'walking in the night about the streets' in an unseemly manner was an unrepresentative one; and not simply because, in contrast to so many of the sons of Belial anathematized by Milton, he was imprisoned for it. Poor people, not rich people, were in general charged with nightwalking. The propertyless, not the propertied, were usually accused of attacking merchants.

'The greatest offence against property', as E. P. Thompson puts it, in this period as in subsequent ones, 'was to have none.'[19] And to have none was to make oneself susceptible to criminalization. Perhaps the most telling detail of the story about Surrey is the assumption among respectable inhabitants of the city that the damage to property had been caused by either vagabonds or apprentices. For the authorities tended to accuse vagrants and (to a lesser extent) apprentices and prostitutes of this crime. These subalterns inhabited a city that, in contrast to the dramatically illuminated one of court masques or aristocratic parties, remained distinctly obscure. They made ideal scapegoats for the offence of sabotaging the city's peace and security at night.

Apprentices, many of whom had originally migrated from the countryside in search of regular wages, just like those who ended up as vagrants, were for their part regarded as a significant agent of social disruption at night in the early modern period. These young men, who fiercely defended their rather limited rights, tended to be central to political and religious demonstrations in the capital. They were also often responsible for social disturbances that had little to do with principled challenges to authority, both individually and collectively. In 1517, for example, apprentices were responsible for the Evil May Day Riots, a xenophobic demonstration inspired by a preacher at St Paul's Cross (and dramatized by Shakespeare and others in *Sir Thomas More* [c. 1592]). The authorities, which suppressed this outburst with troops, punished the perpetrators severely: they arrested 400, and, once they had hanged, drawn and quartered the leaders, gibbeted their remains.

By 1600 roughly 30,000 apprentices – comprising approximately 15 per cent of the city's population – filled London's proliferating workshops and warehouses. They tended to be unmarried male adolescents from the outlying regions of London who hoped, after their seven-year tenure, to rise through the lower ranks of metropolitan society and become shopkeepers or master craftsmen. In return for being trained in a trade – as drapers or grocers or mercers or skinners – they were paid a limited stipend and accommodated with their master's family.

But many of these apprentices, not least those with a predilection for alcohol, chafed under the imposition of their masters' domestic discipline. Popularly depicted as 'idle', they were often prosecuted for acts identified as 'vagrant' (almost three-quarters of the Londoners whose occupations were listed in the records of Bridewell between 1597 and 1608 were apprentices).[20] The nighttime – when they were freed from their duties to their employer but were nonetheless expected to remain indoors – was their particular domain. They had a reputation for unpredictable, violent behaviour in the night – specifically, as Peter Ackroyd states, for victimizing 'foreigners, "night-walkers", or the servants of noblemen who were considered to take on the airs of their superiors'.[21]

An uncontainable mass of class contradictions, these cocky, drunken adolescents blustered about after dark, drinking and looking for trouble – 'lying-out', it was called. They picked on vagrants or nightwalkers because they were poor and weak, and on servants because they were lackeys to the rich and powerful. Like the upper-class roisterers they aped, they too were self-aggrandizing walkers in the night who aggressively persecuted common nightwalkers. In addition, again like their social superiors, they liked to humiliate London's nightwatchmen, mocking them or beating them up. Some of them even styled themselves 'masters of the night'. Hence Anthony Nixon's advice to apprentices in 1613, which included the admonition to 'please thy master, / And all the night keep close within his doors'; and to 'Rove not about the suburbs and the streets / When he doth think you wrapped between his sheets'.[22]

In *The English Rogue* (1665), the story of an idle, thieving apprentice by Richard Head and Francis Kirkman, the protagonist's elderly master is characterized as 'a man of so strange a temper, that he delighted to invert the course of Nature, lying in bed by day, and walking in the night, the rain seldome deterring him'. But if the master's nightwalking is eccentric, the apprentice's nocturnal activities are riotous and villainous. Head and Kirkman's English Rogue steals from his master's bedchamber when the latter 'walk[s] abroad according to his custom at night'. This apprentice is identified in the book's subtitle as a 'witty extravagant'.[23] If the noun 'extravagant' indicates that the apprentice is 'a wasteful person, a spendthrift', then its etymological origin implies, according to the OED, that he is also 'one who strays or wanders from a place; a vagrant, wanderer', and, furthermore, 'a fanatic'. Throughout its history, the nightwalker circulates between two identities, both inflected by class – those of the eccentric and the fanatic.

Nightwalking Strumpets

Prostitutes were increasingly charged with being nightwalkers during the seventeenth century (and in certain contexts the words 'walk' and 'wander' were themselves no more than slang for strolling about with the intent of soliciting sexual custom). A court record from 1629 states that one Sara Powell's 'night walking and day walking got her noe good name and [that] she was accompted noe better than she should be'.[24] By the late seventeenth and early eighteenth centuries, as the Proceedings of the Old Bailey indicate, the term 'common nightwalker' was in legal discourse associated exclusively with female prostitutes. But, partly perhaps because of the rising obsession with crimes against property, in an increasingly capitalistic society, even female prostitutes were rarely convicted as common nightwalkers after the Restoration.

Instead, women convicted of minor crimes against property might be identified as nightwalkers only incidentally. In 1697, for instance, a prostitute called Christian Callow was convicted not for soliciting but for pick-pocketing – the legal record simply notes in passing that she was 'known to be a Common Nightwalker'. And in 1722 the phrase cropped up in a case of highway robbery, where the Proceedings record in evocative prose that, during the trial, Jonathan Wild, the 'Thief-Taker General', who was later exposed as a masterful criminal, took the common nightwalker Mary Floyd by the arm, and, 'looking wishfully in her Face; said, he had an Information against her, for picking a Gentlemans Pocket of a Watch'.[25] The term 'common nightwalker' had by this time largely lost its legal signification, though it no doubt retained a social referent. It had gradually boiled down into a term of abuse.

In his *Letters from the Dead to the Living* (1702), the satirist Thomas Browne refers almost proverbially to the fright given by 'the *Bridewell* Flog-Master to a Night-walking Strumpet'.[26] In this colloquial sense, as in the legal sense that preceded it, the term 'nightwalker' tended to be applied to common prostitutes, whose lives – in contrast to those of courtesans – were shaped by itinerancy and transiency. *The Wandring Whore* and *The Wandring Whore Continued*, which were published in rapid succession in 1660, contain for the reader's titillation and convenience a 'List of the names of the Crafty Bauds, Common Whores, Wanderers, Pick-pockets, Night-walkers, Decoys, Hectors, Pimps and Trapanners, in and about the City, and Suburbs of *London*'. Among the 180 or so names on this list, which include 'Toothless Betty', 'Butter and Eggs', 'Mrs Love' and 'Cock Birch', a woman known as 'Sugar-C' is the only one singled out as 'a constant wanderer & night-walker'. But, as its title indicates, this is a guidebook to a population that was inherently mobile and unsettled – one that lived according to the mantra that 'mony and Cunny are good Commodities'.[27] Prostitutes classified in these terms rarely had regular relationships with clients; and they earned their wages, as John McMullan has put it, 'on a mass production basis'.[28]

A luridly detailed image of the prostitutes that peopled the city streets at night in the mid seventeenth century emerges in two poems by the Protestant reformer and constable Humphrey Mill – *A Night's Search: Discovering the Nature and Condition of all sorts of Night-walkers* (1640) and *The Second Part of the Night's Search* (1646). Mill, who embroiders these volumes' authority with innumerable dedicatory and congratulatory verses, provides a pious but at the same time almost pornographic compendium of the nocturnal crimes he comes across while perambulating the city after dusk. Rambling in a double sense, the poems comprise sketches or case histories, in heroic couplets, of the vicious denizens of the London night, including 'penniless letchers', pimps and common prostitutes. Mill is at his most moralistic when condemning the latter, whom he holds responsible for corrupting both 'country clownes' and susceptible gentlemen (though as a good Puritan he also loathes 'the degenerate Nobility and new found Gentry').[29]

In the first *Night's Search* in particular, Mill provides misogynistic and racist descriptions of the prostitutes whose presence he allegedly monitors and polices. The forty-eighth section, for instance, is a portrait of 'a black impudent Slut that wore a dressing of faire hayre on her head'. 'But couldst thou change thy skin', he mocks in malicious tones, 'then thou might'st passe / For current ware, though thou art nasty trash.' Most of these depraved women, he is gratified to report, end up incarcerated in Bridewell. This volume concludes with verses by other hands that pay handsome tribute to the moral achievements of Mill's enterprise. The author of one of these congratulates him 'on his exact description of the Night-walkers of our time', and boasts that he himself 'lately walk'd your round, took full survey / Of all'.[30] Mill's itinerary thus provides the template for a guided tour of the sins of the metropolis.

Noctambulants of this prurient sort, who appointed themselves the guardians of the nocturnal city's morals, in spite of dubious motives for doing so, reappear in especially large numbers in the eighteenth century, as London becomes an increasingly rampant capital of the culture of consumption.

Vagrant and Wicked Persons

Mill's poems, which castigate nightwalkers as 'a brood of darknesses that do hate the light', direct their vituperation at the idle and criminal poor as well as prostitutes. Here, in clumsy heroic couplets, is a typical scene from Mill's second volume:

> I Walk'd alone, my brain on Fancies fed,
> The man i'th'Moone being newly gone to bed,
> My light was all confin'd within my brest,
> My eares were open, forward, still I prest,
> Till at the last I spi'd a glimmering shine,
> And heard a voice, which made my Muse incline
> To tune her song anew.[31]

The noctambulant, nurturing the flame of spiritual enlightenment in his breast, picks a solitary path through the pitch-black city, his senses sharpened by the moral imperative he obeys. He is like a knight on a journey through some darkened forest haunted by those Shakespeare calls 'night wanderers'.

The 'glimmering shine' that Mill glimpses in the distance signals no more than another example of the benightedness and corruption of the urban poor. Approaching it, he comes across three 'mandies', or professional beggars, who are removing their costumes and makeup after a day spent importuning passersby ('His arme's restor'd, his sores were made by Art', he comments about one of them). He sees them apportioning their ill-gotten gains, and also overhears them dividing up the locations in which they plan to beg the next day – 'Fleet-street shall be thine, / Turn-style is his, the Temple-lane is mine.' But it transpires that, in reality, they lead positively comfortable lives, for when they return to their homes, as one of them brags, 'I am no beggar then. / What e're I ask, I have for my delight.' This discovery inspires a violent diatribe from Mill: 'So do this brood of vermine, baske all day / To suck the spoyle; at night they part the prey.'[32] They are parasites, sucking the life from the industrious, virtuous city that prevails in the daytime, and conspiring, after dark, to tear it apart.

Most people prosecuted for nightwalking in the sixteenth and seventeenth centuries either lacked dependable, stable employment or had no occupation at all. These were the vagabonds and rogues of early modern England, some of whom had started out as apprentices but later resorted to petty crime because of the collapse, for one reason or another, of the master-servant relationship in which they had been indentured. They were among the most visible victims of the emergence of agrarian capitalism, which entailed the abolition not only of common land but of the customary rights that had hitherto shaped it. As one historian has commented, they were 'the complete obverse of all that was acceptable'.[33] In *The Poore Mans Hope* (1635), to give an example of the standard attitude to these economic migrants among the respectable classes, John Gore condemned vagrants as 'the very Sodomites of the land, children of Belial, without god, without magistrate, without minister; dissolute, disobedient, and reprobate to every good work'.[34] These sons and daughters of Belial, in contrast to those at the opposite end of the social scale – the ones Milton castigated in *Paradise Lost* – were not 'flown' or flushed with insolence, as he put it, so much as forlorn.

Displaced from the countryside by the enclosure of land, and impelled to the city by the hope of employment, rural labourers found themselves forced, throughout the early modern period, to compete in a market that, as food prices, rents and taxes rose and real wages declined, simply failed to accommodate them. The problem was exacerbated by additional demographic shifts, caused for example by Henry VII's abolition of private armies and the Dissolution of the Monasteries under Henry VIII. Injured and unemployed soldiers and sailors, on the one hand, and cooks, gardeners and launderers, on the other, ended up in London, attracted by the promise of higher wages in the metropolis but probably ill-prepared for both the poor employment prospects there and the paucity of secure accommodation. In spite of the high number of deaths from disease, especially the plague, London's population thus leaped from approximately 85,000 in 1565 to 140,000 in 1603, largely as a result of migration from the countryside. At a time of depression in the wool trade, when England suddenly found itself competing with countries across Europe, all these factors created the conditions for mass unemployment.

A large number of these jobless, mobile people, if they were not actually homeless, were forced to find temporary footholds in poorly built and collapsing buildings in London's slums and suburbs. In pursuit of profits, landlords brutally subdivided these boarding houses, which were made from little more than lath and plaster, and rammed them full of tenants. In 1582, for instance, a survey of St Margaret's, Westminster, discovered that one building in Tothill Street, which might formerly have been an inn, had been divided into seventeen tenements containing fifty-three lodgers in total.[35] The hasty construction of new buildings, in addition to the partition of existing ones, led in 1592 to an Act of Parliament which asserted that 'great Infection of Sickness and dearth of Victuals and Fuel hath growen and ensued and many idle vagrant and wicked persons have harboured themselves there'.[36] This was creative destruction, of an especially chaotic and exploitative kind, on an unprecedented scale.

Nursery of a Naughty and Lewd People

At night, except when a full or gibbous moon shone, London's densely populated, dirty and disease-ridden 'sinks' escaped illumination almost completely. These Stygian precincts, especially the foggy, tangled alleys close to the Thames, seemed even more deadly to outsiders after nightfall than they did in the day. During the sixteenth and seventeenth centuries lighting regulations were gradually introduced. Individual householders were required, on nights either side of the new moon, to provide candles overlooking the street between dusk and the nine o'clock curfew. But these candles, which were often of inadequate size or quality, produced a dirty, smoky, guttering flame. And, in any case, at other times of the month, when the moon was not 'dark', there was rarely a requirement to illuminate the streets at all. So on cloudy nights even the main thoroughfares of London were pitched into darkness soon after 9 p.m.[37]

The capital's slums also acquired a toxic reputation for being thieves' colonies. The most notorious of these during the early modern period was Whitefriars, the dangerously overcrowded area between Fleet Street and the Thames that, in a laconic reference to the territory fought over by France and Germany on the continent, was known as Alsatia. This region, which had once been the domain of mendicant monks, as its original name suggested, and which for a time had then been the domain of nobles, stood outside the city's secular jurisdiction. It was the most anarchic of London's 'liberties'. It therefore became popular as a refuge from the law in the seventeenth century, even after it was ravaged by the Great Fire of 1666. Daniel Defoe, accused of sedition, fled there in 1692 after seeing posters detailing his appearance pasted up in Fleet Street taverns.

Alsatia was a rotten honeycomb of dilapidated hovels that – in spite of repeated government proclamations intended to prevent precisely this happening – had been hastily constructed by speculative builders and partitioned into impossibly small rooms. Its alleys and foot passages pullulated with the poorest, most renegade members of society (including, after the Restoration, revolutionaries from the 1640s who had been forced underground). In *The Fortunes of Nigel* (1822), a novel set in the early seventeenth century, Walter Scott depicts the place as 'abound[ing] with desperadoes of every description', including 'bankrupt citizens, ruined gamesters, irreclaimable prodigals, desperate duellists, bravoes, homicides, and debauched profligates of every description'. They were all busy 'devouring each other for very poverty', he observes.[38]

Some of the suburbs to the south of the River Thames, particularly Southwark, along with places like Cripplegate and Newgate, and the precincts of Westminster Abbey, rivalled the reputations of the inner-city slums. These areas too consisted of 'small and strait roomes and habitations' crammed with 'idle, indigent, dissolute and dangerous persons', as a parliamentary stricture from 1603 put it.[39] Collectively, Sir Stephen Soame condemned them in 1601 as 'the nurcery of a naughty and lewd people, the harbour of rogues, theeves and beggars, and maintainers of idle persons'.[40]

It was these pockets of anarchic poverty, where constables and watchmen were scarce, which appeared to give credence to the rumours of an 'anti-society' of rogues, with its own elaborate rules and hierarchies, that were sponsored by the authors of so-called 'cony-catching' pamphlets such as Robert Greene and Thomas Harman. These tracts reinforced the idea that vagrants were sexually promiscuous, politically subversive, and organized along professional lines. In *A Caveat or Warning for Common Cursitors, Vulgarly Called Vagabonds* (1566), for example, the Kentish justice of the peace Harman defined no less than twenty-four types of vagabond, each with a specialized criminal skill. These included 'counterfeit cranks', who pretended to have the falling sickness, and 'anglers' or 'hookers', who used a staff to pilfer people's houses from the road (opportunistic thieves still employ this method in London, inserting a fishing rod through the letter box in order to reel in the resident's house keys). In truth, most urban crime involved casual and relatively disorganized theft for the purposes of subsistence.

But if many unemployed or chronically underemployed people were forced to inhabit dangerously overcrowded, jerry-built accommodation, a substantial number of the itinerant poor simply ended up homeless. In 'The Highway to the Spital-House' (1535–1536), a poem organized as a dialogue with a porter, Robert Copland complained about 'beggars and vagabonds' who go about 'Loitering and wandering from place to place'. During the summer, people of this sort 'keep ditches and busks [bushes] ... But in the winter they draw to the town, /And will do nothing but go up and down / And all for lodging that they have here at night.'[41]

Vagabonds arrived in the capital in particularly large numbers during the winter months, in part because the opportunities for labour in the countryside were more restricted then, and in part, presumably, because the social opportunities and sociability of the city made it slightly easier to resist a cold, hostile climate, especially at night. In his comments on the city, Copland marvelled 'that in the night so many lodge without', and boasted of finding them beside brick walls, under stalls, and in porches, sheepcotes and church doors. Sheepcotes were especially popular because, as in meat markets such as Smithfield, the bodies and breath of the closely packed animals produced desperately needed heat. Copland's porter is scornful of these 'michers' – that is, petty thieves and sneaks – 'that live in truandise'. 'Hospitality doth them always despise' is his complacent dismissal of them.[42]

The list of burials from parishes like St Botolph's, in Aldgate, in the 1590s, with its references to nameless, homeless vagrants who had died in the street, still delivers a shock more than four hundred years later (not least because, in a city that still suffers from pervasive homelessness, it remains all too resonant). 'A young man vagrant having no abiding place', it reads at one point, 'who died in the street before the door of Joseph Hayes, a brazier dwelling at the sign of Robin Hood in the High Street.' 'He was about 18 years old', the author of the list adds; 'I could not learn his name.'[43] One maid, of no address, is recorded as having died in the street near the postern. Other individuals, even more poignantly, are identified only by the clothes in which their bodies were found.

The men and women who suffered this sort of fate were of course illiterate, and the archives of the sixteenth and seventeenth centuries consequently contain few testaments from the victims of epidemic unemployment. The voices of vagrants are only to be found in what the medievalist Jacques Le Goff has called 'the archives of silence'.[44] The historian is therefore forced to imagine the desolate conditions in which they lived on the streets, or fought for life at least, and died: the cold; the loneliness; the days filled with people, pressing against one another, competing to subsist; the nights filled for the most part with emptiness, though never with complete silence; the sour smell of dirt; the sweeter smell of shit, animal and human … In the city, daily and nightly, derelicts of one description or another were unceremoniously deposited, as if by night-men, on the dust-heap of an ascendant capitalist system.

Enemies to the Common Weal

In a legal sense, vagabonds in early modern England were defined as the able-bodied, as opposed to disabled, poor. They were 'sturdy rogues', or 'sturdy beggars', in the language of the time. The first poor law of the sixteenth century, the Act of 1531, established the template. It built on earlier legislation against aliens and beggars, including the Egyptians Act of 1530, which sought to expel 'outlandish people calling themselves Egyptians', or gypsies. The language of the Act of 1531 distinguished a vagabond as 'any man or woman being whole and mighty in body and able to labour, having no land, master, nor using any lawful merchandise, craft or mystery whereby he might get his living'.[45]

No fewer than thirteen poor law acts between 1560 and 1640 reinforced this distinction between 'aged and impotent poor people' and poor people who were physically fit but idle. The former were to receive charitable relief, the latter to be apprehended and punished. According to the 'Acte for the punishment of Vacabondes' of 1572, for example, those 'Roges Vacaboundes and Sturdy Beggars' caught 'wandering, and mis-ordering themselves' were 'outrageous enemies to the common weal' who, once convicted, should be 'whipped and burnt through the gristle of the right ear with a hot iron, manifesting his or her roguish kind of life'.[46] Who were these rogues, vagabonds and sturdy beggars? In general, 'all and everye persone and persones beynge whole and mightye in Body and able to labour, havinge not Lord or Maister, nor using any lawfull Marchaundize Crafter [*sic*] or Mysterye whereby hee or shee might get his or her Lyvinge'. More specifically, those 'adjuged and deemed' to be vagrant included 'Fencers Bearewardes Comon Players [i.e. unlicensed actors]', as well as 'Juglers Pedlars Tynkers and Petye Chapmen'.[47]

This Act did make some slightly more humane concessions: it identified certain legitimate circumstances, including discharge from service, which temporarily excused the able-bodied unemployed from punishment; and it introduced the so-called 'poor rates', in order to provide assistance at parish level for the deserving poor. But the cumulative effect of this legislation, at a time of rising population and deepening unemployment, was to make itinerancy, and signs of inactivity, morally and socially unacceptable. Technically, even the death penalty could still be used against vagrants until 1597. Wandering by day and walking by night were both in practice outlawed.

Respectable Londoners, and those who aspired to be respectable, were distinctly alarmed by the presence of the mobile unemployed in the capital. During the Tudor period, the City of London – in contrast to developments to the east and west, which were less cramped and more uniform in social terms – teemed with people from the wealthy, the middling and the poorer classes. The physical proximity that these quite different sorts of citizens enjoyed or endured created the sense of chaotic excitement at which foreign visitors to the English capital frequently stood in amazement. Frederick, Duke of Wirtemberg, for example, observed at the turn of the seventeenth century that 'it is a very populous city, so that one can scarcely pass along the streets, on account of the throng'.[48] But the collision of bodies also reinforced class tensions. Specifically, it generated fear and misunderstanding of the unemployed among the middling and wealthy. 'The jobless, hanging about church steps and street corners, roaming the streets and alleys at night, were regarded as vagrants and potential criminals', as two historians of the city have recently observed, 'masterless men and women who, by dropping out of the Chain of Being, threatened the social order.'[49]

The Chain of Being, or *scala naturae*, was the religious ideology of hierarchical degrees, running from God, through angels, humans of all classes, and animals, to the minerals of the earth, that the Elizabethans had inherited from the Neoplatonists. In *Troilus and Cressida* (c. 1602), Shakespeare's Ulysses, a slippery politician, presents a potent, if disingenuous, image of disruption to the Chain of Being when he describes commotions of all kinds that 'rend and deracinate / The unity and married calm of states / Quite from their fixture'.[50] In 1602, the year in which Shakespeare probably wrote *Troilus and Cressida*, a government inquiry estimated that there were as many as 30,000 vagrants in London.[51] No doubt this was a considerable exaggeration, but they comprised an army of the unemployed all the same, and were therefore far too numerous to ignore. As 'servants to nobody', these people were not merely 'anomalies', as Christopher Hill puts it, but 'potential dissolvents of the society'.[52] Like the planets that 'in evil mixture to disorder wander', as Ulysses puts it,[53] these errant itinerants threatened to undermine the elaborately calibrated social order of communities and cities.

The 'impudent' as opposed to 'impotent' poor, the Devil's as opposed to God's poor, vitiated the discipline both of productive labour, centred in the guilds, and the patriarchal family, along with the religious doctrines that underpinned these spheres. In *The Poores Advocate* (1654), Richard Younge expressed his distaste for the 'horrible uncleanness' of 'vagrant Rogues', and explained that 'they have not particular wives, neither do they range themselves into Families: but consort together as *beasts*'.[54] They didn't fit into the hierarchical categories of an agrarian capitalist regime – which, in contrast to the feudal regime it was transforming, had little respect for poverty. Nor, transparently, could they keep pace with the rapid economic shift according to which the city was becoming a centre of finance capital dominated by successful merchants who had set up overseas trading companies. At night, furthermore, often forced to roam or loiter aimlessly in the streets, the unemployed undermined the stable rhythms of the labouring day and, more broadly, the urban economy.

To dismiss these itinerant men and women as 'idle', as official discourse did, and to criminalize them, as the courts did, was to declare that the accelerating process of modernization had already discarded them. In time, during the late eighteenth and nineteenth centuries, their rootlessness, and their relative lack of kinship ties, would make them ideal soldiers in the industrial army; for the moment, though, there was no economic mechanism that could exploit these qualities on a mass scale.

Bellman's Cry

If the destitute were conspicuous enough in the day, they attracted especially dubious attention after nightfall. The activities of the poor were popularly assumed to be more suspicious after dark, as the medieval nightwalker statutes had indicated. Moreover, respectable citizens, if not asleep, tended like most people to be more apprehensive in the night, when the slightest noise – a heavy footfall, the murmur of voices, or the sinister tinkle of breaking glass – created an ominous sense of tension.

Magistrates certainly adopted a more punitive attitude to people who were apprehended at night. 'The law is not the same at morning and at night', wrote the poet George Herbert in a collection of proverbs in 1652.[55] As in the Middle Ages, the night was in effect an 'aggravating circumstance', to use Jean Verdon's formulation: 'Malefactors were not merely infringing the rules of public order;

acting under cover of darkness, they were demonstrating their evil intentions, their deep perversity, and premeditation.'[56] And, until the mid eighteenth century, the moral and even mythological associations of the night in the cultural imagination, its innately malign connotations, were reflected in the fact that the principal police forces in Europe's cities, if they can be called police forces at all, were the nightwatches. Certainly, they comprised 'the centerpiece of London law enforcement'.[57]

The watchmen, or 'bellmen', who operated under the supervision of 'constables of the night', were organized according to local wards. They worked in pairs, so that one could patrol the streets while the other remained in the watch-house or 'watch-box'. These men, whose professional hours were between 9 p.m. and 7 a.m. in the winter months and 10 p.m. and 5 a.m. in the summer, were expected to perform a number of duties, including calling the hours, announcing the state of the weather, preventing the spread of fires, checking locks, clearing the taverns and – most importantly – deterring or pre-empting criminal activity.

Of these tasks, perhaps the least pressing, and the most curious, was that of calling the hours. A characteristic example of a watchman's chorus can be found in Thomas Dekker's 'The Bellman's Cry' (1608):

> Midnight feastings are great wasters,
> Servants' riots undo masters.
> When you hear this ringing bell,
> Think it is your latest knell.[58]

Another one is recorded in Thomas Ravenscroft's *City Rounds* (1611):

> Give ear to the clock,
> Beware your lock,
> Your fire and your light,
> And God give you good night.
> One o'clock![59]

Cries such as these, repeated at hourly intervals throughout the night, combined time-keeping, which was undoubtedly useful in an age when most people had no clocks, with ritualized and rather pointless advice about either domestic security (as in Ravenscroft's example) or moral welfare (as in Dekker's). People who weren't used to this ritual, such as those who had recently arrived from the countryside, complained vociferously about the interruption to their sleep. For their part, seasoned inhabitants of the city presumably became inured to these habitual disturbances. In either case, it is difficult to understand why the cries were deemed necessary.

'To whom did officers address their cries?' the historian Roger Ekirch asks with comic emphasis; 'Who possibly could have been listening in the late hours of the evening?' He offers two explanations: first, that 'the calls were designed to verify that the watchmen had not themselves drifted asleep, slumped in some alley'; second, that fitful sleep of the kind produced by these interruptions 'heightened people's vigilance to perils of all sorts, including enemy attacks, criminal violence, and fire'.[60] I prefer the former reason (in part because the deleterious effect of these cries on people's ability to labour productively during the day renders the latter reason rather implausible). The watchman's calls were phatic; that is, instead of communicating information, they simply imparted a minimal sense of the community, almost subliminally reinforcing the idea that someone was policing it.

Dogberries

The Compleat Constable (1692) set out the primary commitment of the nightwatchmen in these terms: 'You shall do your best endeavour that the Watch in your Town be duly kept, and that Hue and Cry be duly pursued according to the Statutes; and that the Statute made for punishment of Rogues, Vagabonds, and Night-Walkers, and such other idle wandring Persons coming within your Liberties be duly put in execution.'[61] In particular, then, watchmen were expected to apprehend nightwalkers, prostitutes and others who loitered or straggled in the streets. 'You shall comprehend all vagrom [or vagrant] men; you are to bid any man stand, in the Prince's name', Dogberry instructs the Second Watchman in *Much Ado About Nothing* (1598), congratulating him for being 'the most senseless and fit man for the constable of the watch'.[62]

According to a recognizance, these idle, wandering persons could be bound over to keep the peace not because there was proof that they had committed a crime but simply because their appearance was suspicious. 'Persons apprehended late at night by the watch were often bound over if they were unable to "give a good account" of themselves', as a scholar of petty crime in the period has explained.[63] This generally meant that the watchmen or constable detained the defendants in the watch-house for the remainder of the night, and conveyed them to the justice of the peace the next morning, possibly housing them in the counter – the prison attached to the court – in the meantime. It was from there that they could be consigned to a house of correction such as Bridewell.

The night watch was originally the civic duty of all able-bodied and respectable citizens, who could be indicted for not serving their community in this capacity. Later, as popular concern about rising crime in the metropolis increased across Europe over the course of the sixteenth and seventeenth centuries, it became a salaried role. If it became professionalized, though, this did not necessarily make it more efficient. It simply meant that the task of policing the city was subcontracted to people who, generally recruited from the lower orders, were paid a minimal, if not derisory, sum for performing their duties.

These incumbents, who often had a job in the daytime too, tended to be desperate for any kind of employment. They were by no means qualified or trained to patrol the streets. And they didn't have a uniform. Instead, they put on thick, dark cloaks or coats to insulate them from the cold, and shrouded their heads in hats or long pieces of rag. Furthermore, though some of them carried halberds or staffs, they were often armed with no more than candle-lanterns. At least before the introduction of public lighting in the main thoroughfares of London, which took place from the mid 1680s, they had inadequate means of illuminating the streets of the city – especially those in which crime was most likely to be committed, or to which criminals were most likely to retreat. It is therefore not a complete overstatement to claim that public order in the metropolis at night in the sixteenth and seventeenth centuries depended on elderly, infirm, often inebriated, occasionally nefarious individuals – in short, on Dogberries.[64]

In a letter of 1620, James Howell, the author of *Londinopolis* (1657), bragged to a friend about 'the excellent nocturnal government of our city of London'. His claim was no doubt exaggerated; but, as Paul Griffiths has argued, even though the city's administration, finances and lighting all became considerably more effective in the eighteenth century, 'the essential elements of the night-watch were performing competently by the middle of the seventeenth century'.[65] I have no reason to doubt his claim, but if the night watch in the early modern period was indeed competent, it seems scarcely more than miraculous. It was a poorly paid and haphazardly organized form of employment. And its incumbents were frequently criticized for sleeping and drinking on duty, and for proving broadly inadequate to the task of policing the streets.

For these lapses they were popularly abused. Sometimes they were also beaten, or even killed. 'It would be difficult to exaggerate the extent of popular contempt for nightwatchmen', Ekirch writes.[66] Certainly, there were plenty of commentators in the early modern period who thought them incompetent. Or corrupt. Shakespeare is probably typical of public opinion when he depicts Dogberry advising his watchman that 'the most peaceable way for you, if you do take a thief, is to let him show himself what he is, and steal out of your company'.[67] For Shakespeare's constable, 'stealing' is a matter not of thieving but, rather more positively, of escaping. Peaceableness, not the prevention of crime or the detention of criminals, is his priority.

Unscrupulous watchmen, as opposed to simply supine ones, operated at the profitable interface between crime and law enforcement. They fenced stolen goods, or confiscated them and secretly sold them on. And they used and exploited prostitutes. In Act V of *Microcosmus: A Morall Maske* (1637), Thomas Nabbes, who shortly after contributed a dedicatory verse to Humphrey Mill's *A Night's Search*, introduced a whore who has fallen on hard times and is consequently forced to consort with 'inferiour customers'. This 'desperate piece of neglected mortality' confesses that 'Night-walking' – in the sense of soliciting sex on the streets – 'supply'd me, whil'st I had any thing to pleasure a constable, or relieve the mortified watch with a snatch [or hasty sexual act] and away'.[68] Some of the watchmen probably pimped prostitutes too. Others abused their authority in order to assault women. In 1705, to give a later example, a constable called Thomas Bayly was bound over to appear at the Westminster Quarter Sessions, where he was accused of using one Elizabeth King 'in an Undecent manner of rudeness', which entailed 'having taken her upp for a common Nightwalker and … offering to put his hand up her coats'.[69]

Watchmen also accepted money in exchange for certain deals and dispensations, including unimpeded access to the streets at night. In Samuel Rowley's play *When You See Me, You Know Me* (1603–1604), the legendary criminal known as Black Will, who is subsequently co-opted by Henry VIII into becoming a soldier, has cut a deal with the corrupt watchmen, and is therefore at liberty to walk through the streets of London at night: 'Doe but walke with me through the streetes of *London*, and let mee see the proudest watche disturbe us', he boasts.[70] Semi-professional, watchmen were also semi-criminal.

Night-watchers

In *Londinopolis*, Howell neatly polarized the denizens of London's night in terms of nightwatchers and nightwalkers: 'To this Prison', he wrote of the Tun, 'the Night-watchers to this City, committed not only Night-walkers, but also other persons, as well spiritual as temporal, whom they suspected of incontinency.'[71] In practice, however, there was no simple opposition between these groups of people. Those who watched at night were often confused with those who walked at night. Both were routinely identified as spies or eavesdroppers. In her study of late medieval and early modern court records, Marjorie McIntosh notes that, in the sixteenth century, the term *vigilator* was used in legal discourse to signal someone who watched and walked at night, and comments that it 'implied a destructive inversion of the responsible role played by those who maintained the official night-time patrol of the community, known as the *vigilatio*'.[72]

The dictionaries and glossaries of the sixteenth and seventeenth centuries testified to this persistent confusion of identities. The Latin term *tenebrio*, for example, was sometimes translated as 'night watcher', as in Richard Huloet's *Dictionary* (1552), and sometimes as 'micher', a thief who skulks about or keeps out of sight, as in Charles Hoole's *An Easie Entrance to the Latin Tongue* (1649), published a century later.[73] In both cases, watching and walking at night are darkly intertwined.

A similar ambiguity obtains, long after the Renaissance, in the definitions of various nocturnal activities included in the seventeenth volume of the *Encyclopaedia Londinensis* (1820). A 'night-walker', according to the authors of this Enlightenment dictionary, is 'one who roves in the night upon ill designs'. A 'night-watcher', meanwhile, is 'one who watches through the night upon some ill design'.[74] In both cases, an inversion of the role played by the authorities is once more apparent. To nightwalk is to enact a malign parody of the watchman's patrol; to nightwatch is to enact a malign parody of his supervision or surveillance of the community and its individuals.

The watchman was regularly guilty of malign or corrupt behaviour, or of acting from dubious motives, so he often collapses into his opposite. His nightwalking, his nightwatching, was often quite as nefarious as that of the itinerants and prostitutes he was supposed to apprehend. Required for official reasons to be suspicious of other people, the watch was also, in a more colloquial sense, suspicious – that is, suspect. Here is an early instance of that entanglement of the identities of detective and criminal that is characteristic of noir cinema and fiction in the mid twentieth century. On the mean streets of the sixteenth and seventeenth centuries, before the introduction of public lighting, but perhaps right up to the introduction of a professional metropolitan police force in the early nineteenth century, nightwalkers and nightwatchmen, dressed alike in tattered, ragged clothes, could be hard to discriminate.

3.

Affairs that Walk at Midnight

Shakespeare, Dekker & Co.

Black Brow of the Night

'No pen can anything eternal write, / That is not steep'd in humour of the Night', insisted George Chapman, the Renaissance dramatist, poet and translator, in *The Shadow of Night* (1594), his first published poem.[1] The plays of William Shakespeare are comprehensively steeped in the humour of the night, its animal and spiritual disposition. So is the poetry and prose of a number of his collaborators, competitors and acquaintances, most prominently Thomas Dekker and John Fletcher. The night, for Shakespeare and his contemporaries, is both a mythology and a psychology. It is also a kind of existential condition. In the definition offered by Roland Barthes, it is a 'state which provokes in the subject the metaphor of the darkness, whether affective, intellective, or existential, in which he struggles or subsides'.[2]

What are the uses and values of the night in Shakespeare? What are its peculiar forces? Shakespeare presents a panorama of people who occupy the night. More than any of his contemporaries, he offers the full assortment of forms assumed by the nightwalker in the early modern period, from the earthy to the ethereal. These diverse activities – from carousing to sleepwalking, conspiring to spirit-walking – appear at first sight to be disparate in their motivation. But it transpires that many of them, even the apparently innocent or innocuous ones, resemble common nightwalking in all its disreputable associations with idleness and vagrancy.

'Who dares not stir by day must walk at night', Philip the Bastard tells Queen Elinor at the beginning of Shakespeare's *King John*, written in the mid 1590s;[3] and, at the end of the play, Hubert de Burgh walks 'in the black brow of the night' in order 'to find [Philip] out'.[4] Those who for one reason or another do not find a home in the day often seek one in the night. Night is the domain of illicit desires, political and sexual, and in Shakespeare's comedies and tragedies, as in those of his often brilliant contemporaries, these can lead to psychological collapse, if not social chaos. 'In the dark and loathsome night, wherein all things are covered and hidden', advised the popular devotional manual *A Pensive Man's Practice* (1584), 'such as intend to work wickedness, are most ready.'[5]

Minions of the Moon

Shakespeare's plays offer fascinating glimpses of the reasons people find themselves seeking or exploiting the protection of darkness – all of them more or less nefarious, more or less mysterious.

Carousing in the streets is one nocturnal activity portrayed by Shakespeare, especially in those English history plays that, though set in the fourteenth and early fifteenth centuries, offer compelling glimpses of contemporaneous London life. For example, in the final scene of *The Merry Wives of Windsor* (1597–1598), set at midnight, poor old Falstaff, who has been taunted and taught a humiliating lesson by the other characters, decries the puritanical culture that prevents him from fulfilling his Dionysian desires, and declares, 'This is enough to be the decay of lust and late-walking through the realm.'[6] Lust and 'late-walking' are coupled in this line because the latter implies soliciting prostitutes on the street as well as roistering.

Falstaff loves the night, and aligns himself with its rhythms rather than those of the day. 'We that take purses', he reminds Prince Hal in *I Henry IV* (1596–1597), when he is still an uninhibited libertine and thief, 'go by the moon and the seven stars, and not by Phoebus, he, "that wand'ring knight so fair".'[7] It is Falstaff, not Phoebus, the sun, who wanders about at night, and who is in effect the 'wand'ring knight'. He and Hal are 'gentlemen of the shade, minions of the moon', governed by their 'noble and chaste mistress the moon ... under whose countenance we steal'.[8] Surreptitiously – and inappropriately, since they are knights – they are 'squires of the night's body'.[9]

In a later scene of *I Henry IV*, set in the Boar's Head in Eastcheap, Falstaff berates himself for living 'out of all order, out of all compass', and then abuses his friend Bardolph, whose face is so radiant red from drink that it acts like a beacon in the night: 'Thou has saved me a thousand marks in links and torches', he tells him, 'walking with thee in the night betwixt tavern and tavern'.[10] Falstaff is in social terms a nightwalker not of the common kind; he is a dissolute aristocrat who escapes criminalization because of his class.

Despite his apprenticeship to Falstaff, who has acted as 'the tutor and the feeder of [his] riots', Hal renounces the dissipations of the night when, at the end of *2 Henry IV* (1597–1598), he accedes to the throne and becomes Henry V.[11] Instead, in *Henry V* (1598–1599) itself, he finds other uses for the night, morally redeeming his relation to it in the name of martial solidarity rather than ribald companionship. On the night before the Battle of Agincourt – 'When creeping murmur and the poring dark / Fills the wide vessel of the universe' – Henry disguises himself and goes 'walking from watch to watch, from tent to tent', talking and listening to his demoralized soldiers in order to ascertain their state of mind.[12] In this play, 'a little touch of Harry in the night' implies heroic inspiration rather than corruption.[13]

Henry V was probably first performed in the summer of 1599, the same year in which another play featuring Henry V in disguise appeared. In *Sir John Oldcastle* (1600), by Drayton, Hathaway, Munday and Wilson – though on the title-page of its first edition it is attributed to Shakespeare – the king conducts a kind of surveillance operation on a Protestant conspiracy being fomented in London. In a nod to his riotous past, he refers to himself as one who has 'beene a perfect night-walker' in order to explain the ease with which he conceals his identity.[14]

Four or five years later, Samuel Rowley employed the same device in *When You See Me You Know Me* (1605), a play in which Henry VIII conceals his identity at night in order to patrol the streets and so understand the criminal underside of London:

> This night we meane in some disguised shape,
> To visit *London*, and to walke the round,
> Passe through their watches, and observe the care
> And speciall diligence to keepe our peace.
> They say night-walkers, hourely passe the streets,
> Committing theft, and hated sacriliege:
> And slightly passe unstaied, or unpunished.

Henry is arrested, to comic effect, after a physical fight with Black Will, who has been conducting him on a journey through the streets of the nocturnal city. Black Will is himself a notorious nightwalker and thief who is forced by his infamous reputation, in a delightful phrase, to 'live upon darke nights and mistie mornings'.[15] Once again, nightwatchers and nightwalkers are difficult to distinguish.

Men All in Fire

Conducting clandestine affairs, whether political or sexual, is another of the uses or possibilities Shakespeare ascribes to 'the dark and loathsome night, wherein all things are covered and hidden'.

In the opening scene of *Richard III* (1592), the Duke of Clarence complains to Richard in embittered tones about the 'night-walking heralds' that 'trudge between' Edward IV and his lover Mistress Shore.[16] These discreet but implicitly mercenary intermediaries indicate that the two of them are conducting affairs of state, as well as adulterous relations, in secret. In the final act, at 'dead midnight', after a dream in which he is visited by the ghosts of his victims, Richard suffers an attack of insomnia and paranoia, and asks, 'What do I fear? Myself? There's none else by'.[17] A secret self is fostered, or festers, at midnight – the time when, until the end of the early modern epoch, most people's 'first sleep' ended, as a result of an apparently natural process, and they endured or enjoyed an interval of sleepless contemplation or activity before their 'second sleep'.[18]

In *Julius Caesar* (1599), Shakespeare explores the effect of these conspiratorial possibilities of the night not simply on the state of a nation but on an individual's state of mind. Here, too, nocturnal affairs acquire psychological as well as spiritual meanings. The spirits – including Caesar's, which appears in the shape of a 'monstrous apparition' at the end of Act IV – materialize in the mind of Brutus, with deepening intensity, as the drama proceeds.[19]

From the start of the play, the conspiracy against Caesar is identified with the night. In Act I, Scene iii, set on a street at night during a cataclysmic thunderstorm, the senator Cicero and the conspirator Casca, who have recently accompanied Caesar on his triumphant return to Rome, discuss the portents that point to the destruction of the state. The left hand of a common slave, Casca reports, 'did flame and burn / Like twenty torches join'd', but miraculously left him unscorched.[20] Furthermore:

> there were drawn
> Upon a heap a hundred ghastly women,
> Transformed with their fear, who swore they saw
> Men, all in fire, walk up and down the streets.[21]

Cicero sensibly warns Casca that that 'this disturbed sky / Is not to walk in'.[22]

Cassius, who will also act as one of Caesar's assassins, revels in this menacing nighttime, however, as passive as a lover caught up in a violent passion – 'For my part, I have walk'd about the streets, / Submitting me unto the perilous night', he boasts.[23] Cassius seems positively to savour the fact that – apart from the presence of other conspirators – 'this fearful night, / There is no stir or walking in the streets'.[24] To be out on the streets of the city on a night like this is to align oneself with the signs of an imminent apocalypse. In this context, the nightwalker, 'all in fire', is a political incendiary who flames and burns. One of the provisions included in the Twelve Tables established in Rome in the mid fifth century BCE stipulated that 'no persons shall hold meetings by night in the city' because of the danger of political conspiracy. It was partly this association of nocturnal with conspiratorial activities that persuaded William I to institute the curfew in late eleventh-century England.

In the next scene of *Julius Caesar*, which is also set at night, Brutus finds himself unable to sleep, and paces around his orchard restlessly attempting to decide whether Caesar should be killed.[25] Brutus reconsiders Caesar's political ambition and concludes that its terrible consequences are only likely to be apparent once he has actually been crowned emperor – 'It is the bright day that brings forth the adder, / And that craves wary walking'.[26] Like the other conspirators, Brutus is, in contrast to the bright day, uninhibited when walking in the dark night. Nighttime is the element in which Brutus, who admits he has been incapable of sleep since he first had doubts about Caesar, feels restlessly at home.

'Between the acting of a dreadful thing / And the first motion', Brutus soliloquizes, not unlike both Hamlet and Macbeth, 'all the interim is / Like a phantasma or a hideous dream'.[27] His state of mind, like the night, describes an interval of hallucinatory inaction. And as the night proceeds, inching on into the day, it acquires an even more sickly and feverish quality. When Portia appears, her sleep also interrupted, she anxiously asks her husband, 'Is Brutus sick, and is it physical / To walk unbraced and suck up the humours / Of the dank morning?'[28] But it is less 'the vile contagion of the night' that she fears than the 'sick offence within [his] mind'.[29] Brutus, an insomniac rehearsing a world-historical drama, has interiorized the night.

In *Catiline* (1611), to take an even more lurid example from the period, Shakespeare's rival Ben Jonson also exploited the apocalyptic associations of the conspiratorial night. This Jacobean tragedy, centred on the first-century Roman who conspired to overthrow the Republic and destroy the metropolis, opens shortly before first light in Catiline's house, where the ghost of Sylla, former dictator of Rome, makes an ominous promise 'to engender with the night, and blast the day'. This spectre salutes a day that, already restless with apocalyptic signs that have been 'brought forth by night, with a sinister birth … start[s] away' from the 'half-sphere' of night. Later in the scene, once Catiline has arisen from his sleep, he is visited by Lentulus, another conspirator, who invokes 'a morning full of fate' on which the sun drags itself into the heavens as if 'all the weights of sleep, and death hung at it'.[30]

Lentulus then continues, in remorseless and relentless images, to describe the day breaking in the shadow of what, after the surrealist philosopher Georges Bataille, might be characterized as a 'rotten sun':[31]

> She is not rosy-fingered, but swollen black!
> Her face is like a water, turned to blood,
> And her sick head is bound about with clouds,
> As if she threatened night, ere noon of day![32]

Here, the rosy fingers of the Homeric dawn are blackened and disfigured by necrosis. The morning is an incipient corpse, poisoned and corrupted by a night that is psychopathic, if not necrophiliac. As in Shakespeare's plays about conspiracies of state, the night in Jonson's *Catiline* is a half-sphere that threatens to consume the inner life of individuals, the civilization over which these individuals fight, and finally, perhaps, the entire cosmos.

Sin-Guilty Consciences

The final act of Shakespeare's *Henry VIII*, written with John Fletcher and first performed on 29 June 1613, the date the Globe burnt down, reinforces the conspiratorial meanings of the night, which is the time or dimension when 'such as intend to work wickedness, are most ready'. It opens with an encounter in London, at 1 a.m., between Gardiner, the bishop of Winchester, and Sir Thomas Lovell. 'These should be hours for necessities, / Not for delights', Gardiner comments to his page, who carries a torch before them; 'times to repair our nature / With comforting repose, and not for us / To waste these times'. To waste the night by not sleeping is to waste the body by not repairing it. Political rhythms, especially at a time of conspiratorial intrigue, interrupt organic ones. In Falstaff's phrase, they put them out of order, out of compass.

Alarmed by the political prominence of Cranmer, Cromwell and the new queen, Anne Boleyn, Gardiner demands that Lovell tell him what he is doing out so late, and admonishes him:

> Affairs that walk –
> As they say spirits do – at midnight, have
> In them a wilder nature than the business
> That seeks dispatch by day.[33]

At night, ideas and individuals are all wilder than in the day.[34] As the conjuror Roger Bolingbroke had insisted when he and his accomplices called up a spirit in *2 Henry VI* (1590–1591), 'deep night, dark night, the silent of the night', when 'spirits walk, and ghosts break up their graves', is the time for conspiratorial and criminal acts.[35]

As these pairings of conspirators and criminals with spectres indicate, ghosts are prominent among those that walk at night in the early modern period. Haunting and feeling haunted at night are hard to disassociate. The Swiss theologian Ludwig Lavater's *De Spectris* (1570), translated into English as *Of Ghostes and Spirites Walking by Nyght* (1572), catalogued innumerable cases of otherworldly wandering. An attack on 'Catholic claims that ghosts and purgatorial spirits proved the reality of Purgatory', as Craig Koslofsky explains, the book did not deny the existence of apparitions, but identified them instead as 'a deception of the Devil, intended to tempt Christians into false belief'.[36] Its popularity signalled a shift in thinking about the night.

Increasingly, in the Protestant imagination, the night and its agents, which included witches as well as spectres, became associated with temptation and spiritual darkness. This is reflected, too, in the playwright and poet Thomas Nashe's prose pamphlet *The Terrors of the Night* (1594), which had counselled that 'when Night in her rustie dungeon hath imprisoned our ey-sight, and that we are shut seperatly in our chambers from resort, the divell keepeth his audit in our sin-guilty consciences'. Nashe adds that this scrupulous devil, tabulating our sins according to 'an index of iniquities', is not singular but multiple. He conjures up a corporation of malign spiritual accountants. Furthermore, 'if in one man a whole legion of divells have bin billeted, how manie hundred thousand legions retaine to a Tearme at *London*?'[37] The innumerable inhabitants of the city teem with malign spirits. In the Renaissance, Nashe's pamphlet implies, night was interiorized in the context of mass urbanization.

Hamlet (1600–1601) – in which Shakespeare does rather more than use a spectre simply to spice up the plot, as most revenge tragedies did – probably drew on these religious debates in order to exploit what Stephen Greenblatt has called a 'poetics of Purgatory'.[38] Its action begins at midnight on the battlements of the castle at Elsinore, where the guards discuss the fact that, on two previous occasions, the old king's ghost has processed past them with 'martial stalk' at the 'dead hour'.[39] They have been joined by Hamlet's friend Horatio, who is soon convinced, like the conspirators in Shakespeare's recent play about Caesar, that 'this bodes some strange eruption to our state', and who even recalls that 'a little ere the mightiest Julius fell, / The graves stood tenantless, and the shattered dead / Did squeak and gibber in the Roman streets'.[40] On the succeeding night, Hamlet himself encounters the ghost: 'I am thy father's spirit, / Doom'd for a certain term to walk the night ...'[41]

There is something purgatorial, it might be argued, about almost all forms of walking at night. Nightwalking is caught between a state of freedom and one of confinement. For the nightwalker, as for the spectre, the nighttime represents liberation from what Hamlet's father calls the 'prison-house' in which he is constrained by day[42] – and, at the same time, a sort of sentence.

Walking Too Late

It is in *Macbeth* (1606), the events of which unfold at a time when 'o'er the one half-world, / Nature seems dead, and wicked dreams abuse / The curtain'd sleep', that Shakespeare most comprehensively explores the uses of the night.[43] As the critic A. C. Bradley commented of the play in his classic book on Shakespearean tragedy, 'it is remarkable that almost all the scenes which at once recur to memory take place either at night or in some dark spot'.[44] Here, Shakespeare portrays a range of types of walking that take place at night: the spectral, the criminal, the conspiratorial and the psychopathological.

The witches, 'secret, black, and midnight hags', are of course representatives of the spectral realm.[45] As 'instruments of darkness', shaped and sharpened by the example of both Lavater's and Nashe's tracts, they perform their sinister rituals at night in order to tempt Macbeth into embracing his satanic fate.[46] But Banquo is also a spirit-walker, or becomes one. In Act III, Scene i, he informs Macbeth that, if he fails to make good time riding back to his host at the end of the day, he 'must become a borrower of the night'.[47] When Macbeth next encounters Banquo, in Act III, Scene iv, the latter is a bloodied apparition who takes an empty seat at the feast. For Macbeth has commissioned three murderous thugs to assassinate him in the interim. A borrower of the night, Banquo has been brutally stolen back by it.

Macbeth's murderers – or 'nightwalking cudgeller[s]', to appropriate a wonderfully suggestive phrase from John Milton – have ambushed the 'lated traveller' as he returned to the castle with his son Fleance at nightfall.[48] To be belated is to be benighted. 'Who did strike out the light?' one of the assassins cries as Fleance flees.[49] As Lennox later solemnly reports to another Lord, 'the right-valiant Banquo walk'd too late'.[50] In blunt monosyllables, for stubborn emphasis, he adds that 'men must not walk too late'.[51] As a late walker, Banquo is a victim of the criminal kind of nightwalking at its most casually brutal.

Shakespeare here perhaps leans on the precedent of two plays written in the late 1580s: *The Spanish Tragedy* (c. 1587) by Thomas Kyd; and *The Jew of Malta* (c. 1589) by Christopher Marlowe (who is sometimes conspiratorially identified by critics as a representative of 'the School of Night'). *The Spanish Tragedy* – a seminal revenge tragedy that influenced a number of Jacobean plays, most famously *Hamlet* – had in chillingly clinical tones underlined the dangers of walking too late. There, on the orders of Lorenzo, the king's nephew, the servant Pedringano murders another servant, Serberine, in order to prevent him revealing a plot. When asked by one of the watchmen why he has 'unkindly killed the man', he offers a provocatively inadequate excuse: 'Why? Because he walked abroad so late'. 'Come sir, you had been better kept your bed, / Than have committed this misdeed so late', the same watchman, who is also under Lorenzo's orders, sardonically comments.[52] Pedringano is the nightwalker as sociopath.

But no doubt the most shocking of all portraits, in this period, of a murderer who stalks at night is Barabas in *The Jew of Malta*. In Marlowe's blackly comic play, Barabas is a Jew who loathes Christians so intensely that he coolly eliminates the weakest of them – the lame and the homeless. 'I walk abroad a-nights', he confesses in satisfied tones, 'And kill sick people groaning under walls'.[53] Barabas is the nightwalker as psychopath. He is the prototype of innumerable contemporary serial killers, in film and television especially, who predate on homeless people. In comparison to Barabas, the murderers employed by Macbeth are merely hired hands, careless about what they do 'to spite the world', and pathetically susceptible to his attempts to manipulate their emotions.[54]

Walking Shadow

Macbeth and Lady Macbeth use the night not only for criminal but for conspiratorial purposes. But if their precursors in *Julius Caesar*, when they planned to assassinate their leader, were in part responding to a crisis of state – one paralleled in the cataclysmic convulsions of the cosmos – then Macbeth and Lady Macbeth, in plotting to murder Duncan, create a crisis of state themselves, and open up a breach in nature as a consequence. This is because for them the night is not merely the context in which they can most conveniently discuss their treasonous scheme – 'this night's great business' as she calls it;[55] it is the element in which they must immerse or steep themselves in order to enact it.

Macbeth and Lady Macbeth conspire in the night, then; but they also conspire with the night. They invoke it like an evil spirit, effectively making a Faustian pact with it. This is Lady Macbeth's appeal:

> Come, thick night,
> And pall thee in the dunnest smoke of Hell,
> That my keen knife see not the wound it makes,
> Nor heaven peep through the blanket of the dark
> To cry 'Hold! Hold!'[56]

'Come, seeling Night', echoes Macbeth, 'Scarf up the tender eye of pitiful Day'.[57] The king's murder, according to Lady Macbeth, will create an eternal night: 'O! never / Shall the sun that morrow see!' she tells her husband when he alludes to Duncan's departure from their castle the following day.[58]

And so it comes to pass. Once the act has been committed, universal darkness, in Alexander Pope's phrase, covers all. 'By th'clock 'tis day, / And yet dark night strangles the travelling lamp', Rosse tells the Old Man, asking, 'Is't night's predominance, or the day's shame, / That darkness does the face of earth entomb, / When living light should kiss it?'[59] It is principally night's predominance. For Macbeth and Lady Macbeth, night is not simply a time of temptation but, increasingly, a sort of ontology. It is a condition of being.

Macbeth, who both struggles and subsides in this night, to cite Barthes's definition of its existential dimension again, discovers that its pitch-dark, noisome matter has become an intimate part of his being, and that its associations ineluctably reconstitute him from the inside. 'Stars, hide your fires!' he whispers soon after his first, fateful encounter with the witches; 'Let not light see my black and deep desires'.[60] This is an inner landscape comparable to the unconscious, as Freud will subsequently identify it – a space seething with unacceptable desires that only escape prohibition, and so find expression, at night.

But even at night they do so in displaced and distorted ways. Macbeth suffers from sleeplessness, from a restless noctambulism – in murdering Duncan he murders sleep, the 'balm of hurt minds', and is tormented by a voice that calls out, 'Sleep no more!'[61] Indeed, in a cultural climate that might be characterized as insomniac, so does Banquo – 'yet I would not sleep', he admits in desperation; 'merciful powers, / Restrain in me the cursed thoughts that nature / Gives way to in repose'.[62]

Lady Macbeth, of course, becomes a sleepwalker. She suffers from the 'slumbery agitation' associated with somnambulism. 'A great perturbation in nature', the Doctor comments, 'to receive at once the benefit of sleep, and do the effects of watching'.[63] She walks and watches at night in a state of terminal restlessness. Discussing sleepwalking in his *Religio Medici* (1643), Thomas Browne probed the paradox whereby '*noctambulos* and night-walkers, though in their sleep, do yet enjoy the action of their senses'. He concluded that their relationship to their bodies is comparable to the relationship of ghosts to the physical forms they inhabit: 'those abstracted and ecstatick souls do walk about in their own corpses, as spirits with the bodies they assume ...'[64] Lady Macbeth is one of these abstracted and ecstatic souls; 'ecstatic' here, in its original sense, means 'put out of place', 'beside oneself'. Haunted, she is herself a spectre.

For Macbeth and Lady Macbeth alike, the night, and in particular walking at night, constitutes in the end a psychopathological condition – and an ontological one. In his final soliloquy, Macbeth describes life itself as 'a walking shadow' – a species, perhaps, between a spirit-walker and a sleepwalker.[65] The play's references to late walking and other kinds of walking at night are ultimately compressed into this emblematic image of human subjectivity as no more than the restless materialization of a dark absence.

What Is the Night?

'What is the night?' Macbeth enquires in the banquet scene, once the ghost of Banquo has departed and his wife has dismissed their mystified guests.[66] Deprived of sleep, and half-psychotic, he urgently needs to know the time. But this is also, implicitly, a philosophical question that hints at the ontological meaning of the night.

What is the night? In the most immediate, colloquial sense – the one intended by Banquo when, in Act II, Scene i, he asks his son, 'How goes the night?' – it transpires that the appropriate response is: It is nearly the end of the night. It is moments before the dawn – the time when human beings' circadian cycle is at its nethermost point, their physiology at its most fragile. 'Deaths themselves', as Roger Ekirch has emphasized in his account of the pre-industrial night, 'are most likely to occur during the early morning hours.'[67] And a sense of the embattled status of Macbeth's body, and of the body politic, is indeed palpable at this point. But if Macbeth's question comprises a perfectly mundane, practical expression, it also has deeper implications, as Lady Macbeth's response indicates: 'Almost at odds with morning, which is which'.[68]

This preternaturally calm iambic pentameter, an antidote to Macbeth's feverish state, points to the indistinctness of the boundary separating the territory of the night from that of the day, and hence to the difficulty of defining it at all.[69] 'The west yet glimmers with some streaks of day', the First Murderer had observed in the previous scene, adumbrating an equivalent ambiguous region – the dusk.[70] But Lady Macbeth's response also hints at the moral significance of the night. The phrase 'almost at odds with morning', momentarily isolated by the practically imperceptible pause that succeeds it, underlines a deepening sense that, in Macbeth's universe, infernal as it has become, the night embodies values that are completely incompatible with those of the day. Far from complementing the day, and sustaining it, far from offering opportunities for physical recuperation and spiritual reflection, the night in *Macbeth* is … insomniac, insane, a time of satanic actions. Moreover, in Macbeth's kingdom, night progressively conquers day, and darkness conquers light, so that even when the witches meet on the heath in the daytime it feels like nighttime.

Macbeth, Shakespeare's most elaborate meditation on the night, is a sustained, if not obsessive, exploration of the nocturnal as a realm of alternative values – ones that contradict and threaten to undermine those of the diurnal regime that is ostensibly the domain of politics in the early modern period. In this violent, vengeful tragedy, the language and culture of the medieval night, incarnated above all in the witches, irrupts into the more enlightened language and culture of a purportedly post-medieval epoch. An apocalyptic night, in Macbeth's barbaric court, is one of the forces that shape realpolitik. In the Renaissance, a period in which daily life encroaches more and more on the night, especially in public settings, in the form of elaborately lit masques at court, *Macbeth* thus stages the limits of enlightenment.

At a time when more systematic, socially centralized modes of illumination are increasingly disrupting older patterns of rest, including biphasic sleep – so that, for the early modern ruling class at least, night starts to feel like an extension of the day, its obverse rather than its inverse – Shakespeare dramatizes the tyrannical attraction, the absolutism, of darkness. *Macbeth* describes a process of nocturnalization whereby the night irresistibly colonizes the day, fatally infiltrating both the state and the protagonist's consciousness. To use a word that had some currency in the seventeenth century, but has long since fallen out of use, Shakespeare's drama is a study of 'benightment'.

I Do Haunt You Still

Nightwalkers, in the early modern imagination, are alien in a double sense: they are socially and psychologically alienated; and they are also, potentially, spiritually alien – that is, beings of an altogether different order. If sleep is 'the death of each day's life', as Macbeth puts it in tones of irredeemable loss after murdering Duncan, and 'murdering sleep', too, then nightwalkers are the living dead.[71] The undead.

John Webster presented glimpses of these two kinds of nightwalker – the socially and the spiritually other – in *The Duchess of Malfi* (1612–1613). In Act II, Scene iii, of this gloriously strange Jacobean tragedy, a scene set at night, the sinister, cynical Bosola – a murderer who, after seven years in the galleys, is spying on the Duchess in his role as her 'gentleman of the horse' – creeps about 'with a dark lanthorn' close to her lodgings. When honest Antonio, the Duchess's steward and, secretly, her lover, challenges Bosola with a candle and a drawn sword, he asks him 'what design / When all men were commanded to their lodgings, / Makes [him] a night-walker'.[72]

Bosola – who implausibly pretends he has been seizing the opportunity of saying his prayers while the court is asleep – is of evil disposition. His commonness or meanness is thereby underlined by the accusation, but so is his placelessness. He doesn't fit in. He is an outsider to the Duchess's household, and he constitutes a constant threat to its order; at least, parasitic as he is, he rapaciously exploits the slightest sign of internal disorder, including his mistress's concealed pregnancy. Like other nightwalkers in this period, according to the authorities, he is an opportunist, a barrator, an eavesdropper and a spy.

The Duchess of Malfi, in common with other Jacobean tragedies, is a play in which the night exercises a dangerous, if not lunatic rule or lure. Like *Macbeth*, it narrates the nocturnalization of the court, and anatomizes the process of benightment. Ferdinand, the Duchess's insane twin brother, is an especially colourful example of a character who internalizes the night. He suffers from lycanthropia, and is classified alongside those who 'imagine / Themselves to be transformed into wolves' and so 'Steal forth to churchyards in the dead of night / And dig dead bodies up'. The doctor who offers this diagnosis recounts an anecdote in which he recalls that, 'two nights since', another lycanthrope – in this region they are legion! – had 'met the Duke, 'bout midnight in a lane / Behind St Mark's church, with the leg of a man / Upon his shoulder'.

Here, in a comically grotesque image, is another kind of night-walker – an uncommon one, to be sure. But if this anonymous lycanthrope is explicitly compared to Ferdinand, who claims he is haunted by his shadow, he is compared implicitly to Bosola, whose first line in Act I, Scene i, is: 'I do haunt you still'.[73] Both characters are associated with malign spirits. *The Duchess of Malfi*, too, is a study of benightment.

Black and Burnt Affection

The presiding genius of 'night's black agents', as Macbeth calls them, is Satan himself.[74] He performs a prominent role in the literature of London at night in the early seventeenth century.

In Thomas Middleton's *The Black Book* (1604), Lucifer strides through the nocturnal city 'like a night-walking John Stow', as a recent editor puts it.[75] Middleton designed this scintillating satirical pamphlet as a sequel to Nashe's *Pierce Penniless His Supplication to the Divell* (1592), in which a starving writer, who stands in for Nashe, appeals to Hell for literary patronage. In *The Black Book*, Lucifer appears at the Globe Theatre, in the shabby suburb of Southwark, in response to Pierce's supplication:

> And now that I have vaulted up so high
> Above the stage rails of this earthen Globe,
> I must turn actor, and join companies
> To share my comic sleek-eyed villainies,
> For I must weave a thousand ills in one
> To please my black and burnt affection.[76]

His intention is to take a surreptitious tour of London at night, in a series of disguises, in order to deepen and compound its iniquities.

The first costume Lucifer assumes in order to facilitate this scheme is the clothing of a constable – 'the cunning'st habit that could be'. In this form, he immediately heads to Pickt-hatch, an area close to Old Street that, at this time, was 'the very skirts of all brothel-houses', in Middleton's formulation. Pickt-hatch was named, according to a metonymic logic, after the 'picket-hatch', a familiar term for a brothel door, the upper part of which was surmounted by spikes. In these splendidly seedy surroundings, Lucifer successfully fools the watchmen, who are dismissed as 'poor night crows', into thinking he is the constable, and they duly follow him through the streets and, at his command, search a brothel.[77]

The prostitutes' clients protest, of course; but, after Lucifer has frightened them a little, he congratulates them on their corrupt condition, cheering them 'with the aqua vitae of villainy'. Eventually, after various other adventures, which include infiltrating the Royal Exchange in the 'musty moth-eaten habit' of a usurer in order to mingle with the City's merchants, he decides to amend his 'last will and testament'. As a result, Pierce Penniless is henceforth to receive a pension funded from a cut of the profits of London's 'vaulting-houses' – that is, its houses of prostitution.[78]

Lucifer's name, meaning light-bearer, is an ironic aspect of Middleton's irrepressible satirical attack on the nighttime authorities his anti-hero impersonates. In *The Black Book*, Lucifer gleefully dances along the fragile distinction between the criminals who inhabit the city at night and those employed to apprehend them, between its agents of order and disorder, its benefactors and malefactors. The definition of a 'Night-walker' given in *A New Dictionary of the Terms, Ancient and Modern of the Canting Crew, in Its Several Tribes, of Gypsies, Beggers, Thieves, Cheats* (1699), which has been called 'the first English dictionary of slang', is a representative one, because it accommodates the term's apparently contradictory meanings in the seventeenth century: 'a Bell-man; also a Light Woman, a Thief, a Rogue'.[79] Both nightwatchmen and vagrants get categorized as nightwalkers in the seventeenth century. Lucifer, in Middleton's pamphlet, is at once the arch-nightwatcher and the arch-nightwalker.

Knight-Errant of Hell

Lucifer reappears in the same shape-shifting form in another important representation of the nocturnal city from the opening decade of the seventeenth century, Thomas Dekker's *Lanthorne and Candle-light; or, The Bell-man's Second Nights Walke* (1608). This pamphlet, which Dekker extended in 1612 and amended in 1616, during his seven-year imprisonment in the King's Bench for debt, was a sequel to the *Bellman of London* (also 1608), which had recorded 'the most notorious villainies now practiced in the kingdom'.

Dekker was one of the most productive as well as collaborative playwrights of the 1590s and 1600s (he was involved in the composition of almost fifty plays between 1598 and 1602, though only six of them were printed); and it is no doubt this that, unfairly, reinforced his reputation as a poetaster. Born in London, probably of Dutch extraction, as his name indicates, Dekker was 'passionately dedicated to the City', as Stanley Wells insists, and stands as 'the first prominent dramatist whose work centres on the capital'.[80] But he was also perhaps the most creative and imaginative poet of the London night in the Renaissance, as both his plays and his prose pamphlets reveal.

Like *The Bellman of London*, *Lanthorne and Candle-light* provided its readers with irresistible glimpses of the corrupt life that pullulated in the secret spaces of the metropolis at night. Both pamphlets, like Middleton's *Black Book*, were responses to *Pierce Penniless*, as *The Bellman*'s dedication 'To the Reader', which implicitly refers to Nashe's publication, indicates:

> It is now about eighteen years past since a bed of strange snakes were found. They were then but in the shell, yet when they were fully hatched and began to crawl out their poison spread itself into all parts and veins of the kingdom; but the stench of the venom brake out most in and about London. Candlelight was then the first that discovered that cursed nursery of vipers.

It is at night, when lanterns and candlelight are the sole sources of illumination, that London's iniquities, in both the City and the suburbs, can most easily be discerned. As previous rogue pamphlets had done, the narrator of this one, the peripatetic Bellman, promises to act as a guide to the corrupt underside of the metropolis, the seething life of which is apparent after dark.

'Give me leave to lead you by the hand into a wilderness where are none but monsters', Dekker addresses one of his patrons, Francis Muschamp of Peckam, in the first dedication of *Lanthorne and Candle-light* – monsters 'whose cruelty you need not fear, because I teach the way to tame them'. Commencing with a rich dictionary of contemporary cant – which defines 'darkmans' as 'the night' and 'Romeville' as London – *Lanthorne and Candle-light* provides details of various urban miscreants and their characteristic malpractices. One chapter is about 'cozening inn-keepers, post-masters, and hackney-men'. Another is about 'Moon-Men', which means not madmen but gypsies, who are so called because 'as the moon is never in one shape two nights together but wanders up and down heaven like an antic, so these changeable-stuff companions never tarry one day in a place but are the only, and the only base, runagates upon earth'. As the unnerving but irresistible conclusion to the pamphlet's final dedication, 'To the Reader', had insisted: 'Read and laugh; read and learn; read and loathe. Laugh at the knavery; learn out the mystery; loathe the base villainy.'[81]

The critic William Sharpe, writing about nighttime in New York in the nineteenth century, has proposed that 'the original flâneur was perhaps the Black Man, Satan himself, "wandering to and fro in the earth, and up and down in it" (Job 1: 7)'.[82] Dekker's Black Man reinforces this association. As in *The Black Book*, the Devil in *Lanthorne and Candle-light* is the city's tour-guide, and, in effect, the pamphlet's protagonist. This 'Knight Errant of Hell', as Dekker tells the reader, after relishing the sights of the City and its suburbs in the daytime, 'was glad when he saw Night, having put on the vizard that Hell lends her called darkness, to leap into her coach, because now he knew he should meet with other strange birds and beasts fluttering from their nests and crawling out of their dens'.

The city's exotic bestiary can be seen at night. In the half-light of dusk, 'cozening bankrupts' materialize like owls, and 'certain murderers and thieves' like screech-owls; 'grave and wealthy lechers', for their part, appear 'in the shapes of glow-worms'. And during the night, among other villainous 'comedies', Satan sees hay being stolen from horses, servants secretly disposing of their masters' property, and plague-infected servants being expelled by their masters and left on the streets to die. It is all most enlightening – especially when Candlelight, who is personified, falls 'stark blind', and the darkness becomes almost impenetrable.[83]

Satan, who is something like the patron saint of Renaissance nightwalkers, records what he sees in nocturnal London and decides to return to Hell with the information he has accumulated: 'On therefore he walks with intent to hasten home, as having filled his table-books with notes of sufficient intelligence.' Before he departs from the city, though, he stumbles into the bellman, whom he mistakes for one of his infernal confederates: 'he took him for some churlish hobgoblin, seeing a long staff on his neck, and therefore to be one of his own fellows'. In the end, the Bellman asks Satan what he has discovered in his journey, and 'the mariner of Hell' responds by showing him 'his chart which he had lined with all abuses lying either east, west, north or south'.[84] If *Lanthorne and Candle-light* is about 'the Bell-man's Second Nights Walke', as its subtitle denotes, then this bellman is finally Satan himself. Like Lucifer in *The Black Book*, he is at once a nightwalker and a nightwatcher. He circumnavigates the city at night, in the guise of an inverted moralist, in order both to gather information about its abuses and to luxuriate in them.

In a sequel to this sequel to *The Bellman of London*, however, Dekker presented the nightwatch, in a satirical sketch that seems at the same time ironical and affectionate, as an agent of enlightenment and social order. *O Per Se O; or, A New Cryer of Lanthorne and Candle-light, Being an Addition, or Lengthening, of the Bell-mans Second Night-Walke* (1612) was in part a satire of the contemporary fashion for writing inflated dedicatory epistles to indifferent, if not illiterate, aristocrats. It presented the Bellman as a 'saucie intelligencer' who, in spite of his humble pretensions, and incompetence, threatens fatally to expose the Prince of Darkness and his 'Horned Regiment' to the light. In a letter presented to him in Hell, Satan is warned by one of his spies, who has been sent to London by Beelzebub, of the imminent danger to his dominions:

> *The Childe of Darkenesse, a common Night-walker, a man that had no man to wait upon him but only a Dog, one that was a disordered person, and at midnight would beat at mens dores, bidding them (in meere mockerie) to looke to their candles, when they themselves were in their dead sleeps: and albeit he was an Officer, yet he was but of light carriage, being knowne by the name of the Bel-man of London*, had of late not onely drawne a number of the Devils owne kindred into question for their lives, but also (onely by the help of the Lanthorne and Candle) lookt into the secrets of the best trades that are taught in Hell, laying them open to the broad eye of the world, making them infamous, odious, and ridiculous ...[85]

A 'Childe of Darkenesse' who is almost indistinguishable from a common nightwalker, the Bellman is nonetheless London's final line of defence against Satan's infernal machinations.

Nocturnal Triumph

In *The Seven Deadly Sinnes of London* (1606), published two years before the Bellman's first and second walks, Dekker had figured Candle-light not as an agent of enlightenment but as an instrument that, like Lucifer, facilitated acts of darkness. In this alternative survey of the city and its most iniquitous citizens – its practitioners of 'Citie sinnes', to cite Dekker's delightful pun in *O Per Se* – Candle-light is introduced as one of the pamphlet's eponymous sins.

In a chapter entitled 'Candle-light; Or, The Nocturnall Tryumph', Dekker announces that, though Candle-light once fostered virtuous activities, such as scholarship, craftsmanship, and the pursuit of truth, he has recently become 'a harborer of all kindes of Vices'. Like a pariah, Candle-light sidles into the city at sunset:

> Let the world, therefore, understand that this tallow-facde gentleman (cald Candle-light), so soone as ever the Sunne was gon out of sight, and

> that darknes, like a thief out of a hedge, crept upon the earth, sweate till hee dropt agen with bustling to come into the Cittie. For having no more but one onely eye (and that fierie red with drinking and sitting up late) he was ashamed to be seene by day, knowing he should be laught to scorne and hooted at.

One-eyed, alcoholic and insomniac, Candlelight is like a common nightwalker. Far from the opposite of darkness, this dilapidated Cyclops is its accomplice. Dekker's Darkness is a vagrant too – one who emerges from the 'ditches and busks', as the poet Robert Copland had called them, at the moment when others are ceasing their labours and preparing to sleep. Along with his disreputable friend, then, Candlelight escapes the supervision of the sun and enters the city at Aldersgate, 'because there his glittering would make greatest show'.[86]

As soon as it is rumoured that Candlelight has made his triumphant appearance inside the metropolis, bankrupts, debtors, felons, and everyone who fears 'arrests or justices warrants', creep into the streets. As Dekker puts it in characteristically colourful prose, all those who had 'like so many snayles, kept their houses over their heads al the day before, began now to creep out of their shels, and to stalke up and down the streets as uprightly and with as proud a gate as if they meant to knock against the starres with the crownes of their heads'.[87]

It is a delightful metaphor. Slugs and snails are of course proverbially associated with nocturnal activity: 'I found this Morn upon our furnace Wall', notes a sorcerer's assistant in Nahum Tate's *Brutus of Alba* (1678), 'Mysterious words wrought by a slimy Snail, / Whose Night-walk Fate had guided in that Form …'[88] But they are also horned, like the devil. Here, in Dekker's pamphlet, are the people of whom politicians and divines complained in the late medieval and early modern periods: the unemployed who flouted the capitalist ethic by sleeping in the day and resorting to the streets at night. Here is an entire community of common nightwalkers. And Candlelight delights in their company.

He also appreciates this opportunity to corrupt others, inciting the apprentices 'to make their desperate sallyes out (contarie to the oath of their indentures)' in pursuit of 'pintes', and tempting shopkeepers into 'drinking, dauncing and dicing'. And he is adept at making tattered, tired or adulterated goods into profitable commodities: 'if any in the cittie have badde wares lying deade upon their handes', Dekker tells him in tones of mock admiration, 'thou art better than *aqua vitae* to fetch life into them, and to send them packing'.[89] Indeed, as one of London's deadly sins, at once inverting and transfiguring everything it touches, Candlelight is not unlike gold, which Karl Marx, echoing the famous speech about its transformative power in Act IV, Scene iii, of Shakespeare's *Timon of Athens* (1605), represents as the 'glittering incarnation' of capitalist society's 'innermost principle of life'.[90]

Finally, Dekker describes how Candlelight distracts the befuddled watchmen, stealing into their cots and teaching them 'how to steale nappes into their heades', before making them choke or snore in their sleep. In this manner, he alerts any nightwalkers who happen to be close at hand to the imminent presence of the authorities, thereby enabling them to evade the reach of the law:

> and uppon his warrant snort they so lowde that to those night-walkers (whose wittes are up so late) it serves as a watch-worde to keepe out of the reach of their browne billes: by which meanes they never come to aunswere the matter before maister Constable, and the bench upon which his men (that shoulde watch) doe sitte: so that the Counters are cheated of prisoners, to the great damage of those that shoulde have their mornings draught out of the garnish.[91]

If, earlier in this chapter, Dekker had satirized the city's nightwalkers, affectionately enough, for stalking up and down the streets with the proud and upright gait, as he put it, of people hoping to knock against the stars with the crowns of their heads, in this paragraph he appears to have sided with them completely.

In spite of his praise, in *The Honest Whore* (1604), for Bridewell's programme of reforming beggars and lunatics, Dekker derives a good deal of pleasure from the idea of vagabonds subverting the incompetent regime of the nightwatch.

Passing by the Watch

Dekker displays a similar delight in eluding the city's nocturnal discipline in another sprightly satire from this period, *The Gull's Horn-Book; or, Fashions to Please All Sorts of Gulls* (1609). As its title indicates, this prose pamphlet purports to be an instruction manual for the foolish, fashionable metropolitan types insultingly known as 'gulls'. (A 'horn-book', used to teach children, was a leaf of paper printed with the alphabet, which had been mounted on a wooden tablet and covered with a protective layer of translucent horn – though, in this context, it no doubt also carries the less edifying associations of a cuckold's horns.) The pamphlet's chapters offer advice on how to behave in various social settings, including a playhouse and a tavern.

The eighth and final chapter of *The Gull's Horn-Book* is entitled 'How a Gallant is to behave himselfe passing through the Cittee, at all houres of the night, and how to passe by any watch.' It provides an itinerary from the moment when, as 'the spirit of Wine and Tobacco walkes in [his] braine', the gallant or gull is unceremoniously shoved out of the tavern and must start to make his way home through the streets:

> And if your means cannot reach to the keeping of a boy, hire one of the drawers to be as a lanthorn unto your feet, and to light you home; and, still as you approach near any nightwalker that is up as late as yourself, curse and swear, like one that speaks High Dutch, in a lofty voice, because your men have used you so like a rascal in not waiting upon you, and vow the next morning to pull their blue cases over their ears; though, if your chamber were well searched, you give only sixpence a week to some old woman to make your bed, and that she is all the serving-creatures you give wages to.

At all costs, the gull must keep up the pretence that he is rich and respectable, and to this end he must persuade the common nightwalkers that he encounters on the streets that there is nothing common about him. This might entail speaking in elevated accents and pretending to have a retinue.

The same tactic can be used to circumvent the constable and his watchmen (whose presence is easily detected because 'commonly they eat onions to keep them in sleeping'). Pretending to be a Frenchman or a Dutchman, calling out to an imaginary friend with a title, a 'Sir Giles' or a 'Sir Abram', and talking incessantly about 'such ladies with whom you have played at primero, or danced in the presence', all helps 'to lock up the lips of an inquisitive bellman'. It is necessary at all times, in case 'the sentinel and his court of guard stand strictly upon his martial law, and cry "Stand"', to be able to produce an alibi – 'to shew reason why your ghost walks so late'.[92]

This mischievous attitude both to watchmen and to the more rakish denizens of the city at night is also evident in Dekker's *Blurt, Master-Constable; or, The Spaniards Night-walke* (1602), a play that, like *The Honest Whore*, might have been written in collaboration with Middleton (Benjamin Britten, who set some of it to music in the fourth section of his 1958 *Nocturne*, attributed it to Middleton). Set in Venice, *Blurt* is a slightly clumsy comic romance indebted, in its main plot, to *Romeo and Juliet* (1593–1595), and, in its subplot, to *Much Ado About Nothing* (1598). Oddly, its title is taken from the sub-plot, which centres on the nocturnal antics of both a Spanish captain called Lazarillo and Blurt himself, a constable closely related to Dogberry.

''Tis my office *Signior*, to taken men up a nightes', the former tells the latter in the first act in explanation of his professional duties. The nightwalk alluded to in the play's subtitle is one that the clownish, lustful Lazarillo conducts by accident. In Act IV, Scene ii, he is tricked and sent, 'bareheaded in his shirt', with 'a pair of pantaples' – or slippers – a tobacco pipe and a rapier, to a strange room. 'He seems amazed', the audience is informed, 'and walkes so up and downe', then steps through a trap-door that has deliberately been opened, and falls suddenly into the cellar of a brothel. Blurt finds Lazarillo in his nightshirt, soaked in urine, and arrests him. The hapless Spanish captain is later drily referred to as one of the 'spirits that walke i'th night'.[93] Once again, to comic effect, Dekker underlines the ghostly quality of nightwalkers.

Silent Charnel-House

The redoubtable Dekker invoked the spectral dimension of the city at night to more sinister, apocalyptic effect in *The Wonderful Year*, a pamphlet that he published anonymously in 1603 but assumed responsibility for in 1606. Its ambivalent attitude to the city at night – a city not so much of dreadful delight as of delightful dread – is summed up in this irresistible provocation: 'The dreadfulness of such an hour is inutterable. Let us go further.'

Boldly celebrating the therapeutic properties of laughter, *The Wonderful Year* was a heated, if not feverish, response to two epochal events that occurred in the year it was published. It recorded the shock of Queen Elizabeth's death, and catalogued the devastating effects of the outbreak of bubonic plague. London had been gripped by epidemics of the plague throughout the fourteenth, fifteenth and sixteenth centuries, but the visitation in 1603, which caused two-and-a-half times as many deaths as in 1593, was especially cataclysmic, killing more than 25,000 people – comprising almost 18 per cent of London's population. Dekker's pamphlet, which he followed with another grimly funny piece about the plague, *News from Gravesend* (1604), is written with a terrific sense of urgency and rhetorical energy – 'arm my trembling hand that it may boldly rip up and anatomize the ulcerous body of this anthropophagized plague' is one of his characteristic imprecations.[94] It was an important influence on Daniel Defoe's *Journal of the Plague Year* (1722), which freely plundered from it.

As in 1665, the plague transformed the bustling, vibrant metropolis into a necropolis. At night, according to Dekker in *The Wonderful Year*, this is all the more dramatically apparent. After dark, London is a ghastly, nightmarish place, 'a vast, silent charnel-house hung, to make it more hideous, with lamps dimly and slowly burning in hollow and glimmering corners; where all the pavement should instead of green rushes be strewed with blasted rosemary, withered hyacinths, fatal cypress and yew, thickly mingled with heaps of dead men's bones'. In baroque language that is at times almost suffocating in its pungency, Dekker describes corpses in the street that, crawling with worms and emitting a 'noisome stench', lie 'half mouldered in rotten coffins', and evokes the unearthly sounds of 'toads croaking, screech-owls howling, mandrakes shrieking'.

Dekker's silent protagonist is a man who, as he himself must have done, 'durst in the dead hour of gloomy midnight have been so valiant as to have walked through the still and melancholy streets'. The noises of crying, groaning and dying create what he calls the 'music' of the 'diseased City' at night. 'Were not this an infernal prison?' Dekker's narrator demands, 'Would not the strongest-hearted man beset with such a ghastly horror look wild? And run mad? And die?'[95] It is as if the Earl of Surrey Henry Howard's deepest fears or desires, as expressed in 'London, Has Thou Accused Me', have been realized, and his prison cell has opened out to enclose the entire city. But in Dekker the nightwalker is not some drunken aristocrat careering around the city so much as a spectre stalking a cemetery.

I Forgot 'Twas Darke

John Fletcher, the only dramatist with whom it can confidently be stated that Shakespeare collaborated, achieves a delicate balance of the comic and potentially tragic possibilities of nightwalking in a romantic comedy called *The Night-Walker; or, The Little Theife*. As in the case of Dekker's *Blurt, Master-Constable*, the title of Fletcher's comedy adverts to nightwalking even though the activity does not directly serve the plot. Both presumably exploited the peculiar frisson associated with the term, giving the audience permission to slum it for a couple of hours.

Fletcher probably wrote *The Night-Walker* in 1611 (the year he also produced his provocative, anti-patriarchal sequel to *The Taming of the Shrew*, entitled *The Woman's Prize; or, The Tamer Tamed*). The Master of Revels did not license the play for performance until 1633, though, when James Shirley, principal dramatist of the Queen's Players, revised the script. He put it on first at the Cockpit and then at court in front of Charles I and Henrietta Maria – both venues with privileged audiences. It remained popular, after the interval of the Puritan Revolution, in the later seventeenth-century theatre: Samuel Pepys saw no less than three productions of it in 1661–1662, and it was still regularly produced in the 1690s.

The Night-Walker is a riotous, often melodramatic comedy, but it also betrays an unexpected, sometimes affecting emotional sophistication, and a certain darkness of outlook. Perhaps it is most usefully understood as a 'romantic tragicomedy' – a genre 'which seems especially to have appealed to Fletcher', as Wells has argued, and that Shakespeare too 'found congenial in what turned out to be his last years'.[96] A good deal of the action is set after dark, and several of its scenes involve blundering or wandering around London at night.

Its fiendishly complicated plot centres on a young man, Frank Hartlove, who is in love with a young woman, Maria, whose mother, the Lady, is determined to marry her off to an old usurer, Algripe. Maria's cousin, a hell-raiser called Jacke Wildbraine, tries to prevent this marriage by persuading Hartlove to seduce Maria before it can be consummated. When Algripe discovers the lovers in a compromising relationship, Maria faints from shock and is taken for dead. A thief called Lurcher then mistakes the coffin in which her body has been deposited for a chest containing the wedding gifts, and steals it …

Lurcher, it transpires, is a down-at-heel gentleman who has been forced by circumstances to become a highwayman, and his bracing political philosophy is that 'stealing is the best inheritance'. The scholar Cyrus Hoy has noted that 'unconventional behavior is at a premium' in Fletcher's early comedies, and singles Lurcher out for this reason as 'another penniless gallant who is out to live by his wits and subvert society's norms'.[97] He might have mentioned Wildbraine in the same context, for this gentleman's propensity for nightwalking effectively places him beyond the pale of polite society too.

Nightwalking is a kind of *non sequitur* in *The Night-Walker*; it is of moral or psychological rather than narrative relevance. In Act III, the Lady disinherits Wildbraine and expels him from her home because she believes he is responsible for her daughter's death: 'The most malicious varlet', she chastises him; 'Thy wicked head never at rest, but hammering / And hatching hellish things, and to no purpose, / So thou maist have thy base will.' It is nighttime, and Wildbraine is now homeless. So he borrows a lantern from Toby, the Lady's servant and clown. 'Lend me thy Lanthorne, I forgot 'twas darke', he says rather sadly, in lines freighted with moral significance, 'I had neede looks to my wayes now.' Feeling anguished, he resolves to walk the darkened streets, telling Toby, 'I will wander / I scorne to submit my selfe, ere I have rambled.'[98]

For Wildbraine, morally aimless as he suddenly finds himself, walking in the city at night entails intense self-examination. It thus acquires an almost existential dimension – one that will later define the Romantic and post-Romanic tradition of nightwalking.

Melancholy Walking

Once Wildbraine has exited, Hartlove enters. The stage is still relatively dark, even though performances of the play were presumably held in the afternoon. Throughout this scene the theatre was probably lit by lanterns held in the actors' hands – for, as Andrew Gurr indicates in his classic study of the Shakespearean stage, night scenes in the drama of this period were 'signified in words and by the players or stage hands bringing on flaming torches'.[99] Hartlove too feels partly responsible for Maria's death, as he takes it to be, but he blames Wildbraine for it, and is therefore determined to hunt him down and kill him. He feels courageous, in spite of his unfamiliarity with the streets of the city at night. It must be said, however, that if his courage were less fragile he might not need to affirm: 'The night, and all the evills the night covers, / The goblins, Hagges, and the blacke spawne of darknesse / Cannot fright me.'

Then Wildbraine, the outcast, re-enters with his lantern. Initially unaware of Hartlove's presence, he soliloquizes as follows:

> It is but melancholy walking thus;
> The tavern doors are barricaded too,
> Where I might drinke till morne, in expectation;
> I cannot meete the Watch neither; nothing in

> The likenesses of a Constable, whom I might
> In my distresse abuse, and so be carried,
> For want of other lodging to the Counter.

In these lines Wildbraine gives voice to a state of homelessness that is, in the Renaissance, generally consigned to silence; although for actual vagrants, as distinct from semi-derelict gentlemen, it was less a melancholy condition than a miserable and wretched one. In a song from another of his plays, *The Nice Valour* (c. 1615–1616), probably a collaboration with Middleton, Fletcher gave full expression to the seventeenth-century cult of melancholy. The song hymns Melancholy and praises 'pathlesse Groves' and 'Moon-light walkes, when all the fowles / Are warmly hous'd, save Bats and Owles'.[100] But the nightwalking scenes in *The Night-Walker* are far more edgily urban than this contemplative scene.

Wildbraine underlines his outcast, outlawed identity when he sees Hartlove and explains to him that, 'at this unchristian houre', his aunt has turned him 'out a doores … and I doe walke, / Me thinkes, like *Guido Faux* with my dark Lanthorne, / Stealing to set the towne a fire'. Stalking about in the nocturnal city, he feels like a religious or political terrorist; while 'ith country / I should be tane for William o'the Wispe, / Or Robin Goodfellow'. In spite of his persecuted status, or because of it, he evokes a mischievous, socially disruptive spirit. Throughout the play, Hoy observes, Fletcher 'underscore[s] his farcical plot with a rural folklore of goblins and fiends and spirits walking by night from the surrounding woods and fields into the darkened houses and streets and squares of the nocturnal capital, to plague guilty consciences'.[101]

As the reference to Robin Goodfellow indicates, *The Night-Walker* on occasion resembles an urban version of *A Midsummer Night's Dream* (1595–1596), a play that almost spitefully pits the nocturnal order against the diurnal one.[102] At times, *The Night-Walker* also reads like an urban version of *King Lear* (1605), where the 'foul fiend Flibbertigibbet' – whom Edgar invokes when he sees Gloucester on the Heath with a torch – testifies to the anarchic energies of the night in the folkloric imagination.[103]

I Am the Wandering Jew

King Lear is a significant precedent in another, more important sense too. For it shapes the representation of vagrancy in *The Night-Walker*. In contrast to the sixteenth- and seventeenth-century literature on rogues, *King Lear* accorded homelessness a tragic dignity.[104] Throughout the scenes set during the calamitous storm on the Heath, on a 'cold night' that threatens to turn everyone into 'fools and madmen', Shakespeare portrays his protagonists – Lear, the Fool and, in the guise of Poor Tom, Edgar – as vagrants who have been cast adrift in a society for which 'Man's life is cheap as beast's'.[105] They are 'poor naked wretches' characterized by 'houseless heads and unfed sides'.[106]

The Night-Walker, too, accords homelessness a tragic dignity. In Act IV, Wildbraine and Toby idle about in the streets after midnight again, and are robbed of their clothes by Lurcher (in revenge for Wildbraine's entanglement with Lurcher's mistress). So they find themselves, in Act V, wandering around the nocturnal city in an increasingly destitute state. Toby tries to sell the mat and hassock he carries with him. Wildbraine, who recalls a tragicomic Poor Tom, adrift not on the heath but in the almost empty metropolis, borrows a 'poore shift' from a sexton, but fears he will be apprehended by the watchman.

At this point, Lurcher reappears to sport with Wildbraine, abusing him as a 'rugamuffin' and accusing him of burgling his house the previous night. He then pretends that he plans to report this man who 'walkes disguis'd in this malignant rugge' to the authorities, in order to have him arrested. 'What art thou?' Lurcher asks him in mock contempt. 'I am the wandring Jew, and please your worship', Wildbraine replies with poignant simplicity, alluding to the medieval legend of Ahasverus, the Jewish cobbler who, because he cruelly refused to assist Christ as he stumbled for a third time beneath the weight of the cross on his journey to the crucifixion, was condemned to wander the earth forever. Lurcher's response to Wildbraine is tersely intolerant: 'I will shew you then / A Synagogue, iclip't Bridewell, where you / Under correction may rest your selfe.' Wildbraine's criminality, as a homeless man, is confirmed. And in this recognition of his vagrant state, which Wildbraine has no reason to believe will be anything other than permanent, he is forced to accept that he might have to rest or relinquish altogether his self.

Eventually, of course, after chaotic scenes involving confidence tricks, duels and cases of mistaken identity, a happy ending ensues – Hartlove and Maria marry, and Wildbraine mends relations with the Lady. But the disconcerting effects of the encounter in the street at night between Lurcher and Wildbraine are never fully erased. Like King Lear, the latter must admit that he has finally been ostracized and reduced to the position of a social pariah. He stands for humanity in its most abject, exiled form, as the Wandering Jew does at the level of legend. And he therefore offers a startling, even moving insight, in the midst of a comic plot, into the existential condition of the common nightwalker in the early modern period. The wild-brained, sometimes solipsistic nightwalkers of the eighteenth and nineteenth centuries, including Johnson, Blake and De Quincey, are his spiritual descendants.

PART TWO

4.

Darkness Visible

Night and the Enlightenment in the Eighteenth Century

Face of Night

William Hogarth's 'Night' seethes with the febrile life of the nocturnal city at its most insectile. The supreme portrait of eighteenth-century London's nightlife, it is the fourth composition in his series *Four Times of the Day* (1736). These diaristic paintings, subsequently engraved and reproduced as prints, deliberately reinvented the representation of the so-called *points du jour*, allegorical sequences that were popular in aristocratic homes, by transposing them to an urban context and hence upsetting their pastoral conventions.

'Night' is set in the Charing Cross Road on 29 May – the date when the Restoration of Charles II was commemorated. It is a dystopian glimpse of the anarchy of the nocturnal streets, which are riven and scarred by the most squalid social contradictions. It is as if Hogarth has kicked over a stone and reproduced what he there saw. Beneath the scattered, broken paving stones of eighteenth-century London lies, not the beach – as the Situationists dreamed in twentieth-century Paris – but a collapsing colony of parasites.

The picture's foreground features an inebriated Freemason being accompanied home by his 'tyler', or Masonic guardsman. This vile aristocrat is readily identifiable as Sir Thomas de Veil, a man 'renowned for the gulf between his severity on the bench and his wayward life'.[1] As a Westminster justice, de Veil had opened a magistrate's office in Bow Street in 1740, from where he pioneered practices of corrupt and oppressive policing. The poor held de Veil in particular contempt because in 1736, the year in which *Four Times of the Day* was painted, he had introduced the Gin Act, which controlled the sale of this cheap, sometimes lethal liquid. Gin – the methamphetamine of its time – 'offered speedy if temporary relief from the anxieties of poverty, hunger, homelessness and abuse'.[2]

The years 1735–1736, like 1725–1729 and 1750–1751, were marked by a moral panic among the respectable classes about the poor's addiction to this substance. Henry Fielding, who succeeded de Veil as magistrate in 1749, when he established the Bow Street Runners, fulminated about its addictive and destructive properties in his *Enquiry into the Causes of the late Increase of Robbers* (1751):

> A new Kind of Drunkenness, unknown to our Ancestors, is lately sprung up amongst us, and … if not put a Stop to, will infallibly destroy a great Part of the inferiour People.
>
> The Drunkenness I here intend, is that acquired by the strongest intoxicating Liquors, and particularly by that Poison called *Gin*; which, I have reason to think, is the principal Sustenance (if it may be so called) of more than an hundred thousand People in this Metropolis.[3]

Hogarth's 'Gin Lane' (1751), a print produced in the same year as Fielding's book, when the Gin Act was passed in parliament, was both an expression of this moral panic and a more nuanced attempt to explore the causes of the epidemic levels of alcoholism in terms of the immiseration of the poor.

In 'Night', someone is emptying a chamber pot onto De Veil's head from a first-floor window – a grimly carnivalesque use of excrement to subvert the elaborately calibrated social order. On the ground floor of this building an inebriated barber shaves a grotesque, porcine customer. Beneath the bulk or counter on the street outside it, beside a link-boy who is busy blowing out his flame, homeless children sleep – 'bulkers', they were sometimes nicknamed. The nightwatch is conspicuous by his absence.

In the background of Hogarth's composition, which bristles with bagnios and brothels in the light of the moon, a celebratory bonfire has blocked the street and caused a coach to crash and overturn. This detail recalls a similar scene in *Trivia* (1716), John Gay's glorious hymn to the metropolis, where the heroic couplets, interrupting or upsetting the measured iambic rhythms the reader expects, mime the chaos they describe:

> E'er Night has half roll'd round her Ebon Throne
> In the wide Gulph the shatter'd Coach o'erthrown,
> Sinks with the snorting Steeds; the Reins are broke
> And from the cracking Axle flies the Spoke.

Things fall apart; the centre cannot hold. In Hogarth's painting or print, the conflict between different classes is held in a scarcely containable state of tension, which crackles at the centre of the composition in the fire beneath the upended coach's wheel, and smuts the background in the form of a more serious conflagration several streets away. 'The Face of Night / Is cover'd with a sanguine dreadful Light', as Gay puts it.[4] The anarchic chaos of an urban night in the eighteenth century is in Hogarth's 'Night' concentrated into a single, brutally satirical, dystopian image.

Night of the Mind

But Hogarth's 'Night' is more than simply a satirical or dystopian image; for, as well as being a contemporary cityscape, it is a dreamscape. It is a portrait of a nightmare. In this composition, to take an evocative phrase from John Keats's lexicon in the early nineteenth century, London is 'be-nightmared'.[5]

In the realm of nightmare, the promise of the Enlightenment, and the emergent culture of rationalism, collapse or deliquesce into their opposite. *El sueño de la razón produce monstruos*, as Francisco Goya put it in one of his etchings for the series known as *Los Caprichos* (1799). The sleep of reason brings forth monsters. Or, alternatively, the dream of reason – the cryptic expression of its deepest desires – produces monsters. From this alternative perspective, unreason is the product not simply of the cessation or suspension of reason but of the elaboration of its secret logic. As Gilles Deleuze and Félix Guattari put it, glossing Goya's legend, 'it is not the slumber of reason that engenders monsters, but vigilant and insomniac rationality'.[6]

Contemporaneous descriptions of the inner space of the sleeping subject resemble descriptions of the city's Cimmerian atmosphere at night. In *Nocturnal Revels; or, A General History of Dreams* (1707), for example, the anonymous author writes that, during an individual's dreams, 'those bright Intellectual Beams planted in his Nature by the Father of Light' are eclipsed, and 'he is become a meer Chaos of gross Imaginations and Earthly Affections, clouded with the Bituminous Smoak of the Infernal Pit, and invelop'd with a Pitchy Darkness, like that which was brought upon *Egypt*, and was so thick it might be felt'.[7] This clogged, clotted sentence, with its Miltonic imagery, reads like a moralistic sketch of those impoverished and infernal areas of the eighteenth-century city that eluded the official project of urban illumination, which concentrated on the streets and thoroughfares used by the rich for the purposes of promenading and shopping.

In spite of the introduction of public forms of illumination in the most affluent thoroughfares of the city at the end of the seventeenth century, London's more labyrinthine lanes and streets continued to be cloistered places thick with grime and soot and sepulchral light. Even in the day, industrial pollutants rendered the air fuliginous. In a pamphlet entitled *Fumifugium* (1661), which he dedicated to Charles II, the diarist John Evelyn professed astonishment that 'this Glorious and Antient City', the centre of a maritime empire reaching to the Antipodes, 'should wrap her stately head in Clowds of Smoake and Sulphur, so full of Stink and Darknesse'. He complained that this smoke, 'ascending in the day-time', was 'by the descending Dew, and Cold, precipitated again at night'.[8] As small-scale industrial forms of production became an increasingly entrenched part of everyday life in the capital in the decades that followed, the poisonous climate described by Evelyn persisted and even thickened. Night in the late seventeenth- and eighteenth-century city, it seems, was an accretion of 'black air'.[9]

If accounts of consciousness in its dreaming condition, like the one in *Nocturnal Revels*, recall the nighttime streets, then, conversely, descriptions of the pitch-black precincts of the metropolis read like an objective correlative of those recesses of the eighteenth-century psyche that escaped the advancing logic of the Enlightenment – but at the same time shaped it from inside like a dark secret. These interior spaces constitute the black underside of the Enlightenment mind. For this is the epoch in which thought itself, as Michel Foucault argued in *The Order of Things*, discovered 'both in itself and outside itself, at its borders yet also in its very warp and woof, an element of darkness, an apparently inert density in which it is embedded, an unthought which it contains entirely, yet in which it is also caught'.[10]

Here, then, in Foucault's formulation, is the 'whole landscape of shadow that has been termed, directly or indirectly, the unconscious'. And it is constitutive of consciousness. The 'obscure space' embedded in what the Enlightenment identifies as 'man's nature' is 'both exterior to him and indispensable to him: in one sense, the shadow cast by man as he emerged in the field of knowledge; in another, the blind stain by which it is possible to know him'. 'The night of the mind', Foucault calls it in another context.[11] The obscure spaces of the metropolitan city, which are at once alien to the bourgeois city's self-image and essential to its project of self-aggrandizement, are also shadows and blind stains.

Eighteenth-century nightwalkers inhabit a city, and indeed a self, that is divided between light and darkness, the rational and the irrational, enlightenment and benightment; between 'bright Intellectual Beams' on the one hand, and, on the other, 'a meer Chaos of gross Imaginations and Earthly Affections' that is 'invelop'd with a Pitchy Darkness'. They traverse the unconscious city as well as the conscious one, the unthought city as well as the thought one. Night, in the eighteenth-century city, marks a crisis for the logic of vigilant and insomniac rationality.

Dark Walks

We have 'thrown business and pleasure into the hours of rest, and by that means made the natural night but half as long as it should be'. So Richard Steele in 1710 expressed his consternation at the fashionable rise of an 'unaccountable disposition to continue awake in the night and sleep in the sunshine'.[12] A significant cultural shift occurred in London and other European cities at night in the late seventeenth and eighteenth centuries, as new lighting technologies emerged and their populations expanded beyond the original medieval boundaries.

This shift might be characterized at its simplest in terms of the development of nightlife. The streets after sunset became more and more populous. They pulsed with restless social activities as middle-class citizens, in addition to aristocrats, encroached on the night, seeking entertainment in shops, taverns and theatres, in coffee-houses and pleasure gardens. Artisans and the poor, for their part, increasingly worked after dark. Bakers, brewers, shoemakers and tailors laboured to meet morning deadlines. Night-men (or 'Tom-Turd-Men'), gold-finders and rag-pickers, meanwhile, sifted the detritus of the streets, or disposed of it, during the dead time of night – in a desperate attempt to alchemize the city's shit into precious pennies. Night in the city was socialized in the seventeenth and eighteenth centuries. And, as a consequence, especially from the 1660s, as J. M. Beattie states, 'the idea behind the curfew – the 9 p.m. closing down of the City – was not so much abolished as overwhelmed'.[13]

A gentrification of the night took place in eighteenth-century London. But its effects were socially ambiguous, as the example of the pleasure gardens suggests. Pleasure gardens such as Ranelagh and Vauxhall – both planted on the banks of the Thames, the former fashionable, the latter more plebeian – staged what one cultural historian has characterized as 'commercial imitations of courtly festive culture'.[14] 'One of the principal entertainments of the citizens here, in summer', Oliver Goldsmith observed, adopting the voice of a foreign traveller visiting Vauxhall for the first time, 'is, to repair, about night-fall to a garden not far from town, where they walk about, show their best clothes, and best faces, and listen to a concert provided for the occasion'.[15]

In reality, though, the pleasure gardens were far less genteel than this pointedly innocent or ingenuous description implied. They were bewitching, at times tawdry, amusement parks where people repaired in order to walk and talk, certainly – but also to eat, drink, gamble, flirt, fumble and fuck. They licensed an acceptable, at times almost dangerous, amount of libertinism; and in their precincts the different social classes both mingled and remained segregated. At once inside and outside the city, they boasted lamp-lit avenues and 'Dark Walks' in which to amble about with a combination of spontaneity and calculated intent.[16] In the pleasure gardens, nighttime in the city was staged as a pastoral or anti-pastoral performance for the privileged and the socially aspirant.

Shows and Outsides

Eighteenth-century London, Robert Shoemaker has insisted, 'was truly a twenty-four-hour city, where the overlapping life-styles of its socially disparate inhabitants meant that as night-time revelers returned home at dawn others were getting up to work or beg'.[17] The proximate cause of the rise of nightlife in this period, after the restoration of the monarchy and the reinstitution of a sometimes rampant culture of sociability, was the introduction of public street lighting in London from the mid 1680s. This technological innovation, combined with these social developments, domesticated the nocturnal city but at the same time rendered it exotic, oddly unfamiliar. Underlying this change, though, profounder shifts were taking place.

The most fundamental of these was the consolidation of urban capitalism and its attendant class formations. In England, the foremost capitalist nation, this pivoted on the alliance between landed and moneyed elites after the Civil War. Here, and in contrast to continental nations, where people were dispersed across a constellation of provincial centres, the metropolis became preeminent because of both the concentration of its population and its social and economic strength. By the end of the eighteenth century London had almost a million inhabitants – nearly double the number of Paris.

Lodged at the core of agrarian capitalism and the industries associated with this mode of production, especially the textile and iron trades, the British metropolis became 'the hub of a self-expanding capitalist system, in a nation-state exceptional for its degree of political and economic integration', as Ellen Wood comments.[18] At the same time, in the decades after the Restoration, the City commenced its rise as a financial centre, a laboratory for banking and overseas trading bristling with rentier capitalists of one kind or another, including 'Agents, Factors, Brokers, Insurers, Bankers, Negotiators, Discounters, Subscribers, Contractors, Remitters, Ticket-Mongers, Stock-Jobbers'.[19] In the eighteenth century, London became the engine of agrarian, industrial and emergent financial capitalism.

These economic shifts, which entailed the expansion of the commodities market and the development of an increasingly elaborate division of labour, facilitated the spectacular rise of a culture of consumption in London. Shopping is an eighteenth-century concept. For those who had time and money to spend, upper-class women in particular, visiting shops for the sheer pleasure of it, and not simply in order to purchase necessities, became a fashionable activity. As a result of improvements to the city's glazing, lighting and paving, especially in the 1760s, when no less than five Acts of Parliament established a framework for modernizing the streets, shops became more and more convenient.

They also became more attractive. Shopkeepers developed strategies for embroidering and prettifying the commodities in which they specialized. Daniel Defoe, in *The Complete English Tradesman* (1732), was fascinated and appalled by the practice of 'fitting up' – a 'modern custom' that, as he explained, involved shopkeepers not simply 'furnishing their shops with wares and goods to sell' but embellishing them with 'painting and gilding, fine shelves, shutters, boxes, glass-doors, sashes and the like'. From this he inferred 'that this age must have more fools than the last', since 'fools only are most taken with shows and outsides'.[20]

Foreign visitors were rather more captivated by the capital's shops. The German scientist and satirist Georg Christoph Lichtenberg produced 'a hasty sketch of an evening in the streets of London' for a friend after strolling from Cheapside to Fleet Street in the 1770s. 'Many thousand candles' lit up the goods displayed behind glass on the ground floors of shops, he reported in amazement, and 'the street looks as though it were illuminated for some festivity'.[21] Numerous commentators noticed that, particularly after dark, goods in shop windows acquired a dazzling sheen that made them seem even more seductive. There is a close, indeed complicit, relationship between nocturnal lighting and the commodity in the eighteenth-century city.

The diffusion of Enlightenment ideas and the rise of scientific rationalism also contributed to the transformation of the night in this period. The night was elucidated. In cities, the darkness no longer held those terrors that persisted among less literate populations in rural settings. In his history of nighttime, Roger Ekirch quotes a newspaper report from 1788 that announces that 'not a single building in all London is perhaps now to be heard of, which bears the repute of being an haunted house'. The city, as he glosses it, 'had given up the ghost'.[22] London was becoming disenchanted under the glare of intellectual and technological innovations.

The verb 'to enlighten', which in the late sixteenth and early seventeenth centuries meant to make luminous, in fact first acquired its displaced significance, in the sense of imparting intellectual light, at the precise moment when street lighting was beginning to transform the European metropolis. The first figurative instance of it cited in the OED is from *Paradise Lost* (1667): 'reveal / To Adam what shall come in future days', God instructs Michael in Book XI, 'As I shall thee enlighten …'[23] From the late seventeenth century, the metropolitan city and the psyche both become susceptible to more rationalistic, and potentially more democratic, forms of illumination.

New Lights

Paris pioneered street lighting in 1667 under the initiative of Louis XIV's 'council for the reform of the policing of the city'. It was succeeded by Lille, capital of Flanders, later the same year; Amsterdam in 1669; Turin in 1675; Berlin in 1682; and London from 1684. By 1700 a number of provincial cities across the continent had been publicly illuminated.

Replacing the candle lanterns that private householders had been required to erect outside their front doors, most European civic authorities used oil lanterns, maintained at public expense, to light the streets. In absolutist France, in contradistinction, the authorities employed standard candle lanterns, suspended on ropes approximately fifteen feet above the middle of the street. Lit up at night between October and March, Paris had by 1702 been fitted with approximately 5,400 of them. In London, a number of patents for oil lamps were registered in the 1680s, most of them originating in rapeseed. Initially, an inventor called Edward Heming was licensed to fit a light in front of every tenth door along broad streets, from six until midnight on nights without a moon. The first report on the 'New Lights' of the metropolis, published in 1690, extolled the effects of this, and noted in rapturous tones that these lights produced 'such a mutual reflection, that they all seem to be but one great Solar-Light'.[24]

By this time, as part of the plan to improve the urban environment after the Great Fire, the authorities in London had decided to contract their lighting to specialist companies. From 1694, the Convex Lights Company became responsible for providing street lamps in the City; and, from 1704, the Conic Lights Company administered Westminster.[25] Dissatisfaction with these monopolies mounted, though, partly because they illuminated the streets only for a limited time and at certain seasons, and partly because they were so little accountable to those citizens inclined to complain of poorly maintained lights.

So in 1736, a year of anti-Irish riots, an Act of Parliament introduced a special lighting rate and insisted that each ward contract its provision for lighting on an annual basis. 'Till this time, the Streets of London were perhaps worse illuminated by Night than those of any other great City, which was entirely owing to bad Management', William Maitland grumbled in 1760.[26] The situation rapidly improved under this dispensation – the new globular lamps remained lit at all hours of the night, even when the moon was shining, and throughout the seasons. Stephen Inwood has calculated that 'this gave the City around 4,000 hours of lighting a year, compared to 300 or 400 before 1694, and 750 from 1694 to 1736'.[27]

In a literal sense, the city at night in the seventeenth and eighteenth centuries became flamboyant. In Europe's main thoroughfares, the demise of the curfew was dramatically confirmed. During a visit to London in 1786, reported in correspondence to her adult children, the German novelist Sophie von La Roche – one of the most eloquent and enthusiastic commentators on the emergent culture of consumption – positively marvelled at the sight of the 'eternal stream of coaches' and the mass of people processing along Oxford Street at 11 p.m.:

> Just imagine, dear children, a street taking half an hour to cover from end to end, with double rows of brightly shining lamps, in the middle of which stands an equally long row of beautifully lacquered coaches, and on either side of these there is room for two coaches to pass one another; and the pavement, inlaid with flag-stones, can stand six people deep and allows one to gaze at the splendidly lit shop fronts in comfort.[28]

Sights like these, at once grandiose and routine, were only possible because of public street lighting.

Lighting transformed the streets at night into a theatre in which the richer classes, commingling with the poorer ones, acted both as performers and spectators. It also created the conditions in which the commodity itself became a form of spectacle. Social and commercial life in the urban centres thus finally appeared to be liberating itself from a dependency on the conditions of natural light – as the social life of the court, at the cynosure of which was the elaborately lit baroque masque, had done since the early seventeenth century. If the irradiation of cities during this period entailed a process of disenchantment, then it also re-enchanted the streets, or the arterial roads at least.

Treacherously Shifting Darkness

So a bright new world beckoned the upper and middle classes. Throughout Europe, though, the efficiency and effectiveness of the new technology, and the social arrangements required to organize it, remained in doubt.

In a revealing entry on 'Réverbères' in *Le Tableau de Paris*, a multi-volume compendium dating from the 1780s, Louis-Sébastien Mercier expressed his relief that 'oil reflectors' had recently replaced lanterns in the French capital. 'In the old days', he complained, 'eight thousand lanterns, their candles askew, or guttering, or blown out by the wind, nightly adorned the city, a feeble and wavering illumination broken by patches of treacherously shifting darkness.' But the 'excellent innovation' of 1,200 oil lamps, he added with emphasis, had been 'marred by misdirected economy', and the lamps themselves made, 'in Milton's words, darkness itself visible … At a distance they dazzle, close to they give little light, and standing underneath you can hardly see your hand before you.'[29] It was the same in London. Early street lighting had the disconcerting effect of obnubilating as well as illuminating urban space.

If street lighting gentrified the commercial and political centres of cities, it relegated other regions to no-go areas. Long after the introduction of the new technology, the 'treacherously shifting darkness' evoked by Mercier defined entire districts of the English metropolis, as well as merely parts or patches of the streets. For until the nineteenth century poorer areas continued to be unlit. At night, as in the sixteenth century, parts of London remained, for migrants and vagrants, 'what the greenwood had been for the medieval outlaw – an anonymous refuge'.[30]

For the respectable classes, conversely, these areas had a reputation for feral lawlessness. In the chapter on 'Laws relating to Vagabonds' in his *Enquiry into the Causes of the Late Increase of Robbers*, Fielding wrote:

> Whoever indeed considers the Cities of *London* and *Westminster*, with the late vast Addition of their Suburbs; the great Irregularity of their Buildings, the immense Number of Lanes, Alleys, Courts and Bye-places; must think, that, had they been intended for the very Purpose of Concealment, they could scarce have been better contrived. Upon such a View, the whole appears as a vast Wood or Forest, in which a Thief may harbour with as great Security, as wild Beasts do in the Desarts of *Africa* or *Arabia*. For by *wandering* from one Part to another, and often shifting his Quarters, he may almost avoid the Possibility of being discovered.

According to Fielding, the idleness of the poor was responsible for the perennial problem of vagrancy, which centuries of legislation had failed to solve – 'so here *Wandering* is the Cause of the Mischief, and that alone to which the Remedy should be applied'. 'Where then is the Redress?' he concluded; 'Is it not *to hinder the Poor from wandering* ...?'[31] At night, to be poor and on the streets was by definition to wander.

In spite of the changing geography of the city, and in particular its expansion westwards, the areas inhabited by the poor persisted as outposts of the Middle Ages. They were neither modernized nor diurnalized. The obscurity of 'the Hotch-Potch of half-moon and serpentine narrow Streets, close, dismal, long Lanes, stinking Allies, dark, gloomy Courts and suffocating Yards', of which one eighteenth-century critic of the capital complained, was exacerbated at night.[32] Regions such as St Giles-in-the-Fields, one of the most noisome and notorious of the slums to materialize in the eighteenth century, were benighted even in the day. The districts where money and power were concentrated – the City and Westminster, as well as the roads linking them – thus flared into life against an almost impenetrable background. Such were the chiaroscuro effects of the eighteenth-century cityscape.

Night Watches

Throughout Europe, as Craig Koslofsky has argued, lighting 'beautified a city and provided convenience and social amenity by encouraging respectable traffic on the streets after dark'; but the principal point of the new means of illumination was to promote law and order in the absence of a centralized police force.[33] For more than a century after the introduction of street lighting, however, London continued to be incompetently policed at night, and not merely in the areas where the employed and unemployed poor subsisted.

'The expectation that when night came the streets of the City would be largely deserted continued to shape the provisioning of urban services well into the eighteenth century', Beattie comments in his authoritative account of crime and punishment in the period.[34] So the explosion of nightlife after the Restoration, detonated in sites of sociability such as the coffee-houses, gambling houses and pleasure gardens, created social problems for which the nightwatch was unprepared. There is a slightly plaintive tone, for example, to one *Oath of a Constable*, published in 1701, which reiterates that, 'in this degenerate Age', the incumbent of this office must, among other things, 'use his Endeavour that Night-Walkers be apprehended' and 'see that the Statutes made for punishing Vagabonds and such idle Persons, coming within his Bounds and Limits, be duly put in Execution'.[35] London's admixture of rich and poor had never seemed more combustible; and there were panicked rumours of rising crime.

Charles II was only the most prominent representative of the ruling class to articulate concern about the problem of law and order in the nocturnal metropolis when, in 1661, he complained to the Lord Mayor of London, John Frederick:

> There is not that care and vigilance in setting the Night Watches in [the City] as for the peace and security thereof there ought to bee, but that the same for the most part consisteth of a few weak and feeble men, who if there were occasion, would not be able to suppresse any such disorders, as in these times of lycence and sedition may easily be apprehended.

'Robinson's Act', named after John Robinson, who succeeded Frederick as Lord Mayor, was instituted in 1663 in order to redress this situation. But, in insisting that it was the duty of householders to participate in the watch so as 'to keep the peace and apprehend night-walkers, malefactors and suspected persons', it did no more than repeat existing arrangements. Watchmen continued to be inadequately armed and insufficiently paid – although, predictably enough, the state of affairs was far better in richer wards than in poorer ones.[36]

Another Act, this time in 1705, constituted an admission that previous provisions had been ineffective, and represented an attempt to professionalize the service. But it too was perceived as a failure. In the winter of 1712–1713, for example, aldermen accused the City's constables of being unable to cope with 'Night Walkers and Malefactors who wander and misbehave themselves in the Night time within the Streets and Passages of this City'.[37]

Finally, in 1737, an Act was passed that, in addition to making the system by which rates were collected more efficient, both increased the number of watches in each ward and standardized their wages. It too left the system organized on a local basis, however: 'There was no thought that it would have been useful – let alone possible – to create a larger, better paid, and centrally organized force.'[38] This situation endured until 1829, when Sir Robert Peel formed the first citywide police force.

Instead of police, the eighteenth-century ruling class, more and more preoccupied with the protection of property, deployed an expanding number of capital statutes to control and intimidate those whom it perceived as a threat to its sanctity (though courts and juries were often reluctant to implement the most severe measures).[39] The *Proceedings* of the Old Bailey for 1768 record the trial for burglary, robbery, theft and murder of 613 people, 246 of whom were convicted and 54 of whom were sentenced to death.[40] In a legal sense, in fact, nighttime in the eighteenth century was defined not in terms of the setting of the sun but according to the law against burglary: 'the Word *Noctanter* [by night]', William Hawkins indicated in his *Treatise of the Pleas of the Crown*, first published in 1716 and thereafter repeatedly reprinted, 'cannot be satisfied in a legal Sense, if it appear upon the Evidence, that there was so much Day-light at the Time, that a Man's Countenance might be discerned thereby'.[41]

Bulks and Markets

The beneficent social effects of the 'twenty-four hour city' hailed by Shoemaker in his comments on eighteenth-century London should not therefore be overstated. Like enlightenment, illumination was the privilege of the middle and upper classes. Long after the disappearance of a legal or official curfew, what Beattie has called a 'moral or social curfew' lingered on; it was intended 'to prevent those without legitimate reason to be abroad' – principally apprentices, nightwalkers and prostitutes – 'from wandering the streets at night'.[42] Industrial labourers, for example, were excluded from the emergent nightlife of the city, even if, at the same time, they were increasingly compelled to work into the night.

Apprentices, for their part, continued to make more or less surreptitious raids on the nocturnal city in their pursuit of ephemeral freedoms and pleasures; but these were rarely tolerated either by their masters or by the metropolitan authorities, who heaped opprobrium on them. 'I have good reason to believe', announced Jonas Hanway, a leading proponent of police reform, in *The Defects of Police, the Cause of Immorality, and the Continual Robberies Committed, Particularly in and about the Metropolis* (1775),

> that there is scarce an apprentice boy, turned of fifteen years of age, who, contrary to the practice of our forebears, is not suffered to go abroad almost every night, as soon as the shop is shut … You will easily conceive it next to impossible the apprentice should wander about, without learning to drink strong liquors: some go further, and game: many keep bad company: the society of each other is dangerous.[43]

Here is the operation of the moral or social curfew, which applied to plebeians rather than members of polite society.

Prostitutes, beggars and vagabonds resided in a different kind of nocturnal city to the brilliant one relished by aristocrats and aspirant bourgeois. When these impoverished people walked at night, it was not because they had been out for dinner and, like Samuel Pepys, felt like coolly strolling home through the incandescent main streets in order to gaze at the commodities, and the prostitutes' bodies, on display. It was because they had little or nothing else to do, or nowhere else to go. It was because they were looking for food, or financial opportunities, or a place to sleep.

The historian Tim Hitchcock has pointed to the resourcefulness of the urban poor in their attempts to find refuge at night:

> Besides the bulks and markets, besides the beds of friends, squats and ruins, they could be found on dunghills for their warmth, in dark houses and in cellars, in Moorfields and in dust tubs, sheltering under the cranes at the quayside, and in the boghouses that serviced the courts and alleys of the capital.[44]

In spite of the socialization of the city at night – or because of the unendurable contrasts that this development revealed in the lives of its inhabitants – the experience of eighteenth-century vagabonds resembled that of their medieval forebears. For these people, nights in the city were nasty, brutish and all too long.

Nocturnal Excursions

The most prominent role assumed by self-appointed moralists who patrolled the streets at night in the late seventeenth and eighteenth centuries – descendants of the reformer Humphrey Mill – was to enumerate and police the activities of prostitutes. They deemed it necessary, no doubt, because legislation concerning prostitution remained vague and relatively negligent throughout the eighteenth century, in spite of the introduction of a statute against bawdy houses in 1752.

Specifically, the laws used against streetwalkers did not distinguish between soliciting and other forms of 'lewd behaviour' in public. So, in order to criminalize women caught on the streets at night, magistrates tended to use a statute dating from as far back as 1604 to charge them with being 'idle and disorderly'. But if these women could not be legally identified as common prostitutes, this was nonetheless the automatic assumption. 'Many poor women who were found wandering the streets late at night were unable to explain how they made a living or why they were abroad at that hour, and so suspected of prostitution', confirms one historian.[45]

In contrast to those who attempted to classify, criminalize or reform them, streetwalking prostitutes themselves were of course disqualified from finding a voice in print. They were almost invariably uneducated and illiterate, and inhabited a different social universe from either their moral protectors or their middle- and upper-class clients. There are, to be sure, traces of them in the records of houses of correction such as Bridewell, where 'idle loose Vagrants, loose and disorderly Servants, Night-wakers [*sic*], Strumpets, &c.' are given 'Correction according to their deserts'.[46] But, in condemning them to ritual public humiliation or compulsory labour, and perhaps even forced emigration, these institutions effectively silenced them. There is little in the archives that testifies directly to prostitutes' experience of the streets at night in the eighteenth century.

If street prostitutes' voices were for the most part muted or silenced, then their movements were comparatively restricted too. They did not traverse large distances in the city, as Tony Henderson has demonstrated: 'Success necessitated relative immobility (at most "wandering back and forward") within a restricted area.' Streetwalking prostitutes therefore tended to station themselves at specific locations, especially in the city's main squares and thoroughfares. By the end of the eighteenth century, however, as a result of improvements to lighting and policing in metropolitan centres, they 'were beginning to desert many of the major streets for the lanes and courts of the poorer quarters leading off them'.[47]

Occasionally, it is possible to catch the voices of prostitutes in publications, even if their meanings have been obscured by the mediation of male authors or simply muffled by time. One intriguing exception, for example, is *The Night-Walkers Declaration; or, The Distressed Whores Advice to All their Sisters in City and Country*, a short pamphlet published in 1676. It declares on behalf of the streetwalkers that it is 'set forth (by way of confession) out of a deep sense of the tribulations they have lately suffered'. And it goes on to offer solicitous advice to women forced to take 'the opportunity of the Night (the fittest season for Deeds of Darkness)', and to remind them, in defiant tones, that 'though *Night-walking* be forbidden, the *day*'s our own'.[48] It seems possible that it is a kind of mock-petition compiled by prostitutes complaining that the more licentious and promiscuous ladies at court are crowding them out of the market.

If prostitutes were for the most part condemned to silence, they are sometimes almost audible in the effusions of male authors who, principally for satirical purposes, ventriloquized their voices. In *The Lady's Ramble; or, The Female Night-walker*, an anonymous poem from about 1720 – one that is manifestly written by a man – a streetwalker who 'ramble[s] in *Fleet-street* oft times with Success' offers advice to the poet: 'Then pray take Example by others Undoing, / And let not a pocky young Whore be your Ruin.'[49] Perhaps inevitably, this pamphlet compromises its compassionate attitude to the prostitute, which it is momentarily possible to infer, because it is so transparently driven by moralistic objectives.

But it is the extraordinary Samuel Johnson, in articles in consecutive issues of *The Rambler* in November 1751, who provides some of the least moralistic, and most striking, impressions of a prostitute's life at night in the eighteenth-century city. Johnson's essays purport to be letters from a correspondent called Misella who claims that, though from a respectable family in the countryside, she has been coerced into prostitution in the city. In the first letter she explains that, at the age of ten, she was taken to London by a wealthy relation who, when she was seventeen, raped her.

In the second, she resumes this gruesome narrative and reports that her relative then exiled her to an obscure part of the city in order to corrupt her: 'I now saw with Horror that he was contriving to perpetuate his Gratification, and was desirous to fit me to his Purpose by complete and radical Corruption.' He eventually abandons her, and the landlord evicts her from her lodgings because she cannot afford the rent. So she is compelled to 'wander about without any settled Purpose'. 'Night at last came on in the midst of my Distraction, and I still continued to wander till the Menaces of the Watch obliged me to shelter myself in a covered Passage.'[50] Here she is a common nightwalker rather than a streetwalker.

After successfully finding employment and accommodation as a needlewoman, Misella is forced to flee the shop in order to escape prosecution when a fellow lodger steals the lace on which she has been labouring. 'Thus driven again into the Streets', she writes, 'I lived upon the least that could support me, and at Night, accommodated myself under Penthouses as well as I could.' Eventually, absolutely penniless, she sells her body to a man who accosts her in the street. Nightwalking is the prelude to streetwalking. Thereafter, Misella's days are devoted to finding those 'whom Folly or Excess may expose to [her] Allurements', and her nights to dealing with the 'Guilt and Terror' she feels.

She concludes, in thunderous tones, with an inspiring and provocative challenge to the readers of the *Rambler*, a community of comparatively enlightened men that implicitly constitutes the progressive minority of a privileged class that is as callous as it is complacent:

> If those who pass their Days in Plenty and Security, could visit, for an Hour, the dismal Receptacles to which the Prostitute retires from her nocturnal Excursions, and see the Wretches that lie crowded together,

> mad with Intemperance, ghastly with Famine, nauseous with Filth, and noisome with Disease, it would not be easy for any Degree of Abhorrence to harden them against Compassion, or to repress the Desire which they must immediately feel to rescue such Numbers of human Beings from a State so dreadful.

In a voice that combines fury and sympathy, Johnson uses Misella's narrative both to advertise the 'abject State' in which prostitutes live and to rage against the libertines who create and perpetuate their plight.

Sauntering Gait

If streetwalking, like begging, was a morally and socially unacceptable means of inhabiting the street, then more respectable means of doing so emerged in the late seventeenth and eighteenth centuries. Promenading – an invention, like shopping, of this period – implicitly treated the street as an interior, albeit an extremely capacious and capricious one. In spite of its often inclement climate, and its sometimes hostile or volatile social conditions, or because of these perhaps, aristocrats and aspirant members of the middle classes increasingly colonized the roads and thoroughfares of London as a site of leisurely activity. The promenade, as in contemporaneous Paris, was central to the rise of a society of spectacle.

Verbs such as 'to stroll' and 'to saunter', which had originally been identified with the activities of vagrants – the former probably derived from the German *strolch*, meaning 'vagabond' – acquired a patina of respectability in the eighteenth century. These words retained their association with idleness; but, for respectable people with social pretensions, this increasingly implied an aristocratic resistance to the industriousness of the ascendant middle class. 'I sauntered up and down all this forenoon', wrote James Boswell in a typical diary entry from 1763.[51] In the divided class context of the time, walking thus inevitably became inflected with conflicting social meanings.

The advice manuals, guidebooks and road directories that proliferated in the eighteenth-century metropolis thus represented an attempt to domesticate the streets, and those who walked in them, by codifying and stratifying them. In 'Rules of Behaviour, of General Use, though Much Disregarded in this Populous City', printed in the *London Magazine* in 1780, several recommendations relate to perambulating the streets, including an admonition not to adopt 'the sauntering gait of a lazy Spaniard'.[52] A 'personal etiquette of acceptable street behavior' was developing, confirms Penelope Corfield: 'The informal code decreed that staring too directly at other people was rude; peering closely through the windows of private houses was unacceptable; belligerent jostling or pushing was disliked; spitting was discouraged; and excessive swearing or drunkenness in public were socially as well as legally proscribed.'[53]

The relentless traffic of people in the metropolis, among them recent immigrants from the countryside, created the constant potential for social confusion. Carts and coaches clipped the posts that were supposed to separate them from pedestrians and shops, generating danger and resentment; angry or uppity individuals argued with one another over who had the prerogative of 'the wall' – that is, the right to walk along the strip of pavement farthest from the congested, muddy conditions of the road; and yeomen who had been herding cattle only days earlier embarrassed themselves by mistaking a female aristocrat for a courtesan, or vice versa. Distinctions of rank were easily lost in the press of bodies. In the ordinary conditions of the eighteenth-century city, all that had seemed socially solid was in a state of ceaseless dissolution.

The streets in the daytime thus simmered with an inchoate and sometimes incomprehensible semiotics. And in the nighttime – when those who loitered on the pavements looking as if they didn't belong among fashionable people seemed all the more alien and threatening – the potential for misunderstandings and social conflict was exacerbated. Public lighting was another means of monitoring and policing the streets. As Koslofsky puts it, citing a contemporary, 'court and city authorities used street lighting to sharpen a distinction between their own growing nocturnal sociability and the night life of "apprentices, boys, maids and such unmarried folk found idly in the streets"'.[54]

The nocturnal city, in addition to becoming more populous, seemed increasingly unstable in class terms, as itinerants, mendicants, pickpockets and prostitutes rubbed up against members of the upper and upper-middle classes pursuing entertainment in the streets – parasitic on a parasitic class. This tension is apparent in publications like *The Foreigner's Guide* (1729), which complained of the 'great croud of people' at night, and the poorly lit streets, which are the more 'troublesome' because of 'the readiness of the pickpockets'; and *A Brief Description of the Cities of London and Westminster* (1776), which claimed that 'the streets are by night polluted with lewd women, or infested by villains, notwithstanding the number of watchmen and the glare of lights'.[55]

The Art of Walking the Streets

It is this chaotic if not catastrophic daily scene that John Gay celebrated and satirized in the irrepressible heroic couplets of *Trivia*. Subtitled *The Art of Walking the Streets of London*, this is perhaps the sharpest and most exuberant poem about everyday life in a metropolitan city ever composed.

Like his friend Jonathan Swift, who was the author of satiric poems including 'A Description of the Morning' (1709) and 'A Description of a City Shower' (1710), Gay drew on both Juvenal's third *Satire* and Virgil's *Georgics* to provide penetrating, sometimes acidic advice on how to survive as a 'prudent Walker' – that is, a cannily strategic pedestrian, though not necessarily a morally upright one – among the 'vicious Walkers' that 'croud the street'.[56] It is in the cut-and-thrust of the streets that – unlike Addison and Steele's Spectator, who implicitly travels by coach more often than he does on foot – Gay's quietly heroic pedestrian 'learns to cope at close hand, rather than from the Augustan detachment of a coach window, with a series of powerful challenges to his physical and spiritual integrity'.[57] Gay, who finally found fame with the phenomenal success of *The Beggar's Opera* (1728), is the poet laureate of the eighteenth-century man in the street.[58]

Echoing the invocation at the start of the *Georgics*, Gay proceeds to open *Trivia* with an exordium to the poet's Muse:

> Through Winter Streets to steer your Course aright,
> How to walk clean by Day, and safe by Night,
> How jostling Crouds, with Prudence, to decline,
> When to assert the Wall, and when resign,
> I sing: Thou, Trivia, Goddess, aid my Song,
> Thro' spacious Streets conduct thy Bard along:
> By thee transported, I securely stray
> Where winding Alleys lead the doubtful Way,
> The silent Court, and op'ning Square explore,
> And long perplexing Lanes untrod before.[59]

In the postlapsarian landscape of the metropolis, with its 'winding alleys and 'long perplexing Lanes' as well as its 'spacious Streets', the poet's ambition, in an almost oxymoronic formulation, is to 'securely stray'. The Old French verb 'to stray', which was once thought to derive from the Latin noun *strata*, meaning 'street', signifies movement that escapes confinement or control, and hints in addition at moral deviance. But this pedestrian proposes, paradoxically, to remain safe and free from apprehension in thus erring or straying. It is a delicate and difficult equilibrium to achieve, and it is only possible with the guidance of Trivia, the Roman goddess of crossroads. At one point Gay refers to her as his 'vagrant Muse'.[60] She is the patron saint of psychogeographers.

If Trivia is the ancient goddess of intersecting roads, then she is also, Gay hints, the eighteenth-century goddess of the ordinary. The word 'trivial' is first recorded in association with the everyday or inconsequential from the late sixteenth century. Shakespeare, for example, refers to 'triviall argument' in 2 *Henry VI* (1590–1591). In this sense, it appears to be derived from the Latin *trivium*, which signified the lower division of the liberal arts – consisting of grammar, rhetoric and logic – in medieval university studies. But the adjective is probably also derived from the Latin *trivialis*, meaning a three-way crossing, which identified it with the behaviour of dubious or simply commonplace characters who loitered about at crossroads and other sites of everyday commerce and transit. 'Before it came to mean insignificant', Ross Chambers claims, 'the trivial was associated with people, places, and practices of ill repute, particularly as they involved the body and the satisfaction of its needs, as opposed to the supposedly higher things of the mind and the soul.'[61]

Traditionally, three-way crossings were busy intersections, often clotted with traffic. Travellers of all kinds, including itinerants, prostitutes and vagrants, collected there in order to eat, drink, gamble or sleep before resuming their journeys. Gay implies that eighteenth-century London is itself finally an immense, complicated site of social intersection.

Dangerous Night

The Roman goddess Trivia is the equivalent of the Greek goddess Hecate, a pre-Olympian deity who was closely associated with the night. So it seems appropriate that Gay devotes the third part of his four-part poem to the challenges of 'Walking the Streets by Night'. 'Oh! May thy Silver Lamp in Heav'n's high Bow'r / Direct my Footsteps in the Midnight Hour', is the appeal with which it commences.[62]

Having sketched the city's atmosphere in the evening, as the first stars appear and night 'inwraps the Air', and when 'swarms the busie Street', Gay goes on to describe the dangers of the darkening streets in detail.[63] First, in a Juvenalian passage, he details the perils of shop windows that are suddenly slammed shut, of low penthouses and of broken pavements. Then he depicts the conflicts that arise when, in an urban dynamic that is all too familiar, masses of frantic pedestrians attempt to cross the road as they commute home through frenzied traffic:

> Crouds heap'd on Crouds appear,
> And wait impatient, 'till the Road grow clear.

> Now all the pavement sounds with tramping Feet,
> And the mixt Hurry barricades the Street.[64]

Goaded by road-rage, drivers leap from their vehicles and attack one another with 'pond'rous Fists' – 'Blow answers Blow, their Cheeks are smear'd with Blood, / 'Till down they fall, and grappling roll in Mud'.[65] One must concentrate unceasingly in the city after dark so as to avoid the threat of collisions, concussions. These are the shocks that Walter Benjamin evoked in his discussion of the individual moving through traffic in the nineteenth-century city: 'At dangerous intersections, nervous impulses flow through him in rapid succession, like the energy from a battery.'[66]

The pedestrian's 'Useful Precepts' are methodically indexed – as in less playful advice manuals – in the form of helpful subtitles: 'Of inadvertent Walkers'; 'Observations concerning keeping the Wall'; 'Of avoiding Paint'. These precepts are summarized in the following lines:

> Let constant Vigilance thy Footsteps guide,
> And wary Circumspection guard thy Side;
> Then shalt thou walk unharm'd the dang'rous Night,
> Nor need th'officous Link-Boy's smoaky Light.[67]

Straying securely in the city at night entails vigilance, circumspection and the skilful circumnavigation of dangers (the ancient topos of the *pericula noctis*). Gay's pedestrian alerts his readers, among other things, to pickpockets who hide 'amid the Swarm'; to City Frauds, Guinea-Droppers, Jugglers and Sharpers; and to rakes, 'scowrers' and other aristocratic 'Kindlers of Riots'.[68] He offers advice about how to stick close to a friend in walking through the most thickly crowded streets. And he criticizes the concupiscent fool who, 'regardless of his Pace, / Turns oft' to pore upon the Damsel's Face', pointing out that his inattentiveness might prove almost fatal.[69]

Finally, Gay offers a negative, if not misogynistic, portrait of a prostitute, 'who nightly strowls with saunt'ring Pace' beneath the lamps (in his account of London in the daytime, he refers to 'the

Night-wandring Harlot').[70] And he offers an oddly positive one of the nightwatchman, 'who with friendly Light, / Will teach thy reeling Steps to tread aright'.[71] The authorities, as this emphasis indicates, do not represent a threat to him. Gay's pedestrian is a virtuous citizen, albeit an unobtrusive or unostentatious one, and he does not appear to feel in the least bit morally compromised in the febrile city at night. As one critic has pointed out, he is 'sympathetic to a seventeenth-century model of classical republicanism which advocated acts of civic good along with a personal regime of honesty, modesty, and independence'.[72]

Gay also pays close attention in the third part of the poem to the specific geography of nocturnal London. He urges walkers to circumvent Lincoln's Inn, where violent thieves conceal themselves at night, and to avoid the 'mazy Courts, and dark Abodes' of Drury Lane, as well as the place 'Where Katherine-street descends into the Strand'.[73] In general, his advice to readers is: Don't retire at night to those 'dark Paths' that, during the day, represent a temptingly clean or peaceful alternative to 'the Hurries of the publick Way'.[74] Instead, in an emblematic image of one of the new street lights – one that brilliantly combines light and dark, the liquid and the brittle or crystalline – he recommends them to 'keep the publick Streets, where oily Rays / Shot from the Crystal Lamp, o'erspread the Ways'.[75] Here, and throughout *Trivia*, Gay is like the 'kaleidoscope endowed with consciousness' that Charles Baudelaire, in his characterization of the urban spectator, celebrated in the nineteenth century.[76]

Even in these obscure precincts of the city, though, the 'dim Gleam' emitted by the 'paly Lanthorn' is insufficient to illuminate the 'heapy Rubbish', the 'arched Vaults' and the 'dark Caves' or cellars that threaten to transform an ordinary journey along the pavement into a hazardous odyssey for the nocturnal pedestrian.[77] These are the porous spaces, the cavities of the city inhabited by the poor and destitute. As these scenes indicate, in *Trivia* London at night is not a conventional neoclassical city so much as a Piranesian one that contains endless, complicated convolutions of space.

Noctambulants

The politics of pedestrianism after dark in the eighteenth-century city are polarized – as Gay's lengthy counsel to what he calls 'the wandring Crew' implies.[78] On the one hand, nightwalking was domesticated and gentrified, in the form of promenading and perambulating. On the other hand, in the poorer districts of the city – the patches of darkness that tainted its civilized and enlightened veneer – the disreputable associations of nightwalking were sustained and, amid ruling-class anxieties about rising crime, deepened. These countervailing situations in the metropolis at night, to put it in schematic terms, reinforced the distinction between two pedestrian archetypes: the noctambulant and the noctivagant.

Nightwalkers at the upper end of the social scale can be characterized as noctambulants, or noctambulists, or noctambules (synonymous words that were coined in the late seventeenth and early eighteenth centuries). These terms indicate a voluntary mode of pedestrianism, and for the most part a relatively sociable one. The category of the noctambulant includes gallants and roués who strolled through the streets carousing and soliciting prostitutes. The sons of Belial ... To appropriate Bryan Palmer's expression, these men enjoyed 'the risqué sensuality and discarded gentility of the frenetic metropolis after dark'.[79]

No doubt the most sensational instance of this aristocratic subculture on the streets of eighteenth-century London at night, and the most antisocial one, was the Mohocks. These violent men – 'rakes reckless and ruthless who were said to be beating and stabbing respectable citizens of the middling sort' – caused a scandal in 1712.[80] They slashed the faces of pedestrians with knives and assaulted women, spitefully standing them on their heads. In the *Spectator*, Steele described them as 'a Set of Men (if you will allow them a Place in that Species of Being) who have lately erected themselves into a nocturnal Fraternity', one named after 'a sort of *Cannibals* in India'. 'An outrageous Ambition of doing all possible Hurt to their Fellow-Creatures, is the great Cement of their Assembly, and the only Qualification required in the Members', he explained, advising the periodical's readers that they 'attack all that are so unfortunate to walk the Streets thro' which they patroll'.[81] This fraternity – a forerunner of one of those cults of enlightened and entitled bloodletting to be found in the late novels of J. G. Ballard – was probably closer to an urban myth than to an actual phenomenon; but, even so, it is indicative of the class conflicts that, overtly or covertly, defined the nocturnal city.

At the opposite end of the moral spectrum, though not the social one, the category of the noctambulant includes those who, appointing themselves the spiritual guardians of the city at night, unofficially attempted either to police it or redeem its fallen inhabitants. These philanthropists, many of whom were equally committed misanthropists when it came to beggars and vagrants, were responding partly to the emergent culture of nocturnal sociability, in particular the excesses of the upper class, and partly to ancient rumours or myths about an 'anti-society' among the poor.

A letter to the *Spectator* in 1711 gives a sense of this vocation. It is from 'one of the Directors of the Society for the Reformation of Manners':

> I can describe every Parish by its Impieties, and can tell you in which of our Streets Lewdness prevails, which Gaming has taken the Possession of, and where Drunkenness has got the better of them both. When I am disposed to raise a Fine for the Poor, I know the Lanes and Allies that are inhabited by common Swearers. When I would encourage the Hospital of *Bridewell* and improve the Hempen Manufacture, I am very well acquainted with all the Haunts and Resorts of Female Night-walkers.[82]

Here is a moral topography of the eighteenth-century city, one that is peopled by prostitutes and, implicitly at least, male nightwalkers too. The author's leaden joke about dispatching more people to Bridewell in order to accelerate the production of hemp is chilling.

The distinction between noctambulants motivated by the desire to socialize and those motivated by the desire to moralize is of course an unstable one. Boswell, who liked to 'sall[y] forth like a roaring Lion after girls, blending philosophy and raking', is a deliciously compromised – indeed tortured – example of this contradiction.[83] But, ultimately, both types were tourists in the city at night, however comfortable they might at times have felt in this foreign territory, and however intimate their understanding of it. They made excursions into the nocturnal streets because they had chosen to do so, not because they had been exiled there by circumstance. They were on the side of illumination and socialization, even if this meant something quite different in the cases of a dissolute nobleman and a puritanical preacher. They were colonizers of the night.

Noctivagants

Nightwalkers at the bottom of the social scale – some of them temporary denizens of the night, some semi-permanent – might in turn be characterized as common nightwalkers, or noctivagants, or noctivagators. These people originated in what George Rudé, in his book on Hanoverian London, classifies as 'the "submerged" and floating population of vagrants and beggars, the "miserable", the destitute, the unemployed and unemployable, the indigent, the aged, the part-time domestic workers, the casual workers, the poorest of the immigrant Irish and Jews'.[84] To the masterless men and women listed by Rudé might be added idle apprentices and prostitutes.

Collectively, this agglomeration of the unemployed and semi-employed has many of the characteristics of what Marx, diagnosing the class composition of Bonapartism in the mid nineteenth century, identified as the lumpenproletariat:

> Alongside decayed roués of doubtful origin and uncertain means of subsistence, alongside ruined and adventurous scions of the bourgeoisie, there [are] vagabonds, discharged soldiers, discharged criminals, escaped galley slaves, swindlers, confidence tricksters, *lazzaroni* [Neapolitan street people], pickpockets, sleight-of-hand experts, gamblers, *maquereaux* [pimps], brothel-keepers, porters, pen-pushers, organ-grinders, rag-and-bone merchants, knife-grinders, tinkers, and beggars: in short, the whole indeterminate, fragmented mass, tossed backwards and forwards, which the French call *la bohème*.

This desiccated, indefinite community, 'living off the garbage of society', as Marx explained in another account of 1848, consists of 'people without a definite trace, vagabonds, *gens sans feu et sans aveu*'.[85] They are people without hearth (literally, without fire) and without home, implicitly condemned to inhabit the streets at night.

From the 1660s, however, this miscellaneous, mongrel population comprised a social class that was at times designated instead as 'proletarian'. In his *Dictionary of the English Language* (1755), Johnson defined this adjective, which had been appropriated from ancient Roman political discourse, as 'mean; wretched; vile; vulgar'.[86] It emerged in the aftermath of the Civil War, as Peter Linebaugh has pointed out – specifically, 'in the counter-revolution of a class that went to Roman history to find a term adequate to express its contempt (and fear) of those "lawless" or "loose and disorderly" persons whom it had just vanquished'. In etymological terms, it described those who, in contrast to plebeians, who had limited amounts of property, were 'good for nothing but the production of workers'.[87]

In the late seventeenth and eighteenth centuries, the 'submerged' population of the metropolis did not for the most part even produce workers. It merely replicated its own abject class position on the margins of a productive and increasingly profit-driven economy. In the course of time, these proto-proletarians, as they might be called, will go on to produce a generation of proletarians. At the onset of the age of large-scale manufacture, at the end of the eighteenth century, their sons, if not their daughters, will form a substantial section of the industrial labour force. For the moment, however, these unemployed and semi-employed people do no more than subsist, improvising or jerry-building their lives on an everyday basis.

Noctivagants, who stumble from their ramshackle ranks among the slums, were forced, as in previous centuries, to make a living from the public spaces of the city at night, or to find a home in them. As Malcolm Falkus has explained, '"night-walking" remained an offence in many towns until after the Restoration, and darkness imposed a discipline on men's lives which was only gradually lifted'.[88] But, as the eighteenth century progressed, people apprehended by the nightwatch in the metropolis at night were less and less likely to be charged as common nightwalkers. In this period, nightwalkers were generally of concern to the legal system only if they could be accused of committing burglary or theft (in which case they could be summarily hanged).

Although they remained suspicious, those who merely loitered in the streets for no apparent purpose were of less interest to the authorities. Indeed, some of them might even have found refuge in the ragged system of nocturnal policing. Hitchcock suggests that, 'if you were sick and friendless, drunk beyond self-knowledge, or lacking a home on a cold night, the watchhouse was a beacon of warmth and relative safety', as well as 'a point of access to the substantial resources available to the very poor in the prisons and hospitals and parishes of the capital'.[89]

But, in spite of the decline in the numbers of prosecutions, and the partial accommodation of homeless people indicated by Hitchcock's speculations, nightwalking of this kind remained socially unacceptable as far as polite society was concerned. Common nightwalkers, subsisting in the pitchy darkness of the urban labyrinth, retained their semi-criminal identity. They were the embodiments of the Enlightenment city's unthought – its unconscious. In a fine formulation taken from Foucault, they inhabited 'the secret night of light'.[90] Simply by subsisting, they continued to infringe the moral or spiritual curfew that persisted in the streets and thoroughfares of the metropolis at night.

5.

The Nocturnal Picaresque

Dunton, Ward and their Descendants

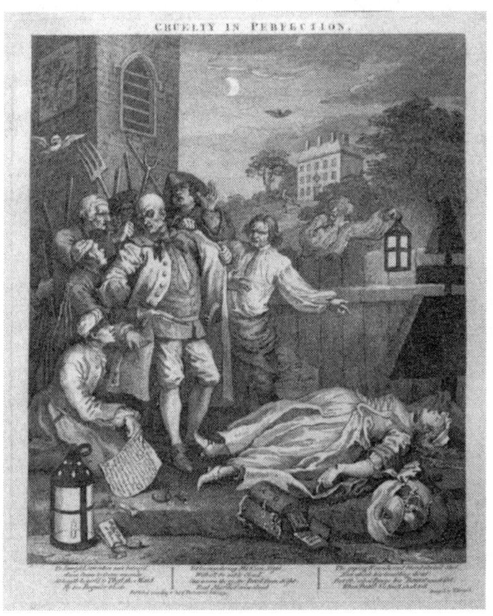

What Passes at Night

At the end of the seventeenth century a new literary genre or subgenre emerged in England, one that can be characterized as the nocturnal picaresque. Its authors, who were moralists or satirists or social tourists, or all of these at the same time, and who were almost invariably male, purported to recount their episodic adventures as pedestrians patrolling the streets of the metropolis at night.

These narratives, which often provided detailed portraits of particular places, especially ones with corrupt reputations, also paid close attention to the precise times when more or less nefarious activities unfolded in the streets. As distinct from diaries, they were noctuaries (in his *Dictionary of the English Language* [1755], Samuel Johnson defined a 'noctuary' simply as 'an account of what passes at night').[1] These apparently unmediated, more or less diaristic accounts of what happened during the course of a night on the street embodied either a tragic or a comic parable of the city, depending on whether their authors intended to celebrate its nightlife or condemn it as satanic.

The nocturnal picaresque, composed more often in prose than verse, was a distinctively modern, metropolitan form that, like several other literary genres that emerged in the late seventeenth and eighteenth centuries, comprised a response to the dramatic social and architectural transformations of the metropolis after the Great Fire of 1666.

This was the epoch when both the West End, which the aristocracy colonized, and the suburbs to the south and east of the city, where the poor were exiled, expanded exponentially. By 1700, when its population reached approximately 550,000, London had outstripped Paris to become the largest city in Europe. Its concentration of imperial trade, industry and government made it the most advanced and energetic metropolitan centre in the world. Leo Hollis has even speculated that 'the true "English Revolution" was seen not in the 1640s, or in 1688, but in the 1690s', when the expansion and recomposition of London 'shattered the traditional urban space into enclaves and modern neighbourhoods' and 'the city at large became a fluid mixture of anonymous and closely knit communities formed by new relationships dependent on work, status, religion and gender'.[2]

These social and topographical changes, especially this segregation, reshaped people's psychogeographical relationship to the metropolis and its proliferating, increasingly complex forms. A number of different types of publication mapped and explored London after the Fire. These included guidebooks, street directories, topographical surveys, urban instruction manuals and antiquarian tour-books. They also included anti-pastoral poems, or 'urban georgics', such as Jonathan Swift's 'Description of a City

Shower' (1710) and John Gay's *Trivia* (1716); and, most prominently, pioneering instances of the novel, as practised in particular by Daniel Defoe – 'probably the first writer to grasp the exotic possibilities of city life with its unpredictable energies tempting the urban adventurer into ever new situations'.[3]

The nocturnal picaresque, which provided a moral map of the metropolitan night, was related to all these genres. But it was above all a type of 'ramble or spy narrative', a form that structured its account of the daily life of the city in terms of the adventures its narrator experienced in the course of a pedestrian stroll through its precincts.[4] The ramble narrative claimed to record these scenes, which were at once sensational and typical of everyday life in the metropolis, as if they had momentarily occurred, at a particular time of day, in precisely located streets.

Like the ramble narrative, the nocturnal picaresque was rendered possible by the fact that, in spite of its rapidly rising population, which leapt by at least 200,000 in the first half of the eighteenth century, London was still not too immense to be circumambulated. The anonymous author of *The Ambulator; or, The Stranger's Companion in a Tour Round London* (1774) measured the metropolis, which included Westminster and Southwark as well as the City itself, as being five miles from east to west and three miles from north to south.[5] It was still a pedestrian's city, in spite of the rising levels of horse-drawn traffic.

The nocturnal picaresque was also rendered possible by the constantly flickering play of light and dark characteristic of the metropolis at night in the era of public street lighting initiated in the mid 1680s. For this technology, inconsistent and intermittent as the oil-burning street lamps were, provided the ideal theatrical conditions for staging the city's social contradictions. The sooty, smutty industrial smoke that thickened and blackened the air in the day – especially in the City, where bakers, brewers, glassmakers, potters and blacksmiths burned quantities of coal in the labyrinthine back streets – intensified these conditions at night.

The pioneering examples of the nocturnal picaresque were, first, John Dunton's *The Night-Walker* (1696), then, most influentially, the nighttime episodes of Ned Ward's *The London Spy* (1698–1700).

For almost a century, Ward reigned as the city's sprightliest, most entertaining tour guide, a dark and distinctly indecorous alternative to the genteel figure of Mr Spectator, Addison and Steele's sparkling creation. *The London Spy* cast a kind of spell on subsequent publications about the urban night. The authors of *The Midnight Rambler; or, New Nocturnal Spy* (1770), *The Complete Modern London Spy* (1781) and *London Unmask'd; or, The New Town Spy* (1784), for example, all more or less opportunistically pointed to it as a precedent. Indeed, *The London Spy* proved so influential that it is tempting to identify a tradition of Nedwardian literature.

Evening Rambles

John Dunton's *The Night-Walker, or, Evening Rambles in Search after Lewd Women, with the Conferences Held with Them* appeared in 1696, roughly a decade after public lighting was first introduced in London.

An author and bookseller who insisted that 'Life is a continued Ramble', Dunton had founded the *Athenian Mercury*, Britain's first successful periodical, in 1691.[6] A committed Anglican whose father, grandfather and great-grandfather had all been ministers in the Church of England, Dunton published *Proposals for a National Reformation of Manners* in 1694 as part of a moral crusade led by Queen Mary. *The Night-Walker*, another periodical, which declared on the title-page of its October 1696 issue that it was '*To be publish'd Monthly*, 'till a Discovery be made of all the chief *Prostitutes* in *England*, from the *Pensionary Miss*, down to the *Common Strumpet*', was a supplementary contribution to Mary II's campaign, albeit one whose crusading ambition was somewhat compromised by its scurrilous content.[7] It folded in 1697 after eight issues – though not, presumably, because it had successfully recorded the identity of every prostitute in London.

The Night-Walker comprised a series of tracts against whoring and whore-mongering among the metropolitan nobility. It was inspired in part by anxieties about the degeneration of aristocratic bloodlines: 'Some of you value your selves as being the *Representatives* of

Ancient and Noble Families; but by the Methods which you take, you will deprive your Posterity of those Pretensions, for you give your Ladies occasion to repay you in your own Coin.' As the Dedication in its first issue indicates, it reserved especially vituperative feelings for clergymen, judges and other hypocritical members of the upper class who, though 'mighty Pretenders to impartial Justice, and zealous Asserters of *Liberty and Property*', had debauched '*poor Maids*' and exposed both them and the 'spurious Issue' they have had by them to 'Poverty, Reproach and Punishment'. *The Night-Walker* detailed Dunton's attempts to pursue these upright representatives of Society, and the 'Suburb Strumpet[s]' with whom they consorted, through the streets of London, which he bemoaned as 'a second Sodom'.[8] The periodical's title thus referred both to the activities of the prostitutes and their clients, and to Dunton's identity as a noctambulant.

Dunton's modus operandi entailed rambling in places like Chancery Lane, Cheapside, Farringdon, Fleet Street, Holborn, St James's Park or the Strand, generally between 8 p.m. and 9 p.m. He pursued this vocation throughout the winter of 1696–1697. In addition to the streets, he visited coffee-houses, music houses, playhouses and pleasure gardens in pursuit of his victims. He liked to take his cue from the coded invitations of prostitutes, as when they pretended to stumble into him or drop their handkerchiefs on the pavement. In order to be morally and socially effective, as he saw it, Dunton masqueraded as the corrupt and sinful individuals whose behaviour he was determined to expose. So on his first night's noctambulation, for example, traversing Pall Mall, he propositioned prostitutes, sequestered them in a convenient tavern, and only then, after several glasses, lectured them on their licentiousness.

This approach, predictably, did not appeal to all his readers, and in the periodical's fourth issue, in December 1696, he was compelled to respond to critics of the enterprise who complained that he acted 'first the part of a Devil to tempt and then the part of a *Parson to Preach*'. In response, he insisted: 'The *Night-Walker* cannot any other way prove the Crime upon each Person with whom he Confers but to *sound their Inclinations*.'[9]

Dunton is a splendid embodiment of the contradictory but symbiotic relationship between puritanical impulses and satanic ones in the nocturnal city. The moral kicks he got from the streets at night cannot be extricated from his sexual kicks. In him the nightwatcher and the nightwalker were in an uncomfortably close relationship. As the historian Joachim Schlör remarks of the 'missionaries' who patrolled the nineteenth-century city at night, 'they too "penetrate" into the nocturnal city, they too seek the extraordinary experience, they too participate in the cycle of chance encounters, they too see how far they can go'.[10]

Night Accidents

Dunton's opinion of his contemporary, Ned Ward, one of the most hedonistic satirists of the time, seems to have alternated between admiration and contempt. On one occasion, Dunton hailed the author of *The Poet's Ramble after Riches* (1691) as 'Ingenious Ward', and praised him for having been 'truly born a Poet, not made, not form'd by Industry'. On another occasion, mistakenly persuaded that Ward had been deriding him in print, he condemned him as 'a harden'd impudent Rake' who likes 'playing at Women, just as he does at Cards'.[11]

Ward's periodical, *The London Spy*, which derived its title from *L'Espion Turc* (1684–1686), a series of fictional letters recently translated from French into English, contains nocturnal episodes that read like a scurrilous riposte to the pious pretences of *The Night-Walker*. If Dunton is a noctambulant, in spite of his troubling moral ambiguity, then Ward's rambunctious and scabrous habits in the streets at night bring him closer to the lowlife he relishes recording; and he therefore begins to resemble the semi-criminal types categorized in the Middle Ages as noctivagants.

The ostensible purpose of *The London Spy*, a comic parable of the metropolis that appeared in eighteen monthly parts from November 1698 to May 1700, was to present 'a complete survey of the most remarkable places, as well as the common vanities and follies of mankind (both day and night)', so that 'Town gentlemen may see the view of the Town (without their experience), and learn the better to avoid those snares and practiced subtleties which trepan many to their ruin'.[12] But Ward's mischievous descriptions of his adventures in London are so rich in Chaucerian relish for lowlife that this rather thin moral rationale rapidly comes to seem irrelevant. His appetite for ribald and titillating experiences, it transpires, is insatiable. And, as an anarchic satirist who identified himself as a high-church Tory opposed to the strict regulation sponsored by the Whig government, he exhibits an irrepressible spirit of anti-authoritarianism too. He seems to have relished any behaviour that subverted the idea of the National Reformation of Manners to which Dunton contributed.

The first issue of *The London Spy* – 'popped into the cautious world as a skilful angler does a new bait among wary fish who have oft been pricked in their nibbling' – opens with the Spy's announcement that, in response to 'an itching inclination' to visit London, he intends to renounce his pastoral life as a scholar living in a 'country hut' like 'Diogenes in his tub'. 'A fig for St Augustine and his doctrines, a fart for Virgil and his elegance, and a turd for Descartes and his philosophy', he declares. At the end of this issue, after spending the evening in a tavern singing songs, the Spy and his companion, who is a surgeon, pay and leave, agreeing 'to give [them]selves the pleasure of two or three hours' ramble in the streets': 'Having spent the time at the tavern till about ten o'clock with mirth and satisfaction, we were now desirous of prying into the dark intrigues of the Town, to experience what pastime the night accidents, the whims and frolics of staggering bravadoes and strolling strumpets, might afford us.' The periodical's second issue – which notes that it is at 9 p.m., 'the miser's bedtime', not 10 p.m., that they leave 'Hymen's palace' – then details the friends' exploits among the denizens of the city after dark.[13]

'A man of low extraction, and who never received any regular education', at least according to contemporary legend, Ned Ward had migrated to London from the Midlands as recently as 1691, when he was in his mid twenties.[14] This might explain the excitement and passion with which he evokes the experience of stepping into the city at night for the first time, as detailed in the first and second numbers of *The London Spy*. For, like a foreign visitor to the capital, the Spy displays an extraordinary openness and sensitivity to the sights and sounds of the streets. 'The streets were all adorned with dazzling lights whose bright reflections so glittered in my eyes that I could see nothing but themselves', he remarks; 'Thus I walked amazed, like a wandering soul in its pilgrimage to Heaven when it passes through the spangled regions.' The Spy's hyperbolic, mock-heroic language conjures up the nocturnal city with contagious energy.

Like his vision, his other senses are almost overwhelmed by the vitality of the streets. 'My ears were so serenaded on every side with the grave music of sundry passing-bells, the rattling of coaches, and the melancholy ditties of "Hot Baked Wardens and Pippins!"', he reports, 'that had I as many eyes as Argos and as many ears as Fame, they would have been all confounded, for nothing could I see but light, and nothing hear but noise.' At the same time, his nose is stimulated by the perfume from 'some odiferous civet-box' – that is, a box containing a sponge probably soaked in ammonia and perfume in order to emit a particularly pungent smell. 'By and by', he divulges, 'came thundering by us a rumbling engine in the dark, which I took for a deadmonger's wagon laden with a stinking corpse (by reason of long keeping), driving post-haste to the next churchyard in order to inter it.'[15] The Spy is completely immersed in the eighteenth-century urban sensorium.

At this point, the Spy's companion, the surgeon – a comparatively sophisticated, metropolitan type – proposes that they retreat to a coffee-house. 'Accordingly, we blundered through the long dark entry of an ancient fabric, groping our way like subterranean labourers in the caverns of a coal-pit, till we found the stairs, which were raised as perpendicular as a tiler's ladder.' The interior of the coffee-house is an 'antiquated Sodom' where they proceed to drink brandy and cock-ale (an ale to which a bag containing a parboiled, skinned and gutted cock was added, along with cloves and raisins and spices, during the brewing process). Here, they encounter two prostitutes preparing to take to the streets, one of whom owes money to the Spy's friend because he allegedly treated her 'last misfortune'. She abuses him as a 'twat-scouring pimp', and delivers a diatribe that leaves him looking 'as tame as a City cuckold chided by his wife'.

As the men depart, a 'grave fornicator' of about sixty – Ward's adjective hints that he is a necrophiliac as well as a relatively old man – arrives in search of the prostitutes' services. The women therefore disappear to look for rods with which to enact his masochist fantasies. Other people are stumbling onto the streets at the same time: 'The brawny topers of the city began now to forsake the warm tavern and stagger hawking after a poop-lantern to their own houses.' It has just turned 11 p.m., according to the jack o' lanterns or watchmen croaking the hour on the streets, and the city is becoming more deserted. 'Strumpets in the street were grown a scarce commodity', the Spy observes, because the threat of the 'compter' or counter – that is, the sheriff's prison – has 'driven them home to their own poor sinful habitations where nothing dwells but shame, poverty and misery, the devil and themselves'.[16]

As it happens, the two men are themselves incarcerated in the compter on the next night, which Ward narrates in the fourth issue of *The London Spy*. How do the Spy and his companion get into this scrape? Drinking and singing in a tavern, the two men collide with a constable, 'a tall, meager, carrionly cony-fumble', along with 'his crazy crew of cornigerous [or horned] halberdiers'.[17] This ragged representative of the state arrests them for infringing the curfew, and promptly commits them to the Poultry Compter, which stood at the eastern end of Cheapside (opposite the bookseller's and printer's shop run by Dunton at the sign of the Black Raven).

More than one poet had ended up in this prison. Thomas Dekker was imprisoned there for debt in 1599; and in the 1740s Samuel Boyse, an impecunious friend of Johnson's, spent many of the final years of his ruined, debt-ridden life in its precincts (at times he could afford only to dress in a blanket, through which he'd cut a hole in order to admit the hand with which he held his pen). The prison, which mainly housed debtors and people committed by the nightwatch, had a reputation for appalling conditions. William Smith described it in 1776 as a place where 'riot, drunkenness, blasphemy and debauchery, echo from the walls, [and] sickness and misery are confined within them'.[18]

In Ward's account in *The London Spy*, the protagonists are thrust into this 'poor man's purgatory' like hogs into a sty. They hear boisterous noises from the Common Side of the prison (as opposed to the Master's Side), which is where, because of their desire to slum it, they persuade the 'under-turnkey' to admit them. 'When we first entered this apartment', the Spy confides to his readers, 'the mixture of scents that arose from mundungus [rank] tobacco, sweaty toes, dirty shirts, the shit-tub, stinking breaths, and uncleanly carcases, poisoned our nostrils far worse than a Southwark ditch, a tanner's yard, or a tallow-chandler's melting-room'. The room is crammed with poor and disreputable people. These 'ill-looking vermin, with long rusty beards, were swaddled up in rags, some with their heads covered with thrum-caps and others thrust into the tops of old stockings'. A number of them circle the two noctambulists 'like so many cannibals, with such devouring countenances as if a man had been but a morsel with 'em, all crying out, "Garnish, garnish," as a rabble in an insurrection crying, "Liberty, liberty!"'[19]

After a night spent in this company, the Spy and his friend are sent before the bench, where – though they fear they will be bound over to the Sessions – they are fined and released. As this sketch of the grotesque scene on the Common Side of the counter indicates, Ward's energetic but not unsympathetic satirical imagination makes him a significant antecedent of Dickens.

His Midnight Majesty

The destination of the Spy's first, most extensive nightwalk in the city is Billingsgate, London's fish market, and it is to a 'dark house' in its precincts that he and the surgeon pursue their meandering path after leaving the coffee-house on their first night together. But, in the approved manner of the picaresque, they have a series of unexpected encounters with other people – all of them archetypal of the social life of the city at night at the turn of the eighteenth century – as they travel through the streets on foot. *The London Spy* comprises a kind of frieze of representative nocturnal scenes.

The first character they meet, on Gracechurch Street, the site of London's corn and hay market in the Middle Ages, is a watchman around whom several rather antiquated nocturnal revellers have excitedly clustered. He has discovered an abandoned baby in a handbasket, accompanied by an inscription in doggerel and lying 'drivelling on a whole slabbering-bin of verses': '"Alack, alack," says Father Midnight, "I'll warrant 'tis some poor poet's bastard".' This literate watchman then proposes taking the child, whom he speculates might be 'a second Ben Jonson', to be warmed at the watch-house fire. So 'away trooped his Midnight Majesty with his feeble band of crippled parish pensioners, to their nocturnal rendezvous'.[20]

The Spy and the surgeon amble on in pursuit of their 'night's felicity', but they are abruptly stopped, before they have 'walked the length of a horse's tether', by a 'dreadful and surprising' noise – as if 'the Devil was riding on [*sic*] hunting through the City, with a pack of deep-mouthed hell-hounds, to catch a brace of tallymen for breakfast'. In trepidation, this nocturnal Quixote and his companion pause:

> At last bolted out from the corner of a street, with an ignis fatuus dancing before them, a parcel of strange hobgoblins covered with long frieze [coarse woollen] rugs and blankets, hooped round with leather girdles from their cruppers [rumps] to their shoulders, and their noddles buttoned up into caps of martial figure, like a knight errant at tilt and tournament with his wooden head locked in an iron helmet. One was armed, as I thought, with a lusty faggot-bat [a bat made from a bundle of sticks], and the rest with strange wooden weapons in their hands in the shape of clyster-pipes [tubes used for injections], but as long, almost, as speaking-trumpets. Of a sudden they clapped them to their mouths and made such a frightful yelling that I thought the world had been dissolving and the terrible sound of the last trumpet to be within an inch of my ears.

It transpires that these cacophonous night wanderers are 'the city waits, who play every winter's night through the streets to rouse each lazy drone to family duty'.[21]

'Waits' were professional musicians, specializing in brass and wind instruments, who were employed to perform for municipal officials on festive occasions, but who were also supposed to entertain and sometimes even discipline the citizens by perambulating the streets at night or in the early morning. Originally, waits were watchmen, but from at least the mid sixteenth century, and notwithstanding the Spy's complaints, they were valued more for their musicianship than their ability to police the streets. According to Walter Woodfill, by the early seventeenth century the typical orders of waits speak of playing music 'evening and morning and say nothing of "the dead time of night," or of "night walkers and robberies"' – which indicates that these rituals had lost their original protective function.[22] The uproarious waits satirized in *The London Spy*, who tumble into the street like the chaotic bacchanalians of Titian's *Bacchus and Ariadne*, are in more than one sense playing their instruments out of time. But Ward evidently finds them discordant partly because they are residually associated with civic authority.

The next scene in the friends' almost allegorical progress through London at night entails an encounter with 'a very young crew of diminutive vagabonds' who are marching along 'in rank and file'. These 'tatterdemalions' are repairing to the Minories Glass House, sometimes called Goodman's Yard Glass House, near Aldgate, where the ashes and the brand-new bottles that had been set aside to cool provided desperately needed heat for those who had no home in which to sleep at night. Collectively, in the seventeenth and eighteenth centuries, these homeless children and youths, who subsisted on the streets by blacking or shining shoes, were known as 'the City Black Guard'. As the Spy's urbane companion informs him, the poor wretches

> are dropped here by gypsies and country beggars when they are so little they can give no account of parents or place or nativity, and the parishes, caring not to bring a charge upon themselves, suffer them to beg about in the daytime, at night sleep at doors, and in holes and corners about the streets till they are so hardened in this sort of misery that they seek no other life till their riper years (for want of being bred to labour) put them upon

> all sorts of villainy. Thus, through the neglect of churchwardens and constables, from beggary they proceed to theft, and from theft to the gallows.

In a sense, the Black Guard was an ideological and literary invention. But there was in fact a rabble of young people who fitted the description of the Blackguards, and rather relished their notorious reputation: 'They did pilfer and steal, and they did sleep rough in the filthy warmth of the annealing yards associated with the glass manufactory.'[23]

The existence of the City Black Guard, or the legend of it, exercised Defoe a good deal. In *Colonel Jack* (1722), a first-person narrative that drew on picaresque novels like *The French Rogue* (1672), Jack records that, as a child, he 'was a dirty Glass-Bottle House Boy, sleeping in the Ashes, and dealing always in the Street Dirt', and that he looked 'like a *Black your Shoes your Honour*, a Beggar Boy, a Black-Guard Boy, or what you please, despicable, and miserable, to the last Degree'.[24]

Defoe also included a diatribe against the Blackguards in *Everybody's Business is Nobody's Business* (1725), a bad-tempered catalogue of the 'private abuses, public grievances' currently disfiguring English society. It declared that it sought 'approbation from the sober and substantial part of mankind', but little cared about the rest: 'As for the vicious and vagabond, their ill-will is my ambition … ' In this book, Defoe accused the Blackguards of being a 'race of caterpillars, who must be swept from out our streets, or we shall be overrun with all manner of wickedness':

> Under the notion of cleaning our shoes, above ten thousand wicked, idle, pilfering vagrants are permitted to patrol about our city and suburbs. These are called the black-guard, who black your honour's shoes, and incorporate themselves under the title of the Worshipful Company of Japanners [to 'japann' meant to apply a thick black varnish].
>
> Were this all, there were no hurt in it, and the whole might terminate in a jest; but the mischief ends not here, they corrupt our youth, especially our men-servants; oaths and impudence are their only flowers of rhetoric; gaming and thieving are the principal parts of their profession; japanning but the pretence.[25]

Defoe held the Blackguards responsible for pilfering and rioting, as well as for corrupting the city's apprentices and servants. Ward appears to have been far more sympathetic. 'We gave the poor wretches a penny', the Spy reports in cheerful tones, 'and away they trooped with a thousand "God Bless-ye's," as ragged as old stocking mops, and, I'll warrant you, as hungry as so many catamountains; yet they seemed as merry as they were poor, and as contented as they were miserable.'[26]

At this moment, 'another midnight King of Clubs' or night-watchman suddenly materializes in front of the Spy and his friend, and commands them to come before the constable. They obey him 'like prudent amblers'. 'He demanded of us, after an austere manner, who and what we were', says the Spy, 'and had as many impertinent questions at his tongue's end as an apothecary has hard words, or a midwife has bawdy stories.' The surgeon pleads: 'we are very sober, civil persons, who have been about our business, and are going quietly to our own habitations'. But this implausible claim proves less persuasive than the shilling they offer him. Mollified by the bribe, the watchman instructs one of his associates to 'light the gentlemen down the hill, [lest] they may chance to stumble in the dark, and break their shins against the Monument' – assistance they tell him they don't need.

Once they have escaped him, the Spy's friend protests in good-natured tones that 'the great good these fellows do in the streets is to disturb people every hour with their bawling, under pretence of taking care they may sleep quietly in their beds, and call every old fool by his name seven times a night, for fear he should rise and forget it next morning'.[27] In *The Expedition of Humphry Clinker* (1771), Tobias Smollett's central character, Matt Bramble, who has recently arrived from the countryside, complains that, after the dissipations of a day spent in London, 'I start every hour from my sleep, at the horrid noise of the watchman bawling the hour through every street, and thundering at every door; a set of useless fellows, who serve no other purpose but that of disturbing the repose of the inhabitants.'[28]

The incompetence and corruptness of the watchman, as well as his ability to seem omnipresent when not needed, continued to make him a serviceable comic device in the eighteenth century, as he had been in the Renaissance. Perhaps these irksome qualities became even more apparent in the epoch of public street lighting, when his anachronistic status, in spite of the pressing need for nocturnal policing, was underlined by the emergent technology.

Dark House

By this time, our imprudent amblers have arrived at their destination. Billingsgate, London's main fish market since at least the Middle Ages, had been declared 'a free and open market for all sorts of fish' in 1698, the year in which *The London Spy* first appeared, when parliament passed an Act to end the monopoly of one especially rapacious group of fishmongers. Billingsgate was notorious for its foul smell, for the compound of fish guts, fish scales and filthy mud underfoot, and for the shouting and cursing of 'fish fags' or fishwives. In the dead time of night, it was no doubt the liveliest and most morally relaxed district of London.

And it is here that the 'dark house' they have been seeking is located:

> In a narrow lane, as dark as a burying-vault, which stunk of stale sprats, piss and sirreverence [human excrement], we groped about like a couple of thieves in a coal-hole, to find the entrance of that nocturnal theatre in whose delightful scenes we proposed to terminate the night's felicity. At last we stumbled upon the threshold of a gloomy cavern where, at a distance, we saw lights burning like candles in a haunted cave where ghosts and goblins keep their midnight revels.

Presumably this is the tavern known as the Dark House, which stood in Dark Lane, a narrow street that became known in the eighteenth century as Dark House Lane.[29] Alexander Pope might have had Dark House Lane in mind when, as early as 1706, he wrote 'The Alley', a Spenserian allegory set in Billingsgate, which features a 'broken Pavement' littered with 'many a stinking Sprat and Herring', 'Hens, and Dogs, and Hogs', and 'Sun-burnt Matrons' who scold one another and sing – 'bad Neighbourhood I ween' is his comically understated dismissal.[30]

At once sordid and strangely magical – its 'lights burning like candles in a haunted cave where ghosts and goblins keep their midnight revels' – the densely packed interior of this 'smoky boozing-ken' is the setting for a midwinter night's dream. A crowd of large, rather motherly alcoholic women are gathered there 'like a litter of squab elephants', and these fishwives proceed to tease the Spy and his friend with scatological insults. One of them hears the surgeon refer to them as 'saucy-tongued old whores' and lashes back at him: 'You white-livered son of a Fleet Street bumsitter, begot upon a chair at noonday between Ludgate and Temple Bar! You puppily offspring of a mangy night-walker who was forced to play the whore an hour before she cried out to pay the bawd, her midwife, for bringing you, you bastard, into the world.'[31] In this context, a 'night-walker' is clearly a prostitute, but the insult inadvertently provides a fictional genealogy for the Spy's friend's identity as an errant, as opposed to strictly upright, noctambulant.

In the face of these curses, the two men scramble into another room, this one populated by an assortment of rakes, seamen and watermen. They watch 'a spruce blade' come in with a prostitute in order to rent a room, rather half-heartedly pretending she is his wife. Then, to the amusement of the company, which falls into 'an extravagant fit of laughter', two drunken sailors bolt into the room and hang 'my little Lord Crowdero' on a tenter hook by the hapless aristocrat's breeches – frightening him so much that he shits himself. Shortly thereafter, the string on his breeches snaps and he lands on the floor in 'his own sauce'. It is a gratifying result.

Finally, a friend of the surgeon's arrives offering to pimp for the people assembled in the room, and the two friends exploit this distraction to slip into another room for some rest. They are delighted with the night's entertainment: 'For the pleasures of the night were so engaging, and every various humour such a wakeful piece of drollery, that a mountebank and his Jack-pudding [buffoon], or a set of morris dancers, could not give more content to a crowd of country spectators than the lively action of what is here only repeated did afford us.'[32] These rural drolleries are innocent and restrained in comparison with the 'pleasures of the night' that culminate in the risible Lord Crowdero's humiliation in the Dark House.

The language with which Ward describes these nocturnal antics, rich in abuses, curses and oaths, and in references to excrement, is the language of the marketplace that, in his celebrated study of Rabelais, the Russian critic and linguist Mikhail Bakhtin designated as 'billingsgate'. It is a language in which 'speech patterns excluded from official intercourse' freely accumulate, and it enacts at the level of form the social inversions represented in the meandering, picaresque plot of the nighttime scenes in *The London Spy*. Carnival, according to Bakhtin, involves 'a temporary suspension of all hierarchic distinctions and barriers among men and of certain norms and prohibitions of usual life'. Ward, it might be concluded, develops a variant of the carnivalesque that is both urban and nocturnal in its emphasis. He is one of the great exponents of 'grotesque realism', as Bakhtin called it, in early modern English literature.[33]

Midnight Ramble

Middle- and upper-middle-class men – those I have identified as noctambulants – were of course far freer in their movements at night than women. In the eighteenth century as in the nineteenth, 'the suspicion of prostitution fell upon women who were about at night unaccompanied and without justification'.[34] Picaresque accounts of the streets at night in the eighteenth century are therefore predicated on a male subject – one who is physically mobile and, more often than not, both patrician in his attitude to the poor and patriarchal in his attitude to women.

The partial exception to this rule, which in the end it probably reinforces, is *The Midnight-Ramble; or, The Adventures of Two Noble Females: Being a True and Impartial Account of their Late Excursion through the Streets of London and Westminster* (1754). For this intriguing fiction, published by an anonymous author who is presumably male, features two gleeful female protagonists who explore the streets of London at night in disguise.

The narrative opens with an account of the reasons for the heroine's social (and perhaps sexual) frustration. Lady Betty, a virtuous young woman, has been married off to Dorimant, a dissolute nobleman who spends 'his Evenings in riotous Mirth and Debauchery at the *Taverns*; and most commonly passe[s] the Remainder of the Night, in the Arms of some Courtezan at a *Bagnio*'. She befriends Mrs Sprightly, the wife of Dorimant's best friend Ned, and the two women resolve to disguise themselves as monks in order to monitor their husbands' nocturnal activities in the city. In prosecuting this plan, they commission their milliner, Mrs Flim, whose name signals that she is adept at idle deception, to bring them 'ordinary Silk Gowns, close Capuchins, and black Hats'. And, having taken care 'to exhilerate their Spirits with a Bottle of excellent *Champain*', the three of them set off in pursuit of the men.

After spying on their husbands at the playhouse, the three women are frustrated in their attempt to follow them by coach to a tavern at Temple Bar because there are so few vehicles on the street. Instead, though it is past 10 p.m., they determine 'upon following their Chace on Foot, at all Hazards'.[35] At a spot between Somerset House and the so-called New Church on the Strand (St Mary le Strand), they meet 'four *Street-Walkers*, that had been long used to tramp those Quarters'. These prostitutes assume that, because of 'the Oddness of our Ladies Disguise', Lady Betty and Mrs Sprightly are 'some Strangers of their own Occupation, that were come thither to trespass upon their Walks'. So they jostle and curse their rivals.

At this point, Mrs Flim intervenes, vociferating with them 'in their own Stile of Language'. For her pains, she is punched in the face and has her false teeth pushed 'directly down her Throat'. The three women promptly call for the Watch, and 'a decrepid old Fellow, with his Staff and Lanthorn' appears. But this 'Midnight Perambulator' is 'in Fee with the *Street-Walkers*', and in any case he too assumes that the women are prostitutes competing for this lucrative spot. An even more violent dispute is only averted when three 'rakish Bucks' who have been drinking in a nearby tavern ascertain that Lady Betty and her companions are not of common rank, and draw their swords against the prostitutes. Once the streetwalkers have fled, and since it is a wet night, these men invite the women into the tavern to drink wine and get warm, which they half-reluctantly do.[36]

Later, at Temple Bar, Mrs Flim happens to see Dorimant and Sprightly climbing into a coach bound for Covent Garden with two conspicuous courtesans. The three respectable women, who already seem morally and socially compromised, consequently decide to track it at a distance. They lose sight of it because the coach they have commandeered clips a post, and end up walking to Covent Garden instead. By the time they reach this centre of eighteenth-century London's nightlife – Vic Gatrell has identified it as 'the first of the world's bohemias' – the men have disappeared.[37] They therefore decide to return to their houses, 'once more, obliged to go on foot'. 'However', the author adds, 'as the Moon was by this Time rose pretty high, they had Light sufficient to conduct them to their Habitations.'[38] It is a reminder that night-time illumination was at best limited even in the eighteenth-century West End.

As they amble home, a foreign gentleman hears their footsteps and takes them for prostitutes returning from the bagnio. He accompanies them 'for some Streets Length', though for scarcely innocent or benign reasons, and the result is that, when they run into a constable, he too assumes that they are 'three of the bettermost sort of *Street-Walkers*'. This constable, who announces that it is 'his Duty to keep the Streets clear of People, that had no real Business in them', threatens to put them in the Roundhouse for the remainder of the night. But the street-smart Mrs Flim bribes him. Finally, resuming their journey home by coach, they pass a couple of men 'pretty much in Liquor, staggering along Arm in Arm together'.[39] It is Dorimant and Sprightly. The two men stop the coach, climb into it, and immediately start kissing the two women, whom they have failed to recognize as their wives. They realize their embarrassing error once the coach has deposited them all at the same address.

The pamphlet's official intention, as its stentorious conclusion indicates, is to serve as 'a Warning to the Female Sex, not to trust themselves abroad on any Frolicks, in this lewd and wicked Town, at unseasonable Hours'. But, until this moment, the tale's moral assignment seems gloriously irrelevant. The women's adventures are so mischievous, and they prove so successful, that it seems unlikely that the effect on them of 'these Adventures of the Night', as the author disingenuously professes to hope, will be to 'prevent their undertaking any more Midnight *Rambles*, lest they should meet with worse Disasters than they experienced in this'.

To the contrary, by the end of the tale, Betty and Mrs Sprightly, like the dubious Mrs Flim from the start, might be said to be 'perfectly acquainted with the Streets', and know 'the Ways of the Town'.[40] Certainly, the *Monthly Review* remained unconvinced by the pamphlet's official moral: it observed in nervous tones that '*probably* this pretended piece of secret history is altogether fabulous'; and righteously dismissed it as 'a low, ill-written tale, bearing the usual marks of a catch penny job'.[41] This response is a clear indication that, in spite of *The Midnight-Ramble*'s claims to rectitude, its account of cross-dressing female aristocrats who spend the night slumming it in the streets is a little bit bent.

The Midnight-Ramble's alternative subtitle, given on the first page of the narrative, is 'The Adventures of Two Noble Night-Walkers'. The juxtaposition of the adjective 'noble' and the noun 'night-walker' is surely designed to transmit an almost inadmissible frisson to the reader. This is after all the period when, in the popular imagination as well as in the discourse of Bridewell and other penal institutions, the term 'night-walker' became increasingly associated not so much with images of maleficent men as with those of 'prostitutes moving along dark streets, gathering on corners, loitering in alleys, touting trade'.[42]

The phrase 'noble night-walkers', in the subtitle of *The Midnight-Ramble*, might distinguish its aristocratic protagonists from all the common kinds of streetwalker – from the 'Jilts, Cracks, Prostitutes, Night-walkers, Whores, She-friends, Kind Women, and others of the Linnen-lifting Tribe' listed in a 1691 broadside against Bartholomew Fair.[43] But it makes them seem morally unreliable at best. It is telling that, in the tale, the 'noble females' are not once mistaken for monks, in spite of their costumes, but on at least three occasions are mistaken for prostitutes. In their disguises, they are highly ambiguous figures, at once masculine and feminine, aristocratic and common, virtuous and perfidious.

According to a predictable formula, the author of *The Midnight-Ramble* thus has it both ways: he contrives a daring fantasy of female independence and, at the last minute, presses it into the service of a patriarchal doctrine. As in the 'Evening Rambles' described in Dunton's *Night-Walker*, hedonistic and moralistic impulses cannot be dissociated in *The Midnight-Ramble*.

Low Life

Low-Life; or, One Half of the World, Knows Not How the Other Half Live (1749), an anonymous nocturnal picaresque manifestly indebted to *The London Spy*, assumes the strict form of a noctuary. A prefatory letter praises 'the Ingenious and Ingenuous Mr Hogarth', and informs him that in the book he 'will find a true Delineation of the various Methods' with which 'the People in and about this Metropolis' have 'contrived to murder' time, especially on the Sabbath. The author, who is perhaps the printer Thomas Legg, then presents an hour-by-hour chronicle of a period of about thirty-six hours that he has spent perambulating the streets of London – its subtitle indicates that it is a *Critical Account of What is Transacted by People of Almost All Religions, Nations, Circumstances, and Sizes of Understanding, in the Twenty-Four Hours between Saturday-Night and Monday-Morning*.

The first hour is from midnight on Saturday to one on Sunday morning, and the book begins by listing all the social types who inhabit the streets at midnight, offering a brief description of their activities. This includes:

> Bawds setting Pimps for Spies at the Avenues to their Houses, to give them timely Notice of the City Marshalls or Constables coming to search their Houses for disorderly Company. Victuallers carrying the Scores of Tradesmen, such as Coachmakers, Carpenters, Smiths, Plaisterers, Plumbers, and others in the Building Branch of Business, to the Pay-Tables in order to clear their last Week's Reckoning, and if possible to get

> a Trifle paid off from an old Score. Gangs of Robbers dividing themselves into Parties, some of whom go to the Watch-House to make the Constable and Watchmen drunk, while the others open Houses, rob them, and make off with their Booty undiscover'd.

The author also mentions 'Constables marching thro' their Liberties with long Staves in their Hands, attended by several Watchmen, to see that the Streets are free from House-Breakers and Night-Walkers'. Nightwalkers in this context are not necessarily prostitutes; implicitly, as in times past, they are men suspected of committing, or being about to commit, some nameless crime.

Midnight, in *Low-Life*, thus presents a populous, if not riotous, scene that has something of the disordered energy of a Hogarth print. But the effect is also dystopian. There is for instance a haunting reference to 'Houses which are left open, and are running to Ruin, fill'd with Beggars, some of whom are asleep, while others are pulling down the Timber, and packing it up, to sell for firing'. The city at night is made up of lives of quiet, and not-so-quiet, desperation. The final group of people to be listed is 'the unhappy Lunaticks in *Bethlehem*-Hospital in *Moorfields*, rattling their Chains, and making a terrible Out-cry'.[44] It was 'within sight' of the walls of Bethlehem Hospital, or Bedlam, which was relocated to Southwark in the early nineteenth century, that Dickens, in the course of one of his nightwalks in the 1850s, had a 'night fancy' – 'and the fancy was this: Are not the sane and the insane equal at night as the sane lie dreaming?'[45]

As the night advances, becoming more tranquil between 3 a.m. and 4 a.m., the cumulative impression created by the author of *Low-Life* is of a rotten city. It is riddled with pitch-black, dead-end lanes, miserable garret rooms, and mephitic night-cellars and other subterranean recesses – in all of which places a multitude of nefarious activities are unfolding. London, in this vision, is like a diseased and rotten hive collapsing in on its foundations. The philosopher Henri Lefebvre once wrote that, in its diversity, urban space has 'a structure far more reminiscent of flaky *mille-feuille* pastry than of the homogeneous and isotropic space of classical (Euclidean/ Cartesian) mathematics'.[46] In the poorer areas of eighteenth-century London, which occupied a confused and conflicted space outside the Euclidean projections of contemporary neoclassicism, this *mille-feuille* pastry is in a state of putrefaction – like something left over from Miss Havisham's wedding feast.

The metropolis was a comparatively well-ordered city by the 1740s, according to Tim Hitchcock, better lit and better maintained than any other European city, with the possible exception of Paris. But, behind its brilliant stone façades, as he underlines, 'it was also a city of stables, barns, outhouses, bog-houses and kitchens', and of 'abandoned houses and half-built ones'. In 1763, one prospective buyer discovered the dead bodies of three emaciated women on the ground floor of the building he was inspecting in Stonecutter Street, as well as two women who had almost starved to death in the garret.[47] In spite of its official appearance of relative order, London was a city in a permanent state of both reconstruction and ruination – a city perpetually shaped and reshaped by the processes of capital accumulation, including property speculation and the dispossession of the poor.

There is in the end a touching humanity to the author of *Low-Life*'s descriptions of the dense but desolate city at night, and even to his lists of the sorts of people on the streets (in this respect he resembles one of the novelists of sensibility who became fashionable from the 1760s). Of course, he is dismissive of 'Black-Guards in the Streets upon full Scent to find out drunken Men sleeping on Benches, that they may pretend to see them Home, and pick their Pockets as they lead them along'; of 'Rakes and Bullies, breaking up from their Nocturnal Debauches'; and of Street-Robbers and House-Breakers and all the other corrupt or rapacious inhabitants of the night. This attitude is almost mandatory.

But he adopts, too, an almost tender tone in relation to the homeless – 'Vagabonds who have been sleeping under Hay-Reeks in the neighbouring Villages and Fields', who 'awaken, begin to rub their Eyes, shake their Rags, and get out of their Nests' between 2 a.m. and 3 a.m. on Sunday. 'Common Beggars, Gypsies and Strollers, who are quite destitute of Friends and Money, creeping into the Farmers Grounds, about the Suburbs of *London*, to find sleeping Places under Hay-Stacks' between 10 p.m. and 11 p.m. on Sunday;

'Lumberers taking a Survey of the Streets and Markets, and preparing to mount Bulks instead of Beds, to sleep away the remaining Part of the Night upon' at this same time; and, finally, 'destitute Whores and run-away Apprentices, who have neither Lodging, Money, nor Friends, carrying Hay, &c. into empty Houses, to make themselves Beds withal'.

In spite of its satirical spirit, there is a deep, melancholic compassion to this book – as its valedictory reference to the 'One Third of the Inhabitants of *London*, *Westminster* and *Southwark*' who, as the day of rest finally ends, lie 'fast a-sleep, and almost Pennyless', movingly avers.[48]

Dark Transactions

In addition to offering its subtitle as a tribute to Ned Ward, the anonymous author of *The Midnight Rambler; or, New Nocturnal Spy* (1770) used its opening chapter to praise *Le Diable Boiteux* (1707), by the French novelist and playwright Alain-René Le Sage, for devising a means of accessing 'the disposition and actions of his fellow creatures'.[49]

Derived from Luis Vélez de Guevara's *El Diablo Cojuelo* (1641), Le Sage's novel was translated into English in 1708 as *The Devil upon Two Sticks* (Richard Steele, who alluded to it in the eleventh issue of *The Tatler*, knew it in this version). Throughout the eighteenth century, like *The London Spy*, *Le Diable Boiteux* spawned numerous imitations and sequels, including *The Devil Upon Crutches in England; or, Night Scenes in London* (1755) and *The Devil Upon Two Sticks in England: Being a Continuation of Le Diable Boiteux of Le Sage* (1790–1791).

In the opening chapter of *Le Diable Boiteux*, a Spanish nobleman and student called Don Cleofas liberates the demon Asmodeus from a bottle. In recompense for this act, Asmodeus flies Don Cleofas up to the highest steeple in Madrid, like Satan tempting Christ, and there tells him that, using his supernatural powers, he will reveal the hidden lives of the city's inhabitants:

> I intend from this high Place to shew you whatever is at present doing in *Madrid*. By my Diabolical Power I will heave up the Roofs of the Houses, and notwithstanding the Darkness of the Night, clearly expose to your View whatever is now under them. At these Words he extended his right Hand, and in an Instant all the Roofs of the Houses seem'd remov'd; and the Scholar saw the Insides of 'em as plainly as if it had been Noon-day.[50]

In the original French edition an additional sentence is included at this point, as a nineteenth-century English translation indicates: 'It was, says Luis Velez de Guevara, like looking into a pasty from which a set of greedy monks had just removed the crust.'[51] Le Sage's novel provides a privileged example of a writer peering into the city at night and exposing its inhabitants' hidden truths. The narrator is interested not simply in the interiors of their homes but 'the Springs of their Actions, and their most secret Thoughts'.[52] As William Sharpe has commented, the misanthropic demon Asmodeus 'is an emotionally crippled flâneur' who 'quickly became a stock character, a device for exposing the sordid secrets of urban society'.[53]

In *The Midnight Rambler*, the 'New Nocturnal Spy', a rather naive scholar, is accosted one evening by a stranger in St James's Park. This enigmatic figure tells the narrator he is his 'Guardian Angel', and offers to act as a guide to London's nightlife – 'and shew you such scenes as you shall behold with real astonishment and indignation'. This 'good Genius' therefore becomes the author's cicerone in the infernal city at night, acting as Virgil to his Dante.[54] He leads him from place to place, providing an inventory of urban types, enumerating people's deceits, and offering moral reflections on them.

Like the London Spy and his companion, the protagonists of *The Midnight Rambler* direct their steps to Billingsgate, which promises to entertain them with 'nocturnal theatre'. But, shortly after 11 p.m., when 'the glittering lamps which about two hours ago sparkled like diamonds, were dwindled many of them to glimmering snuffs, the lighters having confiscated part of the oil allowed them to their own use', they are detained by a constable. The Genius proceeds to inform this officer that they will take legal action against him if he continues to hold them, 'as he knew persons were as free to walk the streets by night as by day, provided they kept the peace'. If in principle this was the case, it was not so in practice. A moral curfew prevailed, above all for the poor. So the constable accedes to them, and they resume their ramble. His action is a reminder of the semi-criminal identity of the nightwalker in the eighteenth century, who continues to be regarded as suspect even when he or she is keeping the peace.

Once they have arrived in Billingsgate and scrutinized the backgrounds and histories of the people congregated there, the two noctambulants decide to head off again, this time 'confin[ing] themselves to no particular spot, so that now uncertainty may be said to be their course, and meer accident their pilot'.[55] This is an eighteenth-century instance of that 'search for an encounter with otherness' that, in the 1950s, the Situationists identified as a *dérive*, or drift.[56]

It is after midnight. The narrator and his tour guide enter a tenement in Wapping in which the laziest and most villainous seamen are lifelessly sitting about eating and drinking in an atmosphere thick with 'fumes of tar, tobacco and toasted cheese'. Their faces, the Genius observes, have 'a downcast, midnight countenance, that would shun the light of day, and skulk in the dreary shades of obscure night'. Heading westwards, 'our peripatetics' stumble upon 'great riots in places that may be deemed lawless, such as courts, alleys, yards and passages'. Meanwhile, coaches roll through the grander streets, 'carrying to their respective habitations such people as were either too drunk, too rich, too proud, too lame, or too lazy to walk'.[57]

In St Bride's, they retire to a tavern for some rest and study an assiduous constable – or 'superintendent of dark transactions' – as he interrogates a man and woman who, having coupled in the street, 'had fallen under the cognizance of one of the reforming patrollers of the streets of this most abominable, most diabolical town'. In a grand square at 3 a.m., the Genius conducts the Spy into a masked ball and exposes the hypocrites who make up fashionable society. From there, for the sake of contrast, in the almost empty streets, he points out the places in which the destitute are secreted: 'Sheds in markets and the bulks of houses were covered with vagrants, that had been picking pockets, carrying links, or skulking about in quest of any thing they could lay their hands on.'[58]

London is a segregated city, according to the Genius; and this is evident above all in the divisions between East and West. The opposing sides of the metropolis have separate populations, and these populations exhibit distinctive relations to the economies of night and day. The man of fashion inhabits Westminster; the tradesman or mechanic inhabits the City. They form 'an absolute contrast' to one another, and are 'a kind of distinct beings, or creatures formed on and actuated by principles diametrically opposite'. They are the Elois and Morlocks of the eighteenth century: 'The purlieus of the squares of the West and the wards of the city, one would imagine to be in different climates, since the inhabitants of the one are more active by night, the other by day. Nay, their very manner of computation seems totally opposite, the one commencing a round of action at sun-setting, the other at sun-rising.' The West End is the nighttime city; the East End is the daytime city. And at this point, between 4 a.m. and 5 a.m., the contrast is particularly acute, since 'the fashionable beau monde, harassed with riot and reveling, are now retiring to rest, while the laborious and useful part having reposed their wearied limbs after the fatigue of the preceding day, during the hours limited and prescribed by nature, arise with renewed vigour and alacrity, to prosecute their ordinary calling and lawful occupations'.

Of course, it remains unclear where the protagonist and his tour guide fit into the moral economy of the twenty-four-hour clock. As nightwalkers they remain distinctly ambiguous, a part of neither of these worlds and both of them. If they are 'moralizing peripatetics', as the author at one point identifies them, then both the nocturnal habits and the sympathies of these mysterious men of sentiment might be characterized as vagrant.[59]

Excentric Mortal

Another, slightly earlier noctuary, *The Midnight Spy* (1766), sketches a contrast, after 3 a.m. and before 5 a.m., between on the one hand 'the votaries of Venus and Bacchus', who are quitting the streets, and on the other the chimney sweeps and market traders, who are returning to them. It refers to the latter as 'the early part of the regular world' – and it notes that these people are preparing for business 'while the excentric mortal is just thinking of repose'.[60]

The bacchanalians who drink and pursue sex in the bagnios, taverns and streets of the eighteenth-century city at night are certainly eccentric in the precise sense that their activities are not concentric with those of 'the regular world'. These upper-class people lead nocturnal rather than diurnal existences. But that does not necessarily make them irregular. Indeed, their behaviour is also routinized and rule-bound. In this respect, they are simply the complement to those who, more conventionally, live by day: they represent the obverse of those who labour.

Far more asymmetrical in his relationship to the night – and to 'the votaries of Venus and Bacchus' on the one hand and the labourers or traders on the other – is the noctambulant. In spite of their countervailing social vocations, neither John Dunton nor Ned Ward, nor indeed their descendants, fit neatly into the moral economy of either the daytime or the nighttime. It is the noctambulant, the midnight rambler, who is eccentric in the sense that develops in the late seventeenth century, when the term is first applied to character and personal attributes. It is the nightwalker who is governed by what the Jacobite conspirator Richard Graham, in his translation of Boethius's *Consolation of Philosophy* (1695), had referred to as 'the Extravagance of Excentrick and irregular desires'.[61]

In a metropolitan culture that, in the eighteenth century, increasingly cultivated concentric and regular desires, because these were consonant with capitalist dispositions of space and time, walking in the streets at night was inherently eccentric. Nightwalkers were, precisely, extravagant. They extravagated – meaning, they wandered away, they strayed beyond reasonable or respectable bounds.

6.

Grub Street at Night

Churchill, Goldsmith and Pattison

I Walk on Foot

By the 1730s, the verb 'to grub', which had originally signified to dig up by the roots, also meant to lead a plodding or grovelling existence – 'to go on, in a mean, servile, covetous, nasty Way or Manner of Living', as *A New General English Dictionary* (1735) formulated it with slightly vindictive emphasis.[1] The noun 'grub', of course, referred to a maggot, the larval form of an insect. It is these senses that Alexander Pope conjured up in *The Dunciad* (1728) when, spitting at the poetasters of his time, he dismissed them as 'maggots half-form'd in rhyme' that 'learn to crawl upon poetic feet'.[2]

In the eighteenth-century city, another category of nightwalker needs to be set beside those of the noctambulant and the noctivagant, or common nightwalker. This category is in social terms distinctly ambiguous. The déclassé artists and writers associated in London with Grub Street – a name that evoked 'fecklessness, eccentricity, and poverty' – inhabited an indeterminate territory between the upper- and lower-class locations I have outlined.[3] For these people, forced to grub along in the streets of the capital – 'where looks are merchandise, and smiles are sold', as Samuel Johnson put it – going on foot meant identifying, consciously or not, reluctantly or not, with the poor, the itinerant, the vagrant; in short, with all those who had to prostitute themselves in the city.[4] Of course, Grub Street authors could not afford the more elevated modes of transport on offer in the metropolis, so pedestrianism was in this sense a compulsory means of circumambulation for them. But to travel on foot was also, implicitly, to adopt a political, or proto-political, stance. It was an expression of *ressentiment*.

This defensive, sometimes militant, attitude informs *Trivia* (1716). There, John Gay compares the righteous walker, whose modest walking-stick is constantly put to use, directing his 'cautious Tread aright, / Though not one glaring Lamp enliven Night', to the idle aristocratic beaux who, 'loll[ing] at Ease' in 'gilded Chariots', carry their 'Amber tipt' canes merely for the sake of fashionable appearance – 'Be theirs for empty Show, but thine for Use'. Some fifty lines later he reiterates his intemperate complaint, attacking the 'griping Broker' who sits in an ostentatious chariot 'and laughs at Honesty, and trudging Wits'. Indeed, in the advertisement to the poem, Gay issues an especially obstinate statement on the same theme: 'The Criticks may see by this Poem, that I walk on Foot, which probably may save me from their Envy.'[5]

The Grub Street authors – exiles from polite society who included Oliver Goldsmith but also Richard Savage and his young companion Johnson – were antecedents of those Romantics who, at the turn of the nineteenth century, asserted the subversive political potential of pedestrianism. They were also the antecedents of those, like De Quincey and Dickens, who reclaimed night in the city. In short, they are among those whom Vic Gatrell has classified as 'the first bohemians'. In defining eighteenth-century bohemianism, he cites T. B. Macaulay's review of a new edition of James Boswell's *Life of Johnson* in 1831, which declared that, in Savage's time, 'all that is squalid and miserable might now be summed up in the one word – Poet'. 'That word', he continued, 'denoted a creature dressed like a scarecrow, familiar with compters and sponging houses.' The poet, according to this evocative caricature, translated 'ten hours a day for the wages of a ditcher', lodged in a garret, dined in a cellar, was 'hunted by bailiffs from one haunt of beggary and pestilence to another', died in a hospital, and was 'buried in a parish vault'.[6]

In the course of the eighteenth century the cultural and legal meanings of nightwalking changed. For men, in an era in which the rise of urban nightlife had progressively obliterated the curfew, it was effectively decriminalized, even though officially it remained on the statute books. The moral curfew persisted, however, and walking at night continued to evoke semi-criminal associations and to threaten to undermine the institution of the family. For this reason – and because, rather than in spite of, the fact that they were no longer liable to being prosecuted for simply walking in the city after dark – Grub Street bohemians and other middle-class malcontents used this still opprobrious form of pedestrianism to express their sense of being excluded from society.

'From the littérateur to the professional conspirator', Walter Benjamin writes of nineteenth-century Paris, 'everyone who belonged to the *bohème* could recognize a bit of himself in the ragpicker.'[7] In eighteenth-century London, all the inhabitants of Grub Street recognized a bit of themselves in the nightwalker.

Manufacturers of Literature

Writing, declared Daniel Defoe in 1725, 'is becoming a very considerable branch of the English Commerce. The Booksellers are the Master Manufacturers or Employers. The several

Writers, Authors, Copyers, Sub-Writers and all other Operators with Pen and Ink are the workmen employed by the said Master Manufacturers.' In the eighteenth century, as the readership for literature expanded among the middle classes and the technological pace of literary production accelerated, the capital's booksellers or publishers, exploiting the decline of aristocratic patronage, mediated the relations between authors, printers and readers, and in the process accumulated both substantial profits and significant social and ideological power. In addition to the books themselves, these booksellers controlled all the important magazines, newspapers and critical reviews. It was a 'virtual monopoly of the channels of opinion [that] brought with it a monopoly of writers'.[8]

As a result of this situation, the community of poorly paid professional writers seeking employment in eighteenth-century London swelled like a dropsical head. Johnson, in an article for the *Rambler* in 1751, noted that he could see no reason to revise Jonathan Swift's earlier calculation that there were 'several Thousands' of authors in the city. Only a handful of these people, he reported, were capable of producing 'new Ideas' or offering 'any uncommon Train of Images or Contexture of Events'. 'The rest, however laborious, however arrogant, can only be considered as the Drudges of the Pen, the Manufacturers of Literature, who have set up for Authors, either with or without a regular Initiation, and like other Artificers, have no other Care than to deliver their Tale of Wares at the stated Time.'[9] Johnson was representative of the generation that realized that the aristocracy – to adapt one of Benjamin's formulations – 'was about to annul its contract with the poet'.[10]

In effect, Johnson and Defoe registered the commodification of literature – the fact that its products were increasingly being sold as quantitative portions of labour time irrespective of the qualitative labour inscribed in them. The producer of literature, like the producer of textiles, was in this period compelled, as Karl Marx later put it, 'to offer for sale as a commodity that very labour-power which exists only in his living body', and was therefore paid no more than 'the value of the means of subsistence necessary for the maintenance of its owner'. The poet, like others who had hitherto been 'looked up to with reverent awe', was becoming merely a paid wage-labourer – his activity 'stripped of its halo'.[11] This shift had palpable social and existential effects on the pamphleteers, periodical journalists and poets of the eighteenth century. Pushed to the margins of a declining patronage system and forced to fight for commissions in an increasingly competitive marketplace, the 'Operators with Pen and Ink' identified by Defoe led an alienated, precarious and often undignified existence in the capital.

When the penniless Scottish poet James Thomson arrived in London from Edinburgh in 1725, he characterized the culture of literary London in these terms:

> The scribbling rhyming generation (lord deliver us!) buzz and swarm here like insects on a summer's day, and are as noxious: so that every coffee-house shop and stall in Town crawl with their maggots. One vengeful hornet (Savage, if you'll indulge me a pun at his name) so plagued and stung me yesterday, with everlasting repetition, as provokes me to this rude – perhaps – complaint ...[12]

Richard Savage, the notorious social renegade, who later became a close friend of both Thomson and Johnson, is the aggressive hornet queen buzzing at the centre of this bristling nest of literary labourers.

Thomson's sketch is a deft satire of everyday life in Grub Street, but the reality was rather less colourful and vibrant. In geographical terms, the name Grub Street served as shorthand for the mean, squalid districts around Moorfields, on the northern edge of the City, which 'were full of narrow alleys, thieves' dens and brothels, and harboured their own literary fences and pimps, the much maligned printers and booksellers'.[13] In these ignoble precincts of the capital – buried today beneath the Barbican Estate – the mass of Grub Street's educated but impecunious inhabitants did little more than subsist, alongside other social outcasts, including actors, beggars, coiners, religious dissenters, political dissidents, fortune-tellers, immigrants, prostitutes and Jews. Like the prostitutes to whom they were often compared, albeit with misogynistic insensitivity, these drudges of the pen manufactured and sold their products piecemeal, and led lives of quiet desperation.

If the so-called hack writers of London in this period lived in close geographical and even physical proximity to prostitutes and thieves, they themselves often led semi-criminal lives. As Pat Rogers has argued in his authoritative study of Grub Street, 'authors lived in social circles where crimes against public decency or public order were a matter of common occurrence'. Many of them, furthermore, inhabited 'such squalid circumstances that they were likely to feel the arm of the law for offences totally unconnected with literature'.[14] Even those who were not imprisoned for debt, drunkenness, theft or violent behaviour, or even incarcerated for lunacy like Christopher Smart, tended to nurse a deep sense of injustice and resentment against those with power and wealth, not least the booksellers and publishers.

Night's Honest Shade

In the literature of the eighteenth century there is a perceptible sense that, in the night, both the self and society, stripped of the elaborate deceits with which they are encased during the day, expose their true character. Charles Churchill, a reckless and rather glamorous satirical poet later admired by Byron, provides a preliminary sense of this in 'Night: An Epistle to Robert Lloyd' (1761).

A priest and schoolmaster, Churchill was forced to become a professional poet in his late twenties as a result of deepening debt (odd as this might sound today). He achieved almost instant success with *The Rosciad* (1761), a satirical attack on the most famous actors of the time, which was modelled on his school friend Robert Lloyd's *The Actor* (1760), as well as on the poetry of John Dryden and Alexander Pope. The money he earned from this poem, said to be as much as £1,000, enabled him to lead a decadent and dandified life in London, dressed in 'a blue coat with metal buttons, a gold-laced waistcoat, a gold-laced hat, and ruffles'. He was 'more a man about town than a clergyman', comments a biographer.[15]

'Night', a product of this hedonistic period, is a splendidly defiant defence of nightlife. Dedicated to Lloyd, his old drinking companion, it is in part a retort to the Scots poet John Armstrong's 'A Day: An Epistle to J. Wilkes' (1761), which encoded an attack on Churchill as the 'new cheat' with whom 'the gaping town is smit' and the 'crazy scribbler' who 'reigns the present wit'.[16] In 'A Day', Armstrong declares in sanctimonious tones that he likes to drink only in moderation and is never tempted to stay up past midnight. He concedes that '*To err is human*, Man's Prerogative', but regards it as deeply regrettable that, hubristic as he is, Man has 'too much Sense by Nature's Laws to live'.[17]

Churchill responds by condemning 'the wretch, bred up in Method's drowsy school, / Whose only merit is to err by rule'. A man of this sort, he complains in exasperated tones, cannot be 'guilty deem'd of one eccentric thought'. And if his mind is deadened by conformity, his 'body's dull machine' travels 'clock-work like', and 'with the same equal pace … through life's insipid space'. 'Night' was thus a spirited attack on all those who 'keep good hours' – a libertine assault on what might be called the ideology of good hours, which had in part underpinned the prohibition against nightwalking from the Middle Ages onwards.

In the context of the eighteenth century, it also amounted to an attack on the Protestant ethic and the emergent spirit of capitalism:

> Let slaves to business, bodies without soul,
> Important blanks in Nature's mighty roll,
> Solemnise nonsense in the day's broad glare,
> We NIGHT prefer, which heals or hides our care.
> Rogues justified, and by success made bold,
> Dull fools and coxcombs sanctified by Gold,
> Freely may bask in fortune's partial ray,
> And spread their feathers opening to the day;
> But *thread-bare* Merit dares not show the head
> 'Till vain Prosperity retires to bed.

Those who keep good hours are those who keep business hours. The poet, in the shape of '*thread-bare* Merit', pits himself against the 'slaves to business' who spend their days acquiring profits and their nights complacently sleeping. 'See where ambition, mean and loathsome, lies.' Churchill is proud to drown 'the galling sneer, the supercilious frown' of these people – who are finally no more than 'upstart knaves grown rich, and fools grown great' – in 'oblivion's grateful cup'.[18]

Churchill is contemptuous of the 'businessman', as he might be called, not least because he is 'purblind to poverty' and 'scarce sees rags an inch beyond his nose'. The pious fools occupied in the pursuit of fortune or fame are incapable of apprehending the truth: 'Through a false medium things are shown by day, / Pomp, wealth, and titles judgment lead astray.' In contrast, the night peels back society's false appearances and reveals the power relations they conceal. At the 'impartial hour', 'beneath NIGHT's honest shade', Churchill insists, it is all too apparent that the 'lordling' is a 'tool of pow'r', and his 'surrounding clients' little more than 'dupes to pride'.[19]

Shadows, it transpires, cast penetrating light. Night illuminates the political relations that an acquisitive society seeks to obscure or repress. It also reveals the presence of individuals occluded in the chaotic circumstances of the city in the day. In *Chrysal* (1760–1765), Charles Johnstone reported a story about Churchill assisting an impoverished girl 'whom he met in the midnight streets' and providing her and her family with proper lodgings.[20] *In nocte veritas*. Or, as Joachim Schlör has it in his book on night in the nineteenth century, *nox revelatrix*: 'the night as revealer – and accuser – of the day'.[21]

Metropolitan culture is in the eighteenth century increasingly shaped by the spectacular hypocrisies of class society. The ostentatious acts of consumption enacted by the rich and their openly contemptuous attitudes to the poor are signs of a constant, half-concealed state of class conflict that occasionally irrupted on the streets in the form of riots and other collective acts of resistance. Against the brutal contrasts that define this background, the city at night functioned for some of the more or less marginalized authors of the eighteenth century as a privileged domain for staging the emergent social contradictions of capitalism.

After nightfall, moreover, as the need to preserve a civilized façade for people's activities slides, the self cannot conceal its secrets. In the words of Edward Young's influential poem *The Complaint; or, Night Thoughts* (1742), which set out to overcome humanity's 'forgetfulness of Death', darkness 'strikes thought inward; it drives back the soul / To settle on herself, our point supreme!'[22] The absence of light, ironically, elucidates people's inner lives. And in the city, these inner lives are defined by alienation. According to this proto-Romantic interpretation of the night, the spaces of the darkened, depopulated metropolis, at once liberated and isolated, are the site of anomie. This is the antisocial night. In contrast to the sociable night of the eighteenth-century city, in which people promenade past brightly illuminated shops, this night is characterized by an empty, solitary experience of the streets.

Thinking of the literary tradition that runs from William Blake to T. S. Eliot, Raymond Williams writes that 'perception of the new qualities of the modern city had been associated, from the beginning, with a man walking, as if alone, in its streets'.[23] It is tempting not simply to antedate this statement, so that it applies to the pre-Romantic period too, but to supplement it: perception of the new qualities of the modern city was from the eighteenth century associated with a man walking, as if alone, in the streets at night.

Wakeful Night

'Let me no longer waste the night over the page of antiquity, or the sallies of contemporary genius, but pursue the solitary walk ...'[24] Goldsmith, one of the glories of Grub Street, and an author who was highly attuned to what he once characterized as 'that fatal revolution whereby writing is converted to a mechanic trade', provides a fascinating, haunting bulletin from the midnight streets of eighteenth-century London.[25]

An Irishman who moved to London in 1756 – when, at least initially, he was homeless – Goldsmith complained that 'the poet's poverty is a standing topic of contempt'. The professional author, he noted, 'taking refuge in garrets and cellars, and living among vermin', is vilified for the living conditions to which he has been condemned by circumstance. It seemed to him a savage irony. 'We keep him poor, and yet revile his poverty', he lamented. Some of Goldsmith's statements are hyperbolic – 'perhaps, of all mankind, an author, in these times is used most hardly', he claims at one point – but their bitter sentiment is not to be doubted. If aspirant critics and poets such as Goldsmith were self-dramatizing, they nonetheless had direct experience of English society's seamiest, grubbiest underside.[26] In his account of London at night, Goldsmith silently leaned on his own experiences of perambulating the city after dark.

In the work for which he is most celebrated, *She Stoops to Conquer; or, The Mistakes of a Night* (1771), Goldsmith has some fun in the fifth act when Mr Hardcastle, the benign patriarch at the centre of the play, accidentally blunders into an elaborate and ridiculous subplot while out strolling along the perimeter of his estate after dark: 'Father-in-law, by all that's unlucky, come to take one of his night walks', the bumpkin Tony Lumpkin whispers in baffled tones.[27] In this panicked aside, a suspicion of some socially inappropriate activity is momentarily evoked. What on earth is Mr Hardcastle doing? *She Stoops to Conquer* is a brilliant comedy that revolves around a series of misunderstandings between, among other categories of people, men and women, the lower and the upper classes, the old and the young, and rural and urban types. In the course of one night, all social certainties are confounded and undermined, so that even Mr Hardcastle's moral innocence seems for an instant doubtful because of his mysterious nocturnal stroll.

But it is in an earlier work, set in the city, that Goldsmith first and most systematically uses a walk at night as a literary device. 'A City Night-Piece', first published in *The Bee* in 1759, exploits the nightwalk not as a comic narrative device but as a diagnostic and even prophetic one. Ben Jonson had originally formulated the term 'night-piece' to refer to a painting of a nocturnal scene designed by Inigo Jones for the set of *The Masque of Blackness* (1605). Robert Herrick then used it for the title of his 'Night-Piece: To Julia', a rather magical lyric poem first printed in his *Hesperides* (1648). A more immediate precedent, though, was 'A Night-Piece on Death' by Thomas Parnell, a Dubliner with whom Goldsmith's father and grandfather had been acquainted. This gloomy, atmospheric poem, which Pope published posthumously in 1722, exerted an important influence on the so-called Graveyard Poets, especially Thomas Gray. In his *Life of Dr Parnell* (1770), Goldsmith wrote in slightly lofty tones that it 'deserves every praise, and I should suppose with very little amendment, might be made to surpass all those night pieces and church yard scenes that have since appeared'.[28]

Parnell's 'Night-Piece' is a meditation on mortality and immortality structured in terms of a nocturnal stroll through a rural churchyard littered with tombs. In its opening lines, the poet decides that he will set aside the scholarly books he has been studying, which 'from Wisdom widely stray, / Or point at best the longest Way', and instead 'seek a readier Path' by stepping out into the moonlit landscape: 'By the blue Tapers trembling Light, / No more I waste the wakeful Night.'[29] Parnell's poem is indebted to *Il Penseroso* (1645), the nocturne with which John Milton rescued the night as a distinct literary topos associated with religious meditation, reclaiming it from the profanities of aristocratic nightlife.

Goldsmith's 'City Night-Piece', for its part, is a kind of prose poem. As one scholar comments, in a rare discussion of this publication, it is at the same time 'an open-ended exercise in the poetic sublime' and an example of 'hazy social criticism'; and in this respect it is uncharacteristic of his periodical prose.[30] But an assessment of this sort underestimates the essay's originality and its poetic and prophetic force, which are considerable not least because of its urban setting. Goldsmith subsequently revised it for republication in *The Citizen of the World* (1760–1761), and in this context its continuities and discontinuities with the contemporaneous form of the nocturnal picaresque become especially apparent.

Undistinguished Heap of Ruin

As its subtitle indicates, *The Citizen of the World*, which first appeared in the *Public Ledger*, purported to be a series of *Letters from a Chinese Philosopher, Residing in London, to His Friends in the East*. Like its precursors, which included *L'Espion Turc* (1684–1686), Montesquieu's *Lettres Persanes* (1721) and, more immediately, Horace Walpole's *A Letter from Xo Ho, a Chinese Philosopher* (1757), it thus used the fiction of a foreigner recording his impressions of the country through which he travels in order to offer a critical panorama of contemporary society (including, in one of its numbers, the satirical battle between actors and poets to which Churchill had contributed). In this context, an excursion into the streets at night enables Goldsmith to scrape the lacquered surface from contemporary society and expose its underside. It also gives him the opportunity to explore the identity of an isolated, alienated individual adrift in the metropolitan city.

The Chinese philosopher, whose name is Lien Chi, is an 'excentric mortal', in the phrase from *The Midnight Spy* (1766).[31] His position as an outsider provides him with a more objective perspective on the society he visits than the one that is accessible to its inhabitants. In his 117th letter, Lien Chi records that, while he is reading ancient books by candlelight in the night, like the poet in Parnell's 'Night-Piece', the sound of a clock striking two suddenly interrupts his scholarly labours and makes him contemplate his surroundings: 'the expiring taper rises and sinks in the socket; the watchman forgets the hour in slumber; the laborious and the happy are at rest; and nothing wakes but meditation, guilt, revelry, and despair'. More specifically, and more melodramatically, he imagines that 'the drunkard once more fills the destroying bowl; the robber walks his midnight round; and the suicide lifts his guilty arm against his own sacred person'.[32]

Lien Chi resolves, then, to venture into the city, in order to 'pursue the solitary walk, where vanity, ever changing, but a few hours past, walked before me; where she kept up the pageant, and now, like a forward child, seems hushed with her own importunities'. Although there might still be some boisterous revellers about, the city cannot be described as sociable. Its nightlife is less jubilant than penitent. 'What a gloom hangs all around!' exclaims Lien Chi once he is outside. This is the dead time of night: 'The dying lamp feebly emits a yellow gleam; no sound is heard, but of the chiming clock, or the distant watch-dog; all the bustle of human pride is forgotten: an hour like this may well display the emptiness of human vanity.'[33]

It was Goldsmith's older acquaintance, the cleric Edward Young, in his melancholic *Night Thoughts*, who consolidated the idea, in the mid eighteenth century, that the dead of night provides an intimation not merely of individual mortality but of some cataclysmic collective death:

> Silence, how dead! and darkness, how profound!
> Nor eye, nor list'ning ear an object finds:
> Creation sleeps. 'Tis as the general pulse
> Of life stood still, and nature made a pause;
> An aweful pause! prophetic of her end.[34]

In Goldsmith's night-piece a deathly stillness pervades the streets, and it is as if civilization itself has acquired a cadaverous quality. The city resembles a still life – *une nature morte*, as the French phrase it; or, more accurately perhaps, it resembles *une culture morte*. Indeed, in an extraordinary shift of perspective, Goldsmith's nightwalker is then prompted to extrapolate from this empty, almost silent scene and to picture it as a post-apocalyptic landscape. 'There will come a time', he muses, 'when this temporary solitude may be made continual, and the city itself, like its inhabitants, fade away, and leave a desert in its room.'[35]

It is a vision derived in part from Defoe's *Journal of the Plague Year* (1722), where the narrator evokes once populous concourses that are suddenly devoid of people, and observes 'a profound silence in the streets'.[36] It is also shaped by contemporary comparisons of London, in its ambition and corruption, to imperial Rome at the point of its collapse. These culminate in the late 1770s and early 1780s with Edward Gibbon's *History of the Decline and Fall of the Roman Empire* (which, in its account of Rome prior to Alaric's invasion in the early fourth century, contains an attack on the 'swarm of dirty and ragged plebeians' who loitered in the streets and gambled, 'and spent the hours of the night in the obscure taverns and brothels in the indulgence of gross and vulgar sensuality').[37]

'What cities, as great as this', Lien Chi asks in London, 'have once triumphed in existence, had their victories as great, joy as just, and as unbounded; and, with short-sighted presumption, promised themselves immortality!' And he goes on to imagine a 'sorrowful traveller' who, circumambulating one of these post-urban cities, 'wanders over the awful ruins' and reaches a rueful understanding of 'the transience of every sublunary possession'.

This prophetic denunciation is relatively conventional. But the vivid details with which Goldsmith renders his vision concrete are different to either of these influences. A fiction inside a fiction, this account of the desolate city that lies before him is offered by Lien Chi's sorrowful traveller:

> Here, he cries, stood their citadel, now grown over with weeds; there, their senate-house, but now the haunt of every noxious reptile: Temples and theatres stood here, now only an undistinguished heap of ruin. They are fallen; for luxury and avarice first made them feeble. The rewards of state were conferred on amusing, and not on useful, members of society. Their riches and opulence invited the invaders, who, though at first repulsed, returned again, conquered by perseverance, and, at last, swept the defendants into undistinguished destruction.[38]

If the effect of this is to summon impressions of post-imperial Rome, it is also to reduce contemporary London to a state of complete ruination.

It is a radical thought experiment, in which implicitly all that remains of the eighteenth-century city, and the civilization for which it stands, is the rubble to which the most tenacious plants and reptiles cleave. And it is one that anticipates a later tradition of portraying the post-apocalyptic city in terms of what might be characterized as the urban picturesque: Mary Shelley's *The Last Man* (1826), Richard Jefferies' *After London* (1885) and, more recently, J. G. Ballard's *The Drowned World* (1962) and Will Self's *The Book of Dave* (2006).[39]

Houseless Creatures

The metropolis at night, in Goldsmith's dystopian parable, provides a presentiment of eighteenth-century civilization's collapse. In its deserted and eerily becalmed streets, Lien Chi discerns the contours of London's death mask. But the city is, according to this Chinese philosopher, already effectively moribund. In a discussion of Defoe, Max Byrd has argued that 'as we turn over in our minds the effects of the *Journal* – the anecdotes of terror and loneliness, the vignettes of a collapsing city – it becomes possible to think of Defoe's vision in another way: is this not only London as it is in plague, but also London as it always is?'[40] An equivalent question might be asked of Goldsmith's night-piece: Is this not only London as it is in the dead time of night, but also London as it always is?

Goldsmith's claim is that the city is already derelict. It is as if the night-piece is composed in the future-perfect tense. The truth that the city reveals at the dead time of night is that, in some proleptic or prophetic sense, it is a dead city. The ruined people he encounters in the nocturnal city are, secretly, its true representatives. 'How few appear in those streets, which, but some few hours ago, were crowded?' Lien Chi comments; 'And those who appear, now no longer wear their daily mask, nor attempt to hide their lewdness or their misery.'[41] As in a dream or nightmare, these people have been thrown up by the city's unconscious. The repressed content of its inhabitants' abject and miserable lives irrupts in the night. And in so doing it anticipates the collapse of civilization into its opposite at some distant point in the future. As the philosopher Ernst Bloch might have formulated it, the city's nightwalkers constitute its Not Yet.[42]

The degraded, feral people who are invisible in the city during the day, Goldsmith goes on to observe, reappear in the streets at night:

> But who are those who make the streets their couch, and find a short repose from wretchedness at the doors of the opulent? These are strangers, wanderers, and orphans, whose circumstances are too humble to expect redress, and whose distresses are too great even for pity. Their wretchedness excites rather horror than pity. Some are without the covering even of rags, and others emaciated with disease: The world has disclaimed them; society turns its back upon their distress, and has given them up to nakedness and hunger.

These homeless people, and especially the prostitutes, are compelled to lie at the doors of the rich people who have exploited and betrayed them. At night, according to Goldsmith, the former constitute a constant rebuke to the latter – those 'wretches, whose hearts are insensible, or debauchees, who may curse, but will not relieve them'. Goldsmith's attitude is admirably combative. And if at times his Chinese philosopher, who seems to correspond to his friend in Peking in the cadences of the King James Bible, sounds oddly like an exponent of the contemporary cult of sensibility, then Goldsmith emphasizes that he is moved more to anger and horror than to pity. He was alert to the egoism concealed in altruism, as Terry Eagleton has pointed out, and in *The Citizen of the World* he 'ridicules the Orientalist vogue of the sentimentalists'.[43] This is a cult of *ressentiment* quite as much as sentiment.

At the end of the night-piece, Goldsmith pointedly refers to the itinerant population on the streets of London at two o'clock in the morning as 'poor houseless creatures'. It is an allusion to King Lear's speech on the heath in Shakespeare's tragedy:

> Poor naked wretches, whereso'er you are,
> That bide the pelting of this pitiless storm,
> How shall your houseless heads and unfed sides,
> Your loop'd and window'd raggedness, defend you
> From seasons such as these? O, I have ta'en
> Too little care of this! Take physic, pomp;
> Expose thyself to feel what wretches feel,
> That thou mayst shake the superflux to them,
> And show the heavens more just.[44]

Goldsmith's complaint, implicitly, is that the rich have failed both to empathize with the poor (to expose themselves 'to feel what wretches feel') and to offer their superfluous wealth to them (to 'shake the superflux to them').

In his correspondence, the Chinese philosopher expresses frustration that, in spite of the emotive and moralistic practice of giving alms, the most affluent members of society are not prepared to relieve these hopeless people in any significant sense. As he tells his silent interlocutors on the streets of the city, 'the world will give you reproaches, but will not give you relief'.[45] Eagleton argues that, if for the upper-class sentimentalists of the eighteenth century charity is little more than 'a quirk of individual disposition, one optional life-style among several', then for Goldsmith it 'is rather the supreme virtue'. He believed in benevolent efforts to instil 'the ordinary, unglamorous petty-bourgeois virtues of sobriety and frugality'. Like his friend Johnson, he was therefore 'the best kind of Tory, one who believes that only such paternalism will protect the poor from the depredations of the free market'.[46]

Houseless Goldsmith

Lien Chi laments the fact that, in contrast to the upper-class sentimentalists, he cannot afford to give financial assistance to the poor. Although his heart too has been 'formed with so much sensibility', his 'fortune' has not been 'adapted to its impulse'.[47] Goldsmith was angered and horrified by the plight of the homeless – as opposed to simply feeling lachrymose about them – in part because of his own experiences of poverty and vagrancy.

Although his articles for the *Public Ledger* amounted to his first literary success, enabling him to move from his shabby lodgings in Green Arbour Court to more salubrious ones in Wine Office Court off Fleet Street, close to Johnson's chambers, Goldsmith did not forget his background. Indeed, throughout his life he 'preserved a secret pact with poverty and failure', and, 'even in his more affluent years, he looked back with fond nostalgia on the low dives he had haunted as a recent immigrant to London'.[48] In his biography of Goldsmith, Washington Irving records with relish that he once 'startled a polite circle at Sir Joshua Reynolds's, by humorously dating an anecdote about the time he "lived among the beggars of Axe Lane"'. 'Poor houseless Goldsmith!' Irving ejaculates in a deliberate echo of *The Citizen of the World* – 'to what shifts he must have been driven to find shelter and sustenance for himself in [his] first venture into London'.[49]

In February 1755, Goldsmith had half-abandoned the medical career for which he had been distractedly studying in Edinburgh and the Netherlands, and set off on foot across the Continent. He was a militant pedestrian. 'A man, who is whirled through Europe in his post-chaise, and the pilgrim, who walks the grand tour on foot, will form very different conclusions', Thomas Percy observed mildly in his memoir of Goldsmith.[50] In the phrase he subsequently used in *The Vicar of Wakefield* (1766), Goldsmith became a 'philosophic Vagabond' in Europe, allegedly funding his peregrinations in Flanders, France, Switzerland, Germany and Italy by tutoring, gambling and playing the flute.[51]

This was a flagrant rejection of the polite conventions that governed the journeys of upper-class English tourists on the continent. Francis Bacon had codified some of these in 'Of Travaile' (1625): 'let his *Travaile* appeare rather in his Discourse, then in his Apparrell, or Gesture', he insisted in his advice to a young man, determined that the civilized rather than the barbaric qualities of travelling on the Continent accrue to him.[52] To go on foot, implicitly, was to go native.

'One thing the traveller never did – walk', wrote Richard Pyke in a sketch of the tradition of the Grand Tour published in 1935; 'Only outlaws and madmen walked.'[53] Goldsmith's ragged journey across the Continent was less a Grand Tour than a poor one. It was an assertion of commonness, if not madness. His poem 'The Traveller' (1764) is a remnant of his time as an itinerant in Europe. Its opening, which conjures up a poet who is 'remote, unfriended, melancholy, slow', and who finds himself in an alpine province where 'the rude Carthinian boor / Against the houseless stranger shuts the door', echoes Ovid's *Ibis*: *Exsul, inops erres, alienaque limina lusres* ('Mayst thou wander an exile and destitute, and haunt the doors of others'). His 'prime of life', he continues, is 'in wandering spent and care': 'My fortune leads to traverse realms alone, / And find no spot of all the world my own.'[54] Here, in contrast to the aristocratic or upper-middle-class tourist, is the poet as a houseless itinerant. He haunts the houses of others – not a guest, nor a host, but a ghost. He is recognizable as a proto-Romantic figure.

Goldsmith reached Dover in February 1756 and, after another

arduous journey on foot, arrived in London, at the age of about twenty-five, in a state of destitution. He had, as he told his brother, 'a pale melancholy visage', a dishevelled appearance, and a pronounced Irish accent, and was instantly identifiable as a déclassé and impoverished exile from the Irish middle class. According to his emotive Victorian biographer, John Forster, 'he had not a single farthing in his pocket', and 'in the middle of February he was wandering without friend or acquaintance, without the knowledge or comfort of even one kind face, in the lonely, terrible, LONDON Streets'. His lodgings in Green Arbour Court, between the Old Bailey and the Fleet Market – a residence of little pastoral charm in spite of its enticing name – were reached by ascending 'Breakneck Steps'. 'Every night', writes Forster, 'he would risk his neck at those steep stone stairs; every day, for his clothes had become too ragged to submit to daylight scrutiny, he would keep within his dirty, naked, unfurnished room, with its single wooden chair and window bench.'[55] At night, groping his way down the precipitous steps in the pitch dark, he reclaimed the streets from which he felt socially excluded in the day.

Goldsmith's biography at this age – because rather than in spite of the fact that it is so threadbare – reads like the supreme Grub Street picaresque. At least until he found employment as an apothecary's assistant, Goldsmith was homeless and jobless in the capital. So the sympathies he exhibits for the prostitutes and vagabonds of his 'City Night-Piece', first published three years after his arrival there, are an expression of social solidarity as much as sensibility. Forster confidently ascribed Goldsmith's description of the 'affecting lonely journey through the London streets, which the *Bee* soon after published with the title of the City Night Piece', to memories of the period in his life when, appalled by the sight of people suffering states of privation far more permanent than his own, he 'would wander through the streets at night, to console and reassure the misery he could not otherwise give help to'. In the night-piece published in *The Bee* and republished in *The Citizen of the World*, Forster discerned 'so much of the past struggle and the lesson it had left, so much of the grief-taught sympathy, so much of the secret of the genius, of tolerant, gentle-hearted Goldsmith'.[56]

Laurence Sterne, in *A Sentimental Journey* (1768), commented that 'the man who either disdains or fears to walk up a dark entry may be an excellent good man, and fit for a hundred things; but he will not do to make a good sentimental traveller. I count little of the many things I see pass at broad noon day, in large and open streets.'[57] As a young man, Goldsmith pressed this logic to its extreme, not simply walking up a dark alley but loitering there and lodging in its dirty shadows. Although Goldsmith did not leave anything more than traces of his ragged, houseless existence in London, he is one of the great nightwalkers in the history of literature in English. For he uses the nightwalk that he and his Chinese philosopher conducted in the streets of the city in order, on the one hand, to imagine the end of eighteenth-century civilization and, on the other, to dramatize the alienation of an emergent urban subject.

All-Sin-Sheltering Grove

In 'National Prejudices' (1763), an essay that opens with an anecdote about a company of gentlemen he has accidentally met on one of his 'late rambles', Goldsmith described himself as 'one of that sauntering tribe of mortals, who spend the greatest part of their time in taverns, coffee houses, and other places of public resort' ('late rambles' hints that they are nocturnal as well as of recent date).[58] A significant number of eighteenth-century critics and poets belonged to this 'sauntering tribe'. Furthermore, many of them walked at night either from necessity or choice. Grub Street was full of rootless intellectuals who led lives that verged on vagrancy.

'I love a straggling life above all things in the world', announces the ragged man whose biography Goldsmith reconstructs in his 'Adventures of a Strolling Player' (1760). Dressed in 'very shabby cloaths', the actor is perched on a bench in St James's Park when Goldsmith, who confesses to being 'fond of amusement in whatever company it is to be found', falls into conversation with him.[59] St James's Park, where 'the first quality blended with the lowest populace', as the Abbé Prévost put it in shocked tones on visiting

London, was a popular place of repose for penniless artists in the eighteenth century.[60] In spite of its reputation for Restoration and post-Restoration chic, and because of it, this park attracted all sorts of illicit activities (its south side, for example, became a notorious resort of homosexual men, perhaps because of the proximity of the barracks at Horse Guards).

The Earl of Rochester's poem 'A Ramble in St James's Park', composed in the early 1670s, is the most celebrated hymn to this titillating scene:

> Unto this all-sin-sheltering grove
> Whores of the bulk and the alcove,
> Great ladies, chambermaids, and drudges,
> The ragpicker, and heiress trudges.
> Carmen, divines, great lords, and tailors,
> Prentices, poets, pimps, and jailers,
> Footmen, fine fops do here arrive,
> And here promiscuously they swive.[61]

The gates of St James's Park were locked at night, but as many as 6,500 people apparently had the keys.[62] It was thus one of those half-private, half-public spaces that, like the pleasure gardens, fostered an alluring and ambiguous moral atmosphere in the eighteenth-century capital. In its precincts it was twilight at all times of the day and night.

St James's Park is the starting point for the rambles around which a number of nocturnal picaresques are structured. In *The Devil Upon Two Sticks in England; or, Night Scenes in London* (1755), an imitation of *Le Diable Boiteux* (1707), Eugenio is visited by Asmodeus while walking one night in St James's Park. In *The Midnight Rambler* (1770), the narrator is accosted by his guide the Good Genius in the same location. And, four years earlier, in *The Midnight Spy* (1766), the adventures of Urbanus and Argestis begin when the former sees the latter seated beside a prostitute and a pimp on a bench in St James's Park, and rescues him from their cunning attempts to con him. The idea that 'garb denotes infamy', Urbanus informs his far less urbane companion 'with a smile of contempt', is a 'mistaken though general notion!' – 'What do you think that a bit of lace constitutes dignity, or that merit is centred in brocade?'[63]

If St James's Park is one of the principal scenes of social dereliction in the capital in the eighteenth century, it is one of the principal scenes of moral instruction too. It might also be understood as the main portal into the alternative universe of the London night.

A Wretched Vagrant

St James's Park is central to the story of the almost forgotten poet William Pattison, a pathetic figure who appears to have spent the night on its benches on a number of occasions. His brief life is a Grub Street tragedy in miniature.

Born in Peasemarch, Sussex, the son of a farmer, Pattison displayed enough intellectual precociousness for his father's landlord, the Earl of Thanet, to send him to a free school in Appleby, Westmorland. At school, he supposedly paid his debts to booksellers by writing odes to local landowners. In the biography of Pattison that prefaces the collection of his poems published shortly after his death, the anonymous author records that on 'many a Moon-light Night' the boy used to retire to a 'Grotto, or Cave' nearby, in order to indulge in 'sadly-pleasing Melancholy'.[64] He left school and attended Sidney Sussex College, Cambridge, but gained a reputation for preferring fishing and writing poetry to studying (apparently he sometimes spent entire summer nights by the banks of a river combining the activities he loved). At the university Pattison developed an erroneous, if not paranoid, conviction that he was about to be expelled, so he carved his name out of the college's record books in order to prevent the authorities from officially erasing it.

In 1726, encouraged by friends to publish a collection of poems by subscription, he left Cambridge before receiving a degree and moved to London. There he was 'reduced to such extreme indigence, as to be no longer able to procure the necessaries of life'. It was during this time, reduced 'by Some Misfortunes in Town', that he probably became homeless. There are rather hopeless references in his correspondence to falling 'in Love with a Lady in the Park', so perhaps this too had something to do with his sleeping on the benches in St James's Park. At this time, Pattison wrote several desperate letters to friends and to the acquaintances of friends in the hope of attracting subscriptions for his poems: 'Spare my blushes – I have not enjoyed the common Necessaries of Life for these two Days ...'. These proved largely ineffective.

It was in this state of distress, 'aggravated by a drooping indisposition', that Edmund Curll, the notorious bookseller, sheltered him in his house in the Strand. According to Pope, who recorded his loathing for Curll in lavish detail in *The Dunciad*, the bookseller starved Pattison to death. It is more likely that, in spite of his unscrupulous practices as a businessman, Curll saved him from starvation.[65] Pattison died of smallpox, at the age of twenty-one, in 1726, a short time after arriving in London.

Pattison's most interesting poem, 'Effigies Authoris', is addressed to Pope's friend Lord Burlington – whom Horace Walpole called 'the Apollo of the Arts' – in the hope of securing him as a patron. Composed in heroic couplets, it is an autobiographical poem, even if it is far too lachrymose and self-dramatizing to be read as strictly factual. It opens with a desperate appeal for compassion: 'Oppress'd with griefs, with poverty, and scorn, / Of all forsaken, and of all forlorn, / What shall I do? Or whither shall I flie?' Pattison identifies himself as 'a wretched vagrant destitute of home' who has roamed 'with restless heart from place to place'. Then he details his three-day journey on foot from Cambridge to London, when he sees 'idle poppies' that he compares to fops, and birds that he compares to bards (because 'both live in want, and unregarded die'). So far, then, the 'Effigies Authoris' is a ridiculous performance that helps explain why Pattison's poetry is almost completely forgotten. It becomes more intriguing when the poet arrives among 'the intermingled multitudes' of London and testifies to his homelessness.[66]

On reaching the city, 'lost in thought', he 'wander[s] up and down / Of all unknowing, and to all unknown'. He searches for a friend or a potential patron, but becomes increasingly hopeless as the little money he possesses runs out. As dusk falls, and the dew too, he repairs to St James's Park, 'solemn in pace, and sadden'd in my look':

> On the first bench my wearied bones I laid,
> For gnawing hunger on my vitals prey'd;
> There faint in melancholy mood I sate,
> And meditated on my future fate.
> Nights sable vapours now the trees invade,
> And gloomy darkness deepen'd ev'ry shade;
> And now, ah! whither shall the helpless fly,
> From the nocturnal horrors of the sky;
> With empty vapours my cruel fate I curse,
> While falling tears bedew my meager purse;
> What shall I do? Or whither shall I run?
> How 'scape the threat'ning fate I cannot shun;
> There, trembling cold, and motionless I lay,
> Till sleep beguil'd the tumults of the day.[67]

In the heart of the aristocratic district of the metropolis, the picturesque surroundings of the park, which in the eighteenth century contained both deer and cattle, acquire a sublime, even horrific quality. The 'sadly-pleasing Melancholy' Pattison allegedly cultivated as a school student when he sequestered himself in a cave in Westmorland, is here transformed into something more like fear. His 'melancholy mood' gradually turns to one of panic. The reference to 'nocturnal horrors', which at first seems embarrassingly hyperbolic, acquires an insidious and unsettling force when the reader recalls that the poet is staring up at the empty, comfortless sky from a cold, hard park bench.

The power of these lines, communicated despite their melodramatic diction, comes from the sense of the poet's isolation at the centre of perhaps the most populous and cosmopolitan city in Europe. The images of night seem relatively familiar, not least because Young and other so-called Graveyard Poets of the mid eighteenth century made them more fashionable. But they transmit a shock, because they record the impact of the night's physical conditions on Pattison's beleaguered body as well as his spirit. It is sadly all too easy to imagine his motionless but trembling form huddled on the bench.

Once asleep, the poet dreams at first of 'tormenting objects'. 'Despairing forms too dreadful for the light' dance in front of his eyes and 'fictious' food materializes before him only to dissolve as he reaches out for it. But then 'a kind, though visionary shade' appears to him. No doubt this angelic agent is another hallucination induced by hunger. No matter. It offers to relieve him, and advises him, 'when morning's beamy rays arise, / And shoot refulgent glories through the skies', to pursue his 'wand'ring path' along the Thames to Chiswick. For there, it tells him, he will find 'great Burlington, the muse's surest friend'. He awakes and reflects on 'the vision of the night', before discovering 'a latent sixpence' in his pocket. 'Surpris'd with transport stood my bristled hair' is Pattison's pitiful, if not laughable, description of his reaction to this change in fortune.[68]

The poet rushes off to 'the first house' he can find, presumably a tavern, and there writes the 'Effigies Authoris' itself. Then he optimistically pursues the road to Chiswick, 'Where now with doubtful hopes, and fears, I wait / Your bounteous lordship's pleasure at your gate. / W. PATTISON.'[69] There is no evidence, tragically, that Lord Burlington – just at this time beginning to build Chiswick House, his Palladian masterpiece – was prepared to indulge Pattison's insignificant ambitions.

It might finally be said of Pattison, as Johnson once noted of Savage, that 'he had seldom any home, or even a lodging in which he could be private; and therefore was driven into public-houses for the common conveniences of life and supports of nature'.[70] Pattison did not even have a home of his own, let alone a dedicated room, in which to sit and write. If his poems had been readable, he might have acquired a reputation as a proto-Romantic, like Thomas Chatterton. But they weren't, so he didn't.

But Pattison deserves nonetheless to be included among the ragged ranks of those eighteenth-century writers whom the author of 'Literary Adventurers', an article in Dickens's periodical *All the Year Round* from 1863, classified in terms of 'vagabond authorship'. These men, the piece underlines, in spite of being 'men of conspicuous abilities and acquirements', were 'intellectual gypsies'. In this category, Savage, Johnson and Goldsmith constitute a ruling triumvirate:

> Savage, compelled by his vices and his needs to herd in cellars with the scum of the town; Goldsmith, composing his Vicar of Wakefield in penury and trouble, and saved from the debtors' prison by the interposition of Johnson; Johnson himself, dining behind the screen at Cave the bookseller's, because he was too shabby to appear, and pacing the streets of London all night with Savage, because neither had the money to procure even the meanest lodging.[71]

7.

Midnight Rambles

Savage and Johnson

Nightwandering

In his *Dictionary of the English Language* (1755), which he began compiling in 1746, Samuel Johnson cited the poetry of his late, lamented friend Richard Savage in some seven entries in order to illustrate the relevant definitions. The associations of some of these words, like 'elevate' and 'fondly', are innocent enough. The associations of others, like 'lone' and 'suicide', seem slightly more pointed, given the baleful and self-destructive character of Savage's life, which ended, not in suicide admittedly, but in a state of indigence and painful infirmity, in a debtors' prison, little more than a decade before the publication of the *Dictionary*.[1] None of the entries that cite Savage's verse relate specifically to the night. But it is nonetheless tempting to think that, when he did come to discriminate the semantics of the night in the *Dictionary*, Johnson had his former comrade in mind.

For during the formative phase of their friendship, in the late 1730s, Johnson and Savage spent a good deal of time together in the nocturnal streets of London – walking, talking, possibly even sleeping rough. Johnson was twenty-seven, Savage approximately forty, when they first met. The former was an aspiring author, almost as impressionable as he was ambitious, the latter a professional poet with a bohemian reputation for glamorous and reckless charm. Savage, impoverished but also temperamentally perverse, and perhaps insane, seems to have been intermittently homeless. In his lifetime, certainly, he was as famous for being a vagrant and criminal who slept in night cellars as for being a sophisticated, if erratic, poet with a reputation for aristocratic arrogance. The two men fostered a friendship that depended in large part on shared beliefs and feelings, forged in the streets at night, of being outcasts or refugees from polite society.

Johnson reconstructed many of Savage's experiences of the city at night when, in the aftermath of his friend's demise in 1743, he composed his brilliantly imaginative, morally biased biography of him, the *Life of Mr Richard Savage* (1744). So it is tempting to speculate that memories of the poet clustered around the term 'night' when the lexicographer came to catalogue its meanings a few years later. In the entries on compound forms of the word 'night' in particular, Johnson's prose seems to contain traces of Savage's acquaintance with the night. There is 'nightfaring', for instance, meaning 'travelling in the night'; and 'nightfoundered', 'lost or distressed in the night'. There is 'nightbrawler', 'one who raises disturbances in the night'; and 'nightwanderer', 'one who wanders by night'.[2] As the court records of the time testify, Savage was given both to nightwandering and nightbrawling. At the end of his life, it might be said, Savage 'nightfoundered'.

Finally, Johnson includes the words 'nightwalk' and 'nightwalker' themselves. He defines a 'nightwalk' – in simple, if rather circular, terms – as a 'walk in the night'. He defines a 'nightwalker' as 'one who roves in the night upon ill designs', citing Roger Ascham as an authority. It is noticeable that Johnson does not specify the nightwalker's gender. He does not directly identify the nightwalker with prostitution. Indeed, the repeated presence of the verb 'to rove' in these definitions hints that he is thinking of a male nightwalker rather than a streetwalker; for, according to the *Dictionary*, roving involves rambling, ranging and wandering – forms of perambulation entailing a freedom of movement that was rarely available to women, especially at night, in the eighteenth century. He might be thinking of Savage in this context.

Johnson is perhaps also conscious of his relationship with Savage when, a few pages later, he defines 'noctivagation' as 'the act of rambling or wandering in the night'. He includes the word 'noctivagant' not as a noun but as an adjective, meaning 'wandering in the night'. In other words, he avoids pinning the act of noctivagation down to a particular social identity. Framed in these terms, it is a temporary habit rather than a permanent condition – a political and spiritual expression of identification with the poor as opposed to a state of absolute poverty. Suggestive of vagrant walking at night, noctivagation closely resembles what Johnson was up to with Savage in the streets of London in the 1730s. It is a form of slumming. Johnson relished the social ambiguity of the city at night as a young man. 'He walked the streets at all hours, and said he was never robbed, for the rogues knew he had little money, nor had the appearance of having much', wrote James Boswell.[3]

Like some of his Grub Street contemporaries, and like Romantic descendants such as De Quincey, Johnson can be usefully characterized as a nightwalker of the uncommon kind. He is not an exile on the streets of the eighteenth-century city at night so much as a sort of self-exile. He is one of those characters whom Iain Sinclair, in a different context, has classified as 'the electively disenfranchised'.[4] Savage, in contradistinction, for all his aristocratic pretensions, cannot completely escape the criminal associations of the common nightwalker that persist in the eighteenth century. He is far more easily assimilated to one of the categories of nocturnal crime set out by the jurist William Hawkins in his *Treatise of the Pleas of the Crown* (1716), which included 'all dangerous and suspicious Persons' and 'those who go abroad in the Night, and sleep in the Day, or those who inordinately haunt Taverns, having no visible Means to live by'.[5] Both Johnson and Savage played a significant part in the transformation of the cultural meanings of nightwalking in the eighteenth century, when its bohemian associations became more and more entrenched.

The biographer Richard Holmes has proposed that the peculiar friendship between the two men was shaped by the relationship of pupil to mentor, and adds that 'Savage can be seen as a sort of urbane Mephistopheles, Johnson as a youthful Faust'.[6] As inhabitants of the city at night, I prefer to see them in terms of another demonic relationship – the one that Alain-René Le Sage mythologized in *Le Diable Boiteux* (1707): Savage is Asmodeus, the crippled demon who heaves the roofs from people's houses after dark and penetrates their deepest secrets; Johnson is Don Cleofas, the student who liberates him from a bottle and is recompensed with glimpses into the hidden life of the metropolis.

Dark Evenings

Perhaps the most infamous and outrageous English poet of the eighteenth century, Savage provides a kind of psychological case history of the vagrant urban poet at night in his most disturbed and unstable state.

Scarcely a single incident in his strange, labyrinthine life can be reconstructed with absolute confidence, but of all its events his birth is probably the most contentious. Throughout his adulthood, he insisted that he was the illegitimate son of Lady Macclesfield and her lover, the fourth Earl of Rivers, also called Richard Savage. Lady Macclesfield, born in 1668, had at the age of fifteen married Viscount Brandon, a vicious, violent individual who had killed a boy in the London streets when drunk. In 1696, two years after her husband inherited the title of Lord Macclesfield, she fell in love with the callous, rakish libertine Lord Rivers. She had two illegitimate children by him, first a daughter, then a son; but she was careful to conceal this fact, and went so far as to wear a mask during labour so that the midwife could not see her face. The son, born in 1697, was christened Richard Smith, and it was this child that the poet Richard Savage claimed to be (though, to add to the confusion, he remained convinced that he had been born in 1698).

Savage maintained that his godmother, a Mrs Lloyd, had reared him, and that, after her death, Lady Macclesfield, in an attempt to suppress her relation to him, had unsuccessfully tried to ship him to the plantations before apprenticing him to a shoemaker in London. He persuaded a number of influential contemporaries of the veracity of this narrative, among them Aaron Hill and Richard Steele, in addition to Johnson (who was unremitting in his hostility to Lady Macclesfield). Lady Macclesfield, who married Colonel Henry Brett in 1700, remained adamant that both of her illegitimate children had died as infants. She was convinced that Savage was either a deliberate imposter, determined to blackmail her, or else a disturbed troublemaker who was in fact the son of one of his nurses.

'The world must vibrate in a state of uncertainty as to what was the truth', Boswell concluded, in tones as measured as they are grandiloquent.[7] Holmes, who has sifted the evidence about Savage's origins with scrupulous care, finally sides with Lady Macclesfield and her version of events. He decides that, rather than being a 'conscious imposter', Savage 'was genuinely deluded about his identity'.[8] Certainly, Savage seems to have staked his entire sense of self on the claim that he was Lady Macclesfield's son – and with increasingly monomaniacal, and self-destructive, intensity.

This is apparent from shortly after his discovery of his mother's identity, as he understood it, when he used to loiter obsessively outside her house on Old Bond Street at night. In Johnson's partial and excessively sympathetic account of his friend's plight, Savage 'was so touched with the discovery of his real mother, that it was his frequent practice to walk in the dark evenings for several hours before her door, in hopes of seeing her as she might come by accident to the window, or cross her apartment with a candle in her hand'.[9] Johnson's pathetic image of the young Savage pacing the nocturnal streets outside Lady Macclesfield's house acquires far more ominous overtones if, instead of merely being deluded, he was delusional.

The nightwalker, in this scene, is a stalker. It is in this sinister shape that Savage appears in a later incident involving Lady Macclesfield and her residence in Old Bond Street. 'One evening walking, as it was his custom, in the street that she inhabited', Johnson explains, rehearsing Savage's version of events, 'he saw the door of her house by accident open; he entered it, and finding no person in the passage to hinder him, went up stairs to salute her.' Discovering him about to enter her chamber, Lady Macclesfield alerted the members of the household with 'screams' and 'distressful outcries' and 'ordered them to drive out of the house that villain, who had forced himself in upon her, and endeavoured to murder her'. A docile, prudent Savage, according to Johnson, then immediately retreated from the house, appalled at 'so detestable an accusation'.[10]

In the *Life of Savage*, Johnson professes to be shocked that Savage's mother, as he regarded Lady Macclesfield, not only used her account of this 'fictitious assault' to 'set herself free from his embraces and solicitations', but stored it up 'as an instrument of future wickedness' so as to 'deprive him of his life' when, in the most sensational episode of his career, he was later sentenced for murder.[11]

Pauper Convict

The tangled threads of Savage's tragic, at times abject, biography often seem to have knotted themselves around scenes in the streets of eighteenth-century London at night. The most sensational of these was the occasion in 1727 that led to Savage being sentenced to death for committing 'wilful murder'. Here, Savage is at his most savage. Johnson, whose highly partisan account of the drama is derived largely from conversations with Savage, though also from the 'Newgate' pamphlet that had been commissioned by Aaron Hill in an attempt to rehabilitate the poet's reputation after the trial, cannot decide 'whether it ought to be mentioned as a crime or a calamity'.[12]

On the night of 20 November 1727, Savage commuted into London from Richmond in order to discharge his debts to the landlord of his lodgings in Westminster. En route, he encountered two friends, James Gregory and William Merchant, and the three of them set off for a night's drinking. According to Johnson, the coffee-house in which the men initially ensconced themselves could not accommodate all three of them for the night, so 'they agreed to ramble about the streets, and divert themselves with such amusements as should offer themselves till morning'.[13] After a couple of hours, tiring of this nightwalk, which presumably involved predictable rakish activities like picking up prostitutes, they entered Robinson's Coffee-House in Charing Cross, which doubled as a brothel. 'In their Walks', writes Thomas Cooke in the 'Newgate' pamphlet, with considered ambiguity, 'seeing a Light in *Robinson's* Coffee-house, they thought that a proper place to entertain them.'[14]

It was by this time about 2 a.m. In the parlour at Robinson's, a private room that had been rented for the night, Merchant 'petulantly placed himself between the company and the fire, and soon after kicked down the table'.[15] Savage and his friends manifestly assumed that it was their prerogative to use the fireplace, and that everyone else present would defer to this privilege. It was an ugly and unpleasant display of class arrogance. In the course of the scuffle that ensued, Savage drunkenly and recklessly drew his sword and stabbed one of the men he and his friends had provoked. As a witness stated, this man, whose name was James Sinclair, 'bore the character of an idle person, who had no settled place of residence'.[16]

In the ensuing chaos, exacerbated by the fact that the candles had been extinguished and the parlour consequently plunged into darkness, Savage also managed to wound a maid, called Mary Rock, who tried to restrain him. This was far more than simply the rough and tumble of a typical tavern brawl. Sinclair, a man about whom little is known except that he was unemployed and of no fixed address, died of his injuries the next day. Thus the infamous noctambulist – one of the sons of Belial, if not of Lord Rivers – terminated the life of a common nightwalker.

Moments after the affray, Savage 'forced his way with Merchant out of the house', as Johnson narrates it; 'but being intimidated and confused, without resolution to fly or stay, they were taken in back-court by one of the company and some soldiers whom he had called to his assistance'. Disarmed and arrested by the three soldiers, who had been entrenched in a night-cellar nearby, they were taken first to the nearest watch house and then to the Gate House. In the morning, after Sinclair's death had been announced, they were transferred to Newgate Prison, where they were 'exempted from the ignominy of chains', thanks to Savage's claim to be the son of the late Lord Rivers, and allowed to sit out the time before the trial in the Press Yard rather than 'among the common criminals'.[17]

The trial in the Old Bailey, which was attended by a number of literary celebrities, including Alexander Pope, resulted in the sentencing of Gregory and Savage for murder, and of Merchant, who had not carried a sword, for manslaughter. Returned to Newgate, where he was confined in iron fetters, Savage appealed against the death sentence, due to be carried out in less than a month, while his friends exerted influence on his behalf at court. Savage and Gregory obtained a royal pardon on 6 January 1728, and the poet was therefore freed as a 'pauper Convict in Newgate' a few weeks later.

Savage's life was saved as a result of the intervention of Lord Tyrconnel, Lady Macclesfield's nephew. This kindly and indulgent aristocrat appears to have both pitied the poet and hoped that, in co-opting him, he could protect his persecuted aunt. As a result of his intervention, Savage extorted a pension from Lady Macclesfield. In addition, from 1729, he secured Tyrconnel's official patronage. His patron even recommended him for the post of poet laureate. In the aftermath of the trial, Savage thus achieved considerable fame and acquired a limited fortune. 'This was the golden part of Mr Savage's life', Johnson reported; 'his appearance was splendid, his expenses large, and his acquaintance extensive.'[18]

Some of his contemporaries were contemptuous of this outcome. Henry Fielding, in his *Covent-Garden Journal* (1752), which contains an attack on Grub Street scribblers, refers for instance to 'the case of one Mr Richard Savage, an Author whose Manufactures had long laid uncalled for in the Warehouse, till he happened very fortunately for his Bookseller to be found guilty of a capital Crime at the Old-Bailey'.[19] Johnson, of course, was less cynical. He observed with a certain sceptical pride that, at this time, 'to admire Mr Savage was a proof of discernment; and to be acquainted with him, was a title to poetical reputation'.[20]

Living in Tyrconnel's house in Arlington Street from 1730, Savage benefited both from access to his patron's library (and cellar) and a generous gift of books. Characteristically, he abused these advantages. In Johnson's account, 'Lord Tyrconnel affirmed, that it was the constant practice of Mr Savage to enter a tavern with any company that proposed it, drink the most expensive wines with great profusion, and when the reckoning was demanded, to be without money'. Back in Tyrconnel's apartments, he 'practiced the most licentious frolics, and committed all the outrages of drunkenness'. Moreover, having given Savage 'a collection of valuable books, stamped with his own arms', Tyrconnel then 'had the mortification to see them in a short time exposed to sale upon the stalls'.[21]

The lure of Grub Street was considerable, and it was thus not long before Savage became no more than 'a distressed poet' once again. This afforded his enemies a good deal of satisfaction. 'His degradation', Johnson observes, 'from the condition which he had enjoyed with such wanton thoughtlessness, was considered by many as an occasion of triumph.'[22]

Prostitute Scribbler

Savage failed to publish any poems of substance during the years in which Tyrconnel fostered his career. By 1730 his best and most ambitious poetry was already behind him. So who was this fugitive poet that, in spite of his declining literary reputation, Johnson admired so profoundly when he first pitched up in the capital in 1737?

Reconstructing his literary biography, Johnson explains that, denied financial assistance during the period in which Lady Macclesfield rejected him, Savage 'was reduced to the utmost miseries of want, while he was endeavouring to awaken the affection of a mother. He was therefore obliged to seek some other means of support; and, having no profession, became by necessity an author.'[23] In this respect, he was like Charles Churchill and other less illustrious Grub Street poets. Savage first became a professional writer in the mid-to-late 1710s, when he produced several English adaptations of fashionable Spanish plays. Rather more controversially, he attracted public attention at this time because he also printed a good deal of Jacobite doggerel. In 1717 he was arrested on a charge of political subversion for his 'Ironical Panagerick on his pretended Majesty George'.

Savage's first original publication was *The Tragedy of Sir Thomas Overbury* (1723), which Johnson regarded as 'an uncommon proof of strength and genius, and evenness of mind, of a serenity not to be ruffled, and an imagination not to be suppressed'. Johnson was impressed by this performance not least because, during the time he composed it, like Pattison,

> he was without lodging, and often without meat; nor had he any other conveniences for study than the fields or the street allowed him; there he used to walk and form his speeches and afterwards step into a shop, beg for a few moments the use of pen and ink, and write down what he had composed, upon paper which he had picked up by accident.[24]

This is a vivid, if idealized, insight into the emergence of the poet as 'a vagrant of the soul'.[25]

In the late 1720s Savage supplied Pope with plenty of gossip for his revised, so-called variorum edition of the *Dunciad* (1729), escaping the poem's censure for this reason. In *An Author to be Lett* (1729), printed in the same year, Savage published an equally vituperative, if far less elegant, broadside against a number of Grub Street's most prominent inhabitants, including Edmund Curll. Savage produced this aggressive attack on his peers – which built on his satire against 'The Authors of the Town' (1725) – in the guise of 'a prostitute Scribler' called Iscariot Hackney. The pseudonymous identity of this backbiting Grub Street hack enabled Savage both to bemoan his own mistreatment by the literary establishment and, at the same time, and with characteristic inconstancy, to revile others in the same position as him.

An Author to be Lett begins with an account of Hackney's childhood and early career, and it is in the course of this autobiographical sketch that he explains that, not long ago, he successfully managed to outwit his rapacious employer Curll. 'But some Years after', he goes on, '(just at the time of his starving poor *Pattison*) the Varlet was revenged. He arrested me for several Months Board, brought me back to my Garret, and made me drudge on in my old, dirty Work.' Pattison thus figures as something like the martyred saint of Grub Street. And Savage implicitly positions his avatar Iscariot Hackney as another Pattison: the dead poet's representative on earth. At the conclusion of the pamphlet, Hackney makes a pointed reference to the coffee shops and night-cellars in which – in the unlikely event that the 'Knights, Esquires, [and] Gentlemen' to whom he has addressed his pleas on the title-page decide to commission him – he can be found.[26] At once self-pitying and self-promoting, Savage is only half-joking.

Savage's most interesting and energetic poems, 'The Bastard' (1728) and *The Wanderer* (1729), composed immediately before and after Sinclair's murder and the ensuing trial, are more artful and sophisticated exercises in self-fashioning. The former, inscribed with sarcasm to 'Mrs Brett, once Countess of Macclesfield', is an affirmation of his illegitimate aristocratic origins, as he understood them, and a vehement attack on the woman he claimed had denied them: 'Blest be the *Bastard*'s birth! through wond'rous ways, / He shines eccentric like a Comet's blaze'. Savage glories in his eccentric, exilic status:

> Born to himself, by no possession led,
> In freedom foster'd, and by fortune fed;
> Nor Guides, nor Rules, his sov'reign choice controul,
> His body independant, as his soul.
> Loos'd to the world's wide range – enjoyn'd no aim;

> Prescrib'd no duty, and assign'd no Name:
> Nature's unbounded son, he stands alone,
> His heart unbiass'd, and his mind his own.[27]

The poet is as aimless as he is nameless, and this condition is at the same time a form of bondage and of freedom. Stripped of his social identity, he is in two distinct meanings of the term 'natural': he is both illegitimate and, in some transcendent sense, pre-social. Excluded from polite society, he completely escapes or circumvents the petty and demeaning claims of civilization. He is thus Shakespeare's Edmund and Edgar, or Poor Tom, rolled into one – both an evil bastard and a spiritually liberated vagabond. In spite of its outrageous egotism, or because of it, there is a violent creativity to this verse that proves irresistible.

Delve Obscene

The most authoritative editor of Savage's poetry, Clarence Tracy, has admitted that 'a great deal of it is rubbish, as eighteenth-century readers themselves recognized'. But he rightly admires the fact that, formless and incoherent though it is, *The Wanderer* is 'a defence of a concept of the poet that we have grown accustomed to call romantic'.[28] This strange poem contains several significant reinscriptions of Savage's nighttime experiences, which appear – according to a dreamlike logic – in condensed and displaced form.

Savage wrote *The Wanderer*, completed at Tyrconnel's house off Piccadilly in 1728, in dialogue with several friends, including John Dyer, David Mallet and, most significantly, James Thomson, the author of *The Seasons* (1730). 'The agreed aim' of this loose grouping, Holmes comments, 'was to develop a genre of long, meditative, Nature poems capable of carrying deep personal feeling and observation, but also with a unified dramatic structure and philosophy.'[29] *The Wanderer* both conforms and fails to conform to Thomson's paradigm, because Savage expresses this personal feeling and observation in a poetic voice so profoundly autobiographical and solipsistic that the poem's form seems to buckle under the pressure.

Composed in five cantos, Savage's poem is subtitled 'A Vision', and this ascription gives the reader a premonitory glimpse of its elusive, even hallucinogenic, qualities. The poet is a youthful Wanderer who stands 'Estrang'd, advent'rous on a foreign Land!'[30] The first Canto offers a potent sense of the protagonist's battle with the brutal climate he encounters in his self-imposed exile from the city and from civilization. He inhabits an alpine landscape in which mountainsides and ridges are battered by cataracts that plunge into gorges. The wintry conditions he endures are concentrated in the east wind, whose 'cutting Influence aches in ev'ry Pore'.[31]

It is tempting to imagine that, in spite of this setting, Savage is writing from the personal experience of being homeless on the bitter streets of London at night. The Wanderer's very nerves and fibres, he tells us, are 'Pinch'd, pierc'd, and torn, enflam'd, and unassuag'd, / They smart, and swell, and throb, and shoot enrag'd!'[32] The Wanderer retreats from this inhospitable environment and meets the Hermit, who leads him to his bleak mansion on the mountainside and there shows him his library, which is conveniently stocked with volumes of poetry by several of Savage's friends, including Hill, Pope and Thomson. 'Of Youth his Form!' the Wanderer comments on the Hermit, 'But why with Anguish bent? / Why pin'd with sallow Marks of Discontent?'[33] In the second Canto, the Hermit explains that, though born 'a wealthy, and illustrious Heir', his wife Olympia died three years ago, and in his grief he has forsworn everything he once owned: 'Mid cloistr'd, solitary Tombs I stray, / Despair, and Horror lead the cheerless Way!'[34] He leads the Wanderer around a grotto dedicated to Olympia's memory.

The third Canto, set at night, is an account of the Wanderer's return to the city on foot under the Hermit's guidance. In its opening lines the sun slopes into the sea and the moon climbs over the mountains, and the two solitaries soon find themselves in a sublime landscape beneath a sky blazing and bursting with comets. Here, in a double sense, is a sublimation of Savage's nightwalking in the city – the act of walking at night is at the same time relocated to a sublime landscape and idealized or ennobled. The journey is an arduous, tortuous one, and in the course of it, in a succession of dream-like images, they conjure up and survey 'How Men, and Spirits chace the Night away'.[35]

Eventually, the city heaves into view, and the Hermit demands that the Wanderer 'mark what *Deeds* adorn, or shame the Night!'[36] Predictably, these include the deeds of '*cruel Mothers*'.[37] At 'the interval 'twixt Night and Morn', the Hermit and the Wanderer stand on the threshold of the city:

> Now *Sleep* to *Fancy* parts with half his Pow'r,
> And broken Slumbers drag the restless Hour.
> The Murder'd seems alive, and ghastly glares,
> And in dire Dreams the conscious Murd'rer scares,
> Shews the yet-spouting Wound, th'ensanguin'd Floor,
> The Walls yet smoaking with the spatter'd Gore;
> Or shrieks to dozing Justice, and reveals
> The Deed, which fraudful Art from Day conceals;
> The Delve obscene, where no Suspicion pries;
> Where the disfigur'd Coarse unshrouded lies;
> The sure, the striking Proof, so strong maintain'd,
> Pale Guilt starts self-convicted, when arraign'd.[38]

In these unsettling lines, the poet evokes a moral universe that, like his lonely, half-lost protagonist, is suspended in a state of feverish equipoise not only between night and day, between the country and the city, but also between dream and reality. And the reader too feels as if caught in some restless, conscience-stricken condition between sleeping and waking.

It is impossible not to assume that Savage is here speaking in an autobiographical voice, albeit one that is thick with Macbeth's febrile, self-accusatory tones. The images of the murdered and the murderer – the former undead, the latter unalive – and of floors and walls at the scene of the crime that are slick with blood, are like a nightmarish collage of his guilty memories of the night of 20 November 1727. Savage thus portrays a landscape that, realized in concrete details of oneiric intensity, is as much mental as physical. Its most significant feature is 'the Delve obscene, where no Suspicion pries'. A 'delve' is a cavity in or under the ground, and here it stands both for the improvised grave in which 'the disfigur'd Coarse [or corpse] unshrouded lies', and for some recess of the poet's psyche that is resistant not only to suspicion but to the intrusions of conscience. The entire passage comprises a pre-Romantic example of what Alfred Tennyson, in *Maud* (1855), his great dramatic monologue of madness and murder, subsequently labelled a 'monodrama' – a form in which the speaker's psychology becomes the stage for a Jacobean revenge tragedy.

The Matin Bell interrupts the nightmarish spell of these lines, and the Hermit is promptly led back to his retreat by a vision of Olympia. But, as the first lines of Canto IV make clear, even though day breaks and the Wanderer gains the city, the night still lies heavy on his consciousness: 'Still o'er my Mind wild *Fancy* holds her Sway, / Still on strange, visionary Land I stray'.[39]

The fourth and fifth cantos of Savage's febrile poem, also organized around the ongoing dialogue between the Hermit and the Wanderer as they journey together through strange landscapes, are even more discontinuous and fragmentary than the previous ones. Here, the poet introduces additional characters – first, a Bard, an inspired and sapient poet who, as Tracy puts it, 'is one of "God's spies", an omniscient being able to see through walls in order to report on the doings of men';[40] second, a Beggar, 'a meagre Mendicant' in rags who, it transpires, is himself an incarnation of the Bard.[41] But, like the Hermit and the Wanderer themselves, into whose identities they seem to dissolve, these men too are in the end no more than emanations of Savage's ego. Full of hieroglyphic episodes, including one set in a prison, the poem's phantasmagoric and finally enigmatic power persists until its conclusion, when the Hermit abruptly soars into the sky, leaving the Wanderer to contemplate his vision.

Like Canto III, Canto V features a nightwalk that commences at dusk: 'Distinction now gives way; yet on we talk, / Full Darkness deep'ning o'er the formless Walk'.[42] This nightwalk offers a clue to the formal problems posed by the improvisatory, sometimes incoherent – it is tempting to say, rambling – structure of the poem. As Holmes perceptively observes, 'it is as if everything in Savage's life eventually came back, with a kind of fatality, to this grim nocturnal patrol, and the whole poem is encircled and contained in this movement, going relentlessly on and on'.[43] *The Wanderer* describes not so much a pilgrimage as a peregrination – a walk that is 'formless' but nonetheless pregnant with mystical meaning.

Savage dedicated *The Wanderer* to Lord Tyrconnel; but, from 1735, when the latter's tolerant attitude to the former finally reached its limit and their association was terminated, the poet spitefully scored his patron's name from any copies of the poem he happened to come across. From the mid 1730s, then, Savage once again energetically pursued a rake's progress to the gutter. By 1736 he was rapidly relapsing into the state of obscurity and poverty that had preceded his short-lived period of celebrity. It was in precisely this déclassé situation that Samuel Johnson, who arrived in London from Lichfield a year later, encountered him for the first time.

How to Take a Walk

As a young man, Johnson suffered from severe physical and psychological infirmities, and those who became acquainted with him were initially impressed more by the peculiarity of his deportment than by his indisputable intellectual brilliance. Lucy Porter, for example, who was Johnson's stepdaughter, informed Boswell that, when he first met her mother in 1734, 'his appearance was very forbidding: he was then lean and lank, so that his immense structure of bones was hideously striking to the eye, and the scars of the scrophula were deeply visible'. She testified that he also 'often had, seemingly, convulsive starts and odd gesticulations, which tended to excite at once surprise and ridicule'. Boswell claimed that Johnson had the 'struggling gait of one in fetters'.[44] Neither his physical disabilities nor his psychological inhibitions, however, prevented Johnson from being a prodigious walker.

Like Gay, Goldsmith and others among his Grub Street contemporaries, Johnson was a militant pedestrian. In an essay on spring published in the *Rambler* – a periodical that might have derived its title from *The Wanderer* – he noted that 'a French Author has advanced this seeming Paradox, that *very few Men know how to take a Walk*'.[45] What does it mean to know how to take a walk? It means to walk attentively, observantly and thoughtfully, actively delighting in one's surroundings. Thomas Traherne, a seventeenth-century poet generally classified alongside those whom Johnson contemptuously christened 'metaphysical', puts it in these terms:

> To *walk* is by a Thought to go;
> To mov in Spirit to and fro;
> To mind the Good we see;
> To taste the Sweet;
> Observing all the things we meet
> How choice and rich they be.

People who don't know how to walk, according to Traherne, are like 'dead puppets' or 'statues dead'. Their feet 'Like logs of wood, / Move up and down, and see no good'.[46] Johnson, in contrast to these automatons, knew how to take a walk, in both the country and the city. His essay on spring, which argues that 'he that enlarges his Curiosity after the Works of Nature, demonstrably multiplies the Inlets to Happiness', is a self-conscious demonstration of his ability, in Traherne's terms, to 'move in spirit to and fro' and 'mind the good' he sees.[47]

As a student at Pembroke College, Oxford, in the late 1720s, before he was forced to leave the university because of debt, Johnson and his friend Thomas Warton frequently took long evening walks in the surrounding countryside. Johnson's shoes were notoriously shoddy and worn at this time. Warton recalled that on one occasion someone thoughtfully deposited a new pair of shoes for him on the landing outside his rooms, but, in his pride, he immediately disposed of them.[48] (Savage too, incidentally, was distinguished by his dilapidated footwear – Johnson told Adam Smith that he had once seen him attired in the most fashionable of cloaks, 'while, at the same time, his naked toes were peeping through his shoes'.)[49] In 1729, during the university vacation, Johnson regularly walked from Lichfield to Birmingham and back, a distance of about thirty-two miles, in an attempt to obliterate his acute feelings of depression – his 'perpetual irritation, fretfulness, and impatience', his 'dejection, gloom, and despair, which made existence misery'.[50]

When Johnson first moved to London, in the company of his

former pupil David Garrick, in the spring of 1737, he explored the capital on foot, 'rambling from the village of Hampstead to the stairs of Southwark, from Chelsea in the west to Bow in the east' in pursuit of employment.[51] A married but impoverished schoolmaster, he lived at first in the house of a stay-maker in Exeter Street near the Strand. Johnson's Hogarthian sketch of 'the revolutions of a garret' in the *Rambler* provides an insight into his penurious existence at this time. In a letter to Mr Rambler, his fictional correspondent reports that, as a result of interrogating his landlady, he has 'collected the History and Antiquities of the several Garrets' in which he has resided. Previous occupants of his room include a tailor who didn't pay the rent; a young woman from the country who was dismissed for entertaining a male cousin from Cheapside; and a mysterious elderly man who, because he is a 'coiner', is forced to flee from the constable. But the predecessor in whom he is most interested is 'a short meager Man, in a tarnished Waistcoat'.[52]

For some time, this man remains an enigma:

> He was generally in Bed at Noon, but from Evening to Midnight he sometimes talked aloud with great Vehemence, sometimes stamped as in a Rage, sometimes threw down his Poker, then clattered his Chairs, then sat down in deep Thought, and again burst out into loud Vociferations; sometimes he would sigh as oppressed with Misery, and sometimes shake with convulsive Laughter.

Like Goldsmith, according to John Forster's biography, he 'keep[s] within his dirty, naked, unfurnished room', in part perhaps because 'his clothes had become too ragged to submit to daylight scrutiny'.[53] But, in a sign of this strange man's gentility, déclassé though he no doubt is, he is unfailingly polite to his landlady's family, even if he does often mutter a phrase in Greek as he ascends the stairs. No one knows his profession until, one day, a printer's boy enquires for him. He is an author. His landlady looks for decent reasons to dismiss him, but can find none – 'till one Night he convinced her by setting Fire to his Curtains, that it was not safe to have an Author for her inmate'.

Here is a glimpse of Johnson not as a magisterial sage presiding over the eighteenth-century metropolis, but as a tragicomic, almost Beckettian figure struggling to find a subsistence in Grub Street.

Misfortunes and Misconduct

After revisiting Lichfield for three months in the summer of 1737, Johnson returned to London, living first in Woodstock Street, near Hanover Square, then in Castle Street, off Cavendish Square. It was at this point, by the end of 1737, when Johnson was beginning to publish translations and poems in the *Gentleman's Magazine*, that he probably first met Savage. His visits to St John's Gate in Clerkenwell, where the printing-house of the *Gentleman's Magazine* was lodged above the old medieval arch, 'naturally brought Johnson and him together', Boswell admitted in slightly gloomy tones, for 'Savage's misfortunes and misconduct had reduced him to the lowest state of wretchedness as a writer for bread'.[54]

Soon after their initial encounter, Johnson testified to the strength of his feelings for Savage in 'Ad Ricardum Savage', a Latin epigraph printed by Edward Cave in the *Gentleman's Magazine* in 1738: 'May the human race cherish him, in whose breast burns the love of humankind.' Boswell professed himself mystified, if not a little mortified still, by his hero's affection for Savage. He refers to him in the *Life* as

> a man of whom it is difficult to speak impartially, without wondering that he was for some time the intimate companion of Johnson; for his character was marked by profligacy, insolence, and ingratitude: yet, as he undoubtedly had a warm and vigorous, though unregulated mind, had seen life in all its varieties, and been much in the company of the statesmen and wits of his time, he could communicate to Johnson an abundant supply of such materials as his philosophical curiosity most eagerly desired ...[55]

Johnson and Savage were united by their political commitments quite as much as by their intellectual or literary aspirations (or their palpable relish for gossip). 'What particularly attracted Johnson to

Savage, apart from his reputation as a poet', according to one biographer, 'was his rebelliousness and readiness to challenge authority, as well as his poverty and hostility towards a society that he felt had deprived him of wealth and fame.'[56] Boswell depoliticizes their relationship. In this respect he is a less effective guide to the impulses that shaped it than his immediate predecessor as a biographer, John Hawkins.

Hawkins, who published the first *Life of Samuel Johnson* in 1787, underlined Savage's superficial charm. He admitted that the older man's handsome appearance and courteous 'modes of salutation' appealed to Johnson, but contended that these attributes 'hid from his view th[e] baser qualities' of the older poet (which included both the facts that he was less intelligent than Johnson and that 'his vagrant life had made him acquainted with the town and its vices'). Hawkins also conceded that they held in common profound feelings of anger and resentment against the prime minister, Robert Walpole, and the entire Whig administration he led. 'They both with the same eye saw, or believed they saw', he wrote, 'that the then minister meditated the ruin of this country; that excise laws, standing armies, and penal statutes were the means by which he meant to effect it; and, at the risk of their liberty, they were bent to oppose his measures.'[57]

Johnson joined his Jacobite sympathies to Savage's in the mid-to-late 1730s. The Hanoverian accession of the early decades of the eighteenth century represented, as Peter Linebaugh notes, 'peace among the European imperialist powers, slavery for Africa and America and repression at home'.[58] Johnson and Savage, who regarded themselves as 'patriots' militantly opposed to the monarchy, which was tainted with German associations, together inveighed against both the colonial oppression and the domestic repression sponsored by Walpole's regime.

In the *Life of Mr Richard Savage*, Johnson emphasized that his subject 'was very far from approving the conduct of Sir Robert Walpole, and in conversation mentioned him sometimes with acrimony, and generally with contempt'; and, furthermore, that 'he was one of those who were always zealous in their assertions of the justice of the late opposition, jealous of the rights of the people, and alarmed by the long-continued triumph of the court'. (Because of these sentiments, Johnson continued to feel distressed that, under Tyrconnel's patronage, Savage had published a panegyric in praise of the prime minister, 'who was, in his opinion, an enemy to liberty, and an oppressor of his country'.)[59]

Johnson also recorded in admiration his friend's anti-imperialist opinions. Savage had affirmed these to forceful effect in a poem he published in 1737, 'Of Public Spirit in Regard to Public Works'. Here, the goddess Public Spirit, addressing the colonizers, attacks both the East Indian trade in commodities and, with particular vehemence, the West African trade in slaves:

> 'Why must I *Afric*'s sable Children see
> 'Vended for Slaves, though form'd by Nature free,
> 'The nameless Tortures cruel Minds invent,
> 'Those to subject, whom Nature equal meant?'[60]

'Savage has not forgotten', Johnson wrote, as if conjuring his spirit, 'to censure those crimes which have been generally committed by the discoverers of new regions, and to expose the enormous wickedness of making war upon barbarous nations because they cannot resist, and of invading countries because they are fruitful.'[61] This critique of colonialism, like Savage's condemnation of the bloody criminal code of the early eighteenth century, had a determinate effect on the development of Johnson's politics.

These views might in turn have contributed to the deepening of Johnson's differences with his wife Elizabeth. He had married 'Tetty', the widow of a Birmingham textile dealer – a blowsy, maternal woman who was two decades older than Johnson – in 1735. She joined him in their cramped but comparatively fashionable accommodation at Castle Street in the winter of 1737.

No doubt their connubial relations were for a number of reasons less than idyllic during the years in which he attempted to establish a literary reputation in London. Walter Jackson Bate has, for example, speculated that the guilt Johnson felt about living off Tetty's fortune – indeed, in his failed efforts to set up a school in Lichfield, squandering it – created an emotional distance between them, leading him 'to estrange himself, and, with something of self-punishment as well as pride, to live deliberately as a kind of adult waif'.[62] But, as Bate's colourful reference to Johnson living like an 'adult waif' suggests, the nightwalking Savage is a protagonist, or antagonist, in most accounts of their marriage at this time. Certainly, although it is difficult to disentangle the relationship of cause and effect, Johnson became intimate with Savage at the precise time he became estranged from Tetty.

Hawkins, who had been acquainted with Johnson since the mid 1740s, insisted that Savage's malign moral example 'was contagious, and tended to confirm Johnson in his indolence and those other evil habits which it was the labour of his life to conquer'. He blamed the 'temporary separation' of Johnson and Tetty on what he delicately described as an 'indifference in the discharge' of his domestic responsibilities arising from the friends' 'nocturnal excursions'.[63] Johnson himself, in the *Life*, makes a sly suggestion that because Savage was 'always accustomed to an irregular manner of life he could not confine himself to any stated hours, or pay any regard to the rules of a family'.[64]

A recent biographer, David Nokes, corroborates the idea that the two men used to stay up all night in Castle Street drinking wine, and that, in consequence, Tetty 'found Johnson's new acquaintance rather wearing … Soon, rather than discompose his wife's slumbers, Johnson began embarking with Savage on night-time rambles through the squares and alleyways of London, discoursing volubly all the while.'[65]

Casual Wanderers

Whatever the reason for Johnson's withdrawal from Tetty, it seems that he started resorting to lodgings in or close to Fleet Street by the winter of 1738, in addition to their residence in Castle Street. It is at about the same time that he began to engage in his 'midnight rambles' with Savage, in Hawkins's formulation. 'They had both felt the pangs of poverty and the want of patronage', according to him, and 'they seemed both to agree in the vulgar opinion, that the world is divided into two classes, of men of merit without riches, and men of wealth without merit'. It was in walking and talking in the streets of the city at night that they gave vent to these sentiments, consolidating their sense of being social and political outsiders:

> Johnson has told me, that whole nights have been spent by him and Savage in conversations of this kind, not under the hospitable roof of a tavern, where warmth might have invigorated their spirits, and wine dispelled their care; but in a perambulation round the squares of Westminster, St James's in particular, when all the money they could both raise was less than sufficient to purchase for them the shelter and sordid comforts of a night cellar.[66]

Three or four years later, Boswell confirmed that Johnson and Savage 'were sometimes in such extreme indigence, that they could not pay for a lodging; so that they have wandered together whole nights in the streets'. He then added in the succeeding sentence an allusion to 'these almost incredible scenes of distress' that was slightly more pointed. Boswell did not doubt Johnson's description of joining his disreputable friend in these nightwalks, but it is possible he did not believe that Johnson was impoverished enough to have been forced to sleep rough (he confines additional 'proof of Johnson's extreme indigence' to a distinctly ambiguous anecdote included in the book's footnotes).[67] Can Johnson really have been indigent? Thomas Kaminksi has argued convincingly that, even if Johnson's income was limited at this time, he did not suffer from 'enduring poverty', for 'there can be no doubt that he earned a competence'. Johnson and Savage wandered the streets, he concludes, 'not because they lacked the means to procure a room, but because they cherished one another's company more than sleep'.[68]

Holmes speculates that 'the episode of their night-walks exists as a kind of composite memory rather than as a specific event which anyone witnessed'. It seems probable, as Johnson's earliest biographers imply, that he and Savage rambled throughout the night, and perhaps slept rough, on a number of occasions. But contemporary accounts of this habit, by his friends Arthur Murphy and Joshua

Reynolds as well as by Boswell and Hawkins, all of whom relied on Johnson's own testimony, tended to concentrate on an archetypal night spent circumambulating St James's Square. This tableau is central to the Grub Street legend of the nightwalks. Here is Boswell again:

> He told Sir Joshua Reynolds, that one night in particular, when Savage and he walked round St James's-square for want of a lodging, they were not at all depressed by their situation; but in high spirits, and brimful of patriotism, traversed the square for several hours, inveighed against the [prime] minister, and 'resolved they would *stand by their country*.'[69]

St James's Square, built from the 1670s, was the most fashionable address in London. Simple, spacious and grand, it was inhabited by some of the richest and most influential aristocrats in the land, largely because of its proximity to St James's Palace. It is here, according to legend, at the heart of the royalist city, that Johnson and Savage, in the role of political seditionaries, chose to conduct their nightwalks. In Murphy's version, which is set in Grosvenor Square, they spent the night 'reforming the world, dethroning princes, establishing new forms of government, and giving laws to the several states of Europe' – at least in conversation. In either location, 'they were walking in enemy territory, the land to be conquered', as Holmes writes in his richly evocative prose, 'and they came like spies in the night, their very presence a provocation'.[70]

What of Johnson's own chronicle of these nightwalks? The *Life of Mr Richard Savage* offer a strangely refracted image of them, for in its pages Johnson attests in some detail to his friend's homelessness but at no point mentions the fact that, perhaps over several months in 1738, he was his companion in the streets at night. In a description of Savage's living conditions during the period in which he was closest to him, Johnson writes:

> He lodged as much by accident as he dined, and passed the night sometimes in mean houses, which are set open at night to any casual wanderers, sometimes in cellars, among the riot and filth of the meanest and most profligate of the rabble; and sometimes, when he had not money to

> support even the expenses of these receptacles, walked about the streets till he was weary, and lay down in the summer upon a bulk, or in the winter, with his associates in poverty, among the ashes of a glass-house.[71]

Savage's 'associates in poverty', whom Johnson is careful to distinguish from 'the meanest and most profligate of the rabble', presumably included the Black Guard. As Daniel Defoe's Colonel Jack explained, these vagabond children repaired to London's glass factories, which were dotted throughout the East End, because 'the arches where they neal the bottles after they are made' (that is, toughen them by heating and then cooling them) contained heaps of ashes, so that these 'Caveties in the Brick-work' were as 'warm as the Dressing-room of a *Bagnio*'.[72] If Johnson himself was not precisely one of Savage's associates in poverty, then it seems likely that, during their nightwalks together, before they both retreated to the former's lodgings near Fleet Street, the latter pointed out the bulks, cellars and glass-houses in which he had been forced to sleep.

In 'completely withdraw[ing] himself from the story', Holmes writes, Johnson 'does something extraordinary'. I am not convinced of this. If Johnson had insisted that he himself possessed first-hand experience of Savage's habits in the late 1730s, he might have rendered his account of these years more authoritative, but he might also have rendered the biography in its entirety less persuasive. In the *Life*, Johnson set out to communicate a sense of what he characterizes at one point as the poet's 'rambling manner of life'.[73] To make this impression dependent on his personal testimony during one particular period would be to risk undermining the illusion of intimacy that he cultivates with such subtlety throughout the volume.

Holmes is certainly correct to argue that, in the *Life*, 'Savage 'is essentially, and some might say symbolically, alone'; and that, in underlining his outcast identity, in constructing the poet as one who has 'no place, no social position, no influence on affairs, and literally no home', Johnson 'is in effect making a Romantic claim for him'. In Johnson's mythopoeic biography, Savage is that privileged figure identified by Raymond Williams in his outline of the 'perception of the new qualities of the modern city': 'a man walking, as if alone, in its streets'[74] – or, more precisely, in its streets at night. Johnson must suppress the sociable nature of the night-walks he took with Savage in order to preside over the legendary birth of the nightwalker as an archetypal bohemian outsider.

Wretched Vagrant

Like the *Life of Mr Richard Savage*, Johnson's 'London: A Poem' (1738), his impassioned 'Imitation of the Third Satire of Juvenal', makes a significant contribution to this myth. It too effectively invents or reinvents Savage as a proto-Romantic hero. I side with those critics and biographers who have argued that Thales, its protagonist, 'spurn'd as a beggar, dreaded as a spy', is based on Savage. But even if this is not the case, its portrait of an embittered, prophetic poet who, retiring or retreating into the countryside, denounces the 'degen'rate' culture of the imperial metropolis, both echoes passages of *The Wanderer* and, more generally, is infused with Savage's cantankerous, rebellious spirit.

Johnson later apparently regretted the pastoralist impulse behind 'London'; but it is an attack not so much on the city itself as on those in power who have transformed it into a festering repository of corrupt practices, especially in so far as these exploit or further depress the poor (including impoverished poets).[75] 'All crimes are safe, but hated poverty', complains Thales, 'This, only this, the rigid law pursues, / This, only this, provokes the snarling muse.' 'Quick let us rise', he cries in response to this lamentable situation, 'And bear oppression's insolence no more.' For it is not just that, in contrast to the 'laureat tribe', which is adept at producing its commodities for the marketplace, this poet is impoverished; it is that his genius is in consequence ignored:

> This mournful truth is ev'ry where confess'd,
> SLOW RISES WORTH, BY POVERTY DEPRESS'D;
> But here more slow, where all are slaves to gold,
> Where looks are merchandise, and smiles are sold.[76]

Five or so years later, in the *Life*, Johnson comments in more restrained but equally feeling tones that 'the great hardships of poverty were to Savage not the want of lodging or food, but the neglect and contempt which it drew upon him'.[77]

In 'London', Johnson thus identifies the poet as the victim of a corrupt and hypocritical society: 'Then thro' the world a wretched vagrant roam, / For where can starving merit find a home?' Like Savage, and like Pattison before him, he is homeless and itinerant. But if for this reason Savage is implicitly the poem's hero, in another disguise he is perhaps its villain. In the last fifty lines of the poem, Johnson includes a denunciation of London at night that blames its barbarous street-life on arrogant, violent aristocrats who bear more than a passing resemblance to his capricious and unpredictable friend.

Here, Johnson establishes a moral contrast between the 'evening walk' taken in the countryside, on which 'security shall smile', and the nightwalk taken in the city, which is fraught with danger:

> Prepare for death, if here at night you roam,
> And sign your will before you sup from home.
> Some fiery fop, with new commission vain,
> Who sleeps on brambles till he kills his man;
> Some frolic drunkard, reeling from a feast,
> Provokes a broil, and stabs you for a jest.
> Yet ev'n these heroes, mischievously gay,
> Lords of the street, and terrors of the way;
> Flush'd as they are with folly, youth, and wine,
> Their prudent insults to the poor confine;
> Afar they mark the flambeau's bright approach,
> And shun the shining train, and golden coach.[78]

The minatory tone of these lines, which grimly refuse to find amusement in the scenes they conjure up, in contrast to so many indulgent descriptions of the antics of the upper classes, is chilling. The danger to those who 'roam' at night in London – the verb implies purposeless movement across a considerable amount of space – lies not in the poor or vagrant but in the rich and decadent.

It lies in the 'lords of the street', whom the poet despises. These dissolute aristocrats, like the 'sons of Belial' censured by Milton in *Paradise Lost*, or perhaps even the Mohocks, persecute the impoverished and the unprotected on the streets at night, then scatter strategically as soon as a rich family's carriage appears at the end of the road. But these brutal, vicious bacchanalians also conjure up memories of Savage and his confederates on the night in 1727 when, flushed with folly, youth and wine, they murdered James Sinclair, an 'idle Person', in Robinson's coffee-house.[79]

It is possible that Johnson, who is himself one of those who roam at night, underlines the connection with his companion when, in the succeeding lines, he informs the reader that, even when 'your doors you close', you are still not safe in London at night:

> Cruel with guilt, and daring with despair,
> The midnight murd'rer bursts the faithless bar;
> Invades the sacred hour of silent rest,
> And leaves, unseen, a dagger in your breast.[80]

Although neither cruel with guilt, exactly, nor daring with despair, Savage was nonetheless a midnight murderer. He did not invade the sacred hour of silent rest, precisely, or murder sleep, as Shakespeare puts it, but he irrupted into a private room and wounded two people with a sword, one of them fatally. In 'London', then, Johnson seems secretly to admit to an ambiguous attitude to Savage and his uses of the night. Alongside the image of him as a vagrant poet, he represents him more covertly, perhaps according to his reputation, as a 'lord of the street' too. If he identifies with the déclassé poet, he anathematizes the pseudo-aristocrat.

The concluding paragraphs of the *Life*, in spite of Johnson's fierce and sometimes moving loyalty to Savage, also betray an ambivalent attitude. Johnson defends his friend's celebrated inability to keep good hours, pointing out that his refusal to retire for the night 'was not the defect of his judgment, but of his fortune; when he left his company, he was frequently to spend the remaining part of the night in the street ...' But, more censoriously, he adds that 'an irregular and dissipated life had made him the slave of every passion that happened to be excited by the presence of its object, and that slavery to his passions reciprocally produced a life irregular and dissipated'.[81]

Nocturnal Intrusions

'Skulking in obscure parts of the town, of which he was no stranger to the remotest corners', Savage plunged into deeper and deeper debt in the late 1730s; and, in 1739, Johnson and some of the poet's other remaining friends, including Pope and Thomson, successfully raised a subscription for him and persuaded him, after an interval spent in the Fleet Prison, where he briefly eluded his creditors, to exile himself to Wales.[82]

Savage's benefactors intended him to move there permanently, but he evidently pictured himself returning to the capital in triumph after briefly acting out a pastoralist fantasy. It is as if he was addicted to London, and in particular its nightlife.[83] He left London in July 1739 – 'having taken leave with great tenderness of his friends', Johnson writes in the *Life*'s single confession to his autobiographical presence, 'and parted from the author of this narrative with tears in his eyes'. 'Deprived of Savage's comforting and exhilarating company', according to Christopher Hibbert, 'Johnson became more and more depressed.'[84] Savage, in the meantime, led a restless, half-settled existence in and around Swansea, before resurfacing in Bristol in 1741 or 1742.

Here, he resumed the urban habits that had got him into trouble in London, running up debts, for instance, and alienating acquaintances with his 'nocturnal intrusions' (Johnson emphasizes his 'practice of prolonging his visits to unseasonable hours, and disconcerting all the families into which he was admitted'). He became more and more derelict, suffering 'the utmost extremities of poverty' and keeping antisocial hours ('he could neither be persuaded to go to bed in the night, nor to rise in the day').[85] He kept to this routine partly because, as Holmes explains, bailiffs were not allowed to arrest people for debt between sunset and sunrise: 'Night thus became the only time Savage could venture out from his hiding-place, which was a back-street tavern called the White Lion.'[86] But he was eventually arrested for his debt to a coffee-house, and in consequence confined to Bristol's Newgate Prison. He died there, in his mid forties, in July 1743.

Savage was at the same time eighteenth-century Grub Street's most aristocratic and most abject representative. Both as an elitist and as a social outcast, he was committed to rejecting and outraging the emergent values of the bourgeoisie. He was a member of the lumpen aristocracy, so to speak. In this respect, he was satanic – for it is characteristic of 'the dual aspect of Satan', as Walter Benjamin writes in relation to Baudelaire, that 'Satan spoke not only for the upper crust but for the lower classes as well'.[87]

Savage's entire life constituted a refusal of middle-class respectability, at least according to Johnson. In the *Life* of Savage, Johnson cites 'a poem written by him in his youth' in which 'he declares his contempt of the contracted views and narrow prospects of the middle state of life, and declares his resolution either to tower like a cedar, or be trampled like the shrub'.[88] In fact, this poem – presumably 'A Poem, Sacred to the Glorious Memory of Our Late Most Gracious Sovereign Lord King George' (1727) – contains no such unqualified declaration of defiance or contempt: 'Wealth, Want, Rank, Power, here each alike partakes, / As the shrub bends, the lofty Cedar shakes', is the couplet Johnson must be recollecting.[89] The poem is in truth a sycophantic appeal for patronage in the style of Iscariot Hackney. Savage's politics were as slippery as his daily life was precarious.

It is extremely revealing that Johnson – perhaps responding to Savage's retrospective attempts to makes his poetry seem more radical than it was – idealizes him as a fugitive and rebel disdainful of the 'middle state of life'. Rogers has suggested that Johnson depicts Savage, prior to his departure for Wales, in terms that, because they emphasize his 'radical innocence', anticipate the 'modern existentialist hero … Savage is presented pretty well as the first Outsider'.[90] Johnson's account of Savage's noctivagant activities in London is of crucial importance to the emergent myth of the bohemian poet in the eighteenth century.

PART THREE

8.

Night on the Lengthening Road

Wordsworth, Clare and Romantic Vagrancy

A Shabby-Looking Pedestrian

On his trip to England in 1782, the German clergyman and poet Karl Philipp Moritz strode out of London with a copy of Milton's poems in one pocket and a change of clothing in the other. He was a 'shabby-looking pedestrian without a knapsack', as a late nineteenth-century editor of his English journals put it.[1]

England, Moritz pointedly noted in these journals, is a 'land of carriages and horses'. In a tone of apparent bemusement, he commented that 'a traveller on foot in this country seems to be considered as a sort of wild man, or an out-of-the-way-being, who is stared at, pitied, suspected, and shunned by every body that meets him'. One night, returning from the banks of the Thames at Windsor after 'a long walk by moon-light', he recorded being 'roughly accosted' by a maid in an inn, who openly sneered at him. A pedestrian, Moritz confirmed with a certain satisfaction, 'is sure to be looked upon, and considered as either a beggar, or a vagabond, or some necessitous wretch, which is a character not much more popular than that of a rogue'.[2]

The examples of Savage, Johnson and Goldsmith, among other 'philosophic vagabonds' of the mid eighteenth century, are evidence that, some time before the rise of a Romantic ideology, going on foot in England was the privilege of déclassé poets as well as the inescapable prerogative of plebeians. The closing decades of the eighteenth century nonetheless signalled a shift in the semiotics of walking, most clearly in a rural context, as the example of Moritz suggests. It is not much of an over-statement to claim that, before this time, there were no pedestrians – there were simply people who travelled on foot. It was during the Romantic period that, no longer merely a means to an end, walking became an end in itself.

The adjective 'pedestrian', which originally referred, metaphorically, to prosaic or uninspired writing, only acquired its more literal meaning of 'something conducted or performed on foot' in the 1740s. As a noun, moreover, 'pedestrian' came to mean a person who travels on foot – as opposed to on a horse or in a vehicle – as late as the third quarter of the eighteenth century. The OED's first example is *The Adventures of an Actor* (1770), where the individual in question, returning to London, 'set out in the character of a Pedestrian, his finances not allowing any other mode of travelling'. Initially, as this indicates, there was a satirical quality to the use of the noun 'pedestrian'. Pedestrians are other people. Going on foot, as a means of travelling from one place to another, denoted poverty and even hinted at depravity. The taint of moral turpitude adhered to pedestrians of all kinds, especially at night.

The ethics and politics of pedestrianism in the late eighteenth and early nineteenth centuries, and in particular the Romantic walker's identification with the figure of the vagrant, play a crucial part in the ongoing history of nightwalking as a dissident activity. The act of walking, for the Romantics, inscribed a coded rebellion against the culture of agrarian and industrial capitalism onto both the material surfaces of city and countryside – the streets, the roads, the footpaths – and their social relations. The act of nightwalking, moreover, carved out dark spaces in the landscape, cityscape and psyche that promised an escape from the penetrating glare of the Enlightenment.

Alone and on Foot

In the late eighteenth and early nineteenth centuries, pedestrianism assumed the form of an intellectual, political, even spiritual vocation. To travel long distances on foot through towns and cities and through the countryside was to invoke the spirit of vagrancy.

From the 1790s – more precisely, in the aftermath of the French Revolution – it was a utopian affirmation of freedom that, in spite of its apparent individualism, implied a collective affiliation of some kind. When William Wordsworth and his friend Robert Jones, both students at Cambridge University, conducted their journey across France to the Swiss Alps in 1790, they were deliberately rebuking the culture of respectability in which they had been conditioned back at home. In his *Descriptive Sketches* of this journey, published in 1793, Wordsworth flaunted the 'great difference between two companions lolling in a post chaise', as Thomas Gray and Horace Walpole had done on their Grand Tour in the late 1730s and early 1740s, 'and two travellers plodding slowly along the road, side by side, each with his little knapsack of necessaries upon his shoulders'.[3] As Rebecca Solnit emphasizes, 'to go on foot and to make Switzerland, rather than Italy, the destination of the trip expressed a radical shift in priorities, away from art and aristocracy toward nature and democracy'.[4]

Romantics like Samuel Taylor Coleridge and Dorothy and William Wordsworth were rural bohemians whose commitment to walking was principled as well as practical. They were determined to find in nature a set of simple values that constituted an alternative to the civilization from which, for moral, social and existential reasons, they felt alienated. And they were determined, too, to encounter on the roads of the countryside the most ordinary, unadorned representatives of humanity. 'The lonely roads / Were schools to me', Wordsworth wrote, 'in which I daily read / With most delight the passions of mankind.'[5] Human nature, like nature itself, was to be experienced in its most pristine and least civilized form, in the shape of uneducated itinerants. Walking thus acquired both an ethical and a philosophical dimension.

Jean-Jacques Rousseau, who praised walking as an exemplary instance of humanity's redemptive, pre-social relationship to nature, was the high priest of this Romantic pedestrianism. His career as a pedestrian commenced in 1728 when, as a fifteen-year-old, locked out of his native city, Geneva, because he returned to its gates after the ringing of the curfew, he set off on foot into a self-imposed exile that effectively lasted his entire lifetime. Thereafter, in Frédéric Gros's formulation, he 'conceived the insane plan to identify – in himself, *homo viator*, walking man – the natural man, one not disfigured by culture, education, art'.[6]

Rousseau's autobiographical reflections effectively determined the Romantic paradigm of the pedestrian. In his *Reveries of the Solitary Walker* (1782), first published four years after he died, the elderly, isolated philosopher carefully recorded his walks and 'the reveries that occupy them'. These were the moments, he mused, 'when I give free rein to my thoughts and let my ideas follow their natural course, unrestricted and unconfined'.[7] Walking in solitude and meditating is thus a humanistic matter – one that entails what Michel Foucault, invoking a Socratic tradition, calls in a different context the 'care of the self'.[8]

In the *Confessions* (1782), published the same year as the *Reveries*, Rousseau recalled his pursuit of Madame de Warens in the early 1730s, and included this paean to pedestrian travel:

> I have never thought so much, existed so much, lived so much, been so much myself, if I may venture to use the phrase, as in the journeys which I have made alone and on foot. There is something in walking which animates and enlivens my ideas. I can scarcely think when I remain still;

> my body must be in motion to make my mind active. The sight of the country, a succession of pleasant views, the open air, a good appetite, the sound health which walking gives me, the free life of the inns, the absence of all that makes me conscious of my dependent position, of all that reminds me of my condition – all this sets my soul free, gives me greater boldness of thought, throws me, so to speak, into the immensity of things, so that I can combine, select, and appropriate them at my pleasure, without fear or restraint.[9]

To ramble across the countryside is to disembarrass oneself of the social and mental constraints with which one is encumbered by civilization.

At night, this ritual gains an almost religious intensity. At one point in the *Confessions*, after recalling his homeless existence in Lyons as a youth, he describes taking a walk by a nearby river one evening after an extremely hot day:

> The night was calm, without a breath of wind; the air was fresh, without being cold; the sun, having gone down, had left in the sky red vapours, the reflection of which cast a rose-red tint upon the water; the trees on the terraces were full of nightingales answering one another. I walked on in a kind of ecstasy, abandoning my heart and senses to the enjoyment of all, only regretting, with a sigh, that I was obliged to enjoy it alone. Absorbed in my delightful reverie, I continued my walk late into the night, without noticing that I was tired.[10]

The epiphanic quality of this experience, which combines an escape from the self and an immersion in it, cannot be dissociated from Rousseau's solitude in the night. He might have half-longed for a companion with whom to share his delight in the night, and the derangement of his senses, but if he hadn't been alone he couldn't have 'walked around in a kind of ecstasy' with the same kind of abandonment and excitement. *Dans la nuit*, as Rimbaud might have put it, *je est un autre*.

Restless Magic

Wordsworth, more than any of his English contemporaries, was a tireless, if not compulsive, walker: 'I would walk alone', he insists in *The Prelude* (1805), 'In storm and tempest, or in starlight nights / Beneath the quiet heavens.'[11]

According to Thomas De Quincey's calculations, Wordsworth's legs, which were serviceable 'beyond the average standard of human requisition', if also a little inelegant, paced in total some '175 to 180,000 English miles'.[12] The relentless iambic rhythms of his poetry are inseparable from this ceaseless pedestrian motion, and from his habit not simply of taking walks but of composing his poems both on the terraces of his homes in the Lake District and on the surrounding roads. In a memorable formulation, Solnit has claimed that, for Wordsworth, walking was 'a mode not of travelling but of being'.[13]

In 'An Evening Walk' (1793), his first published poem, the young Wordsworth, heavily influenced by Rousseau, describes the 'religious awe' with which, as he stands beside a lake, the fading light 'blends with the solemn colouring of the night' while 'the half seen form of Twilight roams astray'. This 'religious awe' is really his own. Lingering a little longer, and striking a rather self-consciously literary attitude to the landscape, the poet also describes the 'dawning moonlight's hoary gleams' as they illuminate the surface of the lake with 'long streaks of fairy light' amid the gloom. ''Tis restless magic all; at once the bright / Breaks on the shade, the shade upon the light', he exclaims in reverential tones; 'Fair Spirits are abroad …'[14]

The Prelude, Wordsworth's greatest poem, is pleated throughout with important, if not epiphanic, incidents that take place at night when he is on foot. Indeed, its narrative of the poet's intellectual and spiritual development is effectively framed by accounts of formative experiences involving nocturnal walking. The poem's first set-piece description, in Book I, evokes the poet's memories of exploring the fells, the hills and mountains, as a school-child after dark; and its final set-piece description, in the opening sections of Book XIII, the 'Conclusion', reconstructs the ascent of Snowdon that he and Jones, his companion on the walking tour of France, made on a summer night in 1791.

'Fair seed-time had my soul, and I grew up / Fostered alike by beauty and by fear', Wordsworth announces in Book I of *The Prelude*.[15] Beauty and fear, the crucial components of the Burkean sublime, structure the dialectic through which his childhood uncoils. He continues:

> Well I call to mind
> ('Twas at an early age, ere I had seen
> Nine summers) when upon the mountain slope
> The frost, and breath of frosty wind, had snapped
> The last autumnal crocus, 'twas my joy
> To wander half the night among the cliffs
> And the smooth hollows where the woodcocks ran,
> Along the open turf. In thought and wish
> That time, my shoulder all with springes hung,
> I was a fell destroyer. On the heights
> Scudding away from snare to snare, I plied
> My anxious visitation, hurrying on,
> Still hurrying, hurrying onward; – moon and stars
> Were shining o'er my head. I was alone,
> And seemed to be a trouble to the peace
> That was among them.[16]

The child plunges freely across the strange nocturnal landscape – and ranges freely through his expanding imagination – as it unfurls before him with an almost vertiginous sense of urgency.

But, hurrying, hurrying, hurrying amid the sublime calm of these mysterious, moonlit mountains at night, he is susceptible to an obscure, feverish guilt. This is in part because he is a 'plunderer', engaged in acts of poaching[17] – and, to compound this crime, in moral if not legal terms, of poaching from poachers. For sometimes 'in these night wanderings', as he confesses, 'a strong desire / O'erpowered my better reason, and the bird / Which was the captive of another's toils / Became my prey'.[18] But he also feels guilt for some deeper, more existential reason. This is because he is secretly conscious that he is violating the serene calm of this nocturnal landscape, which implicitly demands the kind of contemplative attitude that, as an adult, he will self-consciously adopt towards the natural environment. In this scene, set at a time when others are confined at home, perhaps asleep, he is in some fundamental sense an interloper. The fell destroyer, the cruel or ruthless hunter he fantasizes he is, is also a destroyer of the fells.

So when he steals a creature from someone else's snare, and hears 'among the solitary hills / Low breathings coming after me, and sounds / Of undistinguishable motion, steps / Almost as silent as the turf they trod'[19] – when he hears these noises, he is listening to his conscience as much as to the systole and diastole of the land itself. He describes a similar sensation in Book IV, where he recalls an occasion on which, during a walk at dusk, as the 'mountain heights were slowly overspread / With darkness', he sat down in a wood to think, and heard 'a breath-like sound, / A respiration short and quick', which he repeatedly mistakes for the panting of a dog.[20] The landscape is haunted, but principally because his psyche is haunted too.

The *Prelude*'s climactic incident, in Book XIII, the occasion of some of Wordsworth's most self-consciously profound reflections, is also set at night. The poet recounts that, in order to be in time to see the sunrise, the friends ascended Snowdon 'at the dead of night' in a dense mist, and that after about an hour's climbing, 'instantly a light upon the turf / Fell like a flash'.[21] It is not sunlight but moonlight: 'The Moon stood naked in the heavens …'.[22] As distinct from sunlight, moonlight unifies the different components of the landscape – the clouds, the mountains, the water. Everything seems to be made from the same monochromatic substance.

The poet's night-vision is in this sense an intimation of divine vision, for it apprehends the transcendental unity of all things. This is the poem's climactic instance of the sublime, and the meditation it prompts about 'that night' is decisive for Wordsworth's conviction that it is possible, through the mediation of nature, to create a communion between the inner life of the individual and the 'invisible world'.[23] The moonlit landscape spread out beneath the mountain, he affirms:

> appeared to me
> The perfect image of a mighty mind,
> Of one that feeds upon infinity,
> That is exalted by an underpresence,
> The sense of God, or whatso'oer is dim
> Or vast in its own being.[24]

Moonlight, in this scene, becomes a symbol for the unifying power of the poetic imagination.

Nightwalking of the kind practised by Wordsworth was in this respect an experiment in the powers of the imagination; or, as he brilliantly put it in *The Prelude*, of 'a mind beset / With images, and haunted by itself'.[25] It patrolled the nightside of the Enlightenment intellect.

In Search of the Natural

A reconception of walking, then, took place in the European cultural imagination from the end of the eighteenth century. Pedestrian travel, in the everyday conditions of industrializing society, became a means of reconnecting at once with inner and with outer nature. And walking at night, in particular, served to re-enchant the alienated individual's relationship to the world.

In an irony that is characteristic of Romantic ideology, however, going on foot could only be celebrated as a natural activity because it had in some irreversible sense already become a cultural activity, perhaps even an unnatural one. It was because it was no longer a spontaneous activity that the Romantics, who registered this loss with acute sensitivity, felt committed to glorifying it as a spontaneous activity. Pedestrianism is in reality a culturally mediated pursuit that cannot function as some primal, pre-social activity.

William Hazlitt's 'On Going a Journey' (1822), the sprightliest manifesto for Rousseauian walking and thinking published in England in this period, offers an illustration of this irony. Perhaps the finest essayist of the Romantic era, Hazlitt declares at the outset, with characteristic vitality, that the 'the soul of a journey is liberty, perfect liberty, to think, feel, do just as one pleases'. He emphasizes that he likes to leave the city and travel about on foot because it affords him 'a little breathing-space to muse on indifferent matters'. 'We go a journey chiefly to be free of all impediments and of all inconveniences; to leave ourselves behind, much more to get rid of others …'[26]

In Rousseauian fashion, then, it is a question of stripping off one's cultural identity and discarding it – as if it were a stuffy suit of city clothes – in order to expose one's natural, primitive self. 'I laugh, I run, I leap, I sing for joy', Hazlitt writes in one irresistible orientalist effusion; 'I plunge into my past being and revel there, as the sun-burnt Indian plunges into the wave that wafts him to his native shore.'[27] To traverse an open space on foot is to create the conditions for an act of individual liberation. For Hazlitt, walking is a solitary, reflective and at the same time inspiriting activity in which a sense of self can be not only cultivated but set free.

But, as Hazlitt's elaborate rhetorical strategies suggest, to make philosophical claims for the importance of walking in the Romantic period was in effect to confess that this apparently innocent activity had become a fatally artificial, self-conscious one. Pedestrianism's affirmation of the natural was, in a self-cancelling gesture, unnatural. This was the contradiction that the Romantic walker incarnated or enacted. The odd, ill-fitting artificiality of Wordsworth's statement, in the opening line of one of his most famous poems, that he 'wandered lonely as a cloud' is a good indication of this; for it is a surreptitious admission that it is impossible to recapture precisely the instinctive freedom of movement that, in an image of all-too-artful artlessness, the poet strives or strains to evoke.

Percy Bysshe Shelley's 'To a Skylark' (1820), an ode published some thirteen years after Wordsworth's poem, is a more sophisticated, self-reflexive treatment of a comparable Romantic crisis. 'Hail to Thee, blithe Spirit!' it begins, 'Bird thou never wert …'[28] This negation of what might be called, in Marx's terms, the bird's 'species being' is so blunt, in spite of the apostrophe of the first line, that it still shocks the reader. The skylark, Shelley announces, is not a bird, because it is an aesthetic construct. It is always-already an aesthetic construct. So is the walker. An ode to the pedestrian comparable to Shelley's almost post-Romantic poem about the skylark might read: 'Hail to thee, free spirit! / Walker thou never wert …'

The concept of the pedestrian thus implied an aestheticized and unspontaneous relationship to nature that was inescapably post-lapsarian. In this respect, it was like the slightly older concept of the landscape, which in the eighteenth century signified not the countryside itself but a painting or portion of rural scenery framed for the purposes of aesthetic consumption. 'The space of the countryside, as contemplated by the walker in search of the natural, was the outcome of a first violation of nature', Henri Lefebvre observes.[29] In more concrete terms, both the landscape and the pedestrian who inhabited it were indirect products of agrarian capitalism and its singular regime of accumulation by dispossession, which pressed relentlessly for the engrossment of land and the amalgamation of farms.

By the late eighteenth century, farming had systematically transformed the countryside by commodifying its resources for the market. Marx outlined this shift in the *Grundrisse* (1857–1858): 'For the first time, nature becomes purely an object of humankind, purely a matter of utility; ceases to be recognized as a power for itself; and the theoretical discovery of its autonomous laws appears merely as a ruse so as to subjugate it under human needs, whether as an object of consumption or as a means of production.'[30] The presence of the pedestrian in the land is an indelible sign of this alienation. For he or she is either a producer, condemned to roam across it in a restless, rootless pursuit of opportunities to labour, or a consumer, doomed to alienate it as an object of aesthetic satisfaction in the attempt to commune with it. If nature is fetishized at this time, and if its laws are autonomized, then this is definitive proof that it has been instrumentalized.

Rural Scenery

In England, the emergence of an identifiable pedestrian culture among the middle classes needs to be understood in the context of two specific social developments that took place from the mid eighteenth century: the improvement in national transport links, and the extension of the Enclosure Acts. These developments, which helped create the conditions for the consolidation of capitalism at the end of the century, in both its agrarian and industrial forms, were at the same time products of this more profound socio-economic process.

The revolution in transportation, which pivoted on the construction of toll roads built by private companies called Turnpike Trusts, made travel cheaper, faster and safer, especially for the labouring classes. Crucially, this eroded the ancient association of walking with poverty and vagrancy. No longer the only means by which poor people could travel, walking to an unprecedented extent became a matter of choice. This meant that remaining pedestrians were likely either to be the poorest, most desperate plebeians, male and female, forced by extreme social and economic circumstances to travel on foot in search of wage labour; or relatively affluent, if perhaps déclassé, members of the upper-middle classes, principally men, who had decided to go on foot for ideological reasons.

At the same time, an aggressive programme of enclosures, prosecuted by a state that by this time accepted that private profit was the supreme objective of governmental policies, dramatically, indeed violently, reshaped the landscape. It did so in the interests of acquisitive, commercially ambitious landlords and farmers – gentlemen like Mr Knightley and his enterprising tenant Robert Martin in Jane Austen's *Emma* (1815). This campaign, which built on the enclosures of the sixteenth and seventeenth centuries, abolished innumerable public footpaths that had for centuries been used by the members of rural communities. But, as Anne Wallace points out, 'in the controversy over public rights of way through private lands that ensued, walking emerged as a possible mitigation of these ills, for English common law provides that public use itself creates public right of way'. Walking itself thus became a means of what she calls 'unenclosing' paths, or reappropriating them for common use.[31]

It was the improvement of roads and the expropriation of the land that created the material preconditions, in the late eighteenth century, for the increasing popularity of pedestrian tourism. From the 1780s, in England, it became a fashionable activity among undergraduates and the more progressive members of the lower clergy in particular to tour the countryside on foot. For these intellectuals, a walking tour promised to provide the conditions in which, far from the family and other patriarchal institutions, including the university and Church, they might reinvent themselves. It constituted a carefully coded, if quietistic, act of rebellion.

Both at home and on the continent, pedestrian tourism was linked to the cult of the picturesque, the tenets of which were established by William Gilpin and elaborated by Uvedale Price, Richard Payne Knight and others. This aesthetic, which valued nature in a state of delicate equilibrium between order and disorder, at once thrillingly wild and reassuringly tame, and which with some complacency cultivated remnants of the feudal order in the ruined outlines of ancient monasteries and castles, was central to the construction of English national identity in the later eighteenth century. Like the Romantics, who deepened some of the prevailing assumptions of the picturesque even as they reacted against its class politics, its theorists and practitioners, who included gothic novelists like Ann Radcliffe and painters like John Constable, fostered or sponsored a kind of manufactured spontaneity in nature.

The ideology of the picturesque effectively posited England itself as a rough and rugged but elegant landscaped park, like the ones designed by Lancelot 'Capability' Brown. It thereby screened off the brutal transformation of the countryside engineered by agrarian capitalism, distracting from the effects of clearing, drainage, enclosures and reclamation, even as it also idealized them. (Gilpin himself, incidentally, complained that the country had been disfigured by too much agriculture.) In this social topography, a pedestrian tour in places like North Wales and the Lake District increasingly became a component part of an entitled Englishman's education. The events of the French Revolution added impetus to this domestic fashion, because the more violent they appeared to the respectable classes in England the more they made a Grand Tour on the continent seem both less accessible and less appealing.

In spite of its connection to the respectable aesthetic of the picturesque, however, travelling on foot in fields or on public roads retained its nonconformist associations with the lives of migrants and vagrants, at least for self-conscious political dissidents. The experiences of Coleridge and his friend Joseph Hucks during the former's 'pedestrian scheme' in 1794 are a good example of this. Attired in rough workman's clothes and carrying canvas knapsacks, they tramped several hundred miles across England and Wales, explicitly distancing themselves from 'loath'd Aristocracy', which 'careers along', as Coleridge put it, 'on clatt'ring Wheels'.[32] In the Wye Valley, at the heart of their walk, they were often mistaken, as Richard Holmes notes, for either 'French tinkers (dangerously republican) or demobbed soldiers (dangerously drunk)'.[33]

This was at the height of Coleridge's utopian political schemes, which he had hatched in Oxford with Robert Southey, to build the nucleus of a so-called Pantisocratic society – a brotherhood based on egalitarian ideals and a commonality of goods. In a letter to Southey in which he described seeing a beggar girl expelled from an inn because she had asked for food, Coleridge declared, 'When the pure System of Pantisocracy shall have aspheterized the Bounties of Nature, these things will not be so – !'[34] The word 'aspheterize' – a neologism of which he was extremely proud – meant to expropriate property. Coleridge openly proselytized along these lines to people he happened to encounter on the roads. Striding across the countryside dressed as itinerants, he and his rather reluctant comrade Hucks partially, playfully, undid their class identities.

In a sense, Romantics like Coleridge subverted the picturesque by becoming a part of its characteristic landscape themselves. They constituted an almost immanent critique of it. If the aestheticians of the picturesque remained outside the pictorial frame, coolly objectifying both the land and those labouring on it, then the Romantics embedded themselves inside it instead, deliberately identifying with its poorest inhabitants. But, in acting this part, the Romantics also reinforced the logic of the picturesque, which centred on the idea that nature is a form of spectacle, and which integrated gypsies and vagrants, but not ordinary labourers, as colourful, more or less exotic elements of this spectacle. John Thelwall, the fieriest and most famous of the English Jacobins, embarrassed himself in this respect, in spite of his radical credentials. In *The Peripatetic* (1793), his ramshackle compendium of pedestrian itineraries, he described meeting some gypsies in a wood, and called them 'an embellishment of rural scenery'.[35]

More predictably, perhaps, in his *Essay on the Picturesque* (1796), Price categorized gypsies among a set of 'objects' that are supremely picturesque. This was the case because, though not attractive in themselves, they had qualities suited to the art of the painter: 'Among our own species, beggars, gypsies, and all such rough tattered figures as are merely picturesque, bear a close analogy, in all the qualities that make them so, to old hovels and mills, to the wild forest horse, and other objects of the same kind.'[36]

Radical intellectuals like the young Coleridge rejected this pictorial perspective, which coldly objectified the most marginal members of society for aesthetic purposes, reducing them to ornaments. But, as philosophic vagabonds, they inhabited an ambiguous if also privileged position on the edge of a field of vision in which vagabonds proper occupied the background.

Apology for Vagrants

The late eighteenth and early nineteenth centuries were a period in which, because of the systematic displacement of people through enclosures, and as a result of the rapid entrenchment of industrial capitalism, the numbers of unemployed wage-labourers multiplied visibly. Pre-industrial artisans and skilled workers were to an increasing extent recruited or press-ganged into the ranks of the itinerant proletariat – forced into a nomadic existence by the need simply to subsist. Economic migrants, especially from Ireland and Scotland, were familiar figures on rural roads. In England, border counties like Cumberland became especially susceptible to the problem of pauperism, because 'the less liberal poor laws and settlement regulations of Scotland encouraged a persistent movement of destitute persons across the border'.[37]

From the mid 1790s in particular, female vagrants, left with little or no means of subsistence after their husbands had been sent to fight against France on the continent, were an especially striking feature of the social landscape. Several of Wordsworth's poems from this period, in testifying to this parlous situation, developed something like a poetics of vagrancy. In 'An Evening Walk', for example, Wordsworth depicts a female vagrant who, as the neglected wife of a soldier, is one of the forgotten victims of war. As she drags her children along the road in the gathering darkness, the poet demonstrates that he is acutely conscious of her physical pain. He imagines the 'arrowy fire' that shoots 'stinging through her stark o'er-laboured bones' as she hopelessly attempts 'To teach their limbs along the burning road / A few short steps to totter with their load'.[38]

The influence of John Langhorne's *The Country Justice* (1774–1777), which Wordsworth praised as the first poem 'that fairly brought the Muse into the Company of common life', can be felt here. In his 'Apology for Vagrants', Langhorne had invoked a 'houseless Wretch', a soldier who is slain and who leaves behind him a wretched widow and her innocent child.[39] But Langhorne's allusion to society's victims lacks immediacy. In Wordsworth's poem, by contrast, the sense of the female vagrant's acute physical pain as she inches forward on foot – communicated through language that is itself, admittedly, a little 'o'er-laboured' – derives its considerable force from the poet's concrete observations and experiences on the roadside.

More importantly, in 'The Female Vagrant', first published in the *Lyrical Ballads* (1798), Wordsworth instead tried to narrate the life story of one of these victims of war, poverty and the depredations of class society in her own voice. Hence, the eponymous character recapitulates for the poet a devastating series of events. She relates that a rapacious landlord, determined to rid the landscape surrounding his mansion of its labourers' cottages, dispossessed her pious father; that, after her father's death, 'the empty loom, cold hearth, and silent wheel' pushed her and her children into deeper and deeper poverty; that her husband joined the army and, as a consequence, 'dog-like, wading at the heels of war', she was forced to emigrate with him, to 'protract a curst existence, with the brood / That lap (their very nourishment!) their brother's blood'; that, after an agonizing struggle to build a life in America, her husband and children died and she had to return to England in a state of extreme indigence; and finally that, refusing to beg or steal, she has been reduced to foraging and sleeping in fields – consigned to an almost inhuman existence.[40]

'The Female Vagrant' was originally part of a far longer poem, 'Salisbury Plain', which Wordsworth composed in 1793 and 1794, in the aftermath of Britain's declaration of war against France. At this time, incensed by British foreign policy, and penniless, the young poet remained a political radical ('Heroes of Truth pursue your march, uptear / Th' Oppressor's dungeon from its deepest base' is the fiery cry of the final stanza). This first version, shaped by a long walk across the druidic topography of Salisbury Plain in the summer of 1793, depends on a pointed, angry comparison between contemporary victims of social oppression, such as the female vagrant, and the savage who, in primitive society, slept 'at night on [the] unknown plains'.[41]

In this inhospitable landscape, 'naked and unhouzed', as the poet puts it, the fearful savage experienced appalling suffering. In the language of *King Lear* (1605), which Wordsworth's poem self-consciously echoes, this savage is 'the thing itself' – 'a poor, bare, forked animal'.[42] But, in contradistinction to the late-eighteenth-century vagrant, who lives at the edges of an affluent society built on brutal class divisions, the ancient savage evoked by Wordsworth was blissfully ignorant of the fact that, beyond a life of subsistence, a far more comfortable existence is materially possible. For their part, the female vagrant and her kind are 'poor naked wretches', in Lear's language again, who must instead endure 'houseless heads and unfed sides', and a state of 'looped and windowed raggedness';[43] that is, a condition of suffering that is all the more acute because they are conscious of what it is like to be properly housed and fed.

Wordsworth's message to the ruling class in this poem, and his expression of solidarity with the poor, is analogous to that of Lear on the heath, who issues this remarkable challenge:

> Take physic, pomp;
> Expose thyself to feel what wretches feel,

> That thou mayst shake the superflux to them,
> And show the heavens more just.[44]

On 'this tyrannous night' – indeed, throughout Shakespeare's tragedy – vagrancy is the degree zero of humanity.[45] The idea of the 'houseless' in *King Lear*, and the image of the vagrants' torn and ragged clothes, haunt Wordsworth's portrait of the female vagrant.

Wordsworth's poems often involve an encounter between the poet, who is a self-conscious pedestrian, and a working-class itinerant, female or male, who has been displaced either by war or economic developments associated with the advent of the industrial revolution. 'I saw an aged Beggar in my walk', begins 'The Old Cumberland Beggar' (1800), a poem that posits this 'helpless wanderer', paradoxically, as the stable repository of the knowable, organic community through which he circulates.[46] In this respect, the beggar is the double of the poet – even if it is in the form of a 'silent monitor', rather than one who speaks, that he preserves the community's memories and moral continuities.

As Jeffrey Robinson points out, Wordsworth's early poems in particular are populated with characters who in some literal sense 'walk out of their social alienation: outlaws, murderers, people stung to the core with guilt, the dispossessed and disenfranchised, abandoned women, discharged soldiers, beggars and gypsies'.[47] The poet, too, seeks to walk out of his social alienation, in these and many of his more mature poems. In *The Excursion* (1814), for example, which was intended, like *The Prelude* (1805), to form part of *The Recluse*, the poet explicitly identifies himself with the character of the Wanderer as a social and spiritual outsider who cannot be comfortably or conveniently absorbed into the aesthetics, or the cultural logic, of the picturesque. A former pedlar or itinerant salesman, Wordsworth's Wanderer is a simple, sapient man who 'still … loved to pace the public roads / And the wild paths'.[48]

In an Introduction to *The Excursion*, Wordsworth later felt 'called upon freely to acknowledge that the character I have represented in his person is chiefly an idea of what I fancied my own character might have become in his circumstances'.[49] It is a classic dream of déclassement.

Idle and Disorderly Persons

The vagrancy problem reached crisis proportions at the end of the Napoleonic Wars in 1815, when large numbers of discharged soldiers returned to England and, reduced to a homeless and unemployed condition, were forced to beg on the streets of towns and cities and lead lonely, itinerant existences on the roadside.

In a poignant irony, it was at almost exactly this time that, in popular culture, walking came to be institutionalized or professionalized as a form of athleticism. The manifesto for this sporting activity was Walter Thom's *Pedestrianism; or, An Account of the Performances of Celebrated Pedestrians during the Last and Present Century* (1813). It championed walking and running as 'the best species of exercise': 'Exercise on foot is allowed to be the most natural and perfect, as it employs every part of the body, and effectually promotes the circulation of the blood through the arteries and veins.' Thom implied that, during the conflict with France, nothing less than Britain's imperial prospects depended on its inhabitants' pedestrian abilities. Disciplined walking, he insisted, was important 'especially at a time when the physical energies of many of our countrymen are frequently brought into action by the conflicts of war'.[50] In both a physical and a religious or spiritual sense, a nation of proficient, orderly walkers was a fit one.

But England was not a fit nation. In 1816 and 1817 – years of rioting and machine-breaking – impoverished soldiers and their families were joined on the streets and roads by thousands of others who had been ruined by the depression in trade. 'Bankruptcies, seizures, executions, imprisonments, and farmers become parish paupers ...', the liberal journalist Leigh Hunt fulminated in an article for the *Examiner* in 1816 on the 'general distress' caused in the countryside by high taxes and the Corn Laws. 'Great arrears of rent', his list of contemporary social and economic calamities continued; 'tithes and poor-rates unpaid; improvements of every kind generally discontinued; live stock greatly lessened; tradesmen's bills unpaid; and alarming gangs of poachers and other depredators'.[51]

A vast, scattered population, hitherto almost invisible, seemed to have been dispossessed or evicted and to be straggling along the public roads and sleeping in barns and abandoned buildings. John Thomas Smith's *Vagabondiana* (1817), an illustrated guide to some of the more colourful characters living on the streets of London at this time, testified in picturesque and sentimental terms to the effects of this rise in vagrancy in the capital. The Vagrancy Act of 1824 – 'An Act for the Punishment of idle and disorderly Persons, and Rogues and Vagabonds, in England' – was the state's brutal response to the familiar sight, on city pavements and country roadsides, of the mendicant poor catalogued by Smith. It built on a temporary Act passed in 1822, which had insisted on the need for simplifying the current laws relating to vagrants and consolidating them under single legislation.

According to the Act of 1822, several classes of persons who were not subsequently incorporated in the Act of 1824 were 'deemed idle and disorderly', and could therefore be 'committed to the House of Correction' in order to perform hard labour 'for any time not exceeding one calendar month'. These included 'all persons who threaten to run away and leave their wives or children chargeable, all common prostitutes or night-walkers wandering and not giving a satisfactory account of themselves'.[52] 'Night-walkers' here retain a certain ambiguity as a legal entity. They are categorized alongside prostitutes, but they are also implicitly associated with men who abandon their wives and families. So they are not neatly gendered.[53] This legislation leaves room for convicting men as well as women for no other reason than their being outside at night.

The Act of 1824, as its full title indicated, also pressed anachronistic, pre-industrial social categories, above all the 'idle', into legal service – though it silently assimilated 'night-walkers' to the general category of vagrants. Criminalizing beggars, prostitutes and the homeless, and granting magistrates the authority to punish them with up to one month's hard labour, it modernized the late medieval legislation but did not supersede it. The principal problem with this Act, and its main advantage from the authorities' perspective, was that it was so indiscriminate, like the statutes that preceded it. Anybody deemed to be leading an itinerant existence could be prosecuted under its terms. For example, 'every person wandering abroad and lodging in any barn or outhouse, or in any deserted or unoccupied building, or in the open air, or under a tent, or in any cart or wagon, not having any visible means of subsistence and not giving a good account of himself or herself', was liable to arrest.[54] This legislation thus effectively criminalized people on foot.

In his analysis of vagrancy laws in the sixteenth and seventeenth centuries, the historian A. L. Beier concludes that 'offenders were arrested not because of their actions, but because of their position in society'. 'Their status was a criminal one', he adds, 'because it was at odds with the established order.'[55] The same, *mutatis mutandis*, was true of the early-nineteenth-century vagrancy laws.[56]

I Love a Public Road

If biographers and critics have catalogued the importance of walking to Wordsworth, and of the figure of the vagrant, they have nonetheless overlooked the significance he ascribed to walking in the dark, and to nocturnal vagrancy. *The Prelude*, above all, betrays a persistent interest in rural nightwalking and noctivagation.

In Book IV of this poem, Wordsworth describes his attachment to a 'rough terrier', a dog belonging to Ann Tyson (who was a sort of surrogate mother or grandmother to him and his siblings). He records that it used to accompany him on his solitary walks in the Lake District when, as an adolescent, 'affecting private shades / Like a sick Lover', he first began to compose poetry.[57] This creature remained a faithful attendant and friend to him – even if it often seemed frustrated by the dilatory, half-distracted motion of the aspiring poet as, 'busy with the toil of verse', he turned some image over in his mind or tried to force a line to scan.[58]

In addition to keeping him company, the terrier performed one especially useful function. For, 'when in the public roads at eventide / [it] sauntered, like a river murmuring / And talking to itself', it used to jog on in front of him and, if it met 'a passenger approaching', return to signal their presence to him.[59] Immediately:

> Punctual to such admonishment, I hushed
> My voice, composed my gait, and shaped myself
> To give and take a greeting that might save
> My name from piteous rumours, such as wait
> On men suspected to be crazed in brain.[60]

The dog thus regularly recalled the young poet to the fact that, muttering fragments of incomprehensible sentences to himself, his pace stopping and starting as the inspiration took him, and composing extempore, he inadvertently resembled an 'idiot boy', a madman or a vagabond rambling along the public road. The adolescent Wordsworth clearly relished this association with the lunatic, the lover and the poet. He liked to rhyme his wandering mind with his wandering feet; his vagrant imagination with the vagrant image that, in the thickening light of evening, he half-consciously projected. Wondering and wandering. The vague and the vagrant.

Crucially, moreover, the road is where Wordsworth encounters those who are literally as well as metaphorically vagrant. It is the place where Wordsworth momentarily but routinely experiences democratic relations, at the same time intimate and distant, with the poor and the outcast. According to Celeste Langan, 'The poet and the vagrant together constitute a society based on the twin principles of freedom of speech and freedom of movement.'[61] The roadside is the point of intersection of the public and the private, and of these freedoms of speech and movement. It is the scene of social rather than merely individual or psychological epiphanies. 'He loved to pace the public roads / And the wild paths', the poet writes of the Wanderer in *The Excursion*.[62]

'I love a public road', Wordsworth declares, even more openly, in Book XII of *The Prelude*.[63] There he admits that, as a child, he felt intimidated 'by strolling Bedlamites' and 'many other uncouth vagrants'.[64] In the end, though, he acquired the confidence 'to enquire, / To watch and question' those he met, 'the wanderers of the earth'.[65] As a result, he glimpsed into 'the depth of human souls' – 'Souls that appear to have no depth at all / To vulgar eyes'.[66] 'The lonely roads', he underlines, 'Were schools to me in which I daily read / With most delight the passions of mankind'.[67] This education in the passions – passions that are shaped and distorted by class distinctions, but that promise at the same time to redeem these distinctions in the name of 'mankind' – is in both senses of the word pedestrian. It is ordinary, everyday; and it is conducted on foot.

The roadside, particularly at dusk, is in Wordsworth's poetics an important 'chronotope'; perhaps the most important one. A chronotope, in the terms formulated by the Russian literary theorist Mikhail Bakhtin, denotes 'the intrinsic connectedness of temporal and spatial relationships that are artistically expressed in literature'. 'Time', Bakhtin explains, 'thickens, takes on flesh, becomes artistically visible; likewise, space becomes charged and responsive to the movements of time, plot and history'.[68] The road is one of the chronotopes singled out by Bakhtin in his discussion of 'the adventure novel of everyday life'; but what he has to say about it applies to Wordsworth's narrative poetry of everyday life too.

At an allegorical level, the road signifies an ongoing itinerary, like the biographical journey traced by the thirteen books of *The Prelude* (Wordsworth's attempt to write a *bildungsroman* – a novel about the narrator's social and spiritual formation or education – in poetic form). At a symbolic level, more concretely, it signifies the site of contingent encounters, where 'people who are normally kept separate by social and spatial distance can accidentally meet', as Bakhtin puts it.[69] These random encounters then both punctuate and give impetus to the poem's overarching trajectory.

Night Deserted

In *The Prelude*, the roadside meeting that is most pregnant with meaning is the young man's encounter with a discharged soldier at the end of Book IV ('Summer Vacation'). 'From many wanderings', Wordsworth notes, 'I will here / Single out one'.[70] This is perhaps the archetypal democratic encounter with a representative of the itinerant poor on the public road at night. The passage was originally composed as an independent poem in early 1798, some time before the poet's plans for *The Prelude* had properly unfolded, but he later decided to incorporate it into his epic of self-development.

Wordsworth begins by iterating the importance to him of walking on the road, this time emphasizing, however, the peculiar value of doing so at night:

> A favourite pleasure hath it been with me
> From time of earliest youth, to walk alone
> Along the public way, when, for the night
> Deserted, in its silence it assumes
> A character of deeper quietness
> Than pathless solitudes.[71]

At night, as distinct from the muffled silence of the fields and fells, the depopulated roads echo with emptiness. Here, after the intermittent traffic of a summer day, there is a ghostly calm to the solitude.

Wordsworth records that, on one night in particular, he ascended a steep road whose 'watery surface', as he beautifully puts it, 'glittered to the moon'.[72] His mood on this occasion is a tranquil, dreamy one. He intuits from his placid surroundings a deep, restorative sense of peace; his 'body from the stillness drinking in / A restoration like the calm of sleep, / But sweeter far'.[73] He is like a somnambulist. From time to time, objects at the roadside gently obtrude into his consciousness. But it is the 'beauteous pictures' spontaneously produced inside his head that, like a magic lantern, dominate his senses:

> – they rose
> As from some distant region of my soul
> And came along like dreams; yet such as left
> Obscurely mingled with their passing forms
> A consciousness of animal delight,
> A self-possession felt in every pause
> And every gentle movement of my frame.[74]

In the soft, silent night, beneath the moonlight, his physical life and his mental life are perfectly attuned. He pulsates with a sense of … completeness. 'Thus did I steal along that silent road', he writes, as if he feels like a fugitive from the day.[75]

It cannot last. His sense of harmony and serenity is too intense, too exceptional. And it is duly ruptured when, at 'a sudden turning of the road', he glimpses 'an uncouth shape' ahead of him.[76] Reacting instinctively, he slips 'into the shade / Of a thick hawthorn'.[77] He can thus see the man without being seen:

> He was of stature tall,
> A foot above man's common measure tall,
> Stiff in his form, and upright, lank and lean;
> A man more meagre, as it seemed to me,
> Was never seen abroad by night or day.
> His arms were long, and bare his hands; his mouth
> Showed ghastly in the moonlight: from behind,
> A milestone propped him, and his figure seemed
> Half-sitting and half-standing. I could mark
> That he was clad in military garb,
> Though faded, yet entire. He was alone,
> Had no attendant, neither dog nor staff,
> Nor knapsack; in his very dress appeared
> A desolation, a simplicity
> That seemed akin to solitude.[78]

This is not the solitude of redemption; it is the solitude of damnation. It is a permanent state. For a long time, 'with a mingled sense / Of fear and sorrow', the poet watches the ghostly figure a few feet from him in the dark.[79] He listens to him, too, for this strange, unearthly man, who is as motionless as a corpse propped up against the milestone, moves his lips, groans, and murmurs incomprehensible sounds, like someone in the grip of a bad dream.

Wordsworth reports that, eventually, in some trepidation, he revealed his presence to the man and asked him to explain his history. It transpires that he is a soldier, as his costume implies. Returning ten days ago from 'the Tropic Islands' where his troop had been sent, he was abruptly dismissed from service.[80] He has been discarded like a puppet. He is therefore 'travelling to his native home' on foot.[81] The poet, who is keen to assist the discharged soldier, can see that in the nearest village everybody is asleep ('all were gone to rest; the fires all out').[82] But he knows a labourer who lives in a cottage close by, someone who won't mind being woken from his sleep and will happily provide food and lodging for the night. So together they retreat along the road. 'I beheld / With ill-suppressed astonishment his tall / And ghastly figure moving at my side', he comments.[83]

As they walk, Wordsworth cannot resist probing the soldier about 'what he had endured / From hardship, battle, or the pestilence'.[84] The man responds calmly and concisely, and might have seemed 'solemn and sublime', except that 'in all he said / There was a strange half-absence'.[85] The dialogue peters out, and they proceed 'in silence through the shades gloomy and dark'.[86] When they reach the cottage, Wordsworth relinquishes his responsibility, and in parting from the soldier urges him not 'to linger in the public ways' again, but to ask for help.[87] They exchange blessings, but Wordsworth confesses to having himself 'lingered near the door a little space' before seeking his 'distant home'.[88]

So, in spite of his admonition to the soldier, the young poet lingers too. This is not the only respect in which there is a curious doubling of the two men: the stranger's restless mutterings recall Wordsworth's murmurings on the occasions when he walked along the public road at dusk composing poems in the company of the dog; both men are distracted by dreams and by the intermittent drama of their consciousness; and both men are of course nightwalkers, restlessly treading the darkened road while labourers and other ordinary people lie asleep in their beds. The lank, lean, long, solitary man encountered in the moonlight moves like a ghastly, ghostly figure at Wordsworth's side. He is an indigent, vagrant version of the wandering poet, recollecting emotion in a state of stupefaction rather than tranquillity.

The discharged soldier, to put it in Sartre's terms, is 'the negative of one of [the poet's] fondest dreams'.[89] He is the spectral embodiment of an itinerant freedom of movement and speech that is nonetheless inseparable from social and psychological alienation. The glittering, watery surface of the public road in the moonlight is thus a kind of magical mirror in which, in distorted but also mythical form, Wordsworth encounters his other. The road at night is the site on which the commonplace and the mythical, the mundane and the marvellous, intersect.

Creeping in Silence

In the early Romantic period, Robin Jarvis observes, walking was central to 'the emergence of a new form of masculine, middle-class self-fashioning'.[90] So was nightwalking, as Wordsworth's poetry indicates; though walking by night tended to involve the fashioning, or unleashing, of a rather less stable self than walking by day. Jarvis is correct to emphasize, however, that the liberty to use walking of one kind or another for the purpose of self-fashioning was not available to everyone. Women like Dorothy Wordsworth and working-class men like John Clare were not as free as middle-class male poets and writers, at least in public, to cultivate or embroider their selves through the acts of walking and writing about walking.

In spite of this restriction, or precisely because of his origins in the rural working class, Clare was a militant pedestrian who repeatedly affirmed the importance of walking to his sense of self and society. From his youth, he defied enclosure with his feet, asserting the politics of pedestrianism. The son of a landless cottager, he was sixteen when the Act of Parliament that enclosed his native parish of Helpstone was passed in 1809. In 'The Mores' and other poems of the early nineteenth century, he looked back with an acute, embittered sense of loss to a time when 'Unbounded freedom ruled the wandering scene / Nor fence of ownership crept in between'. And he railed against the fact that 'Fence now meets fence in owners little bounds / Of field and meadow large as garden grounds'.[91]

In addition to his commitment to walking as a political act, Clare was probably the English Romantic poet who, apart from Wordsworth, was most attuned to the night's subtle promise of a life that cannot be lived in the common day. For Clare, as an agricultural labourer, the night was a rather more complex phenomenon than it was for Wordsworth. He was more conscious than the poet laureate of the ways in which it is shaped by the political economy of the day. He was acutely aware, for example, that, in a rural setting, for the mass of people, night signifies the cessation of painful physical effort: 'When welcome night shut out the toiling day …'[92] A number of his poems celebrate the restorative value of evening, which in the summer especially descends like a gentle balm. In the night he is free to reclaim both the landscape and his inner self, since at dusk both are liberated from the disciplines of labour. In 'Evening', a relatively late poem, Clare refers to twilight as 'the silent hour when they who roam / Seek shelter', and exclaims: 'Oh! at this hour I love to be abroad, / Gazing upon the moonlit scene around'.[93]

An earlier poem like 'Recollections after an Evening Walk', which opens with Clare's announcement that 'Just as the even bell rung we set out / To wander the fields and the meadows about', reads like an attempt to reclaim the natural world at the end of the labouring day, when humanity is no longer able to exploit it. As the sun sets and a 'blue mist' comes 'creeping with silence and night', the animals and insects that, 'all nameless unnotic'd till now', have retreated from sight during the day, reappear in order to 'live in the silence and sweetness of night'.[94] Moths, snails, frogs, glow-worms, bats and owls all come to life, and the poet records their individual activities at dusk in expressive detail.

In noticing these creatures, in assigning them their names, the poet acts as a benign agent of the night, bringing them back into being, restoring them to an almost prelapsarian existence that is only possible in the absence of people ('almost prelapsarian' because, in spite of their respect for this nocturnal culture, the poet and his anonymous and almost unnoticed companion are a minatory presence on its margins – one that, inevitably, inhibits its inhabitants). At night, nature restores or recreates itself. The poet, whose own recreational excursion into the darkness at the end of the labouring day mimics the creatures' recovery of their environment, even if it also potentially interrupts it, is in turn healed and temporarily made whole as a result of participating in this process.

Clare also understood from experience that, in an impoverished labouring community like the one in which he was raised in Northamptonshire, night meant partial freedom from the intrusive paternalistic order, from the surveillance, that prevails in the day: 'No eyes break undistinguish night / To watch us or reprove'.[95] Since his youth Clare had felt attracted to gypsy culture; and, alongside other characteristic attitudes and practices, including writing poetry, this generated suspicion among local villagers. As Jonathan Bate has noted, 'his reputation as an oddity, an outsider, a wanderer and a trespasser was compounded from an early age by association with the so-called sooty crew'. He had a tendency to ramble about in the countryside at night, and this too prompted the opprobrium of people from his community.

'My odd habits did not escape notice', Clare himself testified; '[some] believed me crazed and some put more criminal interpretation to my rambles and said I was night walking associate [*sic*] with the gypsies, robbing the woods of the hares and pheasants, because I was often in their company'.[96] Poachers had long been associated with nightwalkers in the juridical imagination, not least because of the notorious Black Act, passed in 1723, which imposed the death penalty for some fifty criminal offences, including blacking one's face for the purposes of stealing game after dark.[97] Nightwalking thus retained its semi-criminal associations in a rural context.

Homeless at Home

Clare's relationship to the night, and to being abroad in the moonlight, became more complicated in the summer of 1841, when he was in his late forties. It was at this time that, inspired in part by offers of assistance from an encampment of gypsies, he escaped from Matthew Allen's asylum for the insane in Essex, where he had been treated since 1838, and journeyed home on foot to his cottage in Northborough, a distance of nearly one hundred miles.[98]

As the prose fragment known as the 'Journey out of Essex' testifies, this punishing four-day walk, which left him physically crippled and mentally confused, reduced him to the status of a penniless and houseless vagrant, dependent on acts of charity from passersby. At night, he was forced either to sleep rough or to go on limping along the public road in the direction of his home – and in the direction of the beloved to whom, though she was dead, and despite the uncomfortable fact that he was married to somebody else, he believed he was returning. When he finally reached his destination he noted with unbearable poignancy that he felt 'homeless at home'.[99]

On the first night of this journey, Clare slept on 'some trusses of clover' in a 'shed or hovel' into which he clambered ('I lay down with my head towards the north to show myself the steering point in the morning'). On the second night, after failing to sleep beside a shed under some elm trees because of the cold, Clare tried to reach an inn called The Ram near Potton, which was roughly the midpoint of his journey. 'It now began to grow dark apace', he writes, 'and the odd houses on the road began to light up and show the inside tennants lots very comfortable and my outside lot very uncomfortable and wretched.' He 'hobbled forward' and eventually reached The Ram, but discovered that, having no money, he lacked the courage either to enter the inn, the 'lighted window' of which 'looked very cheering', or to sleep in one of its outbuildings. 'So I still travelled on', he records with grim determination; 'the road was very lonely and dark in places being overshadowed with trees.'[100]

At a fork in the road Clare found a milestone that indicated the direction of London, and realized that, as he feared might happen, he had forgotten 'which was North or South'. He continued 'mile after mile', convinced he was tracking back on himself: 'I was scarcely able to walk yet I could not give up but shuffled along till I saw a lamp shining as bright as the moon.' It then transpired that this lamp was suspended above a tollgate, where a man with a candle, in spite of his suspicions, reassured the derelict poet that he was travelling in the right direction. That night, Clare finally crept into the porch of an 'odd house' near a wood and slept there till daylight – 'the inmates were all gone to roost for I could here them turn over in bed as I lay at full length on the stones in the poach [i.e. porch]'.[101]

Clare's account of the third night of his journey, which followed another debilitating day's travel on foot, is more incoherent – 'I was knocked up and noticed little or nothing', he admitted, alluding to his battered, beaten limbs. He does recall though that he 'lay in a dyke bottom from the wind and went sleep half an hour', waking when he felt 'one side wet through from the sock [boggy ground] in the dyke bottom'. 'So I got out and went on', he concludes in a tone as detached as it is determined. His recollections after this nightwalk, though fragmentary, have a phantasmagoric intensity to them:

> I remember going down a very dark road hung over with trees on both sides very thick which seemed to extend a mile or two I then entered a town and some of the chamber windows had candle lights shineing in them – I felt so weak here that I forced to sit down on the ground to rest myself and while I sat here a Coach that seemed to be heavy laden came rattling up and stopt in the hollow below me and I cannot reccolect its ever passing by me I then got up and pushed onward seeing little to notice for the road very often looked as stupid as myself and I was very often half asleep as I went.[102]

This is the authentic voice of the vagrants that Wordsworth loved to encounter on the public road at night.

But it is also inflected by a poet's self-conscious attention to dreamlike detail: the blackened road endlessly tunnelling on into the distance; the blur and flicker of candles in chamber windows; the cumbersome coach that, in a kind of jump-cut, bustles past him without him noticing it; then the road again ... By the time he resumes his journey after stopping to sit for a moment, Clare's consciousness has become inseparable from the relentless repetitions, the deadening continuities and equally deadening discontinuities, of the public road at night. Like the discharged soldier described by Wordsworth, he is characterized by 'a strange half-absence'. Both the road and his mind feel stupid, stupefied. The nightwalk has collapsed almost completely into a sleepwalk, the noctambulist into a somnambulist.

In one of his untitled poems about Mary, the idealized woman to whom he had deluded himself he was returning, Clare reimagined aspects of this painful journey on foot. 'I love to stretch my length 'tween earth and sky / And see the inky foliage oer me wave', he writes, in lines that, if they refer to him lying stretched out between earth and sky, also conjure up the more heroic image of him striding along between earth and sky. 'Midnight when sleep takes charge of natures rest / Finds me awake and friendless – not distrest', he emphasizes.[103] The poem thus represents an attempt to redeem his homelessness, his compulsion to keep walking at night, by reaffirming that this journey was a pilgrimage to Mary.

'I'm not an outlaw in this midnight deep', the itinerant, almost mendicant poet insists. But, in spite of his protestations, the poem cannot finally eliminate the sense that he is a damned spirit condemned to a state of spiritual darkness, like that of Limbo, on the empty public road at night: 'Day seems my night and night seems blackest hell'.[104] 'Limbo' seems appropriate because, derived from the Latin meaning edge or boundary, it refers to the margins of Hell. In the 'Journey out of Essex', the 'edge of the orison' to which Clare once referred in a different context is also the edge of Hell. It is the perimeter of Hell that he tramps at night.

A Dream that Never Wakes

Clare's account of his travels or travails on the road in 1841 constitutes a forceful challenge to the Romantics' love of walking at night in the countryside, because it stages a violent collision between metaphorical and literal forms of vagrancy. The mental solitude relished by Romantic poets who liked to walk at night is in Clare pressed to the point of an almost pathological response to his indigent and itinerant social condition. 'Life is to me a dream that never wakes / Night finds me on this lengthening road alone', he admits, with a sense of pathos all the more painful because of the matter-of-fact tone in which it is expressed.[105]

This brutal night is far from the tender night evoked by John Keats, Clare's almost exact contemporary, in his 'Ode to a Nightingale' (1819). 'Was it a vision, or a waking dream?' Keats had asked when the nightingale's song faded from the garden; 'Do

I wake or sleep?'[106] Clare's apprehension of the night, as he pursues the relentless public road in a semi-deranged, somnambulant state, is a vision, a waking dream – and a nightmare.

Homeless at home. Clare's poignant phrase – scored into his diary as he arrived in Northamptonshire after his four-day walk from Essex, at once relieved and utterly defeated – might serve as a definition of the archetypal nightwalker's existential condition. If the common nightwalker had often simply been homeless, then his or her Romantic descendant, the uncommon nightwalker, was instead homeless at home. So he sought a spiritual asylum in the night. Vagrancy is in the case of a poet like Wordsworth principally a psychological or philosophical rather than a social state of affairs. Clare, cut adrift between the working class and the middle class, the country and the city, obscurity and fame, can instead be identified as a point of transition between the common and the uncommon kinds of nightwalker.

9.

London's Darkness

William Blake

I Must Walk without the Sun

There is a woodcut by William Blake that movingly interweaves the associations of impoverished itinerants and poets, vagrants and philosophic vagabonds, in the Romantic period. It depicts a lonely pedestrian pacing quietly along an empty, meandering rural road lit by the milky, luminous light of the moon. In the background, among the shadowy hills, is a small city, surmounted by a cathedral spire, which glimmers in the light like a pile of bleached bones. At a bend in the road behind him, to his right, is a cross, which resembles a gibbet. The man has just passed a milestone, to his left, that reads: 'LXII / Miles / London'. Sixty-two miles to London … It is an arduous walk to undertake at night.

Blake's solitary traveller wears a cloak and hat, but he doesn't carry a knapsack on his back – an accoutrement that might have lent some sense of purpose, or an air of semi-respectability, to his appearance. (For practical reasons, Wordsworth and Coleridge had both carried knapsacks on their pedestrian travels in the 1790s, in spite of their political commitments.) In his right hand he holds a shepherd's crook. It resembles a pilgrim's staff, and therefore distantly recalls Bunyan's protagonist in *The Pilgrim's Progress* (1678). 'I must walk without the sun, darkness must cover the path of my feet', Christian moans when, after accidentally slipping into a sinful sleep, he is benighted on his journey.[1]

Blake's enigmatic pilgrim proceeds at a slow, measured pace. His stride is short, and there is a palpable heaviness to his gait, almost as if he is sleepwalking. But his back is straight, and his head, which is very slightly lowered beneath the brim of his hat, is fixed with melancholic determination in the direction in which he is travelling. If he is an itinerant, even a vagrant, his form nonetheless embodies a mournful sense of dignity and solemnity. This is a troubling, deeply affecting portrait of social and spiritual exile. It emanates an eerie silence; and any movement conveyed by the woodcut, apart from that of the almost static pedestrian, seems to come from the unsettling landscape, which gently swarms in the unearthly light. Isolation; desolation. It is one of the saddest pictures I know.

Wandering Feet Unblessed

Blake's beautiful, doleful engraving is one of the illustrations he was commissioned to produce for the third edition of Robert Thornton's *Pastorals of Virgil, with a Course of English Reading, Adapted for Schools* (1821). It is designed to accompany the poet Ambrose Philips's Spenserian imitation of Virgil's first Eclogue, which was composed in the opening years of the eighteenth century. In Philips's poem, a fairly conventional neoclassical inscription of the pastoral tradition, two shepherds are conversing with one another: an older, happier one called Thenot (Virgil's Tityrus), and a younger, unhappier one called Colinet (Virgil's Meliboeus). The former gently interrogates the latter about his 'mournful manner'. Comparing him to the lark and the linnet, which joyfully sing of the coming of spring, he accuses him of being an 'unthankful lad'.[2] Colinet replies that, if these birds were to suffer his 'wayward fate', they would not be able to sing:

> Each Creature, Thenot, to his task is born,
> As they to mirth and musick, I to mourn.
> Waking, at Midnight, I my woes renew,
> My tears oft mingling with the falling Dew.

Remonstrating more forcefully, Thenot then hints that his miserable companion 'in hapless hour of time wast born' – as 'when the moon by wizard charm'd, foreshows, / Blood-stain'd in foul eclipse, impending woes'. And he continues to probe the other shepherd's character, forcefully hinting that the latter must originally have left home in pursuit of wealth. Colinet admits to having had 'a lewd desire, strange lands and swains to know'. But he maintains that he was driven too by some deeper compulsion – a restless longing for fame as a poet, and also for a simple sense of identity. 'With wandering feet unblest, and fond of fame', he tells Thenot, 'I sought I know not what besides a name.'[3]

This itinerant existence, according to Colinet's testimony, left him physically and spiritually vagrant. In drifting across the countryside, he ground his sheep into a state of raggedness; and, forced to make his 'nightly bed' on the cold, damp earth, he found himself gradually reduced to a state of destitution. The most agonizing aspect of Colinet's existence, however, is the stinging abuse he has received for his songs: 'But neither want, nor pinching cold, is hard, / To blasting storms of calumny compar'd.'[4] This couplet must have resonated all too poignantly for Blake, whose life-long struggle for recognition as an engraver, painter, printer and poet in London, which he once characterized as 'a City of Assassinations', proved increasingly hopeless.[5]

Thornton loathed the strange, expressionistic illustrations that Blake executed for his book – an anthology, aimed at school children, which was supposed to celebrate the peaceful spirit of the pastoral tradition. They were only printed because, along with several other distinguished artists, Blake's patron, John Linnell, who had secured the commission in the first place, insisted on defending them. In an irony characteristic of Blake's cursed career, the cold wind of calumny can therefore be felt seeping into the introductory note that Thornton added to the title-page, which nervously and superciliously apologized to the reader that the book's engravings 'display less of art than genius, and are admired by some eminent painters'. (Blake's resentment can still be felt six years later, in a note he made in the margin of a pamphlet by Thornton on the Lord's Prayer, which condemns it as a 'Tory Translation' and complains that the God celebrated by the man who once commissioned him 'Creates Nothing but what can be Touch'd & Weighed & Taxed & Measured'.)[6]

Thornton's statement of disavowal reinforces the suspicion that Blake's illustration of Colinet on the road to London is a self-portrait. Colinet, a shepherd who appears to have lost his sheep, in this woodcut at least, travails as he travels on 'wandering feet unblest'. Blake might have been reimagining his return to London from Felpham in the autumn of 1803, after the humiliating incident in which he was charged with sedition because an intoxicated soldier whom he had evicted from the garden of his thatched cottage vengefully reported him to the authorities. Felpham is approximately sixty-two miles from London, and it seems plausible that the cathedral city in the background is Chichester.[7]

Philips's Colinet tells Thenot that, 'Waking, at Midnight', he renews his woe. Blake's Colinet renews his woe, beneath a charmed moon, by walking at midnight. It is as if, moments before, setting out on those 'wandring Feet unblest', he had intoned these lines from Blake's 'Song':

> And, when night comes, I'll go
> To places fit for woe;

> Walking along the darken'd valley,
> With silent Melancholy.[8]

The melancholic wanderer in the woodcut, pursuing the road through a crepuscular landscape emptied of people, is both a vagrant and a neglected poet. He collapses the figures of the Wordsworthian walker and his vagrant other into one.

Forests of the Night

All his life, Blake was a compulsive walker who endlessly traversed London in his own company. 'His principal childhood memory', according to Peter Ackroyd, was 'of solitary walking'.[9] One evening, when he was in his early twenties, he resolved to walk east along Long Acre in the direction of Great Queen Street, where his former master, the engraver James Basire, lived. It was a perfectly ordinary decision. But it had unexpected and enduring consequences. For this occasion – 6 June 1780 – happened to be the fifth day of the anti-Catholic uprising known as the Gordon Riots.

Suddenly, Blake was swept up in the headlong charge of hundreds of rioters determined to liberate those confined to Newgate Prison in the preceding days. 'He encountered the advancing wave of triumphant Blackguardism', according to his first biographer, Alexander Gilchrist, 'and was forced (for from such a great surging mob there is no disentanglement) to go along in the very front rank, and witness the storm and burning of the fortress-like prison, and release of its three hundred inmates.'[10] The destruction of Newgate, which met with brutal retribution at Tyburn, was the most violent civil disturbance to take place in Britain during Blake's lifetime.

The scenes were apocalyptic. The gates were smashed up and, amid the shouts of rioters and the screams of inmates trapped inside, the walls burst into flames. In his reconstruction of these events for *Barnaby Rudge* (1841), Charles Dickens reported that 'the jail resounded with shrieks and cries for help', and 'the fire bounded up as if each separate flame had had a tiger's life, and roared as though, in every one, there were a hungry voice'.[11] It is an image that irresistibly conjures up Blake's Tyger, 'burning bright, / In the forests of the night'.[12]

Certainly, it is tempting to assume that the images combining conflagration, pain and rage that on numerous occasions erupt in Blake's poetry are partly the result of this experience. In *Jerusalem*, Blake confides that 'To Great Queen Street & Lincolns Inn, all is distress & woe'. 'The throb the dolor the convulsion in soul sickening woes', he thunders in 'Night the Sixth' of *The Four Zoas*, an unfinished prophetic book composed between 1797 and 1807; 'The horrid shapes & sights of torment in burning dungeons & in / Fetters of red hot iron …'[13]

By the time Newgate and several other prisons had been attacked, along with the Bank of England, the Gordon Riots were probably no longer fuelled exclusively by anti-Catholic ideology. They were also driven by anger against the ruling class and its agents and institutions. The riots constituted a strike against London's oppressive penal system, which the British state rebuilt and expanded from the late 1760s.[14] The dissenting tradesmen who, at the start of the week's events, goaded by the demagogue Lord George Gordon, had demonstrated against more tolerant attitudes to Catholics, were by this time outnumbered by apprentices, labourers and servants, as well as some prostitutes and criminals. As E. P. Thompson explains, the social composition of the riots was finally 'something of a mixture of manipulated mob and revolutionary crowd'.[15]

Blake's emotions, as an observer and perhaps an inadvertent participant, must have been correspondingly complex. David Erdman claims that, even if Gilchrist was correct to underline Blake's 'involuntary' participation in the storming of the prison, Blake 'shared the sentiments of Gilchrist's "triumphant black-guardism" insofar as "the mob" believed that freeing their fellows from Newgate was a step towards freeing Albion from an oppressive war'.[16] Ackroyd, both more cautiously and more colourfully, has speculated that 'he went along with the mob willingly, perhaps impulsively, and, when he saw the fire and heard the screaming, he stayed out of sheer panic or overwhelming curiosity'.[17] It is not easy to reconstruct Blake's reaction, though it is tempting to do so.

It is easier to imagine Blake's response to the brutal, repressive justice with which the authorities retaliated after the riots. Another of his recent biographers has noted that Blake's 'anguished recollection' of the night on which Newgate burned 'must have been made more poignant by the subsequent legal retribution, when scores of rioters were hanged at Tyburn, many of them only boys'.[18] In fact, most of those convicted by the courts of rioting were hanged at local sites of public execution scattered across London. This was partly because of the risks of social disorder associated with the elaborate rituals conducted at Tyburn Tree, the city's main centre of spectacular punishment.[19]

In the June 1780 Sessions at the Old Bailey, nonetheless, some thirty-five people were sentenced to hang for rioting or 'pulling down houses' during the Gordon Riots; sixteen were reprieved. The poet Samuel Rogers remembered, or misremembered perhaps, 'seeing a whole cartload of young girls, in dresses of various colours, on their way to be executed at Tyburn': 'They had all been condemned, on one indictment, for having been concerned in (that is, perhaps, for having been spectators of) the burning of some houses during Lord George Gordon's Riots. It was quite horrible.'[20] Presumably Blake was conscious that he too could have been condemned for being 'concerned in' the Riots.

Twenty-five years later, living in South Molton Street, just off the old route from Newgate to Tyburn, seven or eight minutes on foot from the site of the Fatal Tree, Blake surely reflected again and again on the walk he took across London on the evening of 6 June 1780 – a solitary stroll that was suddenly transformed with a phantasmagoric rush into an apocalyptic night in which destruction and liberation could not be dissociated from one another. In the address 'To the Christians' that prefaces Chapter IV of *Jerusalem*, Blake's most ambitious prophetic book, 'a Watcher & a Holy-One' tells the poet to supplicate not to the 'proselytes to tyranny & wrath' but to the prostitutes and sinners – 'For Hell is opend to Heaven; thine eyes beheld / The dungeons burst & the Prisoners set free'.[21] In the liberation of Newgate he was granted a vision of the apocalyptic destruction of the regime of discipline and punishment of which Tyburn was emblematic. Here, at the heart of London's darkness, was a searing flash of light that, in spite of the feverish destruction it caused, remained incandescent for decades.

London in the epoch of ascendant industrial capitalism was in Blake's mythological imagination a city encased in night. The black sun of the Enlightenment obnubilated it; and, at its centre, Tyburn Tree, the ancient scene of execution, cast an impenetrable shade. In his paintings, poems and illuminated books, Blake pitted a kind of anti-Enlightenment light against London's night – in a sustained, if finally doomed, attempt to redeem it.

Paddington Frisk

In the course of its 600-year history, culminating in the late eighteenth century, it is estimated that some 50,000 or 60,000 people died at Tyburn Tree, which is today the site of Marble Arch. At midnight the night before a hanging day or 'hanging fair', which generally took place on a Monday, the bellman of St Sepulchre-without-Newgate recited verses to the men and women who were due to be executed. 'All you that in the condemn'd Holds do lie, / Prepare you, for to Morrow you shall die', he began ...

The next morning, between 9 a.m. and 10 a.m., a procession left the prison, to the deafening sound of church bells – first those of St Sepulchre, then of other churches along the route. The condemned, whose irons were first struck off in the prison's press yard in front of their friends and relations, ascended into a horse-drawn cart that eventually rumbled off along the cobbled streets on its protracted two- or three-hour journey to the gibbet. In the spirit of clemency, the carter might stop at a tavern in Holborn, enabling those about to be executed to inebriate and so anaesthetize themselves.

The three-mile route, which snaked through St Giles before proceeding along Tyburn Road – today's Oxford Street – was dense with curious, sometimes riotous spectators, who packed themselves into the streets and pressed their bodies up against the windows of buildings either side of the road. Some handed measures of ale or gin to the condemned, others lobbed oranges or apples to them. At

Tyburn itself, 50,000 or 100,000 people might be in attendance, jostling one another for standing room, teetering on ladders, sitting precariously along the wall that enclosed Hyde Park, or crowding into 'Mother Proctor's Pews' – the grandstand on the western side of the Edgware Road (originally Watling Street). They had to compete for a glimpse of the moment at which the condemned man or woman – who died from strangulation rather than a broken neck – dangled from the gallows and 'danced the Paddington frisk'. 'The whole vagabond population of London', wrote the diarist Francis Place, 'all the thieves, and all the prostitutes, all those who were evil-minded, and some, a comparatively few curious people made up the mob on those brutalizing occasions.'[22]

From the late sixteenth century, the infamous scaffold at Tyburn took the distinctive form of a 'Triple Tree' design. This consisted of three wooden posts, in a triangular formation, connected across the top by three beams. In addition to ensuring almost indestructible stability, this design facilitated mass executions, since each beam could accommodate up to eight bodies, and on occasion as many as twenty-four people were therefore hanged at one time.

The original gallows, in the Middle Ages, were made from the elms that stood beside Tyburn Brook (a tributary not of the River Tyburn but the River Westbourne – one that today runs as an underground stream into the Serpentine). It was a bucolic site of execution when its first victim, William Longbeard, was hanged in 1196; and even in the mid and later eighteenth century, when on hanging days a temporary scaffold was erected, before being dismantled until needed for the next execution, the area around Tyburn felt like rough countryside.

This entire area, some of it farmed, was open land that belonged to the Bishop of London's Paddington estate. The only building nearby, at least until the 1760s, was Tyburn House, which stood at the junction of Tyburn Road and Watling Street and probably had something to do with the gallows it overlooked. This was the western edge of the capital, with Hyde Park to its south and open land to its north. The outer limits of Georgian London were demarcated by Tyburn Lane, now Park Lane, which ran south-east to Hyde Park Corner, and Tyburn Road, which ran east in the

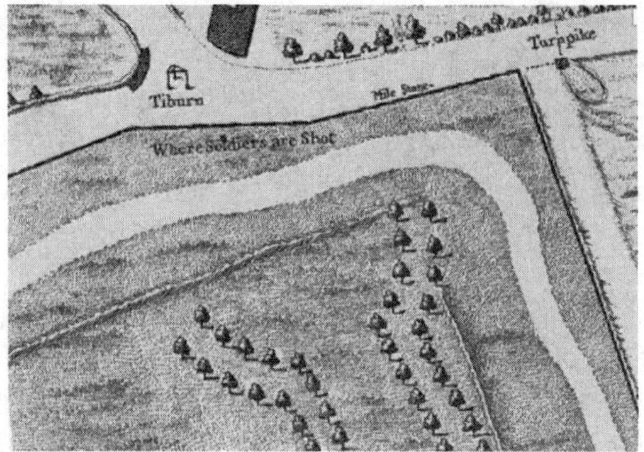

direction of the City. In John Rocque's detailed map of London, first published in 1746, the Triple Tree is starkly marked – printed onto the crook between the roads running west and north like a crude symbol tattooed onto the webbing between index finger and thumb on a prison inmate's hand. Immediately to its south, along the northern fringe of the park, is the legend, 'Where Soldiers are Shot'. These are killing fields.

The last execution at Tyburn – of one John Austen – took place in November 1783. By this time residences around Oxford Street were fashionable, and the social disorder associated with public executions threatened to disrupt the region's increasingly genteel reputation. After 1783 those sentenced for capital offences were hanged at the Debtor's Door, Newgate – a mercifully short journey from the condemned's cell.

Capital Inflictions

There is at Marble Arch today no reference to the mass victims of these infamous gallows (though at Tyburn Convent, overlooking Hyde Park, there is a plaque commemorating 105 Catholics executed from the mid sixteenth century). No doubt it is predictable enough that the obscurest, most desperate members of London's poor population, condemned for committing trifling crimes against property, should remain uncommemorated at

Marble Arch. But even infamous victims of the Tyburn regime are unnamed. There is no mention of Jack Sheppard, the most notorious and popular thief of the eighteenth century, who twice escaped from Newgate, and whose execution in 1724 drew admiring crowds of as many as 200,000 people.

There is not even a memorial to Oliver Cromwell at Marble Arch today – a reminder that Britain continues to function as a monarchy, and organizes its heritage accordingly. The remains of his body, along with those of two other regicides, were disinterred in 1661, after the Restoration, before being carried in coffins by cart from Westminster to Holborn, then dragged on to the Fatal Tree at Tyburn. There, in an undignified posthumous execution, the three men were hanged before a large crowd, and beheaded. According to the diarist John Evelyn, the battered carcasses of the 'arch rebells' were 'then buried under that fatal and ignominious monument in a deepe pitt'.[23] It is possible that Cromwell's bones still lie beneath Marble Arch. The turf at the northeastern corner of Hyde Park, which looks so serene and calm beside the congested, agitated roads that encircle it, should still be soaked in blood.

The British state's regime of terror reached a climax in the late seventeenth and eighteenth centuries, when the country became a 'thanatocracy', in Peter Linebaugh's term: 'a government that ruled by the frequent exercise of the death penalty'.[24] In fact, the application of the death penalty declined in this period; but the state nonetheless used the spectacle of the scaffold, with increasing efficiency and intensity, to terrorize people tempted to challenge or infringe a legal and sociopolitical system to which the protection of property was of more and more totemic importance.

Right up until the early nineteenth century, England lacked a public police force (in spite of the founding of John and Henry Fielding's Runners, who comprised little more than 'a gang of professional thief takers, with a reputation for brutality and corruption', in London in 1749).[25] Moreover, unlike France, the British state did not rely on a network of spies and informers to control its subjects (though in the early 1790s, English Jacobins such as John Thelwall, shadowed by agents of the government at meetings of the London Corresponding Society, apparently used to lecture on the 'moral tendency of spies and informers').[26] 'In place of police, however', as Douglas Hay confirms, 'propertied England had a fat and swelling sheaf of laws which threatened thieves with death.'[27] Approximately 49,000 offences were tried before a jury at the Old Bailey in the course of the eighteenth century, and almost 95 per cent of them were property-related.[28] Through the courts the ruling class prosecuted a pitiless war against the poor. This exacerbated the cruelty of a society built on ever more brutal economic inequalities.

In an essay on 'The Necessity of Proportioning Punishments to Crimes' for the *Rambler* in 1750, Samuel Johnson provided a powerful critique of capital punishment and the eighteenth-century state's business of 'investing lawful Authority with Terrour, and governing by Force rather than Persuasion'. He grimly conceded that 'Rapine and Violence are hourly encreasing', but complained that few law-makers questioned the efficacy of 'capital Inflictions'. 'Of those who employ their Speculations upon the Corruption of the People', as he sarcastically put it, 'some propose the Introduction of more horrid, lingering and terrifick Punishments; some are inclined to accelerate the Executions; some to discourage Pardons; and all seem to think that Lenity has given Confidence to Wickedness, and that we can only be rescued from the Talons of Robbery by inflexible Rigour, and Sanguinary justice.'[29]

Johnson was acutely sensitive to the contradictions of the criminal justice system, and to the hypocrisies of both the elite that sentenced people to death and the populace that relished the spectacle of their execution. He cited the authority of the Dutch humanist Herman Boerhaave, who related 'that he never saw a Criminal dragged to Execution without asking himself "Who knows whether this Man is not less culpable than me?"' On the occasions when 'the Prisons of this City are emptied into the Grave', Johnson added in a pungent image, 'every Spectator of the dreadful Procession should put [a] Question to his own Heart.' And the question was this: 'How few among those that croud in thousands to the legal Massacre, and look with Carelessness or Triumph, on the utmost Exacerbations of human Misery, would be able to return without Horrour and Dejection?' In conclusion, he added: 'For, who can congratulate himself upon a Life passed without some Act more Mischievous to the Peace or Prosperity of others than the Theft of a Piece of Money?'[30]

Tyburn Tree was in the eighteenth century the symbol not of some crude, outdated order of justice, a remnant of feudal times, but of a legal system engineered and rebuilt by the capitalist bourgeoisie. Most of those executed at Tyburn were ordinary men and women who had been reduced by economic circumstances to a state of desperation – apprentices, ill-paid servants, unemployed labourers and vagrants. As Roy Porter points out, 'those committing crimes – notably the 1,200 Londoners hanged in the eighteenth century – were less hardened professionals than servants and seamstresses and the labouring poor, down on their luck or out of work, starving, or just fatally tempted'.[31]

Among them were female nightwalkers, although they were executed not for prostitution but because they had committed crimes against property. Mary Young, for instance – a seamstress from Northern Ireland who became a celebrated thief – was gibbeted at Tyburn in 1741. She had been confined to Bridewell, along with other 'loose idle and disorderly persons & comon Street Walkers', in 1737. She was imprisoned there again in 1738, on this occasion with one other woman, both of them 'Night Walkers'. A minor celebrity by this time, she arrived at the gallows in a mourning coach. Nineteen others died at Tyburn alongside Mary Young the day she hanged, and all of them were executed for crimes against property.[32]

Tyburn's Dreadful Shades

The reader of *Jerusalem: The Emanation of the Giant Albion*, William Blake's finest, most fearsome prophetic poem, composed between approximately 1808 and 1820, must pursue a path through its vast, dense tracts of verse like someone threading their way through an immense, labyrinthine city.

In Chapter II, Blake's reader stumbles into a monumental gate that – in contrast, it might be said, to Marble Arch – promises to liberate, as opposed to entomb, the spirits of those executed at Tyburn Tree. In a dreadful voice, the poet invokes the memory of Britain's 'Victims to Justice' and avers:

> There is in Albion a Gate of precious stones and gold
> Seen only by Emanations, by vegetations viewless,
> Bending across the road of Oxford Street; it from Hyde Park
> To Tyburns deathful shades, admits the wandering souls
> Of multitudes who die from Earth.

This Gate is 'the Gate of Los'. Los is Blake's shape-shifting allegorical embodiment of the imagination. Los's Gate represents the possibility of redemption for the countless spirits of those who, as in an industrial factory, have been sacrificed on the scaffold at Tyburn, which he identifies as a 'Mill, intricate, dreadful / And fill'd with cruel tortures' (181).

Blake insists that the Gate of Los, standing against 'the Mill / Of Satan', 'cannot be found / By Satan's Watch-fiends tho' they search numbering every grain / Of sand on Earth every night'.[33] To these 'Watch-fiends' – who are both Enlightenment rationalists, measuring material reality with their deadly mathematical instruments, and oppressive nightwatchmen, policing the people's city – it is invisible, undetectable. It escapes the oppressive double logic of enlightenment and illumination that is best symbolized, in the late eighteenth century, by the disciplinary regime of the Panopticon, Jeremy Bentham's design for a prison whose 'central point would be both the source of light illuminating everything, and a locus of convergence for everything that must be known'.[34] Concealed as if in some fold in eighteenth-century London's time-space continuum, the Gate of Los is a secret portal into Jerusalem, Blake's city of salvation. It is as if Marble Arch, in all its blankness and coldness, was installed there in the mid nineteenth century not only in order to inter the brutal history of Tyburn, but to block access to Blake's imperceptible 'Gate of precious stones and gold'.

Blake was in his mid twenties when the scaffold at Tyburn was dismantled for the last time in November 1783; but its ominous form haunted him throughout his life. As Jeremy Tambling writes, for Blake 'London in the early nineteenth century retains its ghosts of Tyburn'.[35] In August 1783, an artist and engraver called William Wynne Ryland, whose fashionable and highly successful print-selling business had gone bankrupt in 1771, was hanged at the Tree for forging bills on the East India Company. It was to this professional artist that, in spite of the expense, James Blake had tried to apprentice his son William in 1772. Legend has it that Blake, who was fourteen at the time, deterred his father from committing him to this indenture by commenting, 'Father, I do not like the man's face: *it looks as if he will live to be hanged*.'[36]

Darkness of Old Times

For Blake – an antinomian struggling like an ancient giant in the net of the Enlightenment – Tyburn was an obdurate and inescapable symbol of the oppressiveness of Britain's ruling elite, both in the recent and ancient past and in the present. He identified Tyburn as the altar at the centre of an official cult of sacrifice, and therefore regarded it as the descendant, in a different material form, of Stonehenge, the terrifying abstract forms of which, according to him, encircled a scene of cold-hearted and at the same time frenzied druidic execution.

Stonehenge features in *Jerusalem* as the 'Stone of Trial'. It is here that Luvah, a Christ-like figure who embodies passion and amorous love, but also at times the spirit of revolutionary France, is sacrificed by 'the Spectre Sons of Albion', who derive a vengeful pleasure from 'mocking and deriding at the writhings of their Victim on Salisbury'.[37] The trilithons that comprise Stonehenge, which he illustrated for instance in Plate 4 of *Milton* (1811), are the template for Britain's long and brutal tradition of criminal justice based on capital punishment. If the druid priests ritually killed Luvah on the standing stones of Salisbury Plain, 'drinking his Emanation in intoxicating bliss rejoicing in Giant dance', then their descendants have crucified him, in equally obscene ceremonies, on the hanging tree in the genteel city of Bath nearby: 'They vote the death of Luvah, & they naild him to Albions Tree in Bath'.[38]

But it is above all in London that the 'mighty Polypus nam'd Albions Tree', the criminal justice system, coils itself around the nation and threatens, like an enormous octopoid organism, to strangle the life out of its people: 'Here on the Thames / Where the Victim nightly howls beneath the Druids knife'.[39] It is at Tyburn, where the Tree's despotic form is planted, that it must be uprooted and vanquished. At one point in Chapter III of *Jerusalem*, Jesus invites those that are 'taken to prison & judgment, starved in the streets' to follow him and 'walk thro all the cities'.[40] Jesus is like the Pied Piper of German legend. He expresses the hope that he can avenge the city's oppressive authorities by leading the criminalized and the dispossessed to freedom through the streets of city after city. It is another image that seems to invoke, in redemptive form, Blake's memories of the rioters against Newgate in 1780.

This outburst from the Lamb of God –'Luvah must be created', he proclaims – is the signal for some sort of apocalypse. The poet tells us that 'Luvahs Cloud reddening above / Burst forth in streams of blood upon the heavens & dark night / Involved Jerusalem'; that 'fires blaz'd on Druid Altars'; and that 'the Sun set in Tyburns Brook where Victims howl & cry'.[41] The flames of a cataclysmic sunset, which sink incandescent beneath the horizon to the west of London, consume the bloodstained scene of execution with its purifying fire. Those who have been 'taken to prison & judgment' are liberated into freedom by this symbolic blaze. It is Blake's sublime reinscription both of the destruction of Newgate in 1780 and the liberation of the Bastille in 1789 (an event that he hails at the start of the narrative of *The French Revolution* [1791], where, amid the 'Darkness of old times', 'the Bastile trembles').

This apocalyptic fire melts and frees the chilling, frozen culture of British criminal justice. In the opening lines of Chapter II of *Jerusalem*, Blake had identified Tyburn with ice. There he depicts Albion speaking from his 'secret seat' in London:

> Cold snows drifted around him: ice covered his loins around
> He sat by Tyburns brook, and underneath his heel, shot up!
> A deadly Tree, he nam'd it Moral Virtue, and the Law
> Of God who dwells in Chaos hidden from the human sight.

The Tree spread over him its cold shadows, (Albion groand)
They bent down, they felt the earth and again enrooting
Shot into many a Tree! An endless labyrinth of woe![42]

No doubt the meaning of this 'deadly Tree' is overdetermined.[43] It is a descendant of the Tree of Good and Evil in Eden ('the Tree of Good & Evil sprang from the Rocky Circle & Snake / Of the Druid').[44] And it is related to the Tree of Mystery in 'Night the Seventh' of *The Four Zoas*, where Urizen, who sits 'coverd with snow', is enmazed in 'intricate labyrinths' of roots and branches.[45] But it is also the Fatal Tree at Tyburn. If the many trees enrooting beneath Albion's heel are druidic oaks, then they are also the ancient elms of Tyburn Brook, which have been cut down over the centuries and carved up into scaffolds, so that they form an 'endless labyrinth of woe'.

For the depressed, solipsistic Albion of Chapter II of *Jerusalem*, Tyburn Tree is the embodiment of Moral Virtue. This term carries a bluntly sarcastic inflection in Blake's lexicon. Blake triumphantly implies that, more than merely tautological, it is actually oxymoronic. Moral Virtue is another name for the intellectual, legal, social and spiritual institutions, and the deadly, abstract ideologies, against which Blake pits his breathing, living imagination in a perpetual struggle, an unceasing mental fight. It means enslavement. It entails 'the Slavery of that half of the Human Race who hate [what you call] Moral Virtue', as he wrote in 1810.[46]

The ice and the 'cold snows' that encase Albion as he sits groaning in an agony both physical and spiritual beside Tyburn Brook are the elemental forms of Britain's thanatocratic criminal justice system. But they are also emblematic of the 'naked, shameless, direct, brutal exploitation' that, a generation later, in his polemic against capitalism, Karl Marx will define as the regime of the bourgeoisie. Blake dreams of using the conflagration of the imagination to unfreeze what the *Communist Manifesto* characterizes as 'the icy water of egotistical calculation'.[47]

London Stone

Throughout *Jerusalem* Blake associates Tyburn not only with Stonehenge but with 'London Stone'. 'O God', cries England in Chapter IV, awakening on Albion's bosom as 'storms & snows beat round him': 'In Dreams of Chastity & Moral Law I have Murdered Albion! Ah! / In Stone-henge & on London Stone & in the Oak Groves of Malden / I have Slain him in my Sleep with the Knife of the Druid ...'[48] London Stone is an ancient, probably pre-Roman block of oolitic limestone that stood like a mysterious meteorite on the south side of Cannon Street from 1742 until 1798, when it was shifted to the north side of the road and shoved beside the door of St Swithin's Church.[49]

First mentioned as Lonenstane in the twelfth century, the meaning of this enigmatic fragment of rock has remained obscure. From the Middle Ages, London Stone was totemic of the capital city's safety and authority, and seems to have functioned less as a place of pilgrimage than as a site of political assembly. The rebel leader Jack Cade, entering London from Kent with his band of men in 1450, struck it with his sword in order to assert his insurrectionary claims for social justice; in 2 *Henry VI* (1591), Shakespeare portrayed him 'sitting upon London-stone' and commanding, as if he had pitched up in the Land of Cockaigne, that 'the pissing-conduit run nothing but claret wine this first year of our reign'.[50] In his *Survey of London* (1598), John Stow observed that on the south side of St Swithin's Lane 'is pitched upright a great stone called London Stone, fixed in the ground very deep, fastened with bars of iron'. 'The cause why this stone was set there, the time when, or other memory hereof', he concedes, 'is none, but that the same hath long continued there is manifest.'[51]

The most plausible explanation of its presence in London, whatever its provenance, is that it functioned for the Romans as a milestone (possibly the one from which all distances in Britain were measured). In this sense, too, it is linked to the symbolic landscape of Tyburn. For as Rocque's map indicates, an important Roman milestone, named Ossulston, once stood on the south side of Tyburn Road, at a point roughly equidistant between the turnpike at the top of Tyburn Lane to the east and the Tyburn scaffold to the west. This intriguing monolith, which is mentioned in the Domesday Book in 1086, and which gave its name to the district in Middlesex called the Ossulstone Hundred, was known too as Osulvestane – also Osulfestane, Osolvestoneor, Oselstone, Oswulf's Stone and Oswald's Stone. Antiquarians who have relied on Rocque's map have sometimes conflated the 'Mile Stone', as he marks it, with the site opposite Tyburn House 'Where Soldiers are Shot', thus instinctively, and perhaps correctly, identifying Ossulston with sacrifice.[52]

Conspiratorial or fantastical interpretations of London Stone, which rested on the assumption that it possessed occult properties, circulated from at least the seventeenth century. In the late eighteenth century, when druidism became fashionable at the fringes of British culture, London Stone was assumed by some to be a druidic stone. Blake, who was himself influenced by this cultic, Celtic antiquarianism, as a painting like 'The Bard, from Gray' (c. 1809) indicates, seems to have interpreted it as one more remnant, one more oppressive emblem, of the druids' order of sacrificial justice. In this respect, he imparted a materialist meaning to its elusive spiritual significance.

The Spectre Sons of Albion, Blake fulminates in *Jerusalem*, built their 'stupendous Building on the Plain of Salisbury', a 'building of eternal death', from London Stone – 'with chains / Of rocks round London Stone: of Reasonings'. The druids, he implies, creating 'a wondrous rocky World of cruel destiny', constructing an engine of terror, betrayed London Stone, and appropriated its force or spirit, in building with it.[53] A few pages later, in an image of startling, 3violent eroticism, he depicts 'the beautiful Daughter of Albion' sitting 'naked upon the Stone / Her panting Victim beside her'.[54]

Golgonooza

Blake's clearest, calmest, perhaps most melancholic expression of London's topography of crime and punishment, which incorporates both Tyburn Tree and London Stone, is to be found in the song dedicated 'To the Jews' that he inserted between the first and second chapters of *Jerusalem*. These verses reinforce the geographical and historical continuities – dialectical ones, to be sure – between the druids' cult of sacrifice, the Roman state's persecution and execution of Christ, and Hanoverian England's death-dealing judicial order:

> What are those golden Builders doing
> Near mournful ever-weeping Paddington
> Standing above that mighty Ruin
> Where Satan the first victory won.
>
> Where Albion slept beneath the Fatal Tree
> And the Druids golden Knife,
> Rioted in human gore,
> In Offerings of Human Life
> They groan'd aloud on London Stone
> They groan'd aloud on Tyburns Brook
> Albion gave his deadly groan
> And all the Atlantic mountains shook.[55]

The first of these stanzas evokes the construction of the fashionable suburb of Tyburnia, which took place on the Bishop of London's Paddington Estate in the opening decades of the nineteenth century.

Blake's 'golden Builders' are the migrant Irish labourers who, from 1798, built both the terraces of Tyburnia and the Grand Junction Canal, along with its basin and industrial wharves. These bricklayers rendered the site of execution fit for human habitation, and thereby redeemed it, which is why Blake regarded them as 'golden': 'The stones are pity, and the bricks, well wrought affections: / Enameld with love & kindness, & the tiles engraven gold'.[56] Desperately poor, they squatted on the land in unsanitary huts, sometimes known collectively as Tomlin's Town, where they subsisted on a diet of potatoes tilled from the rough ground surrounding these shacks. The nineteenth-century publisher Charles Knight noted that in 1812 Paddington had 'an evil reputation' because it 'was occupied with the most wretched huts, filled with squatters of the lowest of the community'.[57] Paddington, in Blake's poem, does not weep simply because it personifies some mournful, pastoral impulse, but because it is a festering, open sore on the landscape.

In 1811, in the course of an excavation on the Paddington side of Watling Street, just north of where the scaffold had stood thirty years before, labourers 'dug up a cartload of Tyburn bones and parts of apparel'.[58] Were these the bodies of Cromwell, Ireton and Bradshaw? It is impossible to tell whether these bones belonged to the regicides or to anonymous perpetrators of crimes against property (at least, those that weren't passed on to surgeons for the purpose of public dissection after the institution of the Murder Act in 1752). In either case, if Tyburnia was in one sense built on the backs of Irish bricklayers, in another, even more crudely literal (and richly metaphorical) sense, it was built on the bodies of Tyburn's victims. The bricks from which its elegant residences were constructed might have been 'enameld with love & kindness', as Blake argued, but they were also impregnated with blood and sweat, and their foundations had been sunk in earth enriched by the remains of brutalized bodies. It could be said that Connaught Square, where the former prime minister Tony Blair lives, is a testament to civilization that, as Walter Benjamin might have put it, is at the same time a testament to barbarism.

To Blake, Tyburn is an incarnation of Golgotha, the name in Aramaic for the place of the skull, the site where Christ was nailed to the cross alongside common criminals. 'What are those golden builders doing?' he asks in an earlier reference to 'Tyburns fatal Tree', 'Is that Calvary and Golgotha?'[59] But the site of crucifixion is at least potentially the site of resurrection too. In Blake's idiolect, Golgonooza, the city of art and the imagination, is to be built from Golgotha; and Jerusalem, the city of liberty, is to be built from Golgonooza. Golgonooza is the constant, collective attempt to build Jerusalem. Superimposed on the geography of London, in the form of an invisible force field – battlefield, even – Golgonooza is a redemptive possibility for the city. In order to protect it, Los 'walks round the walls night and day'.[60]

In *Milton*, Blake writes:

From Golgonooza the spiritual Four-fold London eternal
In immense labours & sorrows, ever building, ever falling,
Thro Albions four Forests which overspread all the Earth,
From London Stone to Blackheath east: to Hounslow west …[61]

Golgonooza mediates between the everyday reality of London's streets and the visionary reality of the New Jerusalem. It is the rich, fertile soil in which death and rebirth are indistinguishable. Its strange name – 'combining the place of Christ's sacrifice of self with the primeval ooze of existence' – suggests that the task of constructing Golgonooza starts at Golgotha.[62] Its foundations are set in the terrain where Tyburn Tree once stood. Or, to shift the emphasis slightly, they are built on London Stone.

'They groan'd aloud on London Stone / They groan'd aloud on Tyburns Brook'. In these lines from his message to the Jews in *Jerusalem*, Blake's grammar is ambiguous. The pronoun refers of course to the victims of the criminal justice system, who are sacrificed while Albion slumbers, and groans, beneath the Fatal Tree. But it surely also refers to the druids whose knives riot in human gore. In glorying in 'offerings of human life', the druids and their descendants, agents of a regime of judicial terror, are at the same time relinquishing or destroying their humanity. The groans are their death rattle. In a deft, discreet displacement of the scene he depicts, Blake crucifies the crucifiers. Albion's groan, in this light, is 'deadly' not because it signals his demise but because it deals death to his enemies.

Even as he sees and represents damnation, then, Blake at the same time apprehends it from what Theodor Adorno once called 'the standpoint of redemption'.[63] From this utopian perspective, London Stone is also 'the Stone of Night', the rock that was rolled from in front of Christ's tomb on the night of the resurrection. In *America: A Prophecy* (1793), Blake described this biblical scene: 'The morning comes, the night decays, the watchmen leave their stations; / The grave is burst …' It is a moment of spiritual and political liberation, when the 'inchained soul shut up in darkness' is suddenly released, like freed slaves, or 'redeemed captives', into the light. 'The Sun has left his blackness ...'[64]

Dark and Unknown Night

Like everything in Blake's vast, restlessly evolving oeuvre – it is a body of work, in printed and painted forms, which seems at once monumental and molten – the meaning of London Stone shifts slightly with each mythopoeic inscription or reinscription of the phrase. Much less than the Fatal Tree, the Stone's significance cannot be fixed or confidently identified.

At times, the Stone appears to acquire a general application, and to refer not simply to the monolith in Cannon Street, and the druidic cult of sacrifice for which it stands, but the primal matter from which Britain and its civilization are built. The 'Ancient World of Urizen in the Satanic Void', Blake notes in *Jerusalem*, is created 'from Stone-henge and from London Stone'.[65] In this sense, it is also the fundamental material from which London has been built. So, when Los sits on London Stone in Chapter II of the poem, 'the interiors of Albions fibres & nerves [are] hidden' to him, and to his astonishment he sees 'only the petrified surfaces'.[66]

Here, 'London stone', as Blake has earlier referred to it, is the material substance in which, like an armour, the city is plated.[67] It is cold, resistant, and redolent of fear. London Stone in this abstract rather than particular sense is something like what Sartre calls the 'practico-inert' – 'the worked-over matter that presents an obstacle to human spontaneity', and that 'confronts man as an irreducible other, despite his role in its creation'.[68] It is the sedimentation of objectified, reified relations – alienation realized in the form of petrifaction.

'Chains / Of rocks round London Stone: of Reasonings ...' In abusing London Stone, in using it as a 'Stone of Torture', the Spectre Sons of Albion raised the foundations for the Enlightenment, the petrified forms of which are embodied in the 'Tabernacle of Bacon, Newton & Locke'.[69] In *Jerusalem*, the 'Reasonings' that, like chains, choke the life of London Stone, are a proleptic image of the reified, instrumentalist logic that characterizes what Adorno and Max Horkheimer, little more than a century later, will identify as the totally administered society of the Enlightenment. Night lies in the shade of the Enlightenment but nonetheless illuminates it. As Tambling affirms, 'night thoughts in midnight streets make the night the true Enlightenment, by questioning daytime identity'.[70] To walk in the city at night is to traverse the limits of the Enlightenment.

From Bacon on, Enlightenment ideology prosecuted 'the disenchantment of the world; the dissolution of myths and the substitution of knowledge for fancy' – in short, everything Blake fought against.[71] Enlightenment, according to Blake, means not elucidation but obnubilation. It means benightment. 'The banks of the Thames are clouded! The ancient porches of Albion are / Darkn'd!' he cries in the opening pages of the first chapter; 'they are drawn thro' unbounded space, scatter'd upon / The Void in incoherent despair'.[72] In this spiritual climate, and in 'Londons darkness', the poet sits trembling 'day and night', hoping 'to open the Eternal Worlds'.[73] 'My friends are astonish'd at me', he admits, 'Yet they forgive my wanderings, I rest not from my great task!'[74] In the 'dark and unknown night, indefinite, unmeasurable, without end', he sees 'Abstract Philosophy warring in enmity against Imagination'.[75]

Blake insists in *Milton* that the intellectual and spiritual imperative is 'to cast off Rational Demonstration by Faith in the Saviour'; 'To cast off Bacon, Locke & Newton from Albions covering / To take off his filthy garments, & clothe him with Imagination'.[76] Imagination, in the shape of Los, Blake's blacksmith and poet, must battle against the forces of Reason in order to begin building Jerusalem in Albion. But Los's Spectre, 'a blackning Shadow, blackning dark & opake', divides (and subdivides) from his back and tries to subjugate him, cursing him and 'suggesting murderous thoughts against Albion'. Dismayed that it has not destroyed him, and 'panting like a frighted wolf, and howling', the Spectre stands over 'the Immortal, in the solitude and darkness: Upon the darkening Thames …' Blake applies layer upon layer of opaque, obscure paint to the surface of the poem, until it appears thick and black with impasto.

The Spectre batters at Los with force; it also tries to lure him 'by tears, by arguments of science & by terrors'. It tortures Los, inducing 'Terrors in every Nerve, by spasms & extended pains'. But Los again and again resists the 'opake blackening Fiend'.[77] Blake believed, to take another formulation from Adorno and Horkheimer, that 'the fully enlightened earth radiates disaster'.[78] In Blake's critique of the Enlightenment, to put it in Michel Foucault's terms, he identified 'the darkness that rules at the very heart of what is excessive in light's radiance', and took up the fight against 'the secret night of light'.[79]

In *Jerusalem* and other poems, Blake portrays the rationalistic society radiating darkness. Albion's children, 'trembling victims' of 'Moral Justice', are condemned to '[wander] distant in a dismal Night clouded & dark'.[80] But Blake relentlessly campaigns to redeem Albion through the militant energies of his imagination: Blake against the blackness of Enlightenment.

Travelling through Darkness

Later in this same epic battle between Los and his 'terrible Spectre', the former appears to subdue the latter (in reality, the Spectre is 'hungring & thirsting for Los's life yet pretending obedience'). For a moment, Los compels his Spectre to see 'the tortures of the Victims', and forces him to kneel 'before Los's iron-shod feet on London Stone'.[81] Shackled on the Stone, in spite of his superiority, Los too is one of the justice system's sacrificial victims. Furthermore, even when he is free to roam, he feels compelled to return to the Stone, as if he cannot escape its orbit.

In Chapter II of *Jerusalem*, Los sets out in pursuit of 'the Oppressors of Albion' – the cruel and despotic representatives of the ruling class, who 'mock at the Labourers limbs' and 'at his starved Children', and who 'compell the Poor to live upon a crust of bread by soft mild arts'.[82] He searches for them on foot in a compulsive, restless journey that takes him through the darkest cavities and the deepest interior spaces of the nation. But after failing to find these 'Criminals' he retreats to his seat on London Stone. Los is immured once again, though not forever, amid 'the Rocky Law of Condemnation' built by the oppressors of Albion.[83] At once enervated and innervated, he 'tremble[s] sitting on the Stone / Of London', which is the site of his spiritual crucifixion. But in 'travelling thro darkness & horrid solitude' he has nonetheless had glimpses of redemption: 'And he beheld Jerusalem in Westminster & Marybone'.[84]

Los's travels, or travails, do not seem to him redemptive at the time. His desperate circumambulation of London, in darkness and solitude, presses the nightwalk to its dystopian limits. In the tenebrous spaces of the city he sees 'every Minute Particular of Albion degraded & murderd'. But, though he visits the scenes of these crimes against the poor, he is unable to track down those who have committed them:

> But Los
> Searched in vain: closd from the minutia he walkd, difficult.
> He came down from Highgate thro Hackney & Holloway towards
> London
> Till he came to old Stratford & thence to Stepney & the Isle
> Of Leuthas Dogs, thence thro the narrows of the Rivers side
> And saw every minute particular, the jewels of Albion, running down
> The kennels of the streets & lanes as if they were abhorrd.
> Every Universal Form, was become barren mountains of Moral
> Virtue: and every Minute Particular hardened into grains of sand:
> And all the tenderness of the soul cast forth as filth & mire,
> Among the winding places of deep contemplation intricate
> To where the Tower of London frownd dreadful over Jerusalem.[85]

'He walkd, difficult.' Los's task is a herculean and almost hopeless one (comparable, perhaps, to that of a detective commissioned to search the city for those responsible for the death of God). And Los is conscious that, even if he does find the oppressors, they will escape justice, as all the criminals who comprise the ruling class do, because it is these people, and not the poor, who have created the institutions that dispense punishment. What is standing in the dock, as Bertolt Brecht might have put it, compared to presiding over a court?

'If I could find these Criminals / I could not dare to take vengeance', Blake admits; 'for all things are so constructed / And builded by the Divine Hand, that the sinner shall always escape, / And he who takes vengeance alone is the criminal of Providence.' Indeed, in Britain's corrupt judicial system, which legitimates itself by discriminating against those who resist its regime, to take vengeance is to 'punish the already punishd'.[86] It is to provoke reprisals against the poor. Los is trapped in the circular logic of crime and punishment characteristic of class society. So it makes sense that his dispiriting journey into the metropolis, in which he is forced to confront his cooptation, finishes at London Stone, a fragment of the druid order of condemnation: 'At length he sat on London Stone ...'.[87]

Blake's verse often evokes 'Londons darkness', as if he imagines the city plunged into Stygian gloom during both night and day. Los's solitary journey on foot from Highgate Hill into the East End of London is an exploration of a dystopian city, filled with narrow, filthy, darkened defiles, in which the minute particulars that should have been redeemed by social and spiritual liberation remain damned, and all the tenderness of the soul has been reduced to shit. In this city – to invert a line from *Milton*, where the poet fantasizes about James II calling for the apocalyptic destruction of the decadent metropolis that he has created 'in the night of prosperity and wantonness' – Mathematic Proportion subdues Living Proportion.[88]

But, at the same time, Los's solipsistic journey is a tour of the pedestrian's interior, a labyrinthine space that is structured by 'winding places of deep contemplation intricate'. It reconnoitres what might be called the East End of the mind – the regions of consciousness, as well as of the city, where a sense of humanity has been degraded.[89]

For Blake, London is more than Golgotha, the place of the skull. It is itself a kind of skull.[90] It is Golgonooza, the imaginary city through which Jerusalem might ultimately emerge. Conversely, the mind is labyrinthine like a city. 'My Streets are my, [*sic*] Ideas of Imagination', London cries in *Jerusalem*, 'My Houses are Thoughts'.[91] The poet responds: My ideas of imagination are streets; my thoughts are houses.

Midnight Streets

The topography of Los's infernal journey into the crooked spaces of both the city and his consciousness is recapitulated from a more panoramic perspective in Chapter IV of *Jerusalem*: 'Highgates heights & Hampsteads, to Poplar Hackney & Bow: / To Islington & Paddington & the Brook of Albions River …'[92] This is the voice of the daughters of Albion, who call out to Los, and appeal to him for protection, as he 'all night watches / The stars rising & setting, & the meteors and terrors of night'.[93] It is in these places, they lament, beginning with 'lovely Lambeth', where the Blakes had lived from 1790 until 1800, that they 'builded Jersualem as a City & a Temple'.[94]

But 'Jerusalem lies in ruins'. And, exiled from Jerusalem, London is reduced to a crippled vagrant negotiating the streets of Babylon in a state of perpetual darkness (in this sense he is comparable to Jesus in one version of 'The Everlasting Gospel', who is 'a wandring Vagrant without Home').[95] This is a crucial image: 'I see London blind & age-bent begging thro the Streets / Of Babylon,

led by a child, his tears run down his beard'.[96] In Blake's illustration accompanying these lines, the old man's cramped, stooped loins, in spite of his decrepitude, contain a coiled, curved power that incarnates the promise of a resplendent, upright posture that, like the child's, radiates dignity and resilient strength. London has the social and spiritual potential to be either Jerusalem or Babylon (the former's pavements tiled with 'precious stones', the latter's streets 'paved with Destruction').[97]

But Blake's dialectics, which resist all forms of domestication, are more complicated than this dichotomy implies (as the far-from-simple relationship between Innocence and Experience in his *Songs* of the 1790s implies). For, earlier in the poem, Jerusalem too is personified as an urban outcast: 'I am an outcast', she exclaims; 'I am left to the trampling foot & the spurning heel! / A Harlot I am calld. I am sold from street to street!'[98] Here London is both Jerusalem and Babylon at the same time.

The trope of an aged, blind and infirm itinerant features repeatedly in Blake's poems. In the gallery of derelicts that populate his cityscapes – which, among other 'poor indigents', includes 'an aged Woman raving along the Streets' and a drunken woman 'reeling up the Street of London' – this figure is first among equals.[99] In 'Night the Third' of *The Four Zoas*, for example, the poet insists that where 'Enion blind & age bent wanderd Ahania wanders now / She wanders in Eternal Fear of falling into the indefinite / For her bright eyes behold the Abyss'.[100]

Both this image and, more directly, the one of 'London blind & age-bent begging thro the Streets' in *Jerusalem* lead back to one of Blake's greatest early poems – 'London'. For Blake also illustrated this beautiful prophetic lyric, published in *The Songs of Experience* (1794), with a painting of a child tenderly, perhaps also stridently, conducting a bearded, crippled man along a nocturnal street. This ancient, indigent man, whose presence in the *Songs of Innocence and Experience* encircles all the lost boys and girls, the chimney-sweeps and the little vagabonds of these early poems, is both the poet-prophet and London itself.

In 'London', Blake presents the poet-prophet as a nightwalker; and he presents the city itself, or its personification, as a nightwalker

too – as the illustration indicates. The poem's final stanza is explicitly set in 'midnight streets', but there is a sense that, implicitly, the three stanzas that precede it also depict a pedestrian journey that occurs at night. Here it is in its entirety:

> I wander thro' each charter'd street,
> Near where the charter'd Thames does flow.
> And mark in every face I meet
> Marks of weakness, marks of woe.
>
> In every cry of every Man,
> In every Infants cry of fear,
> In every voice: in every ban,
> The mind-forg'd manacles I hear
>
> How the Chimney-sweepers cry
> Every blackning Church appalls,
> And the hapless Soldiers sigh
> Runs in blood down Palace walls

> But most thro' midnight streets I hear
> How the youthful Harlots curse
> Blasts the new-born Infants tear
> And blights with plagues the Marriage hearse.[101]

The iambic emphasis in the first line of the fourth stanza – 'But most thro' midnight streets I hear' – falls on 'most', not 'night'. This implies that, prior to this climactic point, the poet has been taking it for granted that his circumambulation of the city is taking place in 'midnight streets'. The superlative, to formulate it in slightly different terms, refers not to the setting of the midnight streets but to the sound of 'the youthful Harlots'. What I hear most acutely at night, he is saying, is the prostitutes' curses.

It matters that the entire poem is set in the streets at midnight because it helps to explain both the indistinctness of the speaker's vision and the acuteness of his hearing. The marks that the speaker marks and re-marks in the faces of the impoverished people he meets are relatively abstract, though the reader infers that they take the form of creases, lines and stains, perhaps even injuries, disfigurations – the familiar residues or traces of physical exhaustion, spiritual alienation, and a sense of defeat. These are the crude signatures of an oppressive, rapaciously commercial society. The facial marks that the speaker discerns are not, however, highly individuated. Every face the speaker encounters is reduced to the same dead level of abstraction.

It is as if he cannot discriminate between them both because they are all susceptible to this levelling process of deindividuation and because he simply cannot see them properly. He does not meet people so much as he meets disembodied faces, which appear to him abruptly as he traverses the streets. Why is this the case? He might be blind, like Enion or the incarnation of London in *Jerusalem*, but there is no positive evidence for this in the poem. There is a clear indication, though, in the allusion to 'midnight streets', that it is nighttime. Blake, or London, is walking in the dark, among beggars, vagrants, prostitutes and poor labourers – he is a 'houseless wanderer', to take a phrase from *The Four Zoas*.[102]

The speaker's sight, then, is impaired, probably by the darkness and gloom of unlit or ill-lit streets. But, as a form of compensation, his hearing is acute. In addition to 'every cry of every Man', he hears infants' cries of fear, soldiers' sighs and prostitutes' curses. He hears, that is, the intermittent cacophony of the city at nighttime, which is audible against the background of silence.[103] It is not mere noise, though. These sounds are individuated as well as abstracted. They emanate from bodies, from people; and they punctuate the silence just as the faces materialize in the darkness.

But the speaker's hearing is better than acute – it is preternaturally sensitive. For 'in every voice' and 'every ban' he hears 'the mind-forg'd manacles'. He is tortured by a kind of tinnitus, a condition in which he hears a constant clinking, the sound of the mental shackles with which the poor and indigent have been enchained. Blake's speaker is so attuned to suffering that he can listen in on the most intimate and subtle operations of ideology! It is thus through sounds that he apprehends, in a secondary or visionary sight, the hypocrisies and social contradictions that divide the city and oppress its people. The cry of the chimney-sweeps appals 'every blackning Church'; the sigh of the soldiers 'runs in blood down Palace walls'; and the curse of the prostitutes 'blasts the new-born Infants tear / And blights with plagues the Marriage hearse'. The synaesthetic effects of the poem are a product of the speaker's intense auditory experience of the city at night.

Crooked Roads

'Londons darkness.' Blake insists that London is a city that has been benighted. In the terms he uses in *Europe: A Prophecy* (1794), the 'Stone of Night', an embodiment of violent, vengeful druidic power, comparable to the one rolled aside in Christ's resurrection, and evocative of London Stone, looms above the metropolis and its 'Churches, Palaces, Towers': 'Bleak, dark, abrupt, it stands & overshadows London city'.[104] The blackened churches and bloodied palaces of Blake's nocturnal cityscape in 'London' – the poem is in effect an anti-nocturne – also subsist in its ominous shadow.

But if the city is benighted because it lies in the grip of the eighteenth-century institutions that implement this ancient, deathly cult of oppressive justice, then it is also benighted because it has been choked by the insidious culture of commercial charters. Charters too appal the city; that is, in addition to making it pale or horrifying it, they cover it in a pall, which is both a funeral drape and a dark cloud of smoke. London is trapped in the suffocating apparatus of capital, which marks or stamps everything with the sign of ownership. Its streets are obscured by black print that inscribes proprietary rights. Even the fluid, free-form Thames, chartered by the East India Company, is susceptible to this system – indeed, especially the Thames, since it issues from the centre of an expanding empire and floods the plains of far-distant colonies. London's branded, chartered streets and streams are every bit as repressive in their implications as the blackened churches and bloodied palaces.

The city is blighted by these licences that, prior to the consolidation of commodity capitalism in the nineteenth century, reshape and deform its people and places according to a commercial logic. This is benightment in the name of enlightenment. In a culture in which everything is chartered – commodities, streets, the Thames – these marks of monopolistic privilege signify expropriation, not simply appropriation. 'A charter of liberty', Thompson underlines in his inspiring rereading of 'London', 'is, simultaneously, a denial of these liberties to others.'[105] The people, in this context, have lost their 'right to the city', if they ever possessed it – a collective right 'to change and reinvent the city more after our hearts' desire'.[106]

But, in 'London', Blake's nightwalk through the midnight streets represents a challenge to the logic of accumulation and exploitation that prevails in the city. It affirms the right to the city. It is not simply that, in charting the alienating and exploitative consequences of the charters, the speaker attempts to make its relentless system of accounting … accountable. It is that, in wandering purposelessly through the streets rather than pursuing a direct, purposeful path through them, he resists the commercial organization of the city. 'Improvement makes strait roads', Blake wrote in *The Marriage of Heaven and Hell* at the beginning of the 1790s, 'but the crooked roads without Improvement, are roads of Genius'.[107] Blake opposes the crooked to the straight.

'I wander thro' each charter'd street.' Something that is chartered is mapped and measured as well as licensed. Someone who wanders, inscribing him- or herself on the city, scribbles over these ordered, logical lines. To wander, in its original sense, means, as the OED indicates, 'to roam, ramble, go idly or restlessly about; to have no fixed abode or station'. To wander, then, is to uncharter. Consciously or unconsciously, houseless wandering constitutes a refusal of the chartered city. Here, in the opening line of 'London', is the outline of a political conflict – 'a contradiction between the collective mode of administration and an individual mode of reappropriation', as Michel de Certeau defines it.[108] The wandered city is the unchartered city.

Out of the Cares of Night

To wander through the streets at midnight is not to capitulate to a mood of defeat or despair, as many readers of 'London' have supposed, but to mount a surreptitious political challenge to the city's prevailing social and economic regime. This is far more difficult to achieve in the day, when the individual is invariably overwhelmed by the bustling collective rhythms of the commercial city, than in the night, when there is time and space for the solitary pedestrian to reclaim these rhythms. In 'London', both the poet and the city stand in the tradition of the common nightwalker, taking back the city from which he or she is excluded in the day.

In the late eighteenth century, the city's authorities no longer ring out the curfew in a literal sense; but there is still an engrained ideological sense that anyone on the streets in the dead of night is infringing the rules of polite, respectable, possibly legal society. Foucault speaks of the ruling class's 'fear of darkened spaces' in this period, emphasizing that its 'political and moral order' refused 'to tolerate areas of darkness'.[109] The Enlightenment proscribed the night. And in the aftermath of the French Revolution, when clandestine Jacobin associations met in London and other cities to plot rebellion, there was a widespread fear of 'conspiracies of the night'.[110] In the 1790s, then, and thereafter, a mind-forged curfew continued to be rung.

In Blake's 'London', nightwalking is an attempt to elude this ideological, if not legal, prohibition. It is in a sense an act of 'excarceration'. 'As the theme of incarceration was played out in workhouse, factory, hospital, school and ship' in the eighteenth century, Linebaugh argues, 'so the counterpoint of excarceration was played out in escapes, flights, desertions, migrations and refusals.'[111] Nightwalking is not of course a dramatic act of excarceration, like a desertion or an escape from prison; it is not an openly defiant gesture of rebellion against a despotic regime. It is instead a mundane act of excarceration, which discreetly evades the stifling order of the administered city. It is an attempt to slip free from mind-forg'd manacles rather than to shatter physical ones.

Moreover, nightwalking is an individual rather than a collective act of resistance. But, as Blake portrays in 'London', it nonetheless encodes an expression of solidarity with others in the darkened streets – the constituents of an invisible, plebeian community of common nightwalkers, like the soldiers and prostitutes. I have assumed in my interpretation of the poem, implicitly or explicitly, that London itself is the speaker, in addition to Blake himself, and that, as in a dramatic monologue, its 'pent-up voice', which the critic Harold Bloom describes as 'wandering still at midnight through the streets', cannot be separated from the poet's. London itself – the allegorical embodiment of the industrial metropolis – is then a vagrant condemned to circumnavigate the city. If this is the case, if London is itself a kind of nightwalker, then Blake's scattered community of children, soldiers and prostitutes is contained in the city's collective consciousness, and it is therefore already a unified, almost visible force. For a dystopian poem, 'London' is oddly optimistic.

The relationship between the poem's isolated inhabitants of the night is in the present conditions of society a 'serial' one, to formulate it in Sartre's terms. But there is a possibility that, in the future, it will change from a disaggregated into a 'fused group'. One of Sartre's most important examples of this process is the French Revolution.[111] Blake offers a glimpse of this utopian prospect in his poem about 1789. There, he describes the 'millions of spirits immortal' who, prior to the insurrection, 'when the heavens were seal'd with a stone, and the terrible sun clos'd in an orb', have languished in an almost endless night. Condemned 'to wander inslav'd; black, deprest in dark ignorance, kept in awe with the whip, / To worship terrors', these people are waiting for the dawn of history, which is imminent.[113]

Here is Blake's mythopoeic description of this revolution that is at the same time a resurrection:

> Till dawn, till morning, till the breaking of clouds, and swelling of winds, and the universal voice,
> Till man raise his darken'd limbs out of the caves of night, his eyes and his heart
> Expand: where is space! Where O sun is thy dwelling! Where thy tent, O faint slumb'rous Moon.
> Then the valleys of France shall cry to the soldier, throw down thy sword and musket,
> And run and embrace the meek peasant. Her nobles shall hear and shall weep, and put off
> The red robe of terror, the crown of oppression, the shoes of contempt, and unbuckle
> The girdle of war from the desolate earth.[114]

A nation that has been sentenced to wander in the night is thus liberated into the light.

Perhaps Blake conceals a similar promise in 'London'. The poem's noctambulant speaker assimilates the cries and sighs and curses of the city's victims, its noctivagants, to its own pent-up, prophetic voice. And, in orchestrating them, it commutes them into a collective voice that heralds the passing of the night.

10.

The Nocturnal Labyrinth

Thomas De Quincey

Stealing Away by Night

In London – where, as a destitute eighteen-year-old, he lived a rootless, vagrant existence – Thomas De Quincey's identity was both made and undone. The city exerted what he might have called an elective attraction on him.

The philanthropist John Ritchie Findlay, a friend of the author from his youth, once recalled that, in old age, De Quincey hinted at enigmatic motives for his migration to the metropolis at the turn of the nineteenth century, and 'confessed to occasional accesses of an almost irresistible impulse to flee to the labyrinthine shelter of some great city like London or Paris – there to dwell solitary amid a multitude, buried by day in the cloister-like recesses of mighty libraries, and stealing away by night to some obscure lodging'.[1] De Quincey did indeed lead a solitary life amid the multitude when he first lived in London, stealing among the cloister-like recesses of the mighty city at night, as well as retreating, when he could, to an obscure lodging.

It is in the context of a persistent moral curfew, which long outlasted the rise of nightlife among the metropolitan middle classes, that De Quincey's nocturnal loitering as an adolescent in London needs to be understood. Pacing the streets or squatting on doorsteps, De Quincey might be characterized as a Romantic nightwalker who – half-actively, half-passively – performed the centuries-old role of a common nightwalker. His wanderings at night through the labyrinthine metropolis, which he sketched in *Confessions of an English Opium-Eater* (1821), appear to have been partly a deliberate strategy of self-abnegation and partly the result of a genuinely penurious state. In this respect, as in others, and in spite of his lifetime commitment to a conservative politics, he embodied the Romantic archetype of an itinerant artist or poet condemned to ramble about the city at night in search of … himself.

Casual Hospitalities

Born in Manchester in 1785, De Quincey was the fourth child of a highly educated, liberal-minded textile importer from Lincolnshire who, until his death in 1793, lived mostly abroad because of his tuberculosis. De Quincey's mother was a deeply religious woman who, three years after her husband's death, moved with her sons to Bath, where she joined the evangelical Hannah More's circle. John 'Walking' Stewart, one of the most prodigious and athletic pedestrians of the age, was also living in Bath at this time, and in an article celebrating his 'sublime madness' De Quincey later recalled that, as a thirteen-year-old, he had seen him 'walking up and down, and dispersing his philosophic opinions to the right and the left, like a Grecian Philosopher'.[2]

In 1800, De Quincey's mother sent him to Manchester Grammar School, in the expectation that he would eventually graduate to Brasenose College, Oxford, on a scholarship. A gifted classicist, the precocious De Quincey felt increasingly frustrated in the school's stuffy intellectual environment. So, in July 1802, he absconded and walked to Chester, where his mother was by then living. He carried a copy of Euripides in one pocket and a volume of Wordsworth's poems in the other. In Chester, his mother and guardians agreed to grant him an allowance of one guinea a week. Shortly before his seventeenth birthday, therefore, persuaded of his independence, he set off on a solitary walking tour of North Wales. In this manner, he inaugurated his career as a semi-privileged vagrant – a 'philosophic vagabond', in Oliver Goldsmith's lapidary phrase.

De Quincey's weekly guinea was not a princely sum on which to live, even as a peripatetic, and in order to avoid paying for accommodation in inns he often either lodged with cottagers or, as many as nine days out of every fourteen, identified some rough patch of ground and pitched a canvas tent that he himself had ingeniously devised. 'This tent, as may be imagined, was miserably small', he wrote, 'both to make it more portable, and also on account of the tent-pole, which, to avoid notice and trouble, was no more than a common walking cane.' Sleeping rough like this in fields felt hazardous. De Quincey constantly feared that disturbed cattle would trample on him as he slept. Moreover, the weather became more and more hostile as the autumn advanced. On one occasion he was caught in a storm on Mount Snowdon and wandered about for some six hours before being taken in at midnight, 'cold and perishing', and curling up with a couple of children. He could afford neither books, which he craved, nor adequate quantities of food. 'So long as I remained in Wales, I subsisted either on blackberries, hips, haws &c. or on the casual hospitalities which I now and then received.'[3]

In this desperate but not entirely involuntary condition, De Quincey resolved to move to London, where he hoped, like those who had migrated to Grub Street in the eighteenth century, to promote his emergent literary ambitions. He was conscious that this contravention of the advice his mother and his guardian had given him would involve not only disavowing his chance of going to university but forfeiting his weekly allowance. So he decided instead to borrow £200 from a moneylender and divide it into four lots, living on £50 a year for the next four years, before coming in to his inheritance at the age of twenty-one. There is no consensus among De Quincey's biographers as to why he took this decision, which made no financial and little professional sense. 'There was something distinctly irrational about the London venture', Grevel Lindop observes.[4]

Nightly Asylum

De Quincey arrived in the capital in November 1802. In his *Confessions*, he revealed that, 'generally in Wales, and always for the first two months in London', he 'was houseless, and very seldom slept under a roof'. In a later autobiographical sketch, published in 1835, reflecting again on his experiences both in the valleys of Wales and 'upon the streets of London', he characterized himself as 'a wanderer too often houseless in both situations'.[5] He didn't detail his experience of homelessness at this time; but, even if he exaggerated the extent to which he was unable to afford lodgings, he must have endured some pretty brutal conditions, not least because it was already November when he arrived in the capital.

In the absence of a tent like the one he had devised in North Wales, De Quincey was presumably forced at times to improvise some form of makeshift protection or insulation from the elements. But, whatever it consisted of, it cannot have offered him much warmth or comfort. Moreover, he was far more vulnerable to physical danger in the darkened streets than in the fields. No doubt at nighttime he had to remain alert, and as a consequence did a good deal of fitful sleeping in the daytime, perhaps in the cheaper coffee-houses. Even when he did have accommodation at this time, as he admits, he slept little and 'was apt to fall into transient dozings at all hours'.[6]

De Quincey ascribed the fact that he 'did not sink under [his] torments' during these months to his 'constant exposure to the open air', which implies that, in addition to sitting on doorsteps, he walked at night as well as in the day, and persuaded himself that the exercise was doing him some good. Gazing to the north, in the direction of the Lakes, he nursed his craving for friendship with William Wordsworth, whom he admired more than anyone else alive. 'Oftentimes on moonlight nights', he records,

> my consolation was (if such it could be thought) to gaze from Oxford-street up every avenue in succession which pierces through the heart of Marylebone to the fields and the woods; for *that*, said I, travelling with my eyes up the long vistas which lay part in light and part in shade, '*that* is the road to the North, and therefore to –, and if I had the wings of a dove, *that* way I would fly for comfort.'[7]

The avenues piercing through the heart of Marylebone to the countryside north of the New Road under the moonlight are an objective correlative for the deep stabs of longing he felt for the companionship of the poet, and the comfort and fame such companionship promised. As ever with De Quincey, internal and external topographies are almost indistinguishable.

In January 1803, when he was beginning 'to sink into a more languishing condition' under the effects of an increasingly inclement climate, De Quincey petitioned the attorney to whom he had applied for assistance when he was trying to secure a loan, a Mr Brunell, to give him the use of his large, unoccupied house in Greek Street 'as a nightly asylum from the open air'. This mysterious man, who also called himself Mr Brown, and who slept in a different part of London every night in order to evade the bailiffs, agreed to this arrangement. So the almost derelict eighteen-year-old gratefully moved into the empty, poorly maintained building: 'But I found, on taking possession of my new quarters, that the house already contained one single inmate, a poor friendless child, apparently ten years old.'[8]

Amid the cavernous, dusty spaces of this house, which echoed to the noise of rats because it contained so little furniture, this 'hunger-bitten' girl was pathetically grateful to discover that De Quincey 'was, in future, to be her companion through the hours of darkness'. 'In common with the rats', De Quincey 'sate rent free' (though the child, whom he suspected of being their landlord's illegitimate daughter, was effectively indentured as Mr Brunell's servant). He lived off the crumbs from Brunell's table, and peered longingly into bakers' shops. At night, the two urchins huddled together on the floor beneath 'a sort of large horseman's coat'. During the day, released from his role as the girl's protector, De Quincey 'went off and sate in the parks, or elsewhere, until night-fall'.[9] He was houseless in spite of this house; homeless at home. He must have measured his days in minutes.

De Quincey's recollections of the nameless child with whom he cohabited are marked by a slightly disturbing impatience or intolerance for her charmlessness: 'Apart from her situation, she was not what would be called an interesting child: she was neither pretty, nor quick in understanding, nor remarkably pleasing in manners.' Principally, he admits, he loved the child because she was his 'partner in wretchedness'.[10] But in general De Quincey does not appear to have been particularly open to perceiving others as partners in wretchedness; and in spite of his own semi-vagrant status at this time he seems subsequently to have been disinclined to sympathize with actual vagabonds.

Indeed, quite the reverse. His diary entry for 4 May 1803, when he was living in Everton on the outskirts of Liverpool – a place to which his despairing mother had exiled him – contains this repulsive anecdote:

> walked into the lanes; – met a fellow who counterfeited drunkenness or lunacy or idiocy; – I say *counterfeited*, because I am well convinced he was some vile outcast of society – a pest and disgrace to humanity. I was just on point of hitt[ing] him a dab on his disgust[ing] face when a gentleman (coming up) alarmed him and saved me trouble.[11]

De Quincey's contempt for the vagrant, which is in brutal contrast to his hero Wordsworth's characteristic sympathy for 'vile outcasts of society', is a sign of his social and psychological insecurity – in short, his self-hatred.

Female Peripatetics

Partly, perhaps, because he had been profoundly affected by the death of his eldest sister in 1792, De Quincey nonetheless demonstrated more affection for young women who had been discarded by society than for men. In particular, he felt compassion for street prostitutes. He affirms his sense of identity with them in the *Confessions*:

> Being myself at that time of necessity a peripatetic, or a walker of the streets, I naturally fell in more frequently with those female peripatetics who are technically called street-walkers. Many of these women had occasionally taken my part against the watchmen who wished to drive me off the steps of houses where I was sitting.[12]

He thus points to a double symmetry. Like the prostitutes, De Quincey is criminalized, even though neither he nor they can be prosecuted for anything specific. Like De Quincey, they are peripatetics: by characterizing them as 'female peripatetics', he half-satirically, half-sentimentally dignifies them as philosophers of the street. He might be damned as they fear being; they might be redeemed as he hopes to be.

In defiant tones, then, De Quincey states that he is not ashamed to admit that he 'was then on familiar and friendly terms with many women in that unfortunate condition'. In this attitude – at least in so far as the phrase 'familiar and friendly terms' was not a euphemism for sexual relations – he was far from typical of men of his or other classes at this time. Street prostitutes were popularly regarded as the most corrupt, despicable and disreputable women in the capital, and most middle-class men professed contempt for them (even, or especially, if they paid for their services).

Francis Place, the radical tailor and reformist, is probably more representative than De Quincey in his attitude to street prostitutes.

Place's *Autobiography* (1835) offered a characteristically fastidious but also vivid description of Charing Cross at the turn of the nineteenth century. This was an area in which, on the eastern side at least, opposite the fashionable concert and exhibition rooms, artisans and craftsmen lived alongside soldiers and prostitutes in crowded and chaotic conditions. Place records that on the edge of Privy Gardens, near the top of Parliament Street, there stood a wall daubed with ballads and obscene pictures: 'At night there were a set of prostitutes along this wall, so horridly ragged, dirty and disgusting that I doubt much there are now any such in any part of London. These miserable wretches used to take any customer who would pay them twopence, behind the wall.'[13]

By the mid 1830s, in spite of Place's fond claim, there were still plenty of street prostitutes in London; but two important changes – the introduction of gaslight and the legislation of the Vagrancy Acts in the early 1820s – had rendered them less visible in central London (or rather, these changes had rendered them more visible, and had therefore made their livelihoods less tenable there). The Vagrancy Act, which punished offenders with a prison sentence of up to one month, made it an offence to be a 'common prostitute wandering in the public streets or public highways, or in any place of public resort, and behaving in a riotous or indecent manner'.

De Quincey is a little too defensive, though, in his insistence that his friendly relations with prostitutes prove that he is a 'Catholic creature', an impartial 'philosopher' superior to those who are 'filled with narrow and self-regarding prejudices of birth and education'. He protests too much: 'The truth is, that at no time of my life have I been a person to hold myself polluted by the touch or approach of any creature that wore a human shape.' On the contrary, he emphasizes, 'from my very earliest youth it has been my pride to converse familiarly with all human beings, man, woman, and child, that chance may fling in my way.'[14]

At no time in his life? All human beings? Perhaps the 'pest and disgrace to humanity' he encountered in Everton shortly after this first residence in London simply does not count. Perhaps this poor man did not have a human shape. Far from conversing with this 'vile outcast', De Quincey almost strikes him. He is only saved from committing this shameful assault on the 'disgust[ing]' man by the pre-emptive action of a 'gentleman', a man who is himself apparently filled with precisely those 'narrow and self-regarding prejudices of birth and education' that De Quincey claims to despise. As his most recent biographer points out, De Quincey's solidarity with street prostitutes is 'in defiance of some of his own deep-seated bigotries'.[15] He was a misogynist, as well as someone with almost pathological, if at times sentimental, contempt for the denizens of what subsequently came to be called 'outcast London'.

The most significant portrait painted in the *Confessions* is of 'a young woman, and one of that unhappy class who subsists upon the wages of prostitution' – Ann. De Quincey was on intimate, not simply familiar and friendly, terms with this fifteen-year-old, and formed an intense sentimental attachment to her. 'For many weeks I had walked at nights with this poor friendless girl up and down Oxford Street, or had rested with her on steps and under the shelter of porticos.'[16] The streetwalker and the nightwalker, the common and the uncommon nightwalker, thus found companionship on the lamp-lit streets of the metropolis.

For De Quincey, Ann represents the ideal type of the street prostitute. Her 'simple history', which seems to have turned on the dispossession of 'her little property' by a 'brutal ruffian', is 'a case of ordinary occurrence' in the city; and he regrets the fact that 'London beneficence' is not 'better adapted' to deal with it, and that its laws are used 'to avenge' rather than 'protect' people like her. The 'stream of London charity', he observes, is 'not obvious or readily accessible to poor houseless wanderers', and the 'outside air and framework of London society is harsh, cruel, and repulsive'.[17] Expelled from doorsteps at night by officious watchmen, De Quincey too has experienced this chilling atmosphere, this unfeeling framework.

But if Ann is the archetype of the most oppressed class of prostitutes, then she is also its exception:

> – yet no! let me not class thee, Oh noble minded Ann —, with that order of women; let me find, if it be possible, some gentler name to designate the condition of her whose bounty and compassion, ministering to my

> necessities when all the world had forsaken me, I owe it that I am at this time alive.[18]

Her sisterly kindness to De Quincey, who insists that on one unforgettable occasion she saved his life, lifts her out of the social category to which she has been condemned by circumstance.

'One night', De Quincey explains, 'when we were pacing slowly along Oxford Street, and after a day when I had felt more than usually ill and faint, I requested her to turn off with me into Soho Square.' Together they 'sate down on the steps of a house', and after a short time De Quincey suddenly became far sicker: 'I had been leaning my head against her bosom; and all at once I sank from her arms and fell backwards on the steps.' His 'poor orphan companion' reacted rapidly, running off into Oxford Street and returning 'in less time than could be imagined' with 'a glass of port wine and spices', which instantaneously restored his senses.[19]

Separation for Eternity

'I loved her as affectionately as if she had been my sister', De Quincey testifies in his mournful account of the last night he spent on the streets with Ann. In the course of his ceaseless attempts to secure a loan, De Quincey had persuaded a Jewish moneylender called Dell, a colleague of Mr Brunell, that a young aristocrat of his acquaintance, a student at Eton College, would be prepared to guarantee it. So, accompanied by Ann, 'on a dark winter evening', some time after six o'clock, he set off through the streets, at a dilatory enough pace, in order to catch the Bristol Mail, from which he planned to disembark close to the public school. De Quincey's description is characteristically vague – dream-like, even: 'Our course lay through a part of the town which has now all disappeared, so that I can no longer retrace its ancient boundaries: Swallow-street, I think it was called.'[20]

De Quincey's memories are so enmeshed in the city's intricate medieval geography, even before they are complicated by the phantasmagoria of his opium addiction a few years later, that when the street plan changes, as a direct result of the 'improvements' John Nash implemented on behalf of the Prince Regent in the 1810s and 1820s, they are fatally erased. The 'filthy labyrinthine environs' of Swallow Street, as James Elmes referred to them in his *Metropolitan Improvements of London* (1827), occupied the boundary between the West End and Soho – territories that confronted one another, at the turn of the nineteenth century, like foreign countries.[21] In constructing Regent Street, and destroying Swallow Street, Nash built a bulwark 'between aristocratic London in the west and plebeian London in the east'.[22] This is the social borderland inhabited by De Quincey, emblematic of his own ambiguous class status as someone forced to slum it before going up to Oxford. 'Nowhere, unless perhaps in dreams', Walter Benjamin writes, 'can the phenomenon of the boundary be experienced in a more originary way than in cities.'[23]

On the evening described by De Quincey, he and Ann slipped off into Golden Square and there briefly deposited themselves, 'not wishing to part in the tumult and blaze of Piccadilly'. Clasped on a doorstep in the cold and dark, the two companions must have appeared closely matched in age and social status – in spite of their different backgrounds or divergent trajectories – to those passersby who did more than glimpse at them by the dim, guttering light of nearby lamps. De Quincey discussed his plans and prospects with her; then they made an arrangement to the effect that, from the fifth night after his departure, she would wait every evening for him 'near the bottom of Great Titchfield-street, which had been our customary haven, as it were, of rendezvous, to prevent our missing each other in the great Mediterranean of Oxford-street'. The young man kissed her, and she put her arms around his neck and silently wept (De Quincey's sentimental tableau slyly hints that they had sexual as well as fraternal relations). Finally, he set off, reaching the Gloucester Coffee-House on Piccadilly, the point of departure for many of the city's coaches, just as the Bristol Mail was departing.[24]

He never met Ann again. Once he had returned to London he repaired each evening to their rendezvous, but she never reappeared: 'I sought her daily, and waited for her every night, so long as I staid in London, at the corner of Titchfield-street.' He enquired after her ceaselessly; and, though hampered because he did not know her surname, 'put into activity every means of tracing her that my knowledge of London suggested, and the limited extent of my power made possible'. So he claims in the *Confessions*.[25]

It is entirely possible that these attempts to trace her were a fiction. Robert Morrison suggests that, attracted to aristocrats as well as outcasts, and conscious that his relations with the latter might impede his intellectual and social aspirations, 'he may also have given her the slip'.[26] But it is also possible that Ann herself was a fiction. Biographers and critics have long suspected that she was a composite portrait of a number of prostitutes with whom he became acquainted at this time (perhaps at other times too). What matters is her role as a mythological figure of female suffering and redemption – a Magdalen – and as an emblem of the city's enigmatic logic: 'If she lived, doubtless we must have been sometimes in search of each other, at the very same moment, through the mighty labyrinths of London; perhaps, even within a few feet of each other – a barrier no wider in a London street, often amounting in the end to a separation for eternity.'[27]

In the metropolis the most intense, and characteristic, relationships are at once alienated and intimate.

Dilated Reflection

De Quincey's adventures in pursuit of financial security on the evening he left Ann almost inevitably involved nightwalking. He was in a pretty abject state at this juncture. The moneylender on whom he hoped to depend, Mr Dell, had questioned whether he was indeed the son mentioned in the will left by Thomas Quincey of Greenhay, Manchester. So his 'loss of social identity', as Lindop comments, 'was now virtually complete: not only had he vanished from his guardians to become a shabby stray in a huge city, but his very name and parentage were questioned'.[28] There is something self-punitive about this déclassé individual's desperate, almost hopeless attempt to shore up his crumbling social identity in a journey to Eton, Britain's most celebrated bastion of ruling-class distinction.

Falling into a deep, if restless sleep on his uncomfortable perch on the outside of the coach to Bristol, De Quincey woke to discover that it had already reached Maidenhead. So he clambered off and headed back along the road. 'It must have been nearly midnight', he explains in the *Confessions*, 'but so slowly did I creep along, that I heard a clock in a cottage striking four before I turned down the lane from Slough to Eton.' The distance was no more than seven or eight miles, so he must have moved at a preternaturally slow pace. If a sleepless cottager, rising from her bed as the clock echoed 4 a.m., had happened to peer out into the night, she would have seen a forlorn, ragged figure edging along the road like a somnambulist. Eventually, De Quincey fell asleep at the side of the road, and was woken at dawn by an 'ill-looking fellow' (though not one that was therefore necessarily 'ill-meaning', as he conceded in a rare display of generous feeling for a representative of the working class).[29]

Before he collapsed at the roadside in sleep, De Quincey reflected as he walked that, proceeding in the direction of Hounslow Heath, where a rich man had recently been murdered, he might be unfortunate enough to collide with the assassin in the dark. And he comforted himself with the rather discomforting thought that, in contrast to the aristocrat he sought at Eton, he himself was 'little better than an outcast', and therefore had no reason to fear dying – for it is 'vast power and possessions [that] make a man shamefully afraid of dying'. This precept cannot have been much of a consolation, given his active imagination, as he groped along the desolately empty road. 'It naturally occurred to me', he recalls, 'that I and the accursed murderer, if he were that night abroad, might at every instant be unconsciously approaching each other through the darkness …'[30]

In fact, the man murdered on Hounslow Heath – the owner of a lavender warehouse in the Strand called John Steele – had probably been killed by two men, John Holloway and Owen Haggerty. On a moonlit night in November 1802, the month De Quincey first arrived in London, they had robbed Steele, beaten him about the head with a stick, and left him to die in a ditch (it was not a murder, then, that De Quincey would have considered as a fine art). Holloway was, according to the *Newgate Calendar*, a man of about forty: 'of great muscular strength, tall, and of savage, brutal, and ferocious countenance, with large thick lips, depressed nose, and high cheek bones' – just the kind of caricature of a degenerate criminal that De Quincey presumably imagined as he soldiered along the road in the dark.[31] The men were apprehended in 1806 and sentenced to death at the Old Bailey in 1807, though both of them protested their innocence to the end. In the monstrous crowd that assembled at Newgate to see their execution, which might have numbered as many as 45,000, some thirty people died in the crush.[32]

Throughout his autobiographical writings, De Quincey is interested in the idea of doubles and doubling, as his account in *Suspiria de Profundis* (1845) of 'the Apparition of the Brocken' – a phantom that is 'but a dilated reflection' of the spectator – most clearly indicates.[33] The murderer, tramping through the night in pursuit of his victims, is one of these doppelgangers. So is Ann. As John Barrell has pointed out, De Quincey assumed the identity of the Wandering Jew; and, by association or extension, of the pariah:

> The role of Wandering Jew, adopted after he ran away from school, facilitated his identification with the prostitute Ann, by an associative logic which transforms Wandering Jew into pedestrian, into peripatetic philosopher or 'walker of the streets', into peripatetic as 'street-walker', into Ann 'a lost Pariah woman', untouchable except by those willing to be polluted, and except by fellow-pariahs, fellow-untouchables.[34]

De Quincey's identity as a nightwalker, according to a dreamlike logic, constituted a link in this associative chain.

North-West Passage

De Quincey's notorious addiction to opium – 'dread agent of unimaginable pleasure and pain!' – played an increasingly important part in his relationship to the streets of the metropolis at night. He began using opium, according to the testimony he includes in the *Confessions*, in the autumn of 1804, when he bought some from a pharmacist's shop in order to alleviate toothache. This was during his first visit to the capital after becoming a student, almost a year before, at Worcester (rather than Brasenose) College, Oxford – a time when he lapsed 'into a deep melancholy, from brooding too much on the sufferings which [he] had witnessed in London'.[35] It was as a user of opium, taken in the form of laudanum, that De Quincey resumed his career as a nightwalker.

Initially, as he explains, he was a purely recreational opium-eater – one who consumed it roughly once every three weeks, 'usually on a Tuesday or Saturday night'. These nights 'were the regular Opera nights', when he experimented with the effect of the drug on his appreciation of the music, or vice versa. But, on Saturday nights, the opera competed with another temptation – the ritual of strolling among the poor in the streets of the city as they relaxed at the end of the working week. Most people, he conceded, expressed interest in the poor by sympathizing with their pains; 'I, at that time, was disposed to express my interest by sympathizing with their pleasures.' The life he himself had recently led had been too close to the life of the poor for him to relish observing their miseries; 'but the pleasures of the poor, their consolations of spirit, and their reposes from bodily toil, can never become oppressive to contemplate.'[36]

On a Saturday night, in spite of his own unfamiliarity with the routines of wage-labour, De Quincey vicariously felt as if he too 'were released from some yoke of labour, had some wages to receive, and some luxury of repose to enjoy'. If attending the opera after taking opium entailed immersing himself in the music in order to intensify its sensuous effects, then ambling among the poor as they socialized at the end of the week implied the opposite of immersion – a delicate, perhaps exquisite kind of alienation. Far from collapsing the difference between subject and object, it was symptomatic of a fatal distance between them. The poor perambulating the streets comprised for him a form of opera buffa.

'For the sake of witnessing, upon as large a scale as possible, a spectacle with which my sympathy was so entire', De Quincey confirms in the *Confessions*, 'I used often, on Saturday nights, after I had taken opium, to wander forth, without much regarding the direction or the distance, to all the markets, and other parts of London, to which the poor resort on a Saturday night, for laying out their wages.' He thus 'walks the rounds', like Henry V or Henry VIII; and in benignly spying on the poor, as these illustrious predecessors supposedly did, he acts the part of 'a perfect night-walker'. De Quincey describes eavesdropping on their conversations as they 'stood consulting on their ways and means' or discussing 'the price of household articles'; and observes that, when he could do so 'without appearing to be intrusive', he sometimes even volunteered his opinion on the matter.[37]

De Quincey claims that his interventions were 'always received indulgently', but it is difficult not to imagine that those around whom he floated and hovered with a seraphic smile on his face, or a forehead furrowed in concentration, were frankly bemused by his presence. They must have intuited that he was far more affluent than them. In the *Confessions* he undoubtedly idealized the ephemeral identifications he formed with the poor on these ramblings. His sympathy was scarcely, as he claimed, 'entire'. Barrell is emphatic that, in spite of his apparently indulgent attitude, De Quincey regarded all members of the working class as what he contemptuously called 'latent Jacobins'. He was secretly gripped by 'a fearful suspicion, a paranoia, that in the apparently routine and good-natured transactions of a Saturday-night shopping trip, conspiratorial words are being whispered, glances exchanged'.[38]

De Quincey admits that some of the nightwalking he did under the influence of opium was altogether less sociable, and more solitary, than his opening encomium indicates. 'Some of these rambles led me to great distances: for an opium-eater is too happy to observe the motion of time', he writes.[39] Perhaps it was partly as a release from the oppressive discipline of time, the infinitesimally slow motion of which had dominated the tedious days and nights he spent subsisting in London on his first visit to the metropolis, that opium appealed to him. It must have split open each one of those units of time whose relentless procession had protracted the pain and tedium of his former existence in the capital, plunging him instead into a present of infinite imaginative potential.

'The proportions of time and being are distorted by the innumerable multitude and intensity of sensations and ideas', wrote one of De Quincey's most celebrated acolytes, Charles Baudelaire, in his account of the effects of consuming hashish laced with opium.[40] In the section in the *Confessions* on 'The Pains of Opium', De Quincey registers the drug's impact on his sense of both space and time, which in the end proved debilitating and deleterious. 'Space swelled, and was amplified to an extent of unutterable infinity', he writes; but the 'vast expansion of time' was even more disturbing: 'I sometimes seemed to have lived for 70 or 100 years in one night; nay, sometimes had feelings representative of a millennium passed in that time, or, however, of a duration far beyond the limits of any human experience.'[41]

On occasion, as De Quincey implicitly concedes in the section on 'The Pleasures of Opium' too, his transcendent experience of time rendered his pedestrian experience of space insupportable:

> And sometimes in my attempts to steer homewards, upon nautical principles, by fixing my eye on the pole-star, and seeking ambitiously for a north-west passage, instead of circumnavigating all the capes and headlands I had doubled in my outward voyage, I came suddenly upon such knotty problems of alleys, such enigmatical entries, and such sphinx's riddles of streets without thoroughfares, as must, I conceive, baffle the audacity of porters, and confound the intellects of hackney-coachmen. I could almost believe, at times, that I must be the first discoverer of some of these *terrae incognitae*, and doubted, whether they had yet been laid down in the modern charts of London.[42]

De Quincey's tone expresses exhilaration (the exhilaration of an imperial adventurer or conqueror) and the terror inseparable from it. Opium warped the space of the city at night, transmuting it at every turn into an impossible puzzle. His elaborate, digressive prose style, with its drifting, shifting metaphors and its unpredictable accretion of clauses, mimics the city's labyrinthine logic, its unnerving transitions from one social identity to another, its dead ends and its sudden openings.

But, at least until Nash regimented the area around Regent Street, as Haussmann later did in central Paris, many of the spaces at the core of the metropolis, which took the form of intricate, illogical slums, were already irredeemably distorted. As in his later account of the architecture of his delirious, feverish dreams, they were Piranesian. London itself, in the opium-tinctured nightwalks that De Quincey took at this time, acquired the complexity of consciousness itself. And consciousness resembled a byzantine city for which there was no guidebook or map. Consciousness and the city, the metropolis and mental life ... Both were scenes of creative destruction, abysmal or abyssal building sites.

Stony-Hearted Step-Mother

As a nightwalker, then, De Quincey adopted two different guises in the early 1800s – those of vagrant and drug-taker. A couple of decades later, he assumed a third guise – that of autobiographer. He evidently resumed his nocturnal walks when he researched his own past in composing the *Confessions* for the *London Magazine* in 1821. In this period he and his wife Margaret were living at Fox Ghyll, near Ambleside, as well as paying rent for Dove Cottage, where they had previously lived. But he also took lodgings in York Street, Covent Garden, in an attempt to advance his literary career and pay off his mounting debts. From these premises, revisiting his past, he frequently made 'nightly excursions' (partly perhaps 'to gratify his penchant for prostitutes').[43]

De Quincey's description of the house in Greek Street, for example, contains a kind of postscript in which he notes that, whenever he happens to be in London, he returns to the scene of his abject existence on first arriving in the capital as an eighteen-year-old runaway. With startling immediacy, he even notes that, hours or minutes before writing this section of the *Confessions*, he stood outside its windows:

> about ten o'clock, this very night, August 15, 1821, being my birth-day – I turned aside from my evening walk, down Oxford-street, purposely to

> take a glance at it: it is now occupied by a respectable family; and, by the lights in the front drawing-room, I observed a domestic party, assembled perhaps at tea, and apparently cheerful and gay. Marvellous contrast in my eyes to the darkness – cold – silence – and desolation of that same house eighteen years ago, when its nightly occupants were one famishing scholar, and a neglected child.[44]

It is a ritual designed to manufacture a sense of melancholic relief that he is no longer in the derelict condition he once endured. But it is also tinged with a sense of regret for the innocence he has lost in the meantime, largely because of the agonies of his opium addiction – and with a trace of contempt, too, for the bourgeois family that inhabits it today, which is only 'apparently cheerful and gay'. He is resentful of the process of gentrification, and, in standing outside the house like a ghostly sentinel and so bearing testimony to its former desolation, he casts a kind of blight on it. He distantly recalls Richard Savage loitering on the street outside the house inhabited by the woman he insisted was his mother.

In his reflections on Ann, too, De Quincey offers a glimpse of himself walking at night in order to invoke the past. He has been recounting the events of the night on which, according to him, she saved his life: 'Often, when I walk at this time in Oxford Street by dreamy lamplight, and hear those airs played on a barrel-organ which years ago solaced me and my dear companion (as I must always call her) I shed tears, and muse with myself at the mysterious dispensation which so suddenly and so critically separated us forever.'[45] In the atmospheric conditions of the lamp-lit night, which is by implication far more conducive to romance than the gas-lit night of central London in the early 1820s, De Quincey initiates the cult of Ann, constructing her as a mythical figure. He lights a flame dedicated to a deity not so much of the hearth as of the pavement. As a means of restoring a sense of immediacy to memories, walking in the streets of the city at night is almost as artificial as dosing oneself with laudanum. For De Quincey, it is perhaps a necessary part of the process of writing an autobiography. He nightwalks his way back into the life narrated in the *Confessions*.

In the opening paragraphs of Part II of the *Confessions*, De Quincey apostrophizes the street around which, as if trapped in a compulsive relationship, he obsessively circulated in his youth: 'So then, Oxford-street, stony-hearted step-mother! thou that listenest to the sighs of orphans, and drinkest the tears of orphans …' It is a farewell to its precincts, officially at least, for he has finally reached the point in his autobiography when he can relegate his sufferings as a vagrant to the past – 'the time was come at last that I should no more pace in anguish thy never-ending terraces; no more should dream, and wake, in captivity to the pangs of hunger'. Thenceforth, he emphasizes, 'if again I walked in London, a solitary and contemplative man (as oftentimes I did), I walked for the most part in serenity and peace of mind'.[46] For the most part. The slightest intimation, in Part I of the *Confessions*, of his inner life as an opium addict, whether in a euphoric or dysphoric phase, is enough to undermine this claim.

Certainly, he drops the pretence soon enough. 'Meantime', he writes, after recording his gratitude to Margaret for sustaining him through the mania and insomnia of his addiction,

> Meantime, I am again in London: and again I pace the terraces of Oxford-street by night: and oftentimes, when I am oppressed by anxieties that demand all my philosophy and the comfort of thy presence to support, and yet remember that I am separated from thee by three hundred miles, and the length of three dreary months, – I look up the streets that run northwards from Oxford-street, upon moonlight nights, and recollect my youthful ejaculation of anguish …[47]

He is thinking of his longings, as a young vagrant who stared at night in the direction of the Lake District, for the friendship of Wordsworth. There is a sense here in which, in 1820, forced by a dire financial situation to leave his family in the Lake District and make a foray to London in search of commissions, and physically sick, he is back precisely where he started. Except that the disappointment of his hopes is far more difficult to withstand than their frustration. In this sense, De Quincey's excessively formal leave-taking from Oxford Street is a confession of his failure to take his leave from it. He can never escape the imprint on his consciousness of Oxford Street at night.

Suspicions of Lunacy

Living in the Lake District in the 1810s, when he first became close friends with Wordsworth and his family, before falling out with him in a fit of mutual intemperateness, De Quincey continued to take walks at night. 'I took the very greatest delight in these nocturnal walks through the silent valleys of Cumberland and Westmorland', he wrote in his recollections of 'William Wordsworth and Robert Southey' (1839), adding that these often took place very late at night:

> What I liked in this solitary rambling was, to trace the course of the evening through its house-hold hieroglyphics from the windows which I passed or saw: to see the blazing fires shining through the windows of houses, lurking in nooks far apart from neighbours; sometimes, in solitudes that seemed abandoned to the owl, to catch the sounds of household mirth then, some miles further, to perceive the time of going to bed; then the gradual sinking to silence of the house; then the drowsy reign of cricket; at intervals, to hear church-clocks or a little solitary chapel-bell, under the brows of mighty hills, proclaiming the hours of the night, and flinging out their sullen knells over the graves where 'the rude forefathers of the hamlet slept' … Such was the sort of pleasure which I reaped in my nightly walks – of which, however, considering the suspicions of lunacy which it has sometimes awoke, the less I say, perhaps, the better.[48]

It is a richly evocative description of the sights and sounds that, for the passing pedestrian, are pricked out in the cold darkness of the rural night – the flickering light from fires, the comforting, unsettling noise of laughter, the clang of the church bells as they echo across the emptied landscape. The parochial rituals of civilization are here seen from the outside. De Quincey is an invisible onlooker.

But then, in the last sentence of this passage, he makes a half-satirical reference to the 'suspicions of lunacy' his activities provoked. It was not until some six years after this piece that, under the terms of the Lunacy Act of 1845, the mentally ill were for the first time classified as persons 'of unsound mind'. Before that date they were simply dismissed as social pariahs. In this sentence, De Quincey thus offers the reader a sudden glimpse of himself as a nightwalker. It is as if someone going to blow out a candle at a window casement had momentarily glanced out onto the road and caught sight of a vagrant toiling along in the moonlight. From a comfortable interior, his solitary rambling at night must itself have seemed hieroglyphic, if not ominous.

Wordsworth, whose reputation for egoism was pronounced, had found companionship, or at least a distant comradeship, as well as a solipsistic sense of self, in his nightly walks in the Lake District. De Quincey's nocturnal vagrancy entailed a less sociable attitude. One cannot picture him stepping across the threshold of a labourer's cottage with a decommissioned soldier for whom he is soliciting help. He remains an outsider. In addition to opium, De Quincey was addicted to what Benjamin called 'that most terrible drug – ourselves – which we take in solitude'.[49]

Day into Night

Constitutionally restless, and rendered pathologically restive by his addiction, De Quincey was at home everywhere and nowhere. Living in Edinburgh in 1826 and 1827, when he was writing for *Blackwood's*, his laudanum habit 'turned day into night'.[50] During the day he slept, like the nightwalkers whom the medieval and early modern authorities feared, or like Savage before his final imprisonment and demise; and at night he either socialized until 3 a.m. or 4 a.m. or laboured at his desk until dawn, breaking from his books at about midnight in order to take a walk. He inhabited the city at nighttime because he felt exiled from it in the daytime.

If in the daytime the bohemian is homeless at home, in Clare's painful phrase, then in the nighttime, at least, he feels half at home in an ephemeral state of homelessness. At night in the city one can be someone and no one at the same time. Shedding one's diurnal identity, one can cultivate a nocturnal identity. 'The inner strife of the romantic soul', the art historian Arnold Hauser has written, 'is reflected nowhere so directly and expressively as in the figure of the "second self" which is always present to the romantic mind.' Hauser goes on to associate this second self with 'everything dark and ambiguous, chaotic and ecstatic, demonic and Dionysian'.[51]

De Quincey was expert at creating the artificial conditions in which the 'second self' identified by Hauser could be cultivated. He provided a revealing glimpse of it in the diary he wrote as a seventeen-year-old. At this time, in 1803, he was living in Everton, exhausted and ill after his semi-homeless existence in London. In one entry he records that the previous night he had pictured himself looking through a glass. He ventriloquizes a voice that asks, 'What do you see?' His response is, 'I see a man in the dim and shadowy perspective and (as it were) in a dream. He is a silent, shadowy, mysterious man, a remnant of the past or of "futurity"'. This is his second self. 'He wraps himself up in the dark recesses of his own soul', De Quincey concludes.[52]

Nightwalking, like writing poetry or taking opium, was one of the means by which Romantics like De Quincey, and post-Romantics like Dickens, fostered a second self – a silent, shadowy, mysterious other. It collapsed the dark recesses of the psyche into the labyrinthine spaces of the city.

PART FOUR

II.

Crowded Streets, Empty Streets

The Early Nineteenth-Century City at Night

Urban Emotions

In 1801, in the course of a charming, if provocative, letter to his friend William Wordsworth, the critic and poet Charles Lamb improvised an irresistible hymn to London, and nocturnal London in particular. A militant metropolitan, Lamb politely refused Wordsworth's 'very kind invitation into Cumberland', frankly admitting to the older man that he associated the place with 'dead nature'. (Thomas De Quincey, in contrast, would have given his eye teeth for such an invitation in 1801.) In a tone as playful as it is serious in intent, Lamb then set out his reasons for doing so:

> The Lighted shops of the Strand and Fleet-street, the innumerable trades, tradesmen, and customers, coaches, waggons, playhouses; all the bustle and wickedness round about Covent Garden; [the very women of the Town;] the watchmen, drunken scenes, rattles; – life awake, if you awake, at all hours of the night; the impossibility of being dull in Fleet Street; the crowds, the very dirt and mud, the sun shining upon houses and pavements, the print shops, the old book-stalls, parsons cheapening books, coffee-houses, steams of soups from kitchens, the pantomimes – London itself a pantomime and a masquerade – all these things work themselves into my mind, and feed me without a power of satiating me. The wonder of these sights impels me into night-walks about her crowded streets, and I often shed tears in the motley Strand from fulness of joy at so much Life.

'All these emotions must be strange to you', he adds; but 'so are your rural emotions to me'.[1]

Brilliant and unpredictable, sociable but psychologically troubled, Lamb was one of the most eloquent and rapturous celebrants of the metropolis at the turn of the nineteenth century. Born and brought up in the city, he worked for more than three decades as a clerk in the accountants' department of the East India Company, and at the same time, after shifting his allegiance from verse to prose, became one of the greatest of the Romantic essayists. Although he never published directly on the city at night – through which he routinely, often drunkenly, commuted home after work – it was nonetheless the medium in which, precisely because of the daytime demands of his professional life, he lived and thought.

Lamb is in his letter to Wordsworth completely immersed in the metropolis at night, in both its material and theatrical forms. His vital, moving account of his 'urban emotions', as he almost calls them, identifies the nocturnal city, in its most sociable form, as the site of epiphanies that routinely offer both to affirm his sense of self and cancel it out. For Lamb, the 'motley' streets of the metropolis at night, 'a pantomime and a masquerade', constitute a visionary city. For others, including Wordsworth, who remained appalled by its alienated conditions and its chaos, it was the empty as opposed to crowded streets of the city, when 'all that mighty heart is lying still', as he put it in 1802, contemplating sunrise over the river, that contained redemptive possibilities.[2]

Masterless Feet

As Lamb's ecstatic hymn to the urban night implies, London in the late eighteenth and early nineteenth centuries, the ascendant epoch of industrial capitalism, was shaped by the uninterrupted disturbance of both its social relations and its concrete conditions. The city's sense of excitement could not be dissociated from its state of disorder.

For Lamb, because rather than in spite of its ceaseless chaos, the city was a utopian space. Many of his contemporaries experienced it as a dystopian one. Richard Phillips, for example, a prominent radical politician, concluded his correspondence to the *Monthly Magazine* in 1811, which attempted to explain London's explosive expansion, with an apocalyptic prediction of 'premature and rapid decay':

> London will increase, as long as certain causes operate which she cannot controul [*sic*], and after those cease to operate for a season, her population will require to be renewed by new supplies of wealth; these failing, the houses will become too numerous for the inhabitants, and certain districts will be occupied by beggary and vice, or become depopulated. This disease will spread like an atrophy in the human body, and ruin will follow ruin, till the entire city is disgusting to the remnant of the inhabitants; they flee one after another to a more thriving spot; and at length the whole becomes a heap of ruins! Such have been the causes of the decay of all overgrown cities. Nineveh, Babylon, Antioch, and Thebes, are become heaps of ruins, tolerable only to reptiles and wild beasts. Rome, Delhi, and Alexandria, are partaking the same inevitable fate; and London must some time, from similar causes, succumb under the destiny of every thing human.[3]

In Phillips's panorama, imperial London is on the point of becoming a pile of ruins inhabited by reptiles. Half a century earlier, Oliver Goldsmith's 'City Night-Piece' (1759) had proposed that, in the darkened, depopulated spaces of the metropolis, this apocalyptic future is in some proleptic sense already inscribed in the present.

By 1801, when Lamb corresponded with Wordsworth, London had a population of more than a million – almost twice that of Paris. In the daytime, foot passengers fought for room in its dense, sometimes fetid streets, and stumbled on the pocked and pitted surface of its roads. The metropolis at this time heaved with traffic. On one day in 1811, the year Phillips's article appeared, some 90,000 pedestrians, 5,500 vehicles and 764 horse-riders crossed London Bridge. Because of this phenomenal traffic, the ancient bridge was demolished and replaced slightly upstream in the 1820s, by which period three brand-new bridges – at Vauxhall, Waterloo and Southwark – had also been built by private companies sponsored by Acts of Parliament.[4]

London's four competing centres – the City, the West End, Southwark and the East End – created a complicated, ever-shifting play of commercial and industrial forces. In among these areas the slums metastasized. The city was a constant scene of creative destruction. This was especially evident in the 1820s, a decade dominated by John Nash's ambitious architectural developments, which included the construction of Regent Street. Like other 'improvements' conducted at this time, this one involved the clearance or demolition of entire streets, if not districts, and the dispossession of their working-class inhabitants. 'As the big cities grew', Walter Benjamin comments in laconic tones, 'the means of razing them developed in tandem.'[5] These victims of capitalist enterprise were remorselessly driven into slums like the ones at Lambeth and St Giles.

If capitalist enterprise constantly caused collective displacements in the metropolis, its discipline also imposed peculiar, distortive conditions on the individual citizens attempting to live in its competitive, often conflicted environment. Propelled by the accelerating rhythms of industrial capitalist society, and contorted by 'the deformities of crowded life', in Wordsworth's fine formulation, it was difficult in London to protect a sense of self.[6] In particular, the city exerted what the poet, in a scintillating passage from 'Residence in London', Book VII of the *Prelude*, called 'the strife of singularity':

> Folly, vice,
> Extravagance in gesture, mien and dress,
> And all the strife of singularity
> Lies to the ear, and lies to every sense –
> Of these, and of the living shapes they wear,
> There is no end.[7]

Be singular! This is the metropolitan imperative that dictates that people constantly have to prove they are someone as opposed to no one. It is a stringent discipline, as John Clare realized with a deepening sense of dread on his visits to London in the fashionable but rapidly fading role of the 'peasant poet'.[8] In contrast to Lamb, Clare found the 'urban emotions' excessively importunate, oppressive.

The early nineteenth-century metropolis was the site of what Raymond Williams has called 'a new kind of alienation' – one to which Wordsworth, attempting to capture the disorientating dialectic of multitude and solitude characteristic of the city, was exceptionally sensitive: 'Wordsworth saw strangeness, a loss of connection, not at first in social but in perceptual ways: a failure of identity in the crowd of others which worked back to a loss of identity in the self, and then, in these ways, a loss of society itself.'[9] When Wordsworth proclaims that, in the 'overflowing streets' of the capital, 'The face of every one / That passes by me is a mystery', he admits that, just as the faces of others in the crowd are enigmatic, if not completely blank, so too has he become a mystery to himself.[10] In order to resist this loss of self, in order to circumvent the sense of being fatally assimilated to the anonymous mass of people, individuals are compelled perpetually to create the impression, both to others and to themselves, that they possess a definitive identity.

Resisting an entropic impulse to subside into anonymity, inhabitants of the city have to prove at all times that they are not nonentities. In order to see themselves reflected back in a distinctive form from the people they encounter in the streets, they have to impersonate themselves. In Wordsworth's terms, they have to adopt 'living shapes' – in short, to perform themselves, advertise themselves. The capitalist division of labour develops and conditions particular attributes of the individual at the expense of others, and this effect of the fact that 'the individual has become a mere cog in an enormous organization of things and powers' then has to be used to disguise precisely that fact.[11] In capitalist society, furthermore, all identity is levelled according to the logic of exchange value, and individuality is therefore secretly obliterated by this equivalence. Just as, under capitalism, 'the new is the longing for the new, not the new itself', as Theodor Adorno once said, so individuality is the longing for individuality, not individuality itself.[12]

But, in the public roads and streets of the metropolitan city after dark, the nightwalker is partially exempt from the imperative to be someone definite and identifiable amid what Wordsworth, in a description of Bartholomew Fair, called its 'blank confusion'. Like the Fair, Wordsworth implies, the metropolis is shaped by the 'perpetual flow / Of trivial objects, melted and reduced / To one identity, by differences / That have no law, no meaning, and no end'.[13] At the dead of night, in contrast, when the febrile traffic of bodies, commodities and human ambitions characteristic of life in the daylight finally abates, the strife of singularity is mitigated. If the urban night interrupted the ordinary, alienated identities associated with the daytime routines, it also presented opportunities for fostering other, more 'authentic' ones. The Romantic nightwalker carved a limited freedom from both the constraints of domesticity and the restrictive routines of everyday life.

In an earlier passage of 'Residence in London', the poet sets aside for a moment the alienated city he has been depicting and, grateful for the relief, briefly sketches some of the city's other incarnations:

> The peace
> Of night, for instance, the solemnity
> Of nature's intermediate hours of rest,
> When the great tide of human life stands still;

> The business of the day to come, unborn,
> Of that gone by, locked up, as in the grave;
> The calmness, beauty, of the spectacle,
> Sky, stillness, moonshine, empty streets, and sounds
> Unfrequent as in deserts ...[14]

This is another city, a deserted, unearthly city that resembles some picturesque or sublime landscape – perhaps even a post-apocalyptic one (again comparable to Goldsmith's in the 'City Night-Piece'). Occupying an interval between the death of the previous day and the birth of the next, the city at night is an intermediate state, almost an undead state.

In another poem set in empty streets, 'St Paul's' (1808), Wordsworth describes walking 'through the great City' early one snowy morning and suddenly glimpsing the cathedral at the end of a 'noiseless and unpeopled avenue'. He notes defiantly that, in his pensive state of mind, he has been pacing on 'feet masterless / That were sufficient guide unto themselves'.[15] Such a relief, then, not to have to walk on mastered feet in what William Blake had called 'chartered streets' – such a relief to walk by the rude workings of one's fancies rather than the rule of one's master, to invert the values of the terms used by John Bunyan in *The Pilgrim's Progress*.[16]

At night, especially in a more or less solitary state, feet are a sufficient guide unto themselves. They are provisionally freed from the endless, corrosive demands of the diurnal city. The individual's alienation, in this condition, can be cultivated, even redeemed, as well as merely endured.

Lewdness and Carelessness

The archetypal urban nightwalker of the Romantic period, whether he celebrates the city, like Lamb, or denounces it, as Wordsworth tends to do, is a solitary individual. But more sociable varieties of noctambulist are available for imitation or emulation at this time. The popular journalist Pierce Egan celebrates one of these – the long-familiar figure of the roisterer – in his Regency bestseller *Life in London* (1821). His nocturnal London is one of 'watchmen, drunken scenes, rattles', in Lamb's expression. It is the London of nightlife, not the dead night.

As its subtitle indicates, Egan's book, which was vividly illustrated by his friends and drinking companions George and Robert Cruikshank, details 'the Day and Night Scenes of Jeremy Hawthorn, Esq. and his Elegant Friend Corinthian Tom; Accompanied by Bob Logic, the Oxonian, in their Rambles and Sprees through the Metropolis'. Corinthian Tom, a dandyish metropolitan upstart, and his cousin Jeremy, an *ingénu* from the countryside, are the originals of the cartoon characters Tom and Jerry; and there is a cartoonish energy about their gleeful career through the city that exceeds even that of the Cruikshanks' accompanying images. Peppered throughout with footnotes explaining the slang used to such titillating effect in the text itself, Egan's urban travelogue narrates a series of daytime adventures among the fashionable regions of the city, each of which is capped off by an escapade among its more disreputable nightspots. In the course of these experiences, Jerry's 'rusticity' is rapidly eroded by Tom's beneficial influence.

The most rambunctious of the pair's nocturnal exploits involve that centuries-old comic stereotype, the nightwatchman. One night, for example, after a visit to the playhouse, where they chat happily to 'Cyprians' or prostitutes, and consume a considerable quantity of wine and 'blue ruin' in the 'sluicery' or saloon, they stroll off at about midnight to find a coffee shop.[17] Here, they get into an ugly fight with several people who are determined to fleece them of money, and it quickly spills out onto the street. When the watchmen or 'charleys' arrive, they apprehend Tom and lug him off to the watch-house to see Old Snoozy, the night constable. In an attempt to rescue his cousin, Jerry batters his way past two watchmen and is himself dragged inside. The 'bleeding *mug* of the watchman, together with his *broken lantern*', proves to be powerful evidence against Tom and Jerry, and the two men are booked to see the magistrates at Bow Street and bailed.[18]

At the hearing, the aggrieved watchman gives a fine performance, and convinces the magistrate that he has been comprehensively beaten up (he embellishes his act with props including a ripped

coat and a broken rattle). Tom and Jerry are therefore forced to pay damages. But in the following chapter, at the end of another night's spree, they avenge themselves by 'Getting the best of a Charley' in the empty streets: "Twas silence all around, and clear the coast, / The WATCH, as *usual*, DOZING on his post! / And scarce a lamp display'd a glimmering light.' In this soporific atmosphere, accompanied by a couple of prostitutes, Tom pushes a watch's sentry box over in the dark, thereby 'boxing' or trapping the constable inside. The two cousins skedaddle as another 'guardian of the night', who happens to be circumambulating the streets nearby, responds to his colleague's cries.[19]

Egan insists that the Cruikshanks' illustration of one of the nocturnal scenes he recounts is comparable to William Hogarth's engravings, because it 'displays a complete picture of what is termed "LOW LIFE" in the Metropolis; drunkenness, beggary, lewdness, and carelessness, being its prominent features'.[20] This reference signals clearly enough that, in *Life in London*, Egan was deliberately reviving a late seventeenth- and eighteenth-century tradition – one principally associated with Ned Ward and other practitioners of the urban and nocturnal picaresque. It modernized this tradition partly by rendering it in terms of a contemporary diorama or panorama, partly by exploiting the popularity of sensational 'police literature'. The appeal of this material, for the genteel or 'semi-genteel' reader, as in the past, was that it offered a vicarious, voyeuristic experience of metropolitan lowlife.[21]

Egan's version of 'low-life' literature did not labour to provide its narrative with the sort of moral alibi that had made the revelation of the lives of criminals and prostitutes just about acceptable in late seventeenth- and eighteenth-century predecessors such as John Dunton's *The Night-Walker* (1696). But, if this freedom from moral responsibility must have seemed relatively liberating to its innumerable readers, *Life in London* was not in fact nearly as subversive as, for example, *The London Spy* (1698–1700). Egan, who dedicated the book to George IV, was a Tory, and the rather anodyne incidents that structure it finally left the social hierarchies with which they trifled intact. *Life in London* lacks the scurrilous, carnivalesque energy of its more creative eighteenth-century precursors, which had been characterized by an unstable, dangerously enjoyable, libidinal drive.

In this respect, *Life in London* can finally be classified as pastiche – a form that Fredric Jameson identifies as a 'blank' or 'neutral' practice of mimicry, 'without any of parody's ulterior motives, amputated of the satiric impulse'.[22] In the spirit of nostalgia, it reheats an eighteenth-century literary genre rather than revitalizing or reinventing it for the nineteenth century. It domesticates the form of the urban or nocturnal picaresque. Indeed, the London it portrays resembles the early eighteenth-century city rather than the one that, at the precise moment of the book's publication, was being dramatically reshaped by the forces of industrial capitalism.

Mad-Light

So too does the London that can be glimpsed in 'Walks Home by Night' (1828), an amiable essay by the great liberal editor, journalist and poet Leigh Hunt, the close friend of Keats and Shelley. This piece describes its author's pleasant habit of strolling home to his house outside the metropolis, at about 1 a.m., after a couple of hours spent at the theatre and several more in the company of convivial friends. Originally published in the *Companion*, a journal he edited and published from home, it presents the nightwalker not as a roisterer but as a sort of sojourner in the city.

At this point in his colourful career, in spite of his Cockney credentials, Hunt's commitment to the city was softening into a love of London's outlying countryside, just as he was also drifting 'from politics into recreational literature'; and, as in his articles for the *Indicator* at the beginning of the 1820s, he 'was always attempting to pull his readers away from the busy, smoky, intensely public spaces of the City and its old suburbs and out towards the open fields'.[23] By the later 1820s he was living in a cottage in Highgate Hill, on the semi-rural fringes of north London, where he was a neighbour of Coleridge.

In 'Walks Home by Night', Hunt opens by reminding his readers, in a plebeian spirit evocative of John Gay and other Grub Street authors, that 'we keep no carriage'. Hunt goes on to inform them that, in spite of the fact that it is a matter of necessity, he is 'fond of a walk by night' because 'the mere fact of looking about us, and being conscious of what is going on, is its own reward, if we but notice it in good humour'. His robust Romantic precept is that to become alive to one's environment as a result of stumbling home at night is 'to enrich the stock of our enjoyment'. 'We are great walkers home by night', he confirms, 'and this has made us great acquaintances of watchmen, moonlight, mad-light, and other accompaniments of that interesting hour.' Hunt's journeys to his home in Highgate – sometimes conducted alone, sometimes with a companion – take him, he indicates, through 'streets and suburbs of by no means the worst description'.[24] Or of no description at all, it might be said, for he provides the reader with scarcely any concrete details of the cityscape through which he walks.

Indeed, Hunt's London is a city that, in the night, seems to have acquired a faintly pastoral atmosphere, albeit one that is notably abstract or indistinct: 'The advantage of a late hour is, that everything is silent, and the people fast in their beds. This gives the whole world a tranquil appearance.' Everything from 'inanimate objects' to 'passions and cares' seems calm and motionless. 'Love only is awake', he comments in sentimental tones, hastily insisting that he intends 'to touch profanely upon nothing that ought to be sacred', and that he has in mind only the most refined kind of love – 'love, of no heartless order, legal or illegal'. It is a playful, if slightly complacent, allusion to the presence of prostitutes and their clients in the streets. But it is so discreet that it fails to disturb the atmosphere of genteel calm that characterizes the city he adumbrates. There are no vagrants on the nocturnal streets of this city. Nothing agitates or upsets his inspiriting experience of routinely walking home by night, even in the stormiest conditions. In spite of his insistence, there is no 'mad-light' in Hunt's night.

In his article, Hunt is less interested in prostitutes, the oldest denizens of the city at night, than in their ancient enemies, or accomplices, the watchmen. Hunt describes these 'old friends', in affectionate tones, as 'staid, heavy, indifferent, more coat than man, pondering yet not pondering, old but not reverend, immensely useless'. But he quickly qualifies this last judgement, for the 'inmates of houses' think them useful, and 'in that imagination they do good'. Their role is purely symbolic, their presence merely a phatic one – like the cries of medieval and early modern watchmen as they called the hours when conducting their rounds.

Moreover, Hunt is fond of individual watchmen he has known, and sketches the characters and costumes of some of them in detail. And he finds a certain reassurance, if also a slight sense of rebuke, in the cheerful 'good mornings' with which the 'watchmen and patroles' that he meets greet him as he reaches his house. Certainly, they no more interrupt the bucolic peace of the place than the roosting birds that flutter as he passes them: 'How still the trees! How deliciously asleep the country! How beautifully grim and nocturnal this wooded avenue of ascent, against the cold white sky!'

The article ends with an encomium to home – an idea that is for him concentrated in 'the light in the window, the eye of the warm soul of the house, – one's home.' 'How particular, and yet how universal, is that word', he concludes, 'and how surely does it deposit every one for himself in his own nest.' Everyone? Not Clare, who marched in mad-light as well as moonlight, and finally felt homeless at home.

No doubt Leigh Hunt had good reason for ascribing such importance to the idea of home. During his imprisonment for a libellous attack on the Prince Regent in the *Examiner* in 1813, he had famously transformed his cell in the Surrey County Gaol on

Horsemonger Lane into something like a furnished house – one from which he could entertain his visitors, who included Byron, Hazlitt and Lamb, in domestic comfort and style. And, during his protracted journey through Italy in the early 1820s, in the aftermath of Keats's and Shelley's deaths, he had been desperately homesick for Hampstead, the scene of his friendships with the dead poets.

In 1825, on his return to London which was at that time experiencing an especially brutal phase of development, he felt increasingly 'at odds with the thrusting commercial and imperial spirit of the times', if not as inclined to combat it as he had been; and in Highgate he partially retreated from the metropolis among his family and friends.[25] Hunt was someone to whom, not least perhaps because of his notorious impecuniousness, the idea of 'home' was supremely important, and the idea of being homeless at home almost unimaginable.

But, prior to these travels, in the campaigning phase of his career as a journalist, Hunt had also demonstrated acute sensitivity to the pressing problems of homelessness and vagrancy. In 1817 he wrote a stinging piece for the *Examiner* under the headline 'Fellow-Creatures Suffered to Die in the Streets'. It was prompted by the discovery that a discharged soldier called Robert Johnson had died from exposure after three nights spent homeless in the streets close to the *Examiner*'s office off the Strand. What the man needed, apart from nourishment, Hunt asserted, was warmth – 'not fire warmth, but a little personal trouble – a little *real* charity – a bed'.[26] Instead, the man had been callously neglected by both passersby and the authorities, including watchmen.

By the later 1820s, Hunt seems to have forgotten that, for most people who found themselves on the streets of the metropolis after midnight in the early nineteenth century, watchmen were not necessarily benign agents of the state. For these victims of capitalism and war, like the ones cultivated by Wordsworth in the countryside, nightwalking was a painful struggle for subsistence and brute survival. Shelley had commemorated them in 'The Devil's Walk' (1812), a ballad in which – echoing *King Lear* – he attacked those who thrive because they snatch 'the bread of penury' from the poor, 'And heap the houseless wanderer's store / On the rank pile of luxury'.[27]

New Police Instructions

Sketching an especially timid watchman of his acquaintance in 'Walks Home By Night', Hunt characterizes him as 'an ancient and quiet watchman': 'Such he was in the time of Shakespeare, and such he is now.' Hunt's London at night, the only metropolitan feature of which is its theatres, is in this article so faintly delineated that, like the watchman, it too evokes the early seventeenth century quite as much as the early nineteenth century. The nostalgic figure of the watchman is, for Hunt, the guarantee of this historical continuity. His affectionate caricatures of these 'guardians of the night', as Egan rather more sarcastically called them, offer themselves as proof that, after centuries of change, the city and its environs remain the same.

In fact, both Hunt and Egan were writing at precisely the time when London's antiquated system of policing was in the process of being dramatically modernized in order to make property and people safer at night. These were the dog days of Dogberry. The year in which Hunt published 'Walks Home by Night' – 1828 – was also the year in which, after a series of parliamentary reports that repeatedly complained of the parlous state of policing in the metropolis, Robert Peel formed the committee that revolutionized the police force. This committee concluded that the current system betrayed an 'absence of all union, of all general control and undivided responsibility', and it demanded the institution of a central Office of Police 'under the immediate directions of the Secretary of State for the Home Department'.[28]

In 1829, pressing home this momentum, Peel pushed an Act for Improving the Police in and Near the Metropolis into law:

> Whereas Offences against Property have of late increased in and near the Metropolis; and the local Establishments of Nightly Watch and Nightly Police have been found inadequate to the Prevention and Detection of Crime, by reason of the frequent Unfitness of the individuals employed, the Insufficiency of their Number, the limited Sphere of their Authority, and their Want of Connection and Co-operation with each other: and Whereas it is expedient to substitute a new and more efficient System

> of Police in lieu of such Establishments of Nightly Watch and Nightly Police ... and to constitute an Office of Police, which, acting under the immediate Authority of One of His Majesty's Principal Secretaries of State, shall direct and control the whole of such new System of Police.[29]

Even though the City and the rest of metropolitan London remained as separate jurisdictions, the Act 'went much further in the direction of central government control than the committee had envisaged or public opinion sanctioned'.[30] It professionalized the city's police force. A centralized, regimented body of men replaced the ancient, ramshackle system dependent on parish constables and watchmen. They were properly armed and uniformed, and were expected to conform to the 'New Police Instructions for London', which emphasized the prevention of crime.

By the early 1820s, when some 2,870 nightwatchmen were still operating in London, the city's arrangements for nocturnal policing were both popularly and officially regarded as an embarrassment. The minutes of a meeting of 'the Directors and Governors of the Nightly Watch' in Temple Bar in September 1824 offer a glimpse of this situation. For they contain a letter from the more respectable inhabitants of Serle Lane complaining that the local public houses thereabouts 'are kept open, one or two hours after midnight and are resorted to constantly, by night walkers and vagabonds and other disorderly persons'. In the course of one of the 'disgraceful broils' to have taken place there recently, they add, '*three* watchmen (two of Saint Clement Danes and one of this Liberty) were present who declared their inability to keep the peace and walked away'.[31] The night watch had given up the ghost. This was in spite of the additional presence, from 1800, in response to rising fears of crimes against property, of a Night Foot Patrol (one of whose number, in 1816, was prosecuted for his involvement in crimes in order to claim rewards).[32]

What Jerry White characterizes as 'the fragile backbone of London policing' was utterly sclerotic. The Chief Magistrate at Bow Street declared in 1828 that the nightly watch was 'very defective in every respect', and characterized its incumbents as 'good for nothing decrepid old men, who carry a lantern merely to show a thief where they are'.[33] Hunt's anecdotal account, in 'Walks Home by Night', of the endearing eccentricities of the watchmen, which insists, 'they are not all mere coat, and lump, and indifference', can be read as a coded intervention in contemporary debates about nocturnal policing. It is a tribute to a tribe that is about to become extinct. In the space of a year or two, his journey on foot from central London to Highgate in the dead of night, especially when 'alone, and in bad weather', might have aroused suspicion from the rather more efficient 'Peelers' on patrol, who carried truncheons and wore top hats reinforced with iron.

In the Metropolitan Police Act of 1829, constables were specifically empowered, among other things, to apprehend

> all loose, idle and disorderly Persons whom he shall find disturbing the public Peace, or whom he shall have just Cause to suspect of any evil Designs, and all Persons whom he shall find between sunset and the Hour of Eight in the Forenoon lying in any Highway, Yard, or other Place, or loitering therein, and not giving a satisfactory Account of themselves.[34]

This clause, which sounds archaic in the context of the first modern police force but is consistent with its commitment to crime prevention, was effectively a provision against nightwalkers.

Almost a century and a half after the introduction of public lighting in London, the moral equivalent of a curfew prevailed. Those who loitered on the streets at night, especially if they were working-class, were still regarded as criminal. At night, in the early nineteenth century, prostitutes and vagrants remained common nightwalkers in all but name. In fact, the Metropolitan Police Act of 1839, which extended the remit of its predecessor, prohibited 'every common Prostitute or Nightwalker loitering or being in any Thoroughfare or public Place for the Purpose of Prostitution or Solicitation to the Annoyance of the Inhabitants or Passengers'.[35] Nightwalking remained indirectly criminalized.

How to Light a Street

In *Life in London* the metropolis at night is manifestly illuminated by lamplight; and in 'Walks Home by Night' the only reference to lighting is to the 'lamp-light shining in the gutters' in the rain. There is little sense in either Egan's or Hunt's pages that the introduction of gas lighting – an artificial form of illumination produced from the combustion of gaseous fuel – was in the early nineteenth century fundamentally altering the nocturnal city.

The pioneer of gas lighting, though not its inventor, was Friedrich Winzer, who emigrated from Germany to England at the end of the 1790s, anglicizing his name to Winsor in the process, and pursued a dogged campaign to promote gas lighting in London. In 1804 he became the first person successfully to patent coal-gas lighting, which had been used in tin mines in Cornwall during the early 1790s; and in 1812 his company, the London and Westminster Chartered Gas-Light and Coke Company, was incorporated by royal charter and became the first organization to operate a public gasworks. In the space of a few years London became the first metropolis to be predominantly supplied by gas, though throughout the 1810s many streets continued to be lit by oil lamps. In 1814 Winsor's company possessed a single gasometer with a capacity of 14,000 cubic feet; by 1822 four companies owned forty-seven gasometers with a combined capacity of almost a million cubic feet.[36] This development, which was dependent on capitalization by large joint-stock corporations rather than small-scale entrepreneurs, and which required the technological application of the latest scientific innovations, was exemplary of the new phase of industrial capitalism.

In terms of urban spectacle, the crucial moment came on 4 June 1807, when Winsor mounted an exposition of its benefits in Pall Mall, in the imperial centre of London. Recently forced by inclement weather to cancel a public experiment in 'how to light a street', Winsor had nonetheless managed to persuade the future George IV to let him stage an exhibition of gaslight in the gardens of Carlton House, the prince's palatial residence on the Mall. The engineer ran an elaborate system of pipes, both over- and underground, into the gardens of the house and onto the street, where he strategically positioned a number of lamps. At 8 p.m. a lamplighter lit these in front of an enthusiastic crowd of spectators, and until midnight they remained alight.

A correspondent for the *Monthly Magazine* speculated that, 'from the success of this considerable experiment, in point of number of lights, the distance and length of pipe, hopes may now be entertained, that this long-talked of mode of lighting our streets may at length be realized'. An article in the same periodical six months later claimed that 'one branch of the lamps illuminated with gas affords a greater intensity of light than twenty common lamps lighted with oil', and emphasized that 'the light itself [was] beautifully white and brilliant'.[37] Within less than two decades of this event, almost every town in Britain with a population of more than 10,000 was lit by gas (though it was not until the 1840s that the domestic use of gas was fully in place).[38] By 1823, more than 200 miles of streets in London were lit by almost 40,000 lamps.[39] Light had been industrialized.

The cultural historian Wolfgang Schivelbusch has observed that the light emitted by a gas burner was a measurable improvement on the light that came from the mechanisms it replaced – the candle and the oil lamp. This was the case in three principal respects: it was far brighter, because it had a higher temperature of combustion; it was far more uniform, because its flame was controlled by the even supply of gas from a pipe; and it could be far more easily regulated, because a single person stationed at the gas mains could at the same time adjust all the lamps connected to it by simply turning a stopcock. Schivelbusch summarizes both the technical properties of gas lighting and its impact on visual perception in terms of a single word: distance. 'Not only did its fuel come from the distant gas-works, not only could it be adjusted from a distance, without needing trimming – beyond all this, it was quite literally out of the observer's field of vision.'[40] A gas flame emitted a light so intense that in homes it had to be shaded from consumers, and in the streets it had to be placed out of pedestrians' direct line of sight.

Powers of Darkness

In his comic poem 'The Cap and Bells' (1819), John Keats evoked the emergent culture of gas lighting as evening gathers in the commercial centre of the metropolis:

> It was the time when wholesale houses close
> Their shutters with a moody sense of wealth,
> But retail dealers, diligent, let loose
> The gas (objected to on score of health)
> Convey'd in little solder'd pipes by stealth,
> And make it flare in many a brilliant form,
> That all the powers of darkness it repell'th,
> Which to the oil-trade doth great scaith and harm.[41]

Compared to the intimate forms of illumination associated with the candle and oil-lamp, which lit small areas with an uneven, gently flickering flame, and which consequently generated a kind of contemplative aura, the light from gas lamps seemed to its immediate contemporaries distinctly impersonal. The mechanisms of gaslight were alienated, the light itself alienating. Although fascinated by its secretive, almost sinister force, Keats appears to regret that, in repelling 'all the powers of darkness', gaslight also eliminates the magic of the unenlightened night.

It is this nocturnal magic, increasingly occulted or repressed by the forces of urban and industrial modernization, that Keats attempted to recover or conjure up, as in an experiment, or perhaps a séance, in his 'Ode to a Nightingale' (1819). Composed at his home in Hampstead in May 1819, the poem is set in its garden at night. The ode is a statement of Keats's commitment to the night as a site of enchantment opposed to the routine enlightenments of the metropolis after dark. It is a rejection of the commercial, self-consciously modernizing culture of the city's thoroughfares, in which 'retail dealers' release the gas, as he explains in 'The Cap and Bells', and make it flare into artificial life in their shops, repelling the powers of darkness.

Nicholas Roe, Keats's most recent biographer, who has insisted that the poet suffered from an addiction to laudanum at this time, underlines the opening reference in 'Ode to a Nightingale' to a feeling of 'drowsy numbness' – as of 'some dull opiate' – and identifies the poem as 'one of the greatest re-creations of a drug-inspired dream-vision in English literature'.[42] It is from this perspective a companion-piece to Coleridge's 'Kubla Khan' (1816) and De Quincey's *Confessions of an English Opium-Eater* (1821). In the suburban borderland between city and countryside, Keats's consciousness inhabits a liminal territory distinct from both daydream and sleep. These are the material and mental conditions for an almost hallucinatory invocation of the pre-Enlightenment night. 'Come, seeling night ...' he seems to whisper.

As Keats's nightingale sings, the poet's inability to see, in the heavy, scented darkness, creates a state of such heightened, transcendent sensitivity to his immediate surroundings, and their imaginative associations, that it feels like a dreamy, sensuous premonition of death:

> I cannot see what flowers are at my feet,
> Nor what soft incense hangs upon the boughs,
> But, in embalmed darkness, guess each sweet
> Wherewith the seasonable month endows
> The grass, the thicket, and the fruit-tree wild.

In the night the poet seems to float, as if in a medium of matter that is not matter. It is for this reason that, as Keats's nightingale pours out its soul in ecstasy, evoking the tenderness of night, and death, the poet can imagine what it would be like 'to cease upon the midnight with no pain', to move in an instant from a state of matter to one of not-matter.[43]

Sight fragments the world; it disaggregates it. In the light, I see a universe comprising multiple, competing objects that are perpetually being organized and reorganized, according to a logic that is both spatial and temporal, into a foreground or background. In the 'embalmed darkness' described by Keats, in contrast, I am immersed in a single, harmonious medium that, because the laws of time and space seem for a moment to have been suspended, is experienced as a state of depthlessness, or of pure depth. It is in this sense that, for the Romantics and their descendants, including the Surrealists, the night is a positive alternative to the values of transparency and universal visibility promoted by the scientistic representatives of Enlightenment.

As Roger Caillois wrote in the 1930s, citing the psychiatrist Eugène Minkowski, darkness is in phenomenological terms more than the absence of light:

> There is something positive about it. While light space is eliminated by the materiality of objects, darkness is 'filled', it touches the individual directly, envelops him, penetrates him, and even passes through him: hence 'the ego is *permeable* for darkness while it is not so for light'; the feeling of mystery that one experiences at night would not come from anything else.[44]

The state of being that Keats reconstructs in his ode is precisely this one in which, in the rich, gloaming gloom of the garden at night, the ego is permeated by darkness and the distinction between the environment and the individual or organism at its centre momentarily seems to disappear.

For the Romantics, night was a privileged time for apprehending nature, including human nature, in its least alienated, least mediated forms. The cultural and political theorist Michael Löwy has argued that the German Romantic poet Ludwig Tieck's reference to 'the moonlit enchanted night', which implicitly contains 'a critical attitude towards the disenchanted modern world, illuminated by the blinding sun of instrumental rationality', can usefully be interpreted as a distillation of 'the philosophical and spiritual program of Romanticism'.[45] Keats – who complained in bitter tones of the disenchantment of life in the aftermath of the Enlightenment, when 'the goblin is driven from the heath, and the rainbow is robbed of its mystery!' – exemplifies a 'moonlit enchanted' attitude.[46] He too sought romance in the night. Roe calls him 'a lunar poet of enchanted night'.[47]

In an essay entitled 'Christianity or Europe' (1799), the German poet and thinker Friedrich von Hardenberg, who called himself

Novalis, abused the *philosophes* of the Enlightenment because they programmatically sought to purge poetry 'from nature, the earth, the human soul and the sciences': 'Every trace of the sacred was to be destroyed.' Their 'favourite theme', he added, was light – 'they were pleased that it refracted rather than played with its colours, and so they called their great enterprise "Enlightenment"'. The night, a condition of profound spiritual and philosophical intensity for Novalis, was his antidote to the Enlightenment disposition he outlined in 'Christianity or Europe'. 'Does not all, which inspires us, wear the hue of Night?' he asked in the fourth of his *Hymns to the Night* (1800).[48]

The Romantics pursued a ceaseless search, in the industrializing society to which they felt condemned, for the secret spaces of the night that might redeem them, in both sensual and spiritual terms, from the utilitarian demands of the Enlightenment.

Darkened Spaces

But the city at night was not as brightly or uniformly lit as Keats's satirical image in 'The Cap and Bells' implies. Nor as disenchanted. In spite of gaslight's dramatic improvement over the old pitchy, guttering flames of lamplight, a good deal of what Milton had called 'darkness visible' prevailed on the streets, especially in the more impoverished areas of the metropolis. Gaslight itself, furthermore – as Dickens among others of the generation after Keats testified – quickly came to seem mysterious and magical. The art historian Lynda Nead has insisted that, in psychological terms at least, gaslight was probably closer to 'the archaic form of the lamp flame' than to 'the crude modernity of the electric light'. The gaslit metropolis, notwithstanding Keats's scepticism, 'became a place given over to imagination, dread and dream'.[49]

The early-nineteenth-century city continued to be defined at night by chiaroscuro effects, regardless of the new technology. 'The dim, unsteady clearings of light cast by the gaslamps somehow emphasised the darkness beyond', Al Alvarez has observed.[50] Amid the rutted, often treacherous surfaces of the darkened city, gas created pools of light. The new technology thus did not domesticate the metropolis in any comprehensive sense. There were still innumerable feral streets amid the ones that had been tamed. Indeed, the gaslight that illuminated the main thoroughfares, prettifying its shops after dark, made the labyrinthine passages of the city seem even more dangerous, more mysterious, or simply dirty and shabby, especially in the early hours of the morning on moonless nights.

If the political logic of the Enlightenment, according to Michel Foucault, was 'subjection by "illumination"', then the night, along with 'darkened spaces' more generally, promised a furtive, surreptitious freedom from this disciplinary regime. Night – a condition at once mundane and otherworldly – was for the Romantics and post-Romantics what Foucault called 'the negative of the transparency and visibility' established by the Enlightenment.[51] Inhabiting the night, for the tradition that runs from Blake through De Quincey to Dickens, entailed an invocation of this alternative to the Enlightenment. In the dead of night, the underside of London might be found, and a secret self silently fostered.

12.

The Dead Night

Dickens's Night Walks

Secrets of the Gas

In *Great Expectations* (1861), Pip at one point visits Miss Havisham in her home in Kent in order to inform her and her ward Estella, with whom he is still madly in love, that he has finally discovered the identity of his benefactor, the convict Magwitch. Pip confirms that, because he now knows Miss Havisham was not responsible for his transformation into a gentleman, he realizes that she and Estella have all along treated him not as their protégé but 'as a kind of servant, to gratify a want or a whim'.[1] It is on this occasion, too, that Estella admits she is to be married, as Pip feared, to the odious and oafish aristocrat Bentley Drummle.

Thus discarded, and in a deeply disconsolate state of mind, Pip escapes from Satis House and, as the afternoon light thickens, hides himself for a time 'among some lanes and bypaths'. Then, in a moment of decision, he strikes off 'to walk all the way to London'. 'I could do nothing half so good for myself', he decides, 'as tire myself out'. It is 'past midnight' when he eventually crosses London Bridge. From there he threads his way to his lodgings in Whitefriars, once the site of the 'liberties', weaving a path through 'the narrow intricacies of the streets'. When he arrives at the gate, 'very muddy and weary', the watchman gives him a note. It reads: 'DON'T GO HOME'. He doesn't. Instead, Pip retreats to the Hummums, a hotel in Covent Garden, where he endures an almost sleepless night in which, seeing the phrase 'DON'T GO HOME' wherever he looks, and whatever he thinks, he is beset by 'night-fancies and night-noises'.[2]

Three or four year earlier, Charles Dickens had made roughly the same journey on foot, in reverse. One night in October 1857, when he was in his mid forties, Dickens retired to bed in the family home in Bloomsbury, but found himself completely unable to get to sleep. He had suffered from intermittent insomnia throughout his adult life, but on this occasion he felt particularly agitated. He did not feel at home at home. So at 2 a.m. he climbed out of bed, dressed in warm clothes, and set off through the gas-lit streets of the city. 'The streets of London, to be beheld in the very height of their glory, should be seen on a dark, dull, murky winter's night', Dickens had written more than two decades earlier, 'when the heavy lazy mist, which hangs over every object, makes the gas lamps look brighter.'[3] In the damp silence of the autumn night, beneath the scuffing sound of his boots on the stone pavements, he would have heard the gas whispering its secrets in the softly rasping pipes.

'The seduction of the gaslit night', writes Lynda Nead, 'lay in its invitation to leave the security of the everyday world behind and to experience the hallucinatory images of illuminated darkness.'[4] In *Gaslight and Daylight* (1859), Dickens's young friend, the journalist George Augustus Sala, who also used to 'walk about the streets at night', celebrated the occult magic of gaslight in the city streets – above all its 'endless and always suggestive intercommunings'. 'Gas to guide my footsteps', Sala's encomium continued, 'not over London flags, but through the crooked ways of unseen life and death of the doings of the great Unknown, of the cries of the great Unheard.' Dickens too was attentive to 'the secrets of the gas', whose flickering light offered insights into the hidden life of the city.[5] The novelist often pursued the 'crooked ways of unseen life and death' in the streets of London at night.

Heading south in the direction of the Thames, on that night in October 1857, Dickens walked through London directly to Gad's Hill Place, his country residence in Kent. Like Pip's journey through the night, it was a distance of some thirty miles.

Elastic Novice

On the evening of this nightwalk, Dickens and his wife Catherine had probably quarrelled. They were becoming increasingly estranged, partly because of his relationship with the actress Ellen Ternan, who was then eighteen. For this reason, he visited Tavistock House, the house in Bloomsbury, only rarely at this time. He spent most of the autumn of 1857 at Gad's Hill Place, and, when he needed to be in central London, he tended to stay in a bachelor flat at the offices of his periodical, *Household Words*. It was probably shortly before or after this night that he insisted on partitioning the bedroom he shared with Catherine at Tavistock House so that they could sleep separately.[6]

A couple of years before this incident, in an earlier symptom of his deepening domestic unhappiness, Dickens had written to Maria Winter, the woman with whom he'd fallen in love when he was a twenty-year-old parliamentary reporter, to confess to her that, in his unrequited state in the early 1830s, he had repeatedly loitered outside her house at night. In a letter dated 22 February 1855 – some ten years after she became the wife of a saw-mill manager in Finsbury, prosaically enough – he informed her of these nocturnal walks in pathetic tones:

> When we were falling off from each other, I came from the House of Commons many a night at two or three o'clock in the morning, only to wander past the place you were asleep in. And I have gone over that ground within these twelve months, hoping it was not ungrateful to consider whether any reputation the world can bestow, is repayment to a man for the loss of such a vision of his youth as mine.[7]

Claire Tomalin points out that 'this meant walking from Westminster into the City, and, having patrolled Lombard Street, setting off back to Bentinck Street', an excursion that 'must have taken two hours and got him home not much before morning'.[8] It is tempting to speculate that, for Dickens, going 'over that ground' again entailed doing so physically as well as mentally, and that, in the state of anonymity that night afforded him, the most famous novelist of his generation haunted Lombard Street once again, finding an embattled form of refuge in his memories of Maria. For in the solitary streets at night, in the late 1850s as in the early 1830s, he nursed a profound and painful sense of remaining unfulfilled.

The nighttime journey on foot to Gad's Hill Place, driven by an acute sense of anguish and guilt, took Dickens little more than seven hours. He was a fast walker, who took pride in the fact that he could sustain a pace of at least four miles an hour across long distances. His friends, indeed, frequently complained of the speed and impatience with which he walked. 'Sometimes his perspiring companions gave way to blisters and breathlessness', writes one of his biographers.[9] He himself was boastful of his feats as a pedestrian. 'So much of my travelling is done on foot', he professed in 1860, 'that if I cherished betting propensities, I should probably be found registered in sporting newspapers under some such title as the Elastic Novice, challenging all eleven stone mankind to competition in walking.'[10] No doubt he secretly harboured dreams of bettering Captain Barclay, a celebrated athlete who, in 1809, when pedestrianism first became a sporting activity, walked a thousand miles in a thousand successive hours for a thousand guineas.

In the late 1850s, Dickens remained a fit man precisely because he insisted on walking, both in London and the countryside, whenever he could find the opportunity. Even so, he was increasingly afflicted with ill health at this time. His symptoms included neuralgic and rheumatic pains. His feet also troubled him – 'first his left foot, and then his right, took to swelling intermittently, becoming so painful that during each attack he became unable to take himself on the great walks that were an essential part and pleasure of his life'.[11] Dickens probably had gout, though he was reluctant to accept the idea, claiming instead that he contracted the pain because he had incautiously walked in snowy conditions. This did not deter him from walking in all conditions, clement or inclement. G. K. Chesterton, identifying a 'streak of sickness' in Dickens, which he detected in the novelist's 'fervid' intelligence, nonetheless confirmed that 'he suffered from no formidable malady and could always through life endure a great deal of exertion, even if it was only the exertion of walking violently all night'.[12] Chesterton's understatement is deliberately comic.

For John Hollingshead, who had been apprenticed to Dickens on *Household Words*, and who therefore saw a good deal of him in the 1850s, this proclivity for 'violent walking' was itself a malady. He recalled in retrospect that 'when Dickens lived in Tavistock House he developed a mania for walking long distances, which almost assumed the form of a disease':

> When he was restless, his brain excited by struggling with incidents or characters in the novel he was writing, he would frequently get up and walk through the night over Waterloo Bridge, along the London, New Kent and Old Kent Roads, past all the towns on the old Dover High Road, until he came to his roadside dwelling. His dogs barked when they heard his key in the wicket-gate, and his behaviour must have seemed madness to the ghost of Sir John Falstaff.[13]

The 'roadside dwelling' to which Hollingshead alludes is Gad's Hill Place, which stood opposite the Falstaff Inn, formerly a notorious haunt of robbers and highwaymen, on the old road from London to Dover. It is likely, then, that Dickens conducted his thirty-mile nightwalk to Kent on more than one occasion.

Mania; disease. According to this diagnosis, Dickens's celebrated feat on that night in October 1857 was less about overcoming his physical afflictions than capitulating to his psychological ones. The proximate reasons for Dickens's compulsive walking in the 1850s were, first, the death of his father in 1851, and, second, the deterioration of his marriage to Catherine. But no doubt there were less immediate, more unfathomable, reasons. Dickens had been a manic – not just an energetic – walker for decades. 'If I couldn't walk fast and far, I should just explode and perish', he once told John Forster, his biographer and intimate friend.[14] In some almost terminal sense, to put it in Pip's terms, he wanted to tire himself out.

Gone Astray

In a letter to his friend Lavinia Watson, written some two months after the event, Dickens offered a fairly cheerful sketch of the night he walked to Gad's Hill in the autumn of 1857:

> Six or eight weeks ago, I performed my celebrated feat of getting out of bed at 2 in the morning, and walking down there from Tavistock House – over 30 miles – through the dead night. I had been very much put-out; and I thought, 'After all, it would be better to be up and doing something, than lying here.' So I got up, and did that.[15]

It is a no-nonsense account of his physical achievement – felt put-out; got up; did that. His businesslike use of these bi-syllabic phrases, which seem slightly self-satisfied in tone, creates the superficial impression that, presented with a nameless problem that had made him uncomfortable, he decided to solve it simply by taking a dose of stimulating exercise.

In Dickens's description of his 'celebrated feat', there is no reference to the tormented state of mind that inspired his desperate, solitary act of self-exhaustion. But in the hyphenated phrases of the first sentence – 'over 30 miles – through the dead night' – there is nonetheless a faint hint that the brisk rhythms of his prose cannot entirely conceal a sense of physical or psychological fragmentation. In the second of these clauses – 'through the dead night' – there is a subtle deadening effect, as if it is missing a beat. The phrase 'through the dead of night' might have sustained the forceful, slightly triumphant rhythm of the phrase 'over 30 miles'. Instead, there is a faltering rhythm, as of someone suddenly running out of physical or spiritual energy.

In addition, the expressions 'the dead of night' and 'the dead night' signify subtly different things. The former, a temporal and social category, denotes the deepest, darkest hours of the night, the period between approximately 2 a.m. and 4 a.m. The latter – 'the dead night' – is more like an existential or spiritual category, which in addition connotes the night as a deadly or deathly condition. Shakespeare captures this association when Horatio informs Hamlet that, to the terror of those keeping watch, his father's ghost has been glimpsed on the ramparts 'in the dead vast and middle of the night'.[16] In this line the word 'vast' – from the Latin *vastus*, which indicates a waste or void – lies somewhere between an adjective and a noun. It opens up an immense empty space into which time seems to collapse and disappear. It is a desolate state of being. The dead night, it might be said, like the dead vast of the night, is devastating.

If Dickens's nightwalk to Kent in 1857 was an attempt to preempt an explosion of the kind he alluded to in his comment to Forster, then it was also, like Pip's attempt to tire himself out, an act of self-obliteration. It is probably this nocturnal walk that Dickens described in detail in an article on 'Shy Neighbourhoods' (1860) published in *All the Year Round* some two and a half years later:

> My last special feat was turning out of bed at two, after a hard day, pedestrian and otherwise, and walking thirty miles into the country to breakfast. The road was so lonely in the night, that I fell asleep to the monotonous sound of my own feet, doing their regular four miles an hour. Mile after mile I walked, without the slightest sense of exertion, dozing heavily and dreaming constantly. It was only when I made a stumble like a drunken man, or struck out into the road to avoid a horseman close upon me on the path – who had no existence – that I came to myself and looked about.[17]

The faintly jocular tone in which this anecdote starts, in an echo of the flirtatious letter to Lavinia Watson, darkens incrementally.

The first sentence briskly implies that the object of this thirty-mile walk was breakfast in the country, as if Dickens had simply been working up an appetite for it. But this impression is undermined by the second and third sentences, with their unsettling evocation of the somnambulist on the lonely nighttime road, 'dozing heavily and dreaming constantly'. Dickens's consciousness has become detached from his body, the relentless motions of which are mechanical. If this is the dead time of night, it is also the undead time of night.

In the fourth sentence, despite the residually comic image of him stumbling 'like a drunken man' and getting spooked by a spectral horseman – who recalls the 'hunted phantom' that rides into London at the beginning of *Barnaby Rudge* (1841) – Dickens communicates a sense of profound emptiness. It is as if, in lapsing into a state of semi-consciousness, he himself momentarily 'had no existence'. But, in coming to himself again, he does not fully regain his sense of self. Spiritually speaking, he is still adrift. In spite of the fact he has two homes, he resembles John Clare traipsing along the roads at night in a desperate, automatic motion. Dickens, too, felt homeless at home at this time.

As day breaks, its light penetrating the autumn mist, Dickens starts to hallucinate. His body is evidently famished and exhausted. But his imagination, too, is both exhausted and famished. It is as if his mind, on the obscure, rural roads at night, deprived of the visual material around which it would ordinarily have weaved its endless, restless novelistic fantasies, suddenly sets to work with redoubled feverishness on the inchoate physical forms illuminated by the mysterious early morning light. Dickens's imaginative response to the atmospheric effects of the dawn is comparable to the ecstatic reaction of a starving man for whom a humble crust of bread tastes like the richest, most delicate of dishes.

For in Dickens's somnambulant consciousness, the clouds and mist before him coalesce into a sublime landscape. 'I could not disembarrass myself', he writes, 'of the idea that I had to climb those heights and banks of cloud, and that there was an Alpine Convent somewhere behind the sun, where I was going to breakfast.' He is at the climactic point of a Grand Tour of his own troubled psyche. And he admits that, even once the sun is 'up and bright … I still occasionally caught myself looking about for wooden arms to point the right track up the mountain, and wondering there was no snow yet'. It is as if Dickens is haunted by what Thomas De Quincey, in his description of encountering the Spectre of Brocken at first light in the mountains of North Germany, called his 'Dark Interpreter' – 'an intruder into my dreams'.[18]

Nightwalking was for Dickens a narcotic ('I could do nothing half so good for myself as tire myself out', as Pip puts it). Dickens adds that, in the semi-conscious, somnambulant state that he inhabited on this night, as on other occasions when he suffered from insomnia, his facility for language was strangely loosened:

> It is a curiosity of broken sleep that I made immense quantities of verses on that pedestrian occasion (of course I never make any when I am in my right senses), and that I spoke a certain language once pretty familiar to me, but which I have nearly forgotten from disuse, with fluency. Of both these phenomena I have such frequent experience in the state between sleeping and waking, that I sometimes argue with myself that I know I cannot be awake, for, if I were, I should not be half so ready. The readiness is not imaginary, because I often recall long strings of the verses, and many turns of the fluent speech, after I am broad awake.[19]

The rhythm of his feet, as they pound the roads, provides the impetus needed spontaneously to shape his half-formed thoughts into poems. From a distance, the solitary figure of Dickens recalls that of William Wordsworth, who strode at night along the roads of the Lake District and, rolling fragments of blank verse around his tongue, muttered to himself like a madman. Up close, it becomes apparent that Dickens, speaking a forgotten language as well as making up 'immense quantities of verse' that, in an additional sense, will remain for ever blank, is completely delirious. Locked in 'the state between waking and sleeping', Dickens – unlike the Romantic poet – really is almost mad.

Dickens is, more precisely, a species of 'mad traveller'. Mad travelling is Ian Hacking's term for the 'compulsive aimless wandering' that French psychologists, including Jean-Martin Charcot, sought to diagnose at the end of the nineteenth century. Dickens's walk to Gad's Hill Place, though not aimless, is something like a psychogenic fugue. It is a flight both from his everyday life, including his wife, and from his self. And, like the cases of mad travelling or 'ambulatory automatism' examined by alienists in the 1890s, during what Hacking has characterized as a 'fugue epidemic', Dickens's hypnotic state induces a radical loss of identity.[20] At night, Dickens became a *fugueur*.

From an early age he had been running away from something, or walking 'fast and far' from something. Going astray, he called it. In an article entitled 'Gone Astray', printed in *Household Words* in 1853, he described how he had 'got lost one day in the City of London' as an eight- or nine-year-old child and roamed and strayed and strolled through its precincts all day and into the night, until he found a watchman. 'I have gone astray since, many times, and farther afield', Dickens concludes with a certain sad pride.[21]

Ancient Secrets

In his delightful and profoundly insightful monograph on Dickens, Chesterton argued that the novelist's originality and genius resided in the fact that he possessed, 'in the most sacred and serious sense of the term, the key of the street':

> Few of us understand the street. Even when we step into it, as into a house or a room of strangers. Few of us see through the shining riddle of the street, the strange folk that belong to the street only – the street-walker or the street-Arab, the nomads who, generation after generation, have kept their ancient secrets in the full blaze of the sun. Of the street at night many of us know even less. The street at night is a great house locked up. But Dickens had, if ever man had, the key of the street; his stars were the lamps of the street; his hero was the man in the street. He could open

> the inmost door of his house – the door that leads into that secret passage which is lined with houses and roofed with stars.[22]

Chesterton's emphasis on the importance to Dickens of the street at night was perceptive. Dickens was quite as interested in the nomads that occupied the nocturnal city – the streetwalkers and the night-walkers – as in those who occupied the diurnal one. He wanted to understand those who kept their ancient secrets beneath the cold light of the moon as well as the full blaze of the sun. Indeed, he was himself – in an 'amateur way', to use a characteristic formulation – one of these nomadic people. It was in the streets at night, and among its strange folk, that he sought the solution not only to the riddle of the modern city but to his own inscrutable, often secretive, existence.

It was probably in the late 1830s and early 1840s that Dickens first regularly walked at night in London. These were the years, so the historian Joachim Schlör claims, when night in the European metropolis first came to represent a distinctive challenge both for those who policed it and for the bourgeois imagination itself. From roughly 1840, faced with fears that emerged as a result of the rise of the so-called dangerous classes, 'the complete city-dweller [had] to learn to master the night'. Schlör's claim that, after this time, 'night is more than simply a darker version of the day', seems exaggerated.[23] In the city, night had for centuries been socially, psychologically and even ontologically different to the day, as the career of the common nightwalker and his or her descendants indicated. But he is nonetheless right to emphasize a shift at this time, on the grounds that the night became a pressing social problem in the increasingly conflicted and contradictory centres of industrial capitalism.

As a young man, Dickens regularly strolled in the streets at night for purely companionable or sociable purposes. In his biography of Dickens, Fred Kaplan observes that in the late 1830s Dickens often socialized with Forster and their friend Daniel Maclise, and that together they frequently amused themselves with 'dinners and drinks in city and county inns, rapid overnight trips to Kent, late-night walks through London streets, cigars, brandy, and conversation'. In this guise, exchanging 'elaborate badinage, jokes about women, about eccentricities, about escapades', they are not unlike Tom, Jerry and Logic in Pierce Egan's *Life in London* (1821).[24] This is Dickens the genial roisterer, who inhabited the populous, glittering streets of central London – illuminated in the hours after dusk by the innumerable gaslights that flared from shop windows – as if they were a comfortable, albeit brilliant, interior.

But Dickens was also beginning to roam at night with a darker, more solipsistic sense of purpose at this point – or, with a compulsive sense of purposelessness. It appears likely, for example, that at the start of the 1840s he first returned at night to the site of Warren's, the blacking factory where he had laboured as a twelve-year-old child, labelling bottles, while his father served his prison sentence for debt. In the autobiographical fragment that Dickens wrote for Forster in 1847, he confirmed that, 'in my walks at night I have walked there often, since then, and by degrees I have come to write this'. As in his subsequent recollections of loitering outside Maria Winter's house, the activities of nightwalking and reconstructing decisive or even traumatic events from his past were curiously, elaborately intertwined (in this respect, as in others, he was like De Quincey). 'I often forget in my dreams that I have a dear wife and children; even that I am a man', Dickens wrote of the inexorable pull of the blacking factory, 'and wander desolately back to that time of my life'.[25] Both dreaming and nightwalking involved 'wandering desolately back' into the past.

Black Streets

Increasingly, too, nightwalking seems to have become instrumental to the business of writing, itself a compulsive activity for Dickens. It provided release – sometimes instantaneous, sometimes not – from the uncontainable sense of excitement or frustration he often felt during the composition of his fiction, the serial production of which exerted peculiarly intense demands on his psyche.

On 2 January 1844, for example, Dickens wrote to his friend Cornelius Felton, Professor of Greek at Harvard University, informing him that he had sent a package to him by steamship containing a copy of *A Christmas Carol* (1843): 'Over which Christmas Carol', the novelist writes in the third person, 'Charles Dickens wept and laughed, and wept again, and excited himself in a most extraordinary manner, in the composition; and thinking whereof, he walked about the black streets of London, fifteen and twenty miles, many a night when all the sober folks had gone to bed.'[26] It is as if, but for the freedom to roam through the 'black streets of London', the back streets of the city at night, he might have burst – like the boiler of the steamship that throbbed across the Atlantic with the book he had sent to Felton.

On the occasions when for one reason or another, during the composition of a book, Dickens could not pace freely about the metropolis at night, the absence of the 'black streets' crippled him. 'Put me down on Waterloo-bridge at eight o'clock in the evening, with leave to roam about as long as I like, and I would come home, as you know, panting to go on', he wrote to his confidant Forster from Genoa in 1844, when he was labouring on *The Chimes* (1844); 'I am sadly strange as it is, and can't settle.' 'He so missed his long night-walks before beginning anything', commented Forster, 'that he seemed, as he said, dumbfounded without them.'[27]

Two years later, on the continent once again, Dickens's 'craving for streets' became even more acute. At the end of August 1846, living with his family in Lausanne, where he was writing *Dombey and Son* (1848), he complained to Forster of 'the absence of streets and numbers of figures':

> I can't express how much I want these. It seems as if they supplied something to my brain, which it cannot bear, when busy, to lose. For a week or a fortnight I can write prodigiously in a retired place (as at Broadstairs), and a day in London sets me up again and starts me. But the toil and labour of writing, day after day, without that magic lantern, is IMMENSE!! … I only mention it as a curious fact, which I have never had an opportunity of finding out before. *My* figures seem disposed to stagnate without crowds about them. I wrote very little in Genoa (only the *Chimes*), and fancied myself conscious of some such influence there – but Lord! I had two miles of streets at least, lighted at night, to walk about in; and a great theatre to repair to, every night.[28]

No one in the nineteenth century can have needed London quite as much as Dickens did. It was an addiction.

Dickens sickened when he did not have access to the phantasmagoric effects of the city – especially at night, when it was most like a magic lantern. In October 1846 he informed Forster of his delight at moving from Lausanne to Geneva, though he admitted that in the latter too he suffered from 'occasional giddiness and headache', which he confidently attributed 'to the absence of streets'.[29] Dickens subsisted on the lifeblood of the metropolitan city like a vampire, thriving on its streets and 'figures' as their energies ebbed after nightfall. Even in substantial, sociable urban centres such as Geneva and Genoa, which were extensively lighted at night, he felt claustrophobic because he did not have the same freedom to roam across considerable distances.

Paris, like London, offered Dickens relief from this sense of inhibition that seemed to paralyse both him and his characters. In another slightly desperate letter sent to Forster from Lausanne, this time in September 1846, at a time when he was deeply, painfully embroiled in the composition of *Dombey and Son*, he consoled himself with thoughts of the Parisian streets at night:

> The absence of any accessible streets continues to worry me, now that I have so much to do, in a most singular manner. It is quite a little mental phenomenon. I should not walk in them in the day time, if they were here, I dare say: but at night I want them beyond description. I don't seem to be able to get rid of my spectres unless I can lose them in crowds. However, as you say, there are streets in Paris, and good suggestive streets too; and trips to London will be nothing then.[30]

On the night of his arrival in Paris, shortly after he sent this letter, Dickens escaped from the rest of the family, which had decamped to a small house in the Rue de Courcelles. As Forster reports, invoking Dickens's adjective, he proceeded to take a '"colossal" walk about the city, of which the brilliancy and brightness almost frightened him'.[31]

Nightwalking was a territorial habit, one that enabled Dickens to orientate himself in the city, to realign the relationship between the metropolis and mental life. But it also offered a release from uncontainable emotions. In January 1847, he 'slaughtered' Paul Dombey, to use his term. 'Then he walked through the streets of Paris until dawn', as Peter Ackroyd reports.[32] Thus he attempted to rid himself of one of his spectres. No doubt his nightwalk conjured up other ghosts – in the form of memories or fantasies – which he could not so easily escape or suppress.

Disagreeable Intrusions

The year after his father's death, when Dickens's nightwalking became particularly manic, he openly discussed the conditions that rendered it a kind of psychological necessity to him. 'Lying Awake' (1852) is an autobiographical article about insomnia published in *Household Words*. It is a remarkable rhetorical performance that dramatizes this indeterminate state between waking and sleeping by miming the intermittent and sporadic rhythms with which, in the form of a free association of ideas, phantasmagoric images infiltrate his consciousness. At this time Dickens was writing *Bleak House* (1853), in which Lady Dedlock obsessively 'walks by night' because she is so troubled by her guilty conscience.[33]

At the beginning of 'Lying Awake', Dickens languishes 'glaringly, persistently, and obstinately, broad awake' in bed. As so often in his prose, the comic tone conceals a profound sense of existential apprehension, only thinly encasing it. The philosopher Emmanuel Levinas captures something of this dimension of the Dickensian self when he characterizes insomnia in terms of 'the extinction of the subject' – a state of abstract, anonymous being. Dickens decides, on the night he describes, that he will confront sleep as an intellectual problem rather than a physiological condition, in order to distract his ceaselessly active consciousness from what Levinas, in a scintillating formulation, calls 'the indefectibility of being, where the work of being never lets up'.[34] Throughout his adult life, Dickens was locked into a sense or state of being – in all its indefectibility, its relentless infallibility – that seemed inescapable. The incessant, restless susurration of consciousness …

'I *will* think about Sleep', Dickens writes.[35] But his attempt to discipline his attention is rapidly derailed, and his 'train of thoughts' instead pursues a meandering path through random memories, through mysterious residues of the ancient and recent past. For example, 'for no reason on earth that I can find out, and drawn by no links that are visible to me', he suddenly finds himself, when he should be pondering sleep, climbing a mountain in Switzerland, the Great Saint Bernard, and spending the night in a convent at its summit. Presumably this is the same alpine convent as the one he thinks he is ascending when, some five years later, he has a hallucination in the early morning mist on the nightwalk to Gad's Hill Place. But, no sooner has he reconstructed his memories of this mountain, which he visited in 1846, than a caricature he once saw chalked on a church door as a child, of a terrifying man with 'goggle eyes, and hands like two bunches of carrots', stalks into his consciousness.[36]

In an effort to escape the horror of the scene in the churchyard, which has often haunted him as an adult, Dickens self-consciously resolves instead to reconstruct 'the balloon ascents of this last season'. But this innocent tableau almost instantly slips its moorings. It is replaced, or displaced, by the 'dismal spectacle' of two murderers, George and Maria Manning, 'hanging on the top of Horsemonger Lane Jail' – as if the image of hot-air balloons tugging upwards on their ropes has irresistibly evoked the image of inert bodies tugging down on theirs.[37]

Along with 30,000 other people, Dickens had attended the execution of the Mannings, convicted for killing their lodger with a 'ripping chisel', in 1849. It was an event so unedifying that it shocked him into writing two letters to *The Times* denouncing public executions. In 'Lying Awake', he admits that for weeks afterwards the sight of 'these two forms dangling on the top of the entrance gateway' had made it impossible to imagine the prison 'without presenting it with the two figures still hanging in the morning air'. 'Until, strolling past the gloomy place one night, when the street was deserted and quiet', he adds, 'and actually seeing that the bodies were not there, my fancy was persuaded, as it were, to take them down and bury them within the precincts of the jail, where they have lain ever since.'[38]

Dickens's mental associations, in this restless state between sleeping and waking, dreaming and thinking, have thus led him to recall a recent nightwalk. For Dickens, as an insomniac, night-walking is the alternative to lying awake. It is the physically active as opposed to passive attempt to circumvent the effects of insomnia. And so it is that, at the end of 'Lying Awake', after repeatedly failing to 'return to the balloons', the recollection of which is interrupted again and again by the most 'disagreeable intrusion[s]' – of 'a man with his throat cut, dashing towards me as I lie awake', for example, and of corpses in the Paris Morgue deposited 'like a heap of crushed over-ripe figs' – he decides to search for relief from his sleepless, almost compulsively dystopian imagination in the darkened streets of the metropolis.[39]

After reflecting on the barbarity and inefficacy of flogging as a punishment for 'the late brutal assaults' in London, Dickens offers this explanation:

> I had proceeded thus far, when I found I had been lying awake so long that the very dead began to wake too, and to crowd into my thoughts most sorrowfully. Therefore, I resolved to lie awake no more, but to get up and go out for a night walk – which resolution was an acceptable relief to me, as I dare say it may prove now to a great many more.[40]

Dickens thus resolves to be the protagonist – the 'hero', as David Copperfield might have put it – of his own gothic fiction.

Besieged in his consciousness by an army of the dead, led no doubt by his deceased father, he will try to outflank it by stealing into the nocturnal city and recruiting himself to the scattered army of the undead that, in the form of the homeless, patrol its dirty, shadowy precincts.

Miles upon Miles of Streets

'Night Walks', first published in *All the Year Round* in 1860, then reprinted in *The Uncommercial Traveller* in 1861, was a belated sequel to 'Lying Awake'. It is perhaps Dickens's finest, most haunting piece of non-fictional prose. At once impressionistic and replete with intensely realized detail – like a dream, in fact – it relates his experiences on the streets of the capital between roughly half past midnight and the moment when 'the conscious gas [begins] to grow pale with the knowledge that daylight [is] coming'.[41]

'Some years ago', Dickens's article begins, 'a temporary inability to sleep, referable to a distressing impression, caused me to walk about the streets all night, for a series of several nights.' The 'distressing impression' referred to here, in spite of the interval of almost ten years, appears once again to have been Dickens's grief at his father's death, compounded by surfacing anxieties about his finances as well as by a deepening sense of filial guilt. But if this particular 'series of several nights' in the early 1850s – the most concentrated and intense period of Dickens's career as a nightwalker – provided the inspiration for 'Night Walks', then the oneiric prose of the piece is steeped in a lifetime's experience of the dreamscapes of nocturnal London. Nightwalking was a chronic and at times also an acute condition for Dickens.

Reflecting on his insomnia in the opening paragraph of 'Night Walks', Dickens remarks that this 'disorder might have taken a long time to conquer, if it had been faintly experimented on in bed; but, it was soon defeated by the brisk treatment of getting up directly after lying down, and going out, and coming home tired at sunrise'. In this sentence, Dickens gently mocks the bracing regime of exercise he has prescribed himself. He hints that, in an ironic inversion, his nighttimes acquired the routine character of life in the city in the daytime. Getting up from bed, going out, coming home. It is a comically abbreviated description of a day's commute – one that is roughly contemporaneous with Dickens's portrait of Mr Wemmick in *Great Expectations*, whom Rachel Bowlby has identified as 'the first commuter in literature'.[42]

Except that it doesn't simply invert the logic of the diurnal routine ('getting up directly after lying down, and going out, and coming home tired at sunrise') – it redoubles it, making it seem even more desperate, in spite of the light tone, because it leaves no room at all for sleep, for the restorative pleasures of home so cherished by Wemmick. The image of Dickens getting up directly after lying down at night evokes a daily existence of unsustainable alienation, its comedy darkened by the relentless grind of labour in an industrial society.

Dickens's nightwalking after his father's death is both a prescription and a neurotic compulsion. Cure and poison. For, if it is therapeutic, it also reinforces an almost psychotic sense of solitude. Nightwalking is a ghastly, sometimes horrifying, parody of the comforting, regular life that, in the opening paragraph of 'Night Walks', he pretends it simply mimics. In the somnambulant conditions of the nightwalk, the city cannot be dissociated from the individual's imagination. The metropolis and mental life collapse in on one another. In the couple of hours after midnight, Dickens's own restlessness is mirrored by what he calls 'the restlessness of a great city, and the way in which it tumbles and tosses before it can get to sleep'. This restlessness, a collective restlessness, eventually fades, and London does indeed 'sink to rest', as he puts it.[43]

But Dickens remains terminally restless. 'Walking the streets under the pattering rain', he reports, he 'would walk and walk and walk, seeing nothing but the interminable tangle of streets'. In this state of confused, repetitive solitude, which has the logic of a nightmare, everything is tainted, everything becomes part of some gigantic pathetic fallacy – or neurotic fallacy. The world is restless even when it is at rest. 'The wild moon and clouds were as restless as an evil conscience in a tumbled bed.' Despite his respectability in the early 1850s – which is all the more precious to him because he cannot escape the memories of his father's lack of respectability – Dickens is the archetypal nightwalker. Condemning himself to the emptied city at night, he has 'many miles upon miles of streets' in which he can have his 'own solitary way'.[44]

Dickens's prose evokes a sense of solitude that echoes through his sentences as if they are as empty and hollow as the midnight streets through which he walks. 'When a church clock strikes, on houseless ears in the dead of the night, it may be at first mistaken for company', he explains at one point; but, as 'the spreading circles of vibration' echo out into 'eternal space, the mistake is rectified and the sense of loneliness is profounder.'[45]

But Dickens confesses to having discovered a lonely sense of community in the cold depths of the London night, among men defined by 'a tendency to lurk and lounge; to be at street-corners without intelligible reason' – that is, by what he identifies, in saddened tones imbued with the memory of his father's failure, as 'the Dry Rot in men'. In spite of its oddly indistinct quality, Dry Rot can be unmistakably discerned. In its initial phase, it provokes in the observer no more than an indefinable suspicion that 'the patient [has been] living a little too hard' – like a faintly sour smell clinging to someone's clothes. It soon comes to seem less elusive, for it is indelibly present in 'a certain slovenliness and deterioration, which is not poverty, nor dirt, nor intoxication, nor ill-health, but simply Dry Rot'. In its advanced state, it assumes the form of 'a trembling of the limbs, somnolency, misery, and crumbling to pieces'. As in a wooden plank, 'Dry Rot advances at a compound usury quite incalculable'.[46] So with what Kant called the crooked timber of humanity.

'My principal object being to get through the night', Dickens writes, 'the pursuit of it brought me into sympathetic relations with people who have no other object every night of the year.'[47] These are the everyday casualties of life in the capitalist metropolis – the victims of unemployment, alcoholism and other symptoms of social and spiritual alienation. Sala, a descendant of the eighteenth-century authors of the nocturnal picaresque, sketches this nocturnal species in *Twice Round the Clock* (1859). There he reports that, in London after midnight, 'strange shapes appear of men and women who have lain a-bed all the day and evening, or have remained torpid in holes and corners' (he adds that, at this time, 'the street corners are beset by night prowlers').[48] These are people who, because they are more or less homeless, must conquer time, or defend themselves against its blank emptiness, from minute to minute, moment by moment.

They are the opposite of Wemmick, whose sense of home is excessively pronounced, and who protects himself from the alienation of the day's labour by dividing the evening against it. If Wemmick daily builds a defensive wall around his home, and the promise of recreation it circumscribes in the evening, in order to defend himself against the political economy of the metropolis, then the people inhabiting the streets, for whom time and space are almost completely unbounded, are anti-Wemmicks.

Houseless Creatures

Dickens's nightwalks are partly an experiment in what – once more in deceptively light tones – he calls an 'amateur experience of houselessness'. Homelessness was a pressing problem in nineteenth-century London, especially in the late 1840s and 1850s, when thousands of Irish people, escaping the famine and its effects, fled to the city.

In 1859, when the population of the capital was approximately 3 million, Sala noted that 'it is commonly asserted, and as commonly believed, that there are seventy thousand persons in London who rise every morning without the slightest knowledge as to where they shall lay their heads at night'. Even if this number is overstated, he added, 'a vast quantity of people are daily in the above-mentioned uncertainty regarding sleeping accommodation', and 'a great majority solve the problem in a somewhat (to themselves) disagreeable manner, by not going to bed at all'.[49] Here, in the city at nighttime, was an immense, atomized community.

In 'Night Walks' and other journalistic pieces Dickens depicted the depredations experienced by London's homeless population at night with anger as well as pity. In 'On Duty with Inspector Field' (1851), for example, he records the nocturnal tour of St Giles he took with this charismatic detective, the prototype of Inspector Bucket in *Bleak House*. Field, in Dickens's account, expresses both outrage and disgust at the squalid conditions of a room in a 'tramps' lodging-house': "Ten, twenty, thirty – who can count them! Men, women, children, for the most part naked, heaped upon the floor like maggots in a cheese!'[50]

In 'A Sleep to Startle Us' (1852), Dickens details a visit to the 'Ragged School Dormitory' at the upper end of Farringdon Street, which offered basic shelter to 'houseless creatures', including 'thieves, cadgers, trampers, vagrants, common outcasts of all sorts', who would otherwise be forced 'to hide where they could in heaps of moral and physical pollution'.[51] And in 'A Nightly Scene in London' (1856), printed like the previous articles in *Household Words*, he conducts an interview with five homeless women – 'five dead bodies taken out of graves, tied neck and heels, and covered with rags' – who lie on the muddy pavement beside the wall of the Workhouse in Whitechapel one wet night. He concludes by abominating the 'demented disciples' of political economy.[52]

Dickens revisited the terrain of houselessness in *Little Dorrit* (1857), a novel that betrays an especially intimate relationship with the more polemical pieces he was publishing in periodicals in the early and mid 1850s. One night, along with her idiot friend Maggy, Little Dorrit returns from Covent Garden to the Marshalsea Prison in Southwark, where her father – like Dickens's – has been incarcerated for debt. Forster recounts that Dickens told him of the nights that he and his sister Fanny used to walk back from the Marshalsea Prison to the Royal Academy of Music, where she studied, when he was a child.[53]

Little Dorrit seems 'fragile and defenceless against the bleak damp weather', so the quietly heroic Arthur Clennam follows her at a distance through the streets, from a desire to protect her. Out of delicacy, though, Clennam drifts off when they reach the prison, and he therefore fails to realize that it is locked for the night – 'He had no suspicion that they ran any risk of being houseless until morning.' Little Dorrit, who is fully conscious of this prospect, stops outside a 'poor dwelling all in darkness', in the hope that it might provide them with temporary lodging; but she knocks at its door so tentatively that she fails to rouse its inhabitants. 'If we cannot wake them so', she resolves, 'we must walk about till day.'[54]

And so they do. It is half past one on 'a chill dark night'. They therefore have five and a half hours to kill before the prison reopens in the morning. While the street is 'empty and silent', they perch on Maggy's basket and huddle together beside the prison gate for comfort. When Little Dorrit hears a footstep, however, or sees 'a moving shadow among the street lamps', she panics, and they scramble to their feet and 'wander about a little' before coming back to the gate again. The hulking, uncouth form of Maggy finally falls asleep against Little Dorrit's chest 'in the dead of the night, when the street [is] very still indeed'.[55]

But she soon awakes, 'querulous again', and expresses a desire 'to get up and walk'. It is after 3 a.m. Approximately half an hour later they cross London Bridge:

> They had heard the rush of the tide against obstacles; had looked down, awed, through the dark vapor on the river; had seen little spots of lighted water where the bridge lamps were reflected, shining like demon eyes, with a terrible fascination in them for guilt and misery. They had shrunk past homeless people, lying coiled up in nooks. They had run from drunkards. They had started from slinking men, whistling and signing to one another at bye corners, or running away at full speed.[56]

At one point, a female passerby mistakes Maggy's large form for a mother pimping her daughter as a prostitute.

Eventually, to 'the ghastly dying of the night', the city begins to surface again, as if it were suffering from a fever, or a gin-soaked, guilt-soaked hangover. The flare of gas lamps becomes sickly and feeble in the early morning light; and carts, coaches, wagons and workers gradually stir into life. This is the moment described by James Ewing Ritchie, in *The Night Side of London* (1857), in terms of 'the lamps being extinguished, and the milk carts going round, and the red newspaper expresses tearing along to catch the early train'. It is the moment when, 'in the sober light of day', the experiences of the night 'seem unreal'.[57]

Maggy and Little Dorrit return to the Marshalsea 'in the first grey mist of a rainy morning'. It is the first time in her life that the latter has spent a night outside the precincts of the prison. It has been a shock: 'The shame, desertion, wretchedness, and exposure, of the great capital; the wet, the cold, the slow hours, and the swift clouds, of the dismal night.'[58]

Loose Bundle of Rags

For the police, as Schlör has argued, 'the proof of a home, a legal nocturnal place to stay, is the precondition for the recognition of existence'. So, he continues, 'the situation of *homelessness*, or roaming the night without aim and without rest, represents exclusion from bourgeois society'.[59] It is a form of non-existence, non-being. In his nightwalks, Dickens deliberately patrolled the outer limits of bourgeois society, loitering in its psychological and sociological borderland.

In 'Night Walks', Dickens figures himself in the allegorical guise of 'Houselessness'. Like King Lear on the heath, Dickens on the streets exposes himself to feel what wretches feel. He is an uncommon nightwalker who identifies closely with the condition of the common nightwalker. Dickens's itinerant and vagrant condition is thus an existential rather than a social form of homelessness. It is a state of anomie. He refers at one point to 'the houseless mind', a phrase that, building on Shakespeare's image of 'houseless heads' in *King Lear*, signifies both the mentality of a homeless person and his own homeless state of mind: his anchorless state of consciousness; his displaced or exiled sense of self. But, if he underlines his sense of solidarity with those whom circumstances have rendered materially destitute – especially the children whose naked feet 'are perpetually making a blunt pattering on the pavement' of the piazza at Covent Garden – he is nevertheless not ashamed to admit that, at times, the houseless seem frighteningly foreign or other to him.[60] If he understands their alienation, he also finds them, simply, alien.

This ambivalent attitude is dramatized most sharply in his encounter with an ungendered homeless person on the steps of St Martin-in-the-Fields in Trafalgar Square in the dead of night:

> Once – it was after leaving the Abbey and turning my face north – I came to the great steps of St Martin's Church as the clock was striking three. Suddenly, a thing that in a moment more I should have trodden upon without seeing, rose up at my feet with a cry of loneliness and houselessness, struck out of it by the bell, the like of which I never heard. We then

> stood face to face looking at one another, frightened by one another. The creature was like a beetle-browed hare-lipped youth of twenty, and it had a loose bundle of rags on, which it held together with one of its hands. It shivered from head to foot, and its teeth chattered, and as it stared at me – persecutor, devil, ghost, whatever it thought me – it made with its whining mouth as if it were snapping at me, like a worried dog. Intending to give this ugly object money, I put out my hand to stay it – for it recoiled as it whined and snapped – and laid my hand upon its shoulder. Instantly, it twisted out of its garment, like the young man in the New Testament, and left me standing alone with its rags in my hands.[61]

Here, in Lear's language, is 'unaccommodated man', 'a poor, bare, forked animal'.[62]

In encountering this creature, Dickens confronts the limits of humanity. It is as if he has come face to face with the Night, 'the interior of [human] nature', which Hegel discerned in what he called 'phantasmagorical conceptions', where horrifying forms suddenly appear, 'only to disappear as suddenly'. 'We see this Night', the German philosopher continued, 'when we look a human being in the eye, looking into a Night which turns terrifying.' For, from his eyes, he concluded in an unforgettable image, 'the night of the world hangs out towards us'.[63] The night of the world hangs out towards Dickens from this homeless youth's face.

If in this incident Dickens confronts the limits of humanity, then he also confronts the limits of his own capacity for identifying with the poor; that is, he confronts the limits of his own humanity. A creature, he calls it, and an object. An abject, ugly object. It appears that, once he has laid a patrician, if kindly, hand on its shoulder, the youth is left to run off into the night clothed in nothing at all. 'Poor naked wretches', Lear cries, 'How shall your houseless heads and unfed sides, / Your loop'd and window'd raggedness, defend you / From seasons such as these?'[64] Dickens is evidently moved by this individual's 'cry of loneliness and houselessness', which gives voice to his own inarticulable pain. But, in his description of this incident, there is nonetheless an uncomfortable sense in which he does after all resemble the 'persecutor' that, he assumes, this nameless, homeless person sees in him. So if the houseless youth seems inhuman – that is, 'marked by a terrifying excess which, although negating what we understand as "humanity", is inherent to being human' – then Dickens does too.[65]

This intuition, implicit though it remains, is not one that Dickens's contemporaries, above all the Christian philanthropists who attempted to save fallen women on the streets at night, can countenance. It is alien, for example, to John Blackmore, author and architect of *The London by Moonlight Mission* (1860), an account of his 'midnight cruises' among prostitutes in central London in the 1850s. This book contains the testament of one of Blackmore's confederates, who describes distributing Christian tracts to the women who solicit him in the Haymarket ('at night prostitutes crowd several streets in this quarter by the thousands', Fyodor Dostoevsky wrote of this nightspot on his visit to the English capital in 1862).[66] There he finds himself 'completely possessed by an intense desire to benefit these unhappy creatures'.[67]

Blackmore's colleague thus sublimates his erotic desire into an all-consuming moral desire. Here is a graphic instance of what Jacques Lacan once characterized as 'the aggressivity that underlies the activity of the philanthropist'.[68] Dickens, by comparison, is less philanthropic, less aggressive, far more conflicted and self-divided.

Sanctuaries and Stews

Houselessness has no history. This is an overstatement, of course. For, in the course of centuries, the complicated legal, moral and social superstructure on which the lives of homeless people have depended, shaped above all by economic and political imperatives, has been in a constant state of development; and the balance between their persecution or prosecution and their protection has in consequence shifted ceaselessly. But, in spite of this, and in spite of important material changes to the city, including the introduction of paving and public lighting, the basic homeless experience, which entails searching for shelter and sleeping on the streets, warmed by narcotics and threadbare clothes and blankets, has altered little since the sixteenth or seventeenth centuries.

In a late essay, 'On an Amateur Beat' (1869) – prior to a description of a 'street expedition' in which he accidentally overturned 'a wretched little creature' who 'clutch[ed] at the rags of a pair of trousers with one of its claws, and at its ragged hair with another' – Dickens makes a more general, polemical observation to this effect. At the present time, he states, 'a costly police-system such as was never heard of, has left in London, in the days of steam and gas and photographs of thieves and electric telegraphs, the sanctuaries and stews of the Stuarts'.[69] History moves at a far slower pace for the indigent, especially at night, than it does for the affluent.

When Pip returns in the middle of the night to his lodgings in Whitefriars, the site of the most notorious and anarchic of London's slums in the seventeenth century, at the end of his thirty-mile walk from Miss Havisham's house, the reader is expected to recall these horrifying continuities. Dickens's nighttime street expeditions are an excavation of the past, both a private and a public one, which reveals that it lives, in a state of putrefaction that continues to breed life, just beneath the surface of the present.

13.

A Darkened Walk
The Old Curiosity Shop *and Dickens's Fiction*

Down with Dawdling!

At the beginning of the article on 'Night Walks' (1860), Dickens jokily characterizes nightwalking as a 'brisk treatment' for his inability to sleep. In this context, 'brisk' primarily means fresh, stimulating, tonic in its effect. But it also applies to the action of nightwalking itself. The rapid pace at which Dickens habitually walked probably makes this an objective description, on one level. On another level, however, it seems to function ironically, since although he admits in 'Night Walks' to covering 'miles upon miles of streets', his prose implies that he moves at a relatively dilatory pace, in a desultory way. He gives the impression, most strongly, of 'wandering'.[1]

To wander, according to the OED, means 'to move hither and thither without fixed course or certain aim; to be (in motion) without control or direction; to roam, ramble, go idly or restlessly about; to have no fixed abode or station'. This more aleatory form of ambulation, comparatively aimless, and open to chance happenings, is characteristic of the nightwalking tradition. So it is as if Dickens is half-ashamed to admit how quickly he navigated through the city at night, in case this disqualifies him as a nightwalker. Briskness is incompatible with wandering. One cannot wander briskly, just as one cannot saunter and hurry at the same time. (It might be claimed, though, that this is precisely the paradoxical form of perambulation that Charlie Chaplin's Tramp, a character indebted to Dickensian precedents, achieved.)

'Brisk', a word that first crops up at the end of the fourteenth century in the Old Welsh form *brysg*, 'used of briskness of foot', as the OED puts it, implies industriousness, purposefulness, busyness. In short, it means business. George Eliot, for example, refers in *Romola* (1862–1863) to 'the brisk pace of men who had errands before them', implicitly comparing these men to the 'apparent loungers' who stand about talking to one another.[2] Lounging indicates a more or less studied resistance to the idea, or the disciplinary imperative, of the errand. As the processes of industrial capitalism increasingly shaped people's everyday experiences and perceptions in the course of the nineteenth century, the apparently natural, spontaneous action of walking came to seem more and more culturally determined, and more and more alienated.

For expanding numbers of people, the simple activity of travelling from A to B, from home to work, was in this period subjected to the mechanical rhythms of factory production. The logic of capitalism, its profit motive, valorized 'briskness of foot'. Lounging, by contrast, became unacceptable. The slogan 'Down with dawdling!' sponsored by F. W. Taylor, the American apostle of 'scientific management', in the factories of the late nineteenth century, surely also echoed through factories in Britain half a century earlier.[3] People's most ordinary mode of perambulation was reshaped by the discipline of capitalism. Business required busy-ness, briskness.

In one of the founding texts of capitalist theory, *An Inquiry into the Nature and Causes of the Wealth of Nations* (1776), Adam Smith had argued that the division of labour, the parcelling out of the tasks of production to different workers, or groups of workers, helped to prevent the pernicious habit of sauntering. According to Smith, sauntering was typical of a rural economy, in which the labourer ambled in his or her own time between several tasks, all of which he or she was responsible for executing:

> A man commonly saunters a little in turning his hand from one sort of employment to another. When he first begins the new work, he is seldom very keen and hearty; his mind, as they say, does not go to it, and for some time he rather trifles than applies to good purpose. The habit of sauntering and of indolent careless application, which is naturally, or rather necessarily acquired by every country workman who is obliged to change his work and his tools every half hour, and to apply his hand in twenty different ways almost every day of his life, renders him almost always slothful and lazy, and incapable of any vigorous application even on the most pressing occasions. Independent, therefore, of his deficiency in point of dexterity, this cause alone must always reduce considerably the quantity of work which he is capable of performing.[4]

In an emergent industrial capitalist economy, where profit levels might be affected by the frittering of time, sauntering was by definition unproductive. Lounging, by the same token, was a positively flamboyant rebuke to the principle of productivity. Only briskness of foot was acceptable.

In his *Principles of Political Economy* (1848), John Stuart Mill cited Smith's critique of sauntering, and declared that, in the intervening seventy years, this habit had in effect become an anachronism. Building on Smith's argument, he insisted that factory workers should feel positively refreshed by walking hurriedly between the tasks they had to perform.[5] Hurrying was good for the individual's state of physical and moral health, not merely for the state of the economy. According to this logic, those who had no reason to hurry – the unemployed, for example – felt disqualified from a system that prioritized purposeful, purposive movement. Here is 'the horror of not being in a hurry' that, in a haunting formulation, Theodor Adorno once evoked.[6]

Amateur Vagrancy

To a hitherto unprecedented extent, walking became a self-conscious activity in the nineteenth century. Honoré de Balzac registered this shift when, in his *Theory of Walking* (1833), he demanded: 'Isn't it really quite extraordinary to see that, since man took his first steps, no one has asked himself why he walks, how he walks, if he has ever walked, if he could walk better, what he achieves in walking?' He asserted that these questions were 'tied to all the philosophical, psychological, and political systems which preoccupy the world'.[7] And, it might be added, its economical systems. In the conditions of capitalist society, walking acquired a kind of political economy. The way one walked, as well as when and where one walked, took on socially significant meanings. People's gaits became legible in terms of their position within the division of labour.

Hurried or brisk walking, to polarize rather crudely, marked one's subordination to the industrial system; sauntering or wandering represented an attempt, conscious or unconscious, to escape its labour habits and its time-discipline.[8] Dickens sketches both these kinds of walking, in the guise of Boz, in articles printed in 1835. In 'The Streets – Morning', he describes clerks commuting through London on foot who are too hurried to shake hands with the friends they happen to meet because 'it is not included in their salary'.[9] And in 'The Prisoner's Van', by contrast, he celebrates a more dilatory pace of life: 'We have a most extraordinary partiality for lounging about the streets', he boasts; 'Whenever we have an hour or two to spare, there is nothing we enjoy more than a little amateur vagrancy.'[10]

Dickens was acutely conscious of the emblematic distinction between hurrying and sauntering, in industrial capitalist society, when he adopted the persona of the Uncommercial Traveller in his journalistic sketches of the 1860s. As he explains in the introductory piece, 'the Uncommercial Traveller for the firm of human interest brothers' has 'rather a large collection in the fancy goods way'. He is a collector of human curiosities, who accumulates not in order to sell but solely out of interest – the idea of 'curiosity', here and in *The Old Curiosity Shop* (1841), is partly an attempt to de-commercialize the concept of 'interest'. The Uncommercial Traveller celebrates the use-value of persons and things; that is, he relates to them not as if they are means to an end but as if they are self-delighting ends in themselves. He therefore constitutes an innate challenge to the culture of exchange-value. Like the writers of classical antiquity praised by Karl Marx in the first volume of *Capital* (1867), the Uncommercial Traveller is 'exclusively concerned with quality and use-value' – 'in most striking contrast with [the] accentuation of quantity and exchange-value' maintained by contemporary political economists.[11]

This is evident in the Uncommercial Traveller's means of movement, his mode of transport. In spite of the fact that the train has outmoded many pedestrian journeys, he walks almost everywhere. 'As a country traveller', he confesses, 'I am rarely to be found in a gig, and am never to be encountered by a pleasure train, waiting on the platform of a branch station.' More importantly, perhaps, his manner of walking is scandalous. For, if he sometimes feels forced to hurry purposefully, he far prefers to saunter purposelessly. As he observes: 'My walking is of two kinds: one, straight on end to a definite goal at a round pace; one objectless, loitering and purely vagabond.' 'In the latter state,' he adds, 'no gipsy on earth is a greater vagabond than myself; it is so natural with me, and strong with me, that I think I must be the descendent, at no great distance, of some irreclaimable tramp.'[12]

Dickens's journey on foot to Gad's Hill Place one night in October 1857 no doubt constituted walking of both kinds – at once 'straight on end to a definite goal at a round pace' and objectless, loitering, vagabond. But, in spite of his speed, his nocturnal rambles in the metropolis, like those of the numerous noctambulant or noctivagant characters in his fiction, was generally walking of the latter kind.

Shadows of the Night

There is in Dickens's fiction, which is soaked in the semiotics of walking, 'a quantity of strolling about by night', to cite one of his formulations.[13] A quantity of loitering, prowling, roaming, sauntering, skulking and wandering by night, too – from the more picaresque fiction of the 1830s, through the mature novels of the 1840s, '50s and '60s, to *The Mystery of Edwin Drood* (1870), the one he left unfinished when he died.

The most intimate and sympathetic of Dickens's portraits of the nightwalker is to be found in *The Old Curiosity Shop*, probably composed at the time he was first revisiting the haunts of his youth at night. This novel is arguably also Dickens's most morally ambiguous account of nightwalking. Published as a weekly serial in *Master Humphrey's Clock* from 1840, *The Old Curiosity Shop* was initially conceived as nothing more than a sketch, in a single issue of the miscellany, of the narrator Master Humphrey's encounter with a thirteen-year-old girl called Little Nell in a London street at night. This is a nightwalking scene of seminal importance, partly because of its disconcerting sexual politics. It is in the character of Master Humphrey that, at once tentatively and probingly, Dickens explores the socially unacceptable drives of the nightwalker.

Master Humphrey's Clock proved both unpopular and unprofitable, and Dickens therefore feared that its 'desultory character', as he put it in the Preface to the Cheap Edition of *The Old Curiosity Shop* in 1848, risked undermining his hitherto intimate relationship with his readers. So he extended and reshaped this story, developing Nell's narrative to the point at which it subsumed the weekly publication completely, and thereby saving it from financial collapse. Daringly, and a little desperately, Dickens also discarded his first-person narrator (in spite of the fact that 'Personal Adventures of Master Humphrey: *The Old Curiosity Shop*' was one of the titles he had recently considered for this tale). Master Humphrey is expelled from the narrative at the end of Chapter 3, when he abruptly announces that he is leaving the other characters to 'speak and act for themselves'.[14] An omniscient narrator summarily takes over.

The picaresque plot of *The Old Curiosity Shop* is motivated by the fact that Nell's grandfather, the Old Man, has been gambling in order to support her, and has consequently become indebted to Daniel Quilp, a violent, dwarfish usurer. For it is in order to escape Quilp that Nell and her grandfather steal out of London early one morning, in sunlight that transfigures 'places that had shewn ugly and distrustful all night long' and that 'chase[s] away the shadows of the night', and commence their journey to some resting place in the countryside where they can forget about their past, and about the city:

> The two pilgrims, often pressing each other's hands, or exchanging a smile or cheerful look, pursued their way in silence. Bright and happy as it was, there was something solemn in the long, deserted streets, from which, like bodies without souls, all habitual character and expression had departed, leaving but one dead uniform repose, that made them all alike.

This flight from a dead city, which famously ends in Nell's death, is structured as a pilgrimage. Later in this chapter, in fact, Nell explicitly compares herself and her grandfather to John Bunyan's Christian. So this is a pilgrim's progress – and walking thus serves a spiritual as well as a socially symbolic function in *The Old Curiosity Shop*.[15]

In spite of the eventual success of *The Old Curiosity Shop*, the intensive demands of producing a weekly publication had a corrosive effect on Dickens. In the late autumn and winter of 1840, depressed because of his relative unproductiveness, he took 'long walks at night through the streets of London to restore his spirits'.[16] The composition of this novel was itself shaped by nightwalking, then. But this compulsive activity appears not to have provided much relief. As an antidote, it had a toxic effect. 'All night I have been pursued by the child', he informed John Forster on one occasion in November, alluding to Little Nell; 'and this morning I am unrefreshed and miserable. I don't know what to do with myself ...'[17] *The Old Curiosity Shop* is all about pursuing the child. Almost every character in the novel pursues the child. So does the reader. But, from the reverse perspective opened up by Dickens's comment, the innocent Little Nell acquires a slightly demonic character. She momentarily seems more like Bradley Headstone or Eugene Wrayburn in *Our Mutual Friend* (1865), both of whom are at once hunted and hunter on the streets after dark.

In spite of his apparent innocence, Master Humphrey is one of those individuals who, albeit not in especially obvious ways, pursue the child. He is a character whose oddness has often been overlooked, perhaps because he is superficially less peculiar than so many of Dickens's characters. Readers have tended either to ignore him or to take him at face value and regard him as a benign, if rather eccentric, geriatric.[18] He is a far darker character than an ascription of this kind implies, and not least because he is a nightwalker. In a double sense, he is the novel's most curious character. Some critics have implicitly recognized this. John Bowen, for example, has pointed out that he 'links the archaic and the modern in his nocturnal city strolling'.[19]

But an emphasis on Master Humphrey not only illuminates Dickens's understanding of nightwalking as a deviant, vagrant tradition; it provides an alternative introduction to the novel, and, in a sense, the introduction to an alternative novel. This alternative novel might be called 'The Old Cupiosity Shape', for this is the playful and suggestive pun with which, in *Finnegans Wake* (1939), James Joyce casually and deftly excavates the book's hidden channels of desire.[20]

Ugly Humphrey

At the start of *The Old Curiosity Shop*, Master Humphrey reflects on 'that constant pacing to and fro, that never-ending restlessness, that incessant tread of feet wearing the rough stones smooth and glossy' that typifies life in the metropolis. He characterizes the city as a sort of secular purgatory:

> Think of a sick man in such a place as Saint Martin's Court, listening to the footsteps, and in the midst of pain and weariness obliged, despite himself (as though it were a task he must perform) to detect the child's

> step from the man's, the slipshod beggar from the booted exquisite, the lounging from the busy, the dull heel of the sauntering outcast from the quick tread of an expectant pleasure-seeker – think of the hum and noise always being present to his sense, and of the stream of life that will not stop, pouring on, on, on, through all his restless dreams, as if he were condemned to lie, dead but conscious, in a noisy churchyard, and had no hope of rest for centuries to come.[21]

For the sick man, the activity of physiognomizing people's footsteps, as it might be called, of identifying their relationship to the city, whether it is 'lounging' or 'busy', lazily sauntering or briskly hurrying, becomes a sort of urban mania. The restlessness of London, embodied in the constant, repetitive movement of feet on pavements, shapes the sick man's 'restless dreams', troubling the distinction between the sane and the insane. Indeed, it seems plausible that the nameless man in St Martin's Court is sick precisely because of his obsession with the sound of footsteps; that this febrile attempt exhaustively to classify passing feet is not some palliative response to the sickness, nor even a symptom of it, but the sickness itself.

It is a mental state rather than a physical one. He is at rest; but he is no less restless because of that. In fact, he is probably all the more restless as a result of his immobility. Like the nightwalker, the man in St Martin's Court is one of the urban undead, for it is 'as if he were condemned to lie, dead but conscious, in a noisy churchyard, and had no hope of rest for centuries to come'. This is the urban mania that Alfred Tennyson explores in his extraordinary poem *Maud* (1855). In the fifth section of this 'monodrama', 'the mad scene' as Tennyson called it, the speaker pictures himself dead and buried 'a yard beneath the street', listening to the horses' hooves and the footsteps above him: 'With never an end to the stream of passing feet, / Driving, hurrying, marrying, burying …'[22]

Maud is a poem freely scattered with invective against the corrupt practices of mid-nineteenth-century capitalism. So, in the gerunds that end the line I have cited, which reproduce what Dickens calls the 'hum and noise' of passing feet, it is possible to detect an implicit association of hurrying, and marrying, and indeed burying, with busy-ness, with business – that is, with buying (a word buried in the word 'burying'). Both the speaker of *Maud* and the man in St Martin's Court, immobilized and entombed as they are, embody a protest, conscious or unconscious, against the rhythms of commerce that drive the life of the metropolis. If sauntering and lounging constitute a muted form of social protest in the conditions of industrial capitalism, then the state of physical paralysis imagined by the speaker of *Maud* represents a pathological refusal of its logic.

Master Humphrey distances himself from the 'sick man' about whom he fantasises, then; but he does so because of an uncomfortable proximity to him. For he is himself a cripple, who has suffered from some unnamed 'infirmity' since his childhood, as the first chapter of *Master Humphrey's Clock* testifies. It is presumably partly for this reason that for many years he has 'led a lonely, solitary life'. He lives, he informs us, in an old house in a 'venerable suburb' of London that was once a celebrated resort for 'merry roysterers and peerless ladies, long since departed. It is a silent, shady place, with a paved courtyard so full of echoes, that sometimes I am tempted to believe that faint responses to the noises of old times linger there yet, and that these ghosts of sound haunt my footsteps as I pace it up and down.'[23]

This courtyard full of the echoes of older footfalls is of course sequestered in a quiet suburb; and Master Humphrey seems quite sane, albeit a little quaint. But the haunted footsteps evoked by this urbane sentence, and the footsteps that haunt them, are indelible symptoms of an urban mania, as the slightly unsettling image of Humphrey perpetually pacing this confined space implies. There is evidently some kind of secret kinship, perhaps even an identity, between Humphrey and the sick man he subsequently mentions, who inhabits another courtyard, St Martin's Court, although the former's obsessiveness is far less intense than the latter's, and his infirmity more chronic than acute.

For the frail Humphrey, it could be said, as for the convalescent sketched in Charles Baudelaire's 'The Painter of Modern Life' (1863), 'curiosity had become a fatal, irresistible passion'.[24] It impels him into the city's streets. In fact, the 'Curiosity Shop' of the title refers not merely to Nell's grandfather's home, stuffed with fantastical commodities, but the city itself. In *Master Humphrey's Clock*, offering a first bulletin from his home in St Humphrey's Court, as it might be called, Humphrey announces that he has lived there 'for a long time without any friend or acquaintance'. He goes on: 'In the course of my wanderings by night and day, at all hours and seasons, in city streets and quiet country parts, I came to be familiar with certain faces, and to take it to heart as quite a heavy disappointment if they failed to present themselves each at its accustomed spot.' For Humphrey, implicitly, faces are curiosities to be collected, just as 'the inanimate objects that people [his] chamber' have acquired anthropomorphic qualities.[25]

But if he likes to amble around the lumber-room that is the city, Humphrey is manifestly not completely comfortable in it. Embattled because of his disability, he does not feel at home in the crowd. In contrast to the Baudelairean hero of modernity, the déclassé bourgeois stroller who revels in being 'at the centre of the world' but at the same time 'hidden from the world', Humphrey is in the inverse, and unenviable, position of a socially marginal figure who is nonetheless the object of public fascination.[26] He is 'a misshapen, deformed old man', as he himself puts it. And when he first moved to the suburb in which he presently lives, he explains, he was variously regarded as 'a spy, an infidel, a conjuror, a kidnapper of children, a refugee, a priest, a monster': 'I was the object of suspicion and distrust – ay, of downright hatred too.' At that time he was known as 'Ugly Humphrey'.[27] So, according to his neighbours, who identify him with the feudal, the foreign and the folkloric, he is outside the pale of modernity.

The identities initially ascribed to Humphrey by his suspicious-minded neighbours – spy, infidel, conjuror, kidnapper of children, refugee, priest, monster – might be the consequence of his eccentric nocturnal habits as much as his peculiar physical condition. Humphrey is the victim of popular prejudices about men of slightly odd appearance who walk about the metropolis at night because they do not feel at home in it during the day. He is a 'sauntering outcast', like one of the archetypes whose footsteps the sick man in St Martin's Court hears pacing about. But he feels half at home at least in the city at night, when there is nobody around to monitor his 'objectless, loitering, purely vagabond' mode of walking, as the Uncommercial Traveller had put it.

Humphrey is like Neville Landless in *The Mystery of Edwin Drood* (1870), who for different reasons feels he 'cannot go about in the daylight', and therefore makes solitary expeditions through the streets at night: 'I feel marked and tainted, even when I go out – as I do only – at night. But the darkness covers me then, and I take courage from it.'[28] Both men are nineteenth-century descendants of the tradition of common nightwalking. 'In the eyes of their respectable neighbours', writes Joachim Schlör in a comment on Karl Josef Friedrich's *Der Nachtwächter Gottes* (1934), 'those who for no obvious reason spend hours walking through the night are behaving strangely, abnormally.'[29]

Inhuman Designs

In *Master Humphrey's Clock*, Humphrey claims to walk in both the country and the city, during both the day and the night. In the opening sentence of *The Old Curiosity Shop*, though, he admits to a particular propensity for walking in the city at night: 'Night is generally my time for walking.'[30]

Humphrey adds that he 'seldom go[es] out until after dark', except in the countryside (where he likes to 'roam about fields and lanes all day'):

> I have fallen insensibly into this habit, both because it favours my infirmity and because it affords me greater opportunity of speculating on the characters and occupations of those who fill the streets. The glare and hurry of broad noon are not adapted to idle pursuits like mine; a glimpse of passing faces caught by the light of a street-lamp or a shop window is often better for my purpose than their full revelation in the daylight; and, if I must add the truth, night is kinder in this respect than day, which too often destroys an air-built castle at the moment of its completion, without the least ceremony or remorse.[31]

Refusing the 'hurry of broad noon', and the brisk rhythms of business, Humphrey prefers 'idle pursuits', like rambling, and speculating about 'those who fill the streets', even when they aren't filled. The city at night, where there are fewer people about to police a loitering mode of perambulation, permits him to wander and wonder at the same time. It is a space of fantasy, one where 'air-built castles', in contrast to the city in the daytime, can be erected and maintained.

Humphrey's narrative begins, then, with an anecdotal account of his encounter with Little Nell – the incident that constitutes the novel's primal scene:

> One night I had roamed into the city, and was walking slowly on in my usual way, musing upon a great many things, when I was arrested by an inquiry, the purport of which did not reach me, but which seemed to be addressed to myself, and was preferred in a soft sweet voice that struck me very pleasantly. I turned hastily round and found at my elbow a pretty little girl, who begged to be directed to a certain street at a considerable distance, and indeed in quite another quarter of the town.[32]

After this paragraph, Dickens delays a fraction before reassuring us of the innocence of Nell's inquiry, and her innate goodness, and we have to suppress an impulse to mistrust her 'soft sweet voice'. Momentarily, we suspect that Little Nell has solicited Master Humphrey. As Catherine Robson notices, 'Nell is alone walking the streets, perilously close to Covent Garden, London's traditional red-light district, when she "solicits" Master Humphrey.'[33]

Is this adolescent girl in the street at night a child prostitute? One of the most visible forms of prostitution in the nineteenth century, as Judith Walkowitz reminds us, was that of 'the isolated activity of the lone streetwalker, a solitary figure in the urban landscape, outside home and hearth, emblematic of urban alienation and the dehumanization of the cash nexus'.[34] Dostoevsky, describing the Haymarket at night on his visit to London in 1862, expressed his sadness that 'little girls around twelve years of age take you by the hand and ask you to go with them'.[35]

No doubt it is because of the risk that his readers might initially identify Nell as a child prostitute that Dickens decided to amend his first draft of the story. Originally, rather more dangerously, he had specified that, when she meets the narrator, Nell is a 'young female, apparently in some agitation', and that she is 'looking archly'. He had also indicated that she has diamonds to sell. Dickens altered the text in order to insist instead that she is simply a 'pretty little girl' who, in spite of the secret that compels her onto the streets at night, is smiling.[36] In this manuscript version, the opening of *The Old Curiosity Shop* is disconcertingly close to a depiction of the encounter between a nightwalker and a streetwalker.

But Dickens does not fully erase the traces of such an encounter in the final version of the novel. 'I have lost my road', Nell announces in the ensuing dialogue, in a sentence that is heavy with moral associations. It is designed once again gently to hint that she might be a fallen female child, or at the least a potentially corruptible one – perhaps in order to transmit an added frisson of excitement to the reader. For if young girls walking alone in the city's streets were not prostitutes, they were, in the popular imagination at least, potential prostitutes, susceptible to predatory pimps.

Henry Mayhew's *London Labour and the London Poor* (1851) included a quotation from the opening address of 'The London Society for the Protection of Young Females, and Prevention of Juvenile Prostitution', founded in 1835. The lecture at one point discusses those who trap, or trepan, girls of between eleven and fifteen in order to prostitute them: 'When an innocent child appears in the streets without a protector, she is insidiously watched by one of these merciless wretches and decoyed under some plausible pretext to an abode of infamy and degradation. No sooner is the unsuspecting helpless one within their grasp than, by a preconcerted measure, she becomes a victim of their inhuman designs.'[37]

Dickens had himself reflected on the exploitation and criminalization of young girls in an article for *Bell's Life in London* from November 1835. There, he describes watching two sisters being placed in a prisoners' van on the street, and sermonizes in these tones: 'Step by step, how many wretched females, within the sphere of every man's observation, have become involved in a career of vice, frightful to contemplate; hopeless at its commencement, loathsome and repulsive in its course; friendless, forlorn, and unpitied, at its miserable conclusion.'[38] So an association with criminalized or victimized young girls on the city's streets, and with the rapacious or pathetic men who exploit them, flickers uneasily at the corners of the reader's consciousness during the description of Humphrey's encounter with Nell at the start of *The Old Curiosity Shop*.

Dickens does not directly identify Nell and Master Humphrey with the social outcasts that people Mayhew's taxonomies and his own sketches. But at the beginning of *The Old Curiosity Shop* the reader nonetheless briefly glimpses an alternative London – the dystopian London that he will explore more fully in his mature novels, like *Bleak House* (1853) and *Our Mutual Friend*, with their persistent concern for repressed secrets. The reader consequently glimpses an alternative novel too.

After all, when Humphrey agrees to take Nell back to her grandfather, he grows fearful that, if she herself recognizes the way home, she will take her farewell of him. So he leads her there by a curiously circuitous route: 'I avoided the most frequented ways and took the most intricate, and thus it was not until we arrived in the street itself that she knew where we were.'[39] This is at the very least an odd, slightly sadistic way of proceeding. In the strict etymological sense, it is a seduction, a leading away. The meeting between Humphrey and Nell, to appropriate a formulation from Freud, is a scene of seduction.

This is not to propose that Master Humphrey is a paedophile – the 'kidnapper of children' or 'monster' that his neighbours once took him for. It is simply to intimate that he is not necessarily what he seems. He too is a collector of curiosities, including human ones, and he too, it seems, is reluctant to relinquish his hold on such curiosities. In Joycean terms, he assumes the shape of cupiosity.

Dickens, for his part, also sometimes assumed the shape of cupiosity. Late one night, for example, when he was living in Paris during the composition of *Little Dorrit* (1857), he visited a dance hall where prostitutes and female escorts were available for hire. He dismissed almost all of these women as either 'wicked and coldly calculating, or haggard and wretched in their worn beauty'. But he was attracted nonetheless to one woman of about thirty dressed in an Indian shawl – 'handsome, regardless, brooding, and yet with some nobler qualities in her forehead'. 'I mean to walk about tonight, and look for her', he wrote to the novelist Wilkie Collins in April 1856; 'I didn't speak to her there, but I have a fancy that I should like to know more about her.'[40]

There is something predatory as well as sadly solitary about this resolution, at once casual and coolly determined, to walk the streets of Paris at night in pursuit of the prostitute. Dickens's initial impulse might be dismissed as a classic instance of what Walter Benjamin, compiling his poetics of the metropolitan city, called 'love at last sight'.[41] But the decision to walk about looking for her is altogether darker.

Dickens squandered a subtle and insidiously unsettling sense of moral and psychological danger when he expelled Master Humphrey from *The Old Curiosity Shop*. In a letter to John Forster in January 1840, he explained his most recent conception of the storytelling mechanism of *Master Humphrey's Clock*, which centres on the relation of Humphrey to the clock: 'Then I mean to tell how he has kept odd manuscripts in the old, deep, dark, silent closet where the weights are; and taken them from thence to read.'[42] Humphrey himself contains a deep, dark, silent interior in which secrets are concealed, as his roaming in the streets of the capital at night in the seminal scene of *The Old Curiosity Shop* seems to imply. Perhaps this is the reason Dickens dismisses him from his role as the narrator of Nell's story. Perhaps it is his darkness rather than his cumbrousness that prompted Dickens to expel him.

Ghost upon the Earth

Other early novels by Dickens feature nightwalking too. In *Oliver Twist* (1838), the eponymous character is born in the workhouse when his mother, who has been found 'lying in the street', is carried there after walking through the night, in shoes that are 'worn to pieces' – 'but where she came from, or where she was going to', comments the narrator, 'nobody knows'. When he finally escapes the workhouse, Oliver himself walks a distance of seventy miles, sleeping rough at night, in order to lose himself in London, which he speculates is 'the very place for a homeless boy, who must die in the streets, unless someone helped him'. The innocent Rose Maylie dies of illness after a moonlit walk.[43]

Most strikingly, after murdering Nancy, Bill Sikes flees on foot and tramps relentlessly through both city and countryside in a doomed attempt to elude both his pursuers and the ghastly image of his guilt. When he leaves the town of Hatfield, for instance, the reader is told that he 'plunged into the solitude and darkness of the road, [and] felt a dread and awe creeping upon him which shook him to the core'.[44] Sikes's nightwalking underlines the fact that, like a number of Dickens's villains, heroes and anti-heroes, he is the scion of a centuries-old tradition of alienation and anomie, if not outlawry. Dickens's fiction is full of fugitives and outcasts of one kind and another who find refuge in the city at night.

Barnaby Rudge (1841), the novel Dickens produced after *The Old Curiosity Shop*, which also appeared in *Master Humphrey's Clock*, is another prolonged meditation on the social and psychological meanings of nighttime London. In this fictional account of the anti-Catholic Gordon Riots of 1780, Dickens demonstrates his fascination with the atmospherics of night in the metropolis prior to the introduction of gas lamps, and hints that these conditions persist in the mid nineteenth century.

Dickens relishes the task of reconstructing a city in which, because of the inefficiency of the 'oil and cotton lamps', a heavy, often impenetrable darkness prevails. 'Many of the courts and lanes were left in total darkness', he explains, and even 'in the lightest thoroughfares, there was at every turn some obscure and dangerous spot whither a thief might fly for shelter, and few would care to follow'. The pavements are in places illuminated by the 'little stream of light' emanating from night-cellars, which 'yawned for the reception and entertainment of the most abandoned of both sexes'. And they are barricaded with sheds and bulks under which 'small groups of link-boys gamed away the earnings of the day; or one more weary than the rest, gave way to sleep, and let the fragment of his torch fall hissing on the puddled ground'. The novel's main setting is the 'dark, houseless night' of late-eighteenth-century London.[45]

In this nocturnal cityscape, shaped by the turbulent forces of anti-Catholic rebellion, as well as the insurgent energies of repressed memories and fantasies, Dickens is especially interested in those 'who trod the streets by night'. He is interested in the anonymous people who, in the climate of fear created by the threat of footpads and other ruffians, 'wended home alone at midnight' and kept to the middle of the road in order to avoid being attacked. He is interested in individuals like Mr Haredale, a respectable Catholic who is forced to search for his niece, missing since Protestants burned their house down, on the night of the riots at Newgate; and who 'found himself, with the night coming on, alone in the streets; and destitute of any place in which to lay his head'.[46]

Above all, Dickens is interested in the mysterious stranger who, it is eventually revealed, is the father of poor Barnaby, and the perpetrator of a long-unsolved murder. This sinister man, who remains nameless for most of the narrative, is an inveterate nightwalker. Indeed, in his character the nightwalker is, initially at least, elevated to the level of a satanic villain. In the fragmented community of nightwalkers that constitutes the subterranean life of the city, he is first among equals. 'Among all the dangerous characters who, in such a state of society, prowled and skulked in the metropolis at night, there was one man, from whom many as uncouth and fierce as he, shrunk with an involuntary dread.'[47]

This man who, 'so surely as the dead of night set in', appeared in the night-cellars like the spectre of Banquo, and 'chilled and haunted' their licentious occupants, has a particular proclivity for 'traversing the streets' after dark:

> Directly it was dark, he was abroad – never in company with anyone, but always alone; never lingering or loitering, but always walking swiftly; and looking (so they said who had seen him) over his shoulder from time to time, and as he did so quickening his pace. In the fields, the lanes, the roads, in all quarters of the town – east, west, north, and south – that man was seen gliding on, like a shadow. He was always hurrying away. Those who encountered him, saw him steal past, caught sight of the backward glance, and so lost him in the darkness.

Haunted and hunted, this nightwalker is in a moral sense lost in the darkness.

Glimpsed briefly by beggars, footpads and other inhabitants of the urban night, he acquires a fantastical or mythical reputation. 'There are tales among us that you have sold yourself to the devil', observes a grave-robber who has the temerity to talk to him. 'I am what you all are, and live as you all do', the stranger admonishes his interrogator. But 'the dread of the man and the mystery that surrounded him' do not dissipate. He leads the life both of 'a haunted beast' and of 'a ghost upon the earth'; and, like the Wandering Jew, he is 'a thing from which all creatures shrink, save those curst beings of another world, who will not leave me'. At the same time subhuman and superhuman, he is the common nightwalker in its legendary or mythical incarnation.[48]

It is after the itinerant stranger's ominous reappearance in her life that Barnaby's mother comments, in tender, mournful tones, that her simple-minded son's existence is itself a 'darkened walk through this sad world'. The father's existential condition imprints itself on the son in the form of an abstract and irresistible fate. Leaving his former wife's house, the stranger plunges back into the nocturnal city, 'gliding along the silent streets, and holding his course where they were darkest and most gloomy':

> It was the dead time of the night, and all was quiet. Now and then a drowsy watchman's footsteps sounded on the pavement, or the lamplighter on his rounds went flashing past, leaving behind a little track of smoke mingled with glowing morsels of his hot red link. He hid himself even from these partakers of his lonely walk, and, shrinking in some arch or doorway while they passed, issued forth again when they were gone and pursued his solitary way.[49]

Concealed in the chiaroscuro shadows of doorways, amid the faint traces of sulphuric smoke, this enigmatic, aggressively solitary individual is the avatar of a kind of nineteenth-century noir.

It is at this point that Dickens's secret sympathy for this outcast starts to become apparent. In the end, it transpires that he is the illegitimate son of Sir John Chester, and that, in both literal and metaphorical senses, he is therefore an aristocrat among common nightwalkers. But in Chapter 18 Dickens identifies him, with incipient compassion, as 'a houseless rejected creature', whose unhappiness is deepened because he is 'wandering up and down where shelter is, and beds and sleepers are by thousands':

> To pace the echoing stones from hour to hour, counting the dull chimes of the clocks; to watch the lights twinkling in chamber windows, to think what happy forgetfulness each house shuts in … to have nothing in common with the slumbering world around, not even sleep, Heaven's gift to all its creatures, and be akin to nothing but despair; to feel, by the wretched contrast with everything on every hand, more utterly alone and cast away than in a trackless desert, – this is a kind of suffering, on which the rivers of great cities close full many a time, and which the solitude in crowds alone awakens.

He looks to the east for relief, in the hope of seeing the first streaks of the sun's light, 'but obdurate night had yet possession of the sky, and his undisturbed and restless walk found no relief'.[50] Here, as elsewhere, the sense of isolation and alienation that, half-consciously, half-unconsciously, Dickens cultivated in the course of his own nightwalking activities, directly informs his fiction.

Vagabond and Restless Habits

'A quantity of strolling about by night'. The phrase is taken from *A Tale of Two Cities* (1859), Dickens's historical novel about the French Revolution, which he wrote in the midst of the emotional crisis that afflicted him in the late 1850s. The most fascinating character in this book, which was heavily influenced by Thomas Carlyle's account of the Revolution, is Sidney Carton, an intellectually brilliant barrister who is tormented by dark, even vicious drives that he ultimately redeems in the novel's climactic act of martyrdom, when he takes the place in prison of his former client, Charles Darnay, and is executed. Carton too is an inveterate nightwalker. Indeed, this is probably one of the signs that Dickens secretly identifies with him. 'I must say that I like my Carton', he admitted in a letter shortly after completing the novel; 'And I have a faint idea sometimes, that if I had acted him, I could have done something with his life and death.'[51] Carton is the nightwalker not as villain but as anti-hero.

Dickens indicates that, in the house of Dr Manette, who is insane after eighteen years' imprisonment in the Bastille, Carton is a 'moody and morose lounger' who exhibits an almost sociopathic attitude to other people: 'the cloud of caring for nothing, which over-shadowed him with such a fatal darkness, was very rarely pierced by the light within him'. But Carton is in love with Lucie, Manette's daughter, who will subsequently marry Darnay, and this hopeless passion incipiently humanizes him. Its redemptive potential is apparent in his poignant attachment to the streets – and 'the senseless stones that made their pavements' – that environ Manette's house in London:

> Many a night he vaguely and unhappily wandered there, when wine had brought no transitory gladness to him; many a dreary daybreak revealed his solitary figure lingering there, and still lingering there when the first beams of the sun brought into strong relief, removed beauties of architecture in spires of churches and lofty buildings, as perhaps the quiet time brought some sense of better things, else forgotten and unattainable, into his mind.

Presumably Dickens is in this passage recalling the nights he haunted the streets surrounding Maria Winter's house when he was in his early twenties. 'I have so far verified what is done and suffered in these pages', he confessed in the Preface to *A Tale of Two Cities*, 'as that I have certainly done and suffered it all myself.'[52]

In the third volume of the novel, shortly after his arrival in France during the Terror, Carton devotes an entire night to walking the streets of Paris. 'You know my vagabond and restless habits', he reassures the benign, fatherly Mr Lorry, who is distressed to learn of Darnay's second arrest; 'If I should prowl about the streets a long time, don't be uneasy.' Ordinarily, it is implied, nightwalking provokes a distinct sense of uneasiness. Leaving Lorry at approximately

10 a.m., he sets off into the 'dark and dirty streets' of the metropolis. He stops briefly 'under a glimmering lamp' in order to scribble on a scrap of paper, before entering a chemist's shop and purchasing 'certain small packets' containing, it seems, the ingredients of ether. But, apart from these momentary interruptions, he pursues a path through the city at once aimless and relentless. 'I can't sleep', Carton announces beneath the moon, in 'the settled manner of a tired man, who had wandered and struggled and got lost, but who at length struck into his road and saw its end.'[53] If he traces an uncertain route through the city on foot, he nonetheless identifies his destiny with certainty.

As Carton walks 'down the dark streets, among the heavy shadows, with the moon and the clouds sailing on high above him', a forgotten fragment of scripture, read at his father's graveside, surfaces in his mind with insistent regularity: 'I am the resurrection and the life, saith the Lord.' It is not so much that, 'in a city dominated by the axe, alone at night', he clings to this sentence; it seems to cling to him. In 'lighted windows' he glimpses people 'going to rest, forgetful through a few calm hours of the horrors surrounding them'. Across lamp-lit streets he sees people pouring out of the theatres. All this time, Christ's minatory comment to Martha in St John's Gospel repeats itself, especially when the city empties: 'Now, that the streets were quiet, and the night wore on, the words were in the echoes of his feet, and were in the air.' The words redeem the 'senseless stones' of the pavement.

Eventually, the day appears, 'coldly, looking like a dead face out of the sky'; and the night turns pale and expires, 'as if Creation were delivered over to Death's dominion'. In fact, this scene heralds not only Carton's execution, in the final chapter of the novel, but his resurrection. Christ's words are echoed again as he dies. Death is delivered over to Creation's dominion.

Carton is transfigured by his brutal martyrdom, which leaves his face looking 'sublime and prophetic'.[54] His mystic nightwalk has been a preparation both for his death and for his redemption. It is a dark night of the soul, endured not in a prison cell, like that of St John of the Cross, the sixteenth-century theologian of the night, but on the deserted city streets. In the second book of the *Dark*

Night of the Soul (1582–1585), John celebrated the liberation of the soul through the night: 'It is not to be supposed that, because in this night and darkness [the soul] has passed through so many tempests of afflictions, doubts, fears, and horrors, as has been said, it has for that reason run any risk of being lost.' No. 'On the contrary', he stresses, '*in the darkness of this night it has gained itself*.'[55]

The dead of night in the city is, according to Dickens, a spiritual as well as a psychological and a social condition. Indeed, in the act of nightwalking, these three categories or dimensions are densely intertangled.

Vast Armies of Dead

In Dickens's city, the dead of night, like the urban crowd characterized by Walter Benjamin, is 'the newest asylum for outlaws' and 'the latest narcotic for those abandoned'.[56] Consciously or unconsciously, the nightwalker refuses the logic of the diurnal city, the ceaseless traffic of its commodities and its commuters. Bohemian or lumpenproletarian, he is an exile from the political economy of the capitalist metropolis. Homeless at home, he seeks a sense of home instead in the state of homelessness afforded by emptied, darkened streets.

In contradistinction to those individuals who, from necessity, travel from one place to another after dark, perhaps because they are compelled either to make a journey or to perform some sort of professional duty, walking at night is for the nightwalker a kind of vocation. The nightwalker's ambition is to lose and find himself in the labyrinth of the city at nighttime. Like Thomas De Quincey, he experiences the city as a form of phantasmagoria. In its tenebrous spaces he confronts the limits of his subjectivity. Every nightwalk is thus a fugue or psychogenic flight – an escape from the self and, at the same time, a plunge into its depths.

In 'Night Walks', Dickens recalls wandering near Bethlehem Hospital and pursuing a 'night fancy' in sight of its walls: 'And the fancy was this: Are not the sane and the insane equal at night as the sane lie a dreaming?' At night in the city, according to Dickens, there is a democracy of dreamers, one in which there is almost no distinction between the thoughts of people in bed and those of the semi-somnambulant nightwalkers who haunt the darkened streets like the undead. One in which, moreover, there is almost no distinction between these undead noctambulants and the ghosts of the city's dead themselves:

> And indeed in those houseless night walks – which even included cemeteries where watchmen went round among the graves at stated times, and moved the tell-tale handle of an index which recorded that they had touched it at such an hour – it was a solemn consideration what enormous hosts of dead belong to one old great city, and how, if they were raised while the living slept, there would not be the space of a pin's point in all the streets and ways for the living to come out into. Not only that, but the vast armies of dead would overflow the hills and valleys beyond the city, and would stretch away all round it, God knows how far.

So many, I had not thought death had undone so many … London at night is a necropolis.

After midnight the metropolitan city is a necropolitan city, and the nightwalker roams through it like those unfortunate individuals in Greek mythology who were condemned to wander the near bank of the Styx in a state of solitary desolation because they could not afford to pay Charon the fee he demanded to ferry them to the kingdom of the dead. In the dead of night, or the dead night, the circadian cycle reaches its nethermost point and the sleeping body settles into a stasis that resembles – death. If this condition is something like the degree-zero of subjectivity, then the dead of night stages the zero-degree identity of the city. It is this city that Dickens, one of the dead of the night, traversed in his solitary nightwalks.

Nightwalking, it might be said, takes place in the realm of the unnight, a liminal zone between the waking and sleeping city, and between the waking and sleeping state of mind – even between the living and the dead. In the final paragraph of 'Night Walks', Dickens refers to 'the real desert region of the night' in which, to his persistent surprise, the 'houseless wanderer' finds himself almost completely alone.[57] The time of night that most accommodates the nightwalker, houseless as he is, and restless, is when respectable people are not only curtained off from the city in their more or less comfortable domestic interiors, their sitting rooms or bedrooms, but when they are helplessly, hopelessly deep in sleep. It is the time of night when the city is almost entirely deserted, but at the same time teems with spectres.

It is almost as if Night itself is a spectral wanderer in London, a city that resembles some vast, labyrinthine 'Ghost's Walk', to cite *Bleak House*. Jeremy Tambling has perceptively observed that, in the title of 'Night Walks', the word 'night' might be either an adjective or a noun: 'if the latter, it is night that "walks", like a spectre haunting London'.[58]

Guilt and Darkness

In 'The Heart of London', an article from *Master Humphrey's Clock* in 1843, Dickens discriminates between two phases of the night. The first of these, the social night as it might be called, is the night of 'lights and pleasures'; the second, the antisocial or asocial phase of the night, is one of 'guilt and darkness'.[59] He makes an equivalent distinction in *Great Expectations*, where Pip implicitly compares 'the London streets, so crowded with people and so brilliantly lighted in the dusk of evening', to those same streets stripped of their nightlife in the 'dead of night'.[60] It is with the second of these phases that Dickens associates nightwalking.

This is the gothic atmosphere evoked by George Augustus Sala in *Twice Round the Clock* (1859) when he discloses that, in the hours after midnight, 'all has a solemn, ghastly, unearthly aspect; the gas-lamps flicker like corpse candles; and the distant scream of a profligate, in conflict with the police, courses up and down the streets in weird and shuddering echoes'.[61] In the night of guilt and darkness, the night that refuses to be domesticated, the nightwalker incarnates the unconscious drives shaping the dreams of those that sleep.

Those who awake from their dreams at this time, and lie listening in their beds, as he describes it in *Barnaby Rudge*, long for the dawn, 'and wish the dead of the night were past'. This phrase, 'the dead of the night', evokes not only the deepest, blackest recess of the nighttime, but those alienated, alien people who, like the undead, colonize its spaces. In the same chapter of *Barnaby Rudge*, Dickens likens a knot of nocturnal labourers, who are building the scaffold on which Barnaby's father is to be hanged outside the ruined remains of Newgate Prison, to 'shadowy creatures toiling at midnight on some ghostly unsubstantial work, which, like themselves, would vanish with the first gleam of day, and leave but morning mist and vapour'.[62]

These too are the city's undead. In the light of day, Dickens observes, the gibbet they have built in the night will be an 'obscene presence' in the street. 'It was better haunting the street like a spectre, when men were in their beds', he concludes, 'and influencing perchance the city's dreams.'[63] At night the architecture of the city and that of the unconscious cannot be dissociated. The nightwalker – like someone trapped in the contradictory spaces of Piranesi's *Carceri*, as depicted by De Quincey, whose dreams were 'chiefly architectural' – occupies both these domains.[64]

'What fancy takes you, then, for walking about in the night?' one of Dickens's characters asks in *Our Mutual Friend*. Extinction, the extinction of the city and the self, is one of the answers Dickens presents in both his journalistic pieces and his fiction. In Benjamin's formulation, Dickens understood that, especially at night, 'the places are countless in the great cities where one stands on the edge of the void', and where prostitutes, and derelicts of one kind and another, are like the household gods and goddesses of 'this cult of nothingness'.[65] But, freed from his connections to a functioning civilization, Dickens's encounter with the non-being of the night entails the liberation of the self as well as its obliteration. In the language of Hegel, 'This is the night, the interior of [human] nature, existing here – pure *Self*.'[66]

14.

Conclusion

The Man of the Crowd

'I have nowhere to sleep at night, but roam about the Streets – I am nearly exhausted.' So Edgar Allan Poe complained to his foster father in 1827, after finally leaving home, in an attempt to extract money from him.[1] In later life, as a penurious alcoholic, Poe often spent the night in a rootless pursuit of oblivion on the streets of Baltimore, Philadelphia or New York. In Dickensian terms, he suffered his entire life from a severe case of Dry Rot.

But if the city at night signifies for Poe a houseless, penniless state, as his biography suggests, it also represents a refuge for those who have exiled themselves in the day from its streets and thoroughfares, as his fiction indicates. In 'The Murders in the Rue Morgue' (1841), often regarded as the first detective story, Poe offered a sense of the importance, for the city's misfits, of recovering the freedom of the city after nightfall. In its introductory paragraphs, the narrator describes how he and the detective Auguste Dupin, cultivating a cerebral, if not sepulchral, existence in Paris, together became 'enamoured of the Night for her own sake'. He reports that, awaiting 'the advent of the true Darkness', the friends used to barricade themselves in shuttered rooms during the day in order to read and talk.[2] Like modern metropolitan mystics, they look to 'the true Darkness' for enlightenment.

Once night had fallen in the city, the two men used to set out: 'Then we sallied forth into the streets, arm in arm, continuing the topics of the day, or roaming far and wide until a late hour, seeking, amid the wild lights and shadows of the populous city, that infinity of mental excitement which quiet observation can afford.' Sometimes they talked to one another. Sometimes – as on an occasion when, 'strolling one night down a long dirty street, in the vicinity of the Palais Royal', Dupin demonstrates the penetration of his ratiocinative mind to particularly scintillating effect – they remained silent.[3] In Poe's fiction, the nightwalker thus assumes the form of the detective, an archetype that will of course acquire enormous cultural significance in the nocturnal city of the late nineteenth and twentieth centuries.

The nightwalker also assumes the form, in Poe's fiction, of a satanic stranger – the demonic embodiment of the industrial metropolitan city at its most alien and unknowable.

À Pas de Loup

Poe's 'The Man of the Crowd' (1840) represents the apotheosis, in the mid nineteenth century, of the metropolitan nightwalker as a sort of modern mythical archetype. In this mysterious short story, he pushes nightwalking to a pathological extreme, exploring it as an irresistible compulsion.

Set in London, 'The Man of the Crowd' explores the nocturnal drama of lights and shadows in the streets – and of 'mental excitement' and 'quiet observation' – with the intensity of a chiaroscuro painting. First published in December 1840, it appeared eight months after the publication of the first chapter of *The Old Curiosity Shop*, which was printed in the April 1840 issue of *Master Humphrey's Clock*. Poe reviewed the first volume of Dickens's periodical for *Graham's Magazine*, so it is almost certain that he was reading instalments of Dickens's novel as he composed his short story. One critic has persuasively argued that Dickens's account of 'the obsessive nocturnal peregrinations of both Master Humphrey and Little Nell's grandfather' directly shaped Poe's portrait of a man obsessively pursuing an enigmatic stranger on foot through the streets of London at night.[4] Dickens's fictional studies of London's eccentrics and derelicts in *Sketches by Boz*, including 'The Drunkard's Death' (1836), also evidently influenced it.

The anonymous narrator of 'The Man of the Crowd', recovering from a fever, sits inside a coffee shop on a busy thoroughfare in central London at dusk. Peering through the 'smoky panes' of the window, he watches the passersby, regarding 'with minute interest the innumerable varieties of details, dress, air, gait, visage and expression of countenance'. Detached from the 'dense and continuous tides of population' that rush past the café as the evening closes in, and from the rhythms of routine production and consumption they collectively embody, this convalescent is fascinated by the people he sees commuting home: 'At this particular period of the evening I had never before been in a similar situation, and the tumultuous sea of human heads filled me, therefore, with a delicious novelty of emotion.'[5] This is what Charles Lamb, forty years earlier, implicitly thought of as 'urban emotion'.

The narrator's sense of curiosity, exacerbated by his convalescent state, is almost boundless. For him, as for Master Humphrey, 'curiosity had become a fatal, irresistible passion', as Charles Baudelaire put it in 'The Painter of Modern Life' (1863).[6] Initially, he examines the mass of human forms that pass him in relatively abstract terms. He is particularly interested in those who seem unconfident on the street, those who 'were restless in their movements, had flushed faces, and talked and gesticulated to themselves, as if feeling in solitude on account of the very denseness of the company around'. Here is that 'dissolution of mankind into monads' that Friedrich Engels diagnosed in his account of the dynamics of the London crowd in *The Condition of the Working Class in England* (1845).[7]

Then Poe's convalescent examines the passersby in more concrete detail, as if they inhabit some grimy aquarium. Sliding down 'the scale of what is termed gentility', as the light thickens, he classifies their physiognomies, their clothes and their step, carefully identifying the aristocrats, the businessmen, the clerks, the 'ragged artizans', the 'exhausted labourers', the pie-men, the dandies, the conmen, the pickpockets, the beggars and the prostitutes. He is fascinated above all by the innumerable drunkards he sees. Their countenances pale, their eyes a livid red, they clutch at passing objects 'with quivering fingers' as they stride though the crowd.[8] These are the sufferers of Dry Rot.

The identities of all the city's inhabitants, it seems, are indelibly inscribed on their bodies. In contrast to Wordsworth, who complained in the *Prelude* that, in the metropolis, 'the face of every one / That passes by me is a mystery!', Poe's narrator finds the passersby transparently readable.[9] It makes him feel almost contemptuous of them. But it is while 'thus occupied in scrutinizing the mob', his forehead pressed against the pane of glass beside his seat, that he abruptly glimpses a 'decrepid old man' of about seventy who, because his face is an irreducible mystery, both fascinates and terrifies him. The narrator finds himself completely unable to classify the old man's physiognomy or physiology, which instantly constitutes an impenetrable enigma.

By this time, the night has deepened, and the 'general character of the crowd' has altered accordingly. The narrator reports that the 'more orderly portion of people' has retired from the streets, and that in their place 'the late hour [has] brought forth every species of infamy from its den'.[10] 'Voici le soir charmant, ami du criminel', Baudelaire writes in 'Le Crépuscule du Soir' (1857), perhaps thinking partly of his hero Poe; 'Il vient comme un complice, à pas de loup …'[11]

The old man, though he is 'short in stature, very thin, and apparently very feeble', embodies precisely this loping, lupine form. His idiosyncratic countenance communicates a series of contradictory ideas to the narrator: 'the ideas of vast mental power, of caution, of penuriousness, of avarice, of coolness, of malice, of blood-thirstiness, of triumph, of merriment, of excessive terror, of intense – of supreme despair'.[12] He seems demonic, in the mass of people on the streets of the city, precisely because of his apparently innate resistance to being reduced to a monadic identity. If he personifies solitude, he contains multitudes.

Death-Hour

It is almost night. 'The rays of the gas-lamps, feeble at first in their struggle with the dying day, had now at length gained ascendancy, and threw over everything a fitful and garish lustre.' This is the onset of what Lynda Nead has called 'London's gas time; the time that passed as the gas burned in the street lamps and when the city became a place given over to imagination, dread and dream'.[13] In a moment of heated decision, responding to 'a craving desire to keep the man in view – to know more of him', Poe's convalescent narrator resolves to follow him.[14]

So, still slightly feverish, he rushes into the street, his curiosity intensified by the snatched sight, beneath the old man's cloak, of a diamond and a dagger, or so he thinks. It is as if, Lazarus-like, the man in St Martin's Court described by Dickens in *Master Humphrey's Clock* had suddenly stood up and, to use one of Walter Benjamin's formulations, 'plunge[d] into the crowd as into a reservoir of energy'.[15] Poe's narrator thus commences his pursuit, determined 'to follow the stranger whithersoever he should go'. 'It was now fully night-fall, and a thick humid fog hung over the city, soon ending in a settled rain.'[16] It is the time of benightment.

The old man roams the streets ceaselessly, sometimes at a ponderous, dilatory pace, sometimes at a preternaturally rapid one, through densely dark alleys and 'brilliantly lighted squares', in both crowded and isolated sections of the city. In 'a large and busy bazaar', he moves for an hour and a half with purposeless purposefulness among the assembled buyers and sellers: 'He entered shop after shop, priced nothing, spoke no word, and looked at all objects with a wild and vacant stare.' This is an image of the metropolitan consumer in the mid nineteenth century as one of the undead. The narrator is 'utterly amazed at his behaviour'.[17] Amazed at his behaviour and enmazed by the city.

From there, 'looking anxiously around him for an instant', the old man runs 'with incredible swiftness through many crooked and people-less lanes', before suddenly arriving back at the populous street containing the coffee-house from which the narrator had started stalking him. But it is approaching midnight, so this 'great thoroughfare' now feels different. The crowds of people have disappeared and the streets have become deserted: 'It was still brilliant with gas; but the rain fell fiercely, and there were few persons to be seen.' The old man abruptly quits this scene, 'plunging through a great variety of devious ways' as if he is tracking the convolutions of his own consciousness. Outside a theatre, he immerses himself in the crowds collected there, and 'the intense agony of his countenance' momentarily seems to diminish; but as soon as these crowds disperse he seems tortured by 'his old uneasiness and vacillation'. Once again, the narrator is left 'at a loss to comprehend the waywardness of his actions'.[18]

All this time the narrator follows him in a more and more futile attempt to understand what motivates him. At one point, the old man trails closely 'some ten or twelve roisterers', but this party eventually disperses and he abruptly becomes 'lost in thought'. Then, in the dead of the night, and 'with every mark of agitation', the stranger pursues a route into the poorest region of the metropolis:

> It was the most noisome quarter of London, where every thing wore the worst impress of the most deplorable poverty, and of the most desperate crime. By the dim light of an accidental lamp, tall, antique, worm-eaten, wooden tenements were seen tottering to their fall, in directions so many and capricious that scarce the semblance of a passage was discernible between them. The paving-stones lay at random, displaced from their beds by the rankly-growing grass. Horrible filth festered in the dammed-up gutters. The whole atmosphere teemed with desolation. Yet, as we proceeded, the sounds of human life revived by sure degrees, and at

> length large bands of the most abandoned of a London populace were seen reeling to and fro. The spirits of the old man again flickered up, as a lamp which is near its death-hour. Once more he strode onward with elastic tread.[19]

Here, still thriving, are 'the sanctuaries and stews of the Stuarts', as Dickens put it.[20] From roisterers to the most ruined representatives of the poor, the old man conducts a demonic tour of the cityscape mapped by the authors of nocturnal picaresques in the late seventeenth and eighteenth centuries. It is a gruesome parody of the kind of 'midnight mission' conducted at precisely this time by nineteenth-century philanthropists. Poe's old man conducts the midnight mission of a nineteenth-century misanthropist.

As the sun rises, the Man of the Crowd once more retraces his steps to the road on which the coffee-house stands: 'Long and swiftly he fled, while I followed him in the wildest amazement, resolute not to abandon a scrutiny in which I now felt an interest all-absorbing.' To the increasing confusion of the narrator, who nonetheless persists in pursuing him, the impenetrable and implacable old man spends the entire day pacing up and down this populous thoroughfare. As dusk falls again, the physically and psychologically exhausted narrator finally admits defeat:

> And, as the shades of the second evening came on, I grew wearied unto death, and, stopping fully in front of the wanderer, gazed at him steadfastly in the face. He noticed me not, but resumed his solemn walk, while I, ceasing to follow, remained absorbed in contemplation. 'This old man,' I said at length, 'is the type and the genius of deep crime. He refuses to be alone. *He is the man of the crowd.* It will be in vain to follow; for I shall learn no more of him, nor of his deeds …'[21]

The old man, as impassive and incomprehensible as a sphinx, seems to be more than human. Or less than human. He is apparently capable of walking without ever stopping. It is as if, in his labyrinthine path through the streets of the city at night, he has traced not the arbitrary trajectory of an individual but the secret form or logic of the corrupt, decrepit metropolis itself. The endless, circuitous restlessness of the city, ancient and modern, and its relentless ability both to seduce and to abandon its inhabitants, is concentrated in the old man. So the narrator finally renounces his pursuit.

Rereading Poe's short story in 'On Some Motifs in Baudelaire' a century later, Benjamin decides that ultimately he cannot identify the Man of the Crowd as a *flâneur*. This is mainly because, in the old man, 'composure has given way to manic behavior'. Instead, according to Benjamin, he exemplifies the destiny of the *flâneur* once this intrinsically urbane figure has been 'deprived of the milieu to which he belonged' (a milieu, he implies, that London probably never provided).[22] The same can be said of Poe's narrator, in whom composure must compete with an increasingly monomaniacal state of mind.

Indeed, it might be argued that 'The Man of the Crowd' dramatizes the process by which, in the hectic conditions of London in the mid nineteenth century, the *flâneur* splits apart and produces two additional metropolitan archetypes. One is driven by a pathological compulsion, the other by a scarcely controlled curiosity. The former is the nightwalker – a disreputable, indeterminately criminal type who embodies the half of the *flâneur* characterized by a state of restless mobility. The latter is the detective – another kind of nocturnal itinerant, who incarnates the half of him characterized by an attitude of relentless inquisitiveness. They are the hunted and the hunter; the stalked and the stalker. For Poe, these archetypes are spectral doubles. In nocturnal London in the mid nineteenth century, their identities are easily confused, easily interchanged. And, as he implies in 'The Murders in the Rue Morgue', their characteristic dispositions, the states of 'mental excitement' and 'quiet observation', cannot be neatly separated.

In the fugitive old man and his pursuer the ancient identities of the noctivagant and the noctambulant can be identified in forms that have been reshaped and distorted by the accelerated conditions of the industrial metropolis at night. This ritualized dance, in the mean streets of the city at night, between criminal and detective, nightwalker and nightstalker, will be extended and elaborated in the noir cinema and fiction of the mid twentieth century.

Genius of Deep Crime

The Man of the Crowd 'refuses to be alone'. But he is committed at the same time to a state of profound solitude – or condemned to it. The narrator, too, looking the old man 'steadfastly in the face' as if staring into a mirror, is at once addicted to the anonymous society of the metropolitan streets and, in the end, asocial. It is this dialectic – of a compulsive desire for the life of the city and a desperate need to flee it – that defines the nightwalker. In the inscrutable character of the Man of the Crowd, in Poe's urban fable, this dialectic attains its finest, and its most satanic, incarnation. As William Sharpe has observed, 'Poe's story hints that the stranger is the Devil' – but the narrator is also one of the damned, so 'the two men of the crowd are fellow fiends, incarnations of the modern night'.[23]

'The Man of the Crowd' dramatizes the range of historical identities or meanings ascribed to the common nightwalker in the metropolitan city – petty criminal, detective, bohemian outcast, stalker, homeless vagrant and, finally, Satan himself. In the character of the Man of the Crowd, who is both damned and redeemed in the darkened streets of the city, the tradition of the nightwalker resurfaces in its most common and uncommon forms. He is the emblem of physical and existential homelessness. If the mysterious old man is the perpetrator of a nameless crime, then in the end perhaps this is no more than the crime of being an outsider in the metropolis. Or, more precisely, it is the crime of appearing both homeless and at home in its precincts – lodged at its centre and at the same time dislodged, terminally marginal. The streets at night intensify the nightwalker's sense of solitude and offer a consolation for it. Poe's protagonist, or antagonist, is an intimate part of the city, but he is also an 'ex-timate' part of it – that is, a sort of foreign body embedded at its core.

'The Man of the Crowd', from this perspective, is an allegory of the criminalization of those who inhabit the nocturnal city. The Man of the Crowd seems suspicious or criminous because he leads an itinerant, possibly houseless existence in the city at night, and because the narrator who so obsessively pursues him is unable to identify or classify him. He is not, as the narrator desperately asserts, 'the type and the genius of deep crime'. At least, he is the type and genius of deep crime only in so far as this entity is an ideological construct. For in the end the Man of the Crowd is simply the repository of popular suspicions about solitary individuals who occupy the metropolitan streets at night. He is an empty signifier for the city's indigents and itinerants: the type and genius of its others, its otherness. In this respect, he resembles the tragic scapegoat who, blessed as well as cursed, assumes the sins of the society from which he is ritually excluded.

In his enigmatic short story, Poe imparts a renewed mythopoeic significance, in the conditions of the industrial capitalist city, to the descendant of a centuries-old metropolitan archetype: the common nightwalker.

Afterword

By Will Self

London, Friday, 20 June 2014 – it was the evening of the shortest night of the year, so was there anything more fitting to do than to walk the sixteen or so miles from my house in Stockwell to the high point of the North Downs near Woldingham? I wanted to capture this view at dawn – I wanted to see the city with the startled provincial eyes of a waking Wordsworth, rather than the gritty ones of a cockney wordsmith. But I also wanted the experience of getting there: the sole-shuffle over tarmac and paving as the city fell into slumber around me. I entertained the notion that since I'd be journeying from the insomniac centre to the always stuporous suburbs, I'd be acting as a twenty-first-century knocker-up, bringing with me the dawn of the longest day in the neoliberal calendar.

For companions I had the writers Nick Papadimitriou and Matthew Beaumont; the former's book *Scarp* is a sort of prose eulogy for another outer-London massif; the latter's, which you now hold in your hand, a cultural history of the human subject cast adrift in the urban darkness. Heading up Stockwell Road, then wending our way through Brixton, we were still paddling in the urban millrace: the Portuguese smack addicts outside the bookie's;

the Afro-Caribbean devotees of the plantain; the evening footballers whooping it up on the greensward of Brockwell Park – we were at one with them all as we strode. A litre flask of espresso sat in my backpack banging against the kidneys it was soon to flush through. From the top of Brockwell Park we had an excellent prospect of Central London, with its new skyline of hypertrophied desktop-toys. It was dusk as we left the park; dusk too when we gained Tulse Hill Station and Nick bought a plastic-encapsulated polypropylene sandwich from Tesco's.

Yet by the time we'd reached the top of Knight's Hill, and Matthew and Nick – I thought this distinctly infra dig – were taking snaps of the Crystal Palace radio mast, night had definitively fallen. It seemed fitting: we were walking through the lofty suburbia immortalized by Patrick Keiller in his short film *Norwood* (1983), a twisted fable of death, disappearance and unclipped privet in the time of Thatcher. *Norwood* is filmed in black and white – and we inhabited a similarly leached environment, with the lights of Croydon beginning to twinkle below us and to the south.

Descending through the darkness from Upper Norwood we passed through a cluster of pubs and takeaways around Norwood Junction that were patronized entirely by shaven-headed men wearing England football shirts and their womenfolk. The fascistic jollity that gusted from the open doors was … bracing.

But within minutes we'd left white-town and entered black-town: African groceries lined the road, men in colourful dish-dashes dashed from their cars to their front doors. We passed a pub that had been transformed into an African-themed nightclub, complete with fake elephant tusks bracketing the doorway, and a sign that announced that 'Fine African Wines' were being served inside.

By then it was already too late for such quaffing – the streets of the world city were emptying of traffic. We stopped somewhere in Addiscombe for a coffee and chocolate; Nick and Matthew bench-bound while I stretched out on the pavement, luxuriating in the bivouac of sodium light pitched by a streetlamp. A police patrol car schmoozed by. Later, coming down the hill towards Shirley, as we trudged in the middle of the shadowy lane, a BMW thrumming bass came up behind us; its driver wound down a window and goggled in marijuana bemusement at these odd tramping magi, acting as if we were kings of the road. On the outskirts of Shirley we halted on a bosky traffic island for another pick-us-up. As we sipped our coffee the moon rose in a cowl of milky, deliquescent mist.

Nick had the better night sight, so he navigated us down avenues of beeches, where we tripped over smoothed roots, kicking up the grey sandy soil.

Dawn winkled us out of the woodland, and we found ourselves blinking by the lychgate of St Leonard's Church, a little thirteenth-century gem tucked away on the outskirts of Warlingham; then came the final slog up the ridge of the North Downs, with the sun not yet risen but the eggshell sky cloudily cracking overhead. In the field were sluggish bullocks my dog was too tired to pester. We sought out the high point, and there it was: the panorama we'd been seeking. I could make out the blocks of flats near my home and the chimneys of Battersea Power Station – Nick thought he could see his own tower block off the Finchley Road. Only Matthew's home, in Kilburn, was lacking the necessary salience.

I stared at London spread out before us, and it seemed as strange to me as any landscape. This might've been an alien planet, or some virtual realm, conjured up in Silicon Valley and downloaded straight to my psyche. It was that much of an inversion of ordinary experience – the nighttime promenade out of the city – that all conventional measures of space and time and urbanity had been abandoned: as the sun rose London was made anew – and so, perhaps, were we.

Notes

Introduction

1. Percy Bysshe Shelley, 'Alastor, or The Spirit of Solitude', l. 30, in *Poetical Works*, ed. Thomas Hutchinson (Oxford: Oxford University Press, 1971), p. 16.
2. A. Alvarez, *Night: An Exploration of Night Life, Night Language, Sleep and Dreams* (London: Vintage, 1996), pp. xiii–xiv.
3. Ford Madox Ford, *The Soul of London: A Survey of a Modern City*, ed. Alan G. Hill (London: Everyman, 1995), p. 102.
4. Guy Debord, 'Introduction to a Critique of Urban Geography', in *The Situationists and the City*, ed. Tom McDonough (London: Verso, 2009), p. 62.
5. Louis Aragon, *Paris Peasant*, trans. Simon Watson Taylor (London: Pan Books, 1987), p. 155.
6. Virginia Woolf, 'Street Haunting' in *Selected Essays*, ed. David Bradshaw (Oxford: Oxford University Press, 2008), p. 177.
7. Bryan D. Palmer, *Cultures of Darkness: Night Travels in the History of Transgression* (New York: Monthly Review Press, 2000), pp. 16–17.
8. Joachim Schlör, *Nights in the Big City: Paris, Berlin, London, 1840–1930* (London: Reaktion, 1998), p. 168.
9. R. M. Lumiansky and David Mills, eds, *The Chester Mystery Cycle*, Vol.

1 (London: Early English Text Society/Oxford University Press, 1974), p. 244.

10. John Milton, *Paradise Lost*, XII. 648–9, IX. 638–41, V. 51–2, ed. Alastair Fowler (London: Longman, 1971), pp. 642, 475, 259.
11. See Jonathan Crary, *24/7: Late Capitalism and the Ends of Sleep* (London: Verso, 2013).
12. Roberto Bolaño, *2666*, trans. Natasha Wimmer (London: Picador, 2009), p. 180.
13. Charles Dickens, 'Shy Neighbourhoods', in *The Uncommercial Traveller and Reprinted Pieces*, ed. Leslie C. Staples (Oxford: Oxford University Press, 1958), p. 95.
14. Marjorie Keniston McIntosh; *Controlling Misbehavior in England, 1370–1600* (Cambridge: Cambridge University Press, 1998), p. 66.
15. Richard Huloet, *Huloet's Dictionarie Newly Corrected, Amended, Set in Order and Enlarged*, 2nd edn, ed. John Higgins (London: In ædibus I. Marshii, 1572), n.p.
16. Daniel Defoe, *The History of the Devil, as Well Ancient as Modern*, 2nd edn (London: T. Warner, 1727), p. 81.
17. William Shakespeare, *King Lear*, III. iv. 113–14, in *The Complete Works*, ed. Peter Alexander (London: Collins, 1951), p. 1,094. Henceforth, throughout this book, citations from Shakespeare are taken from this edition.
18. Rupert Brooke, *Letters from America* (New York: Charles Scribner's Sons, 1913), p. 29.
19. André Breton, *Manifesto of Surrealism*, in *Manifestoes of Surrealism*, trans. Richard Seaver and Helen R. Lane (Ann Arbor: University of Michigan Press, 1972), p. 11.
20. Maurice Blanchot, 'Michel Foucault as I Imagine Him', trans. Jeffrey Mehlman, in *Foucault/Blanchot* (New York: Zone Books, 1990), pp. 84–5.
21. Georg Lukács, *Theory of the Novel: A Historico-Philosophical Essay on the Forms of Great Epic Literature*, trans. Anna Bostock (London: Merlin, 1971), p. 41.
22. Walter Benjamin, 'The Paris of the Second Empire in Baudelaire', in *The Writer of Modern Life: Essays on Charles Baudelaire*, ed. Michael W. Jennings (Cambridge, MA: Harvard University Press, 2006), p. 109.

Chapter 1: Crime and the Common Nightwalker

1. Richard of Devizes, *Chronicle of Richard of Devizes of the Time of Richard the First*, ed. and trans. John T. Appleby (London: Thomas Nelson, 1963), pp. 65–6.

2. See *General Laws of Massachusetts* (2011), Part IV, Chapter 272 ('Crimes against Chastity, Morality, Decency, and Good Order'), Section 53.
3. *Commonwealth v. Boyer*, 400 Mass. 52, 53 (1987).
4. *Thomes v. Commonwealth*, 355 Mass. 203 (1968–1669).
5. Quoted in Martha Grace Duncan, *Romantic Outlaws, Beloved Prisons: The Unconscious Meanings of Crime and Punishment* (New York: New York University Press, 1996), p. 172.
6. David C. Brody, James R. Acker and Wayne A. Logan, *Criminal Law* (Gaithersburg, MD: Aspen, 2001), p. 63.
7. William Henry Whitmore, *The Colonial Laws of Massachusetts. Reprinted from the Edition of 1660, with the Supplements to 1672* (Boston: City Council of Boston, 1889), pp. 198–9.
8. See Roger Thompson, *Sex in Middlesex: Popular Mores in a Massachusetts County, 1649–1699* (Amherst: University of Massachusetts Press, 1986), p. 88.
9. David Charles Douglas and Harry Rothwell, eds, *English Historical Documents, 1189–1327* (London: Routledge, 1996), pp. 457–8.
10. John Stow, A *Survey of London*, ed. Antonia Fraser (Stroud: Sutton, 2005), p. 102.
11. Douglas and Rothwell, *English Historical Documents*, p. 458.
12. The case of the *benandanti* (literally, 'good walkers') in fifteenth- and sixteenth-century Italy offers a sense of the unstable moral meanings ascribed to those who inhabit the night. Members of this strange sect, which conducted nocturnal rituals in order to counteract the malevolent influence of witches, were initially dismissed as vagabonds; but, once the Inquisition became involved, were themselves violently persecuted as evil spirits. Their psychological or spiritual condition was also highly ambiguous, according to the records uncovered by Carlo Ginzburg, since they claimed that their nighttime activities took place in a dream-like state between sleeping and waking. In the eyes of the authorities, these benign walkers were malign walkers. See Carlo Ginzburg, *The Night Battles: Witchcraft and Agrarian Cults in the Sixteenth and Seventeenth Centuries*, trans. John and Anne Tedeschi (Baltimore, MD: Johns Hopkins University Press, 1983).
13. John Fletcher, *The Night-Walker; or, The Little Theife: A Comedy*, revised by James Shirley (London: Andrew Crooke and William Cooke, 1640), n.p.
14. Craig Koslofsky, *Evening's Empire: A History of the Night in Early Modern Europe* (Cambridge: Cambridge University Press, 2011), p. 15.
15. Johan Huizinga, *The Autumn of the Middle Ages*, trans. Rodney J. Paton

and Ulrich Mammitzsch (Chicago: University of Chicago Press, 1996), p. 2.

16. Jean Verdon, *Night and the Middle Ages*, trans. George Holoch (Notre Dame, IN: University of Notre Dame Press, 2002), p. 99.
17. See Edward Coke, *The Second Part of the Institutes of the Laws of England*, 4th edn (London: Richard and Edward Atkins, 1671), p. 52.
18. John Carpenter, *Liber Albus: The White Book of the City of London*, trans. Henry Thomas Riley (London: Griffin, 1861), pp. 240, 334, 518.
19. Anonymous, 'How the Wise Man Taught His Sonne', in *Medieval Conduct Literature: An Anthology of Vernacular Guides to Behaviour for Youths, with English Translations*, ed. Mark D. Johnston (Toronto: University of Toronto Press, 2009), p. 300.
20. James Howell, *Londinopolis: An Historicall Discourse or Perlustration of the City of London* (London: J. Streater, 1657), p. 77.
21. F. J. Snell, *The Customs of Old England* (London: Methuen, 1911), p. 219.
22. John Milton, 'A Masque Presented at Ludlow Castle, 1634 [Comus]', ll. 431, 435, in *Complete Shorter Poems*, ed. John Carey (London: Longman, 1971), p. 198.
23. This is John Stow's account in *A Survey of London*, p. 101.
24. A. Roger Ekirch, *At Day's Close: A History of Nighttime* (London: Weidenfeld & Nicolson, 2005), p. 64.
25. Geoffrey Chaucer, 'The Miller's Tale', l. 3,645, in *The Canterbury Tales*, in *The Riverside Chaucer*, 3rd edn, ed. Larry D. Benson (Oxford: Oxford University Press, 1988), p. 74.
26. On the fascinating topic of 'biphasic sleep', see Ekirch, *At Day's Close*, pp. 300–4.
27. Cited in Wolfgang Schivelbusch, *Disenchanted Night: The Industrialization of Light in the Nineteenth Century*, trans. Angela Davies (Berkeley, CA: University of California Press, 1988), p. 82.
28. Henry Thomas Riley, *Memorials of London and London Life in the XIIIth, XIVth, and XVth Centuries* (London: Longmans, Green & Co., 1868), p. 21.
29. Schivelbusch, *Disenchanted Night*, p. 81.
30. Verdon, *Night and the Middle Ages*, p. 2.
31. Ekirch, *At Day's Close*, p. 65. Anathematized both before and after their expulsion from England in 1290 (the culmination of their religious persecution under Edward I), Jews were often associated with the night – in part because they could not see the light of Christianity, in part presumably because the Jewish calendar is a lunar one. In the popular religious culture of the Middle Ages, they continued to be identified with malign

nocturnal creatures, especially owls. 'The symbolic identification of the owl with sinners in general in medieval visual culture was often refocused to represent the Jews in particular', writes one scholar: 'just as the owl shuns the daylight and prefers the night, so too the Jews obstinately reject Christ and remain in the darkness of ignorance.' Moreover, 'the owl's reputation as a filthy bird that soiled its own nest also resonated with anti-semitic narratives linking the Jews to faeces'. See Brett D. Hirsch, 'From Jew to Puritan: The Emblematic Owl in Early English Culture', in Brett D. Hirsch and Christopher Wortham, eds, *This Earthly Stage: World and Stage in Late Medieval and Early Modern England* (Turnhout: Brepols, 2010), p. 144.

32. 5. Edw. III. See William David Evans, ed., *A Collection of Statutes Connected with the General Administration of the Law*, 3rd edn, vol. 6 (London: Thomas Blenkarn, 1836), p. 236.
33. Henry B. Wheatley, *The Story of London* (London: J. M. Dent, 1904), p. 23.
34. Riley, *Memorials of London and London Life*, p. 86.
35. Quoted in Paul Griffiths, 'Meanings of Nightwalking in Early Modern England', *Seventeenth Century* 13: 2 (Autumn 1998), p. 224.
36. Francis Stoughton Sullivan, *Lectures on the Constitution and Laws of England* (London: J. Johnson, 1776), p. 370.
37. R. W. Chambers and Marjorie Daunt, *A Book of London English 1384–1425* (Oxford: Clarendon Press, 1931), p. 122.
38. See R. H. Tawney, 'Introduction', in Thomas Wilson, *A Discourse upon Usury* (London: G. Bell, 1925), p. 23.
39. Marjorie Keniston McIntosh, *Controlling Misbehavior in England, 1370–1600* (Cambridge: Cambridge University Press, 1998), p. 65.
40. Richard Kilburne, *Choice Presidents upon all Acts of Parliament, Relating to the Office and Duty of a Justice of Peace* (London: Richard and Edward Atkins, 1681), p. 61.
41. Edward Ravenscroft, *The London Cuckolds: A Comedy* (London: Joseph Hindmarsh, 1683), p. 22.
42. William Hawkins, *A Treatise of the Pleas of the Crown*, 5th edn (London: n.p., 1771), vol. 1, p. 132.
43. Cited in McIntosh, *Controlling Misbehavior*, p. 67.
44. See Earl D. Lyon, 'Roger de Ware, Cook', *Modern Language Notes* 52: 7 (1937), p. 492.
45. Geoffrey Chaucer, 'The Cook's Tale', l. 4,414, in *The Riverside Chaucer*, p. 86.
46. Francis Manning, *The Generous Choice: A Comedy* (London: R. Wellington, 1700), n.p.

47. Carpenter, *Liber Albus*, p. 240.
48. Hawkins, *Treatise of the Pleas of the Crown*, vol. 2, p. 77.
49. Thomas Dekker, *The Gull's Horn-Book: or, Fashions to Please All Sort of Gulls*, in E. D. Pendry, ed., *Thomas Dekker* (Stratford-Upon-Avon Library) (Cambridge, MA: Harvard University Press, 1968), p. 107.
50. John Popham, *Reports and Cases Collected by the Learned, Sir John Popham, Knight* (London: Richard and Edward Atkins, 1682), p. 208.
51. A. H. Thomas, ed., *Calendar of Plea and Memoranda Rolls, 1323–1364* (Cambridge: Cambridge University Press, 1926), pp. 125–6, 113.
52. Christopher Hill, 'William Perkins and the Poor', in *Puritanism and Revolution: Studies in Interpretation of the English Revolution of the Seventeenth Century* (London: Secker & Warburg, 1958), p. 218.
53. Raymond Williams, *The Country and the City* (London: Chatto & Windus, 1973), p. 83.
54. Edmonde Dudley, *The Tree of Common Wealth: A Treatise* (Manchester: Charles Simms, 1859), p. 15.
55. R. H. Tawney, *The Agrarian Problem in the Sixteenth Century* (New York: Longmans, Green & Co., 1912), p. 268.
56. Quoted in Christopher Hill, *The World Turned Upside Down: Radical Ideas During the English Revolution* (London: Penguin, 1975), p. 39. Hill notes that '[t]he object of the Geneva comment is to turn the accusation of sedition, of subverting the state of the world, away from religious radicals and to apply it to lower-class itinerants'.
57. John Howes, *John Howes' MS., 1582*, ed. William Lempriere (London: n.p., 1904), p. 14.
58. Thomas Dekker, *The Honest Whore, Part 2*, in *The Dramatic Works of Thomas Dekker*, vol. 2, ed. Fredson Bowers (Cambridge: Cambridge University Press, 1955), p. 204.
59. Quoted in William C. Carroll, *Fat King, Lean Beggar: Representations of Poverty in the Age of Shakespeare* (Ithaca, NY: Cornell University Press, 1996), p. 60.
60. Peter Wilson Coldham, ed., *The Complete Book of Emigrants, 1607–1660* (Baltimore, MD: Genealogical Publishing Company, 1987), p. 198.
61. Again, see Carroll, *Fat King, Lean Beggar*, p. 60.
62. Griffiths, 'Meanings of Nightwalking', pp. 212, 213, 218.
63. Ibid., p. 229.
64. See Koslofsky, *Evening's Empire*, p. 6.
65. Griffiths, 'Meanings of Nightwalking', p. 220.
66. Virginia Woolf, *A Room of One's Own* (London: Penguin, 1945), p. 49.
67. Cited in Paul Griffiths, *Youth and Authority: Formative Experiences in England 1560–1640* (Oxford: Clarendon Press, 1996), p. 204.

68. Geoffrey Chaucer, *The Legend of Good Women*, l. 95, in *The Riverside Chaucer*, p. 591.
69. Geoffrey Chaucer, 'The Wife of Bath's Prologue,' ll. 397–8, in *The Riverside Chaucer*, p. 110.
70. Amanda Flather, *Gender and Space in Early Modern England* (Woodbridge: Boydell, 2007), p. 132.
71. Thomas Dekker, *[English Villanies Discovered by] Lanthorne and Candle-light. Or, The Bell-man's Second Nights walke*, in E. D. Pendry, ed., *Thomas Dekker* (The Stratford-Upon-Avon Library) (Cambridge, MA: Harvard University Press, 1968), pp. 245–6.
72. Barnabe [*sic*] Rich, *My Ladies Looking Glasse: Wherein May Be Discerned a Wise Man from a Foole, A Good Woman from a Bad* (London: Thomas Adams, 1616), p. 44.
73. See Daniel Greenberg, ed., *Jowitt's Dictionary of English Law*, 3rd edn (London: Thomas Reuters, 2010), p. 1,539.
74. See Thomas Dekker, 'On Sleep', in Joyce Carol Oates, ed., *Night Walks: A Bedside Companion* (Princeton: Ontario Review Press, 1982), p. 138.
75. See Douglas Knoop and G. P. Jones, *The Mediaeval Mason: An Economic History of English Stone Building in the Later Middle Ages and Early Modern Times* (Manchester: Manchester University Press, 1933), p. 270.
76. Richard Braithwait, *A Comment upon the Two Tales of Our Ancient, Renowned, and Ever-Living Poet Sr Jeffray Chaucer, Knight* (London: W. Godbid, 1665), p. 44.
77. Michael Dalton, *The Country Justice: Containing the Practice of the Justices of the Peace Out of Their Sessions* (London: William Rawlins and Samuel Roycroft, 1705), p. 140. A 'whistler' was a nocturnal bird whose whistling note was believed to be of ill omen.
78. Cited in Griffiths, 'Meanings of Nightwalking', p. 213.
79. *Miles* v. *Weston*, 60 Ill. 361 (1871).
80. 'The prolongation of the working day beyond the limits of the natural day, into the night', Marx fulminated, 'only slightly quenches the [capitalist's] vampire thirst for the living blood of labour. Capitalist production therefore drives, by its inherent nature, towards the appropriation of labour throughout the whole of the 24 hours in the day.' See *Capital: A Critique of Political Economy, Volume One*, trans. Ben Fowkes (London: Penguin/New Left Review), p. 367.
81. Jonathan Crary, *24/7: Late Capitalism and the Ends of Sleep* (London: Verso, 2013), p. 66.
82. Maurice Blanchot, *The Space of Literature*, trans. Ann Smock (Lincoln, NE: University of Nebraska Press, 1982), p. 265.

83. John Bunyan, *The Pilgrim's Progress*, ed. Roger Pooley (London: Penguin, 2008), pp. 44–9.

Chapter 2: Idle Wandering Persons

1. Quoted in A. Roger Ekirch, *At Day's Close: A History of Nighttime* (London: Weidenfeld & Nicolson, 2005), p. 14.
2. William Baldwin, *Beware the Cat* (London: Halliwell, 1864), p. 58.
3. Jessie Childs, *Henry VIII's Last Victim: The Life and Times of Henry Howard, Earl of Surrey* (London: Jonathan Cape, 2006), p. 189.
4. Ibid., p. 190.
5. John Stow, *A Survey of London*, ed. Antonia Fraser (Stroud: Sutton Publishing, 2005), p. 256.
6. See Edwin Casey, *Henry Howard, Earl of Surrey* (New York: Modern Language Association of America, 1938), p. 98.
7. Ibid., p. 98.
8. Henry Howard, Earl of Surrey, 'A Satire on London', in Lawrence Manley, ed., *London in the Age of Shakespeare: An Anthology* (London: Croom Helm, 1986), p. 159. See Andrew W. Taylor, 'Glass Houses: Surrey, Petrarch, and the Religious Poetics of the "London" Invective', *Review of English Studies* 57: 231 (2006), esp. p. 437.
9. W. A. Sessions, *Henry Howard, The Poet Earl of Surrey: A Life* (Oxford: Oxford University Press, 1999), p. 239.
10. James Shirley, *The Gamester* (London: John Norton, 1637), p. 12.
11. Quoted in Christopher Hill, *Liberty Against the Law: Some Seventeenth-Century Controversies* (London: Penguin, 1996), p. 49.
12. [Anonymous,] *The Night-Walkers; or, The Loyal Huzza … To the Tune of, On the Bank of a River, &c.* (London: P. Brooksby, 1682), p. [1].
13. An abbreviation of Hector, the name of the Trojan warrior, the term 'heck' was at this time slang for a braggart, swaggerer or swashbuckler, as the verb 'to hector' suggests.
14. John Milton, *Paradise Lost*, I. 500–2, ed. Alastair Fowler (London: Longman, 1971), p. 73.
15. Peter Linebaugh, *The London Hanged: Crime and Civil Society in the Eighteenth Century*, 2nd edn (London: Verso, 2006), p. 48. Linebaugh points out that Milton portrays Belial as more sophisticated, more intellectual, than his proverbial reputation indicates: 'he stresses persuasive qualities of good breeding, study, and "reason".' Belial, in Milton, is thus a satanic incarnation of the 'Renaissance man'.
16. John Milton, 'Il Penseroso', ll. 65–74, 141, 160, in *Complete Shorter*

Poems, ed. John Carey (London: Longman, 1971), pp. 142–3, 145–6. 'Il Penseroso', one critic has remarked, 'establishes a holy noctivagant aesthetic at the heart of its poetic ideal'. See Chris Fitter, 'The Poetic Nocturne: From Ancient Motif to Renaissance Genre', *Early Modern Literary Studies* 3: 2 (September 1997), p. 21.

17. John Milton, *A Masque Presented at Ludlow Castle, 1634 [Comus]*, ll. 380–4, in Carey, ed., *Complete Shorter Poems*, p. 195.
18. Craig Koslofsky, *Evening's Empire: A History of the Night in Early Modern Europe* (Cambridge: Cambridge University Press, 2011), p. 92.
19. E. P. Thompson, *The Making of the English Working Class* (London: Penguin, 1968), p. 66.
20. A. L. Beier, *Masterless Men: The Vagrancy Problem in England, 1560–1640* (London: Methuen, 1985), p. 43.
21. Peter Ackroyd, *London: The Biography* (London: Chatto & Windus, 2000), p. 106.
22. Anthony Nixon, 'Advice to Apprentices', in Manley, *London in the Age of Shakespeare*, p. 202.
23. Richard Head and Francis Kirkman, *The English Rogue: Described, in the Life of Meriton Latroon, A Witty Extravagant* (London: Henry Marsh, 1665), pp. 26, 27.
24. Gordon Williams, *A Dictionary of Sexual Language and Imagery in Shakespearean and Stuart Literature*, vol. 3 (London: Athlone Press, 1994), p. 1,497.
25. Old Bailey Proceedings Online (oldbaileyonline.org, version 7.0, 8 April 2014), May 1722, trial of Charles Johns James Bradshaw (t17220510-38).
26. These examples are all taken from Williams, *A Dictionary of Sexual Language and Imagery*, vol. 3, p. 1,497.
27. Anonymous, *The Wandring Whore Continued* (London: John Garfield, 1660), pp. 4, 6, 11.
28. John L. McMullan, *The Canting Crew: London's Criminal Underworld 1550–1700* (New Brunswick: Rutgers University Press, 1984), p. 123.
29. Humphrey Mill, *A Night's Search: Discovering the Nature and Condition of all sorts of Night-walkers; with their Associates* (London, 1640), p. 14.
30. Ibid., pp. 239–40, 285.
31. Humphrey Mill, *The Second Part of the Nights Search: Discovering the Condition of the Various Fowles of Night; or, The Second Great Mystery of Iniquity Exactly Revealed* (London, 1646), p. 123.
32. Ibid., pp. 276, 123, 125, 126.
33. See Paul Slack, *Poverty and Policy in Tudor and Stuart England* (London: Longman, 1988), p. 25.
34. Ibid.

35. See Robert O. Bucholz and Joseph P. Ward, *London: A Social and Cultural History, 1550–1750* (Cambridge: Cambridge University Press, 2012), p. 224.
36. Quoted in Stephen Porter, *Shakespeare's London: Everyday Life in London 1580–1616* (Stroud: Amberley, 2009), p. 51.
37. On these lighting regulations, see Malcolm Falkus, 'Lighting in the Dark Ages of English Economic History: Town Streets before the Industrial Revolution', in D. C. Coleman and A. H. John, eds, *Trade, Government and Economy in Pre-Industrial England: Essays Presented to F. J. Fisher* (London: Weidenfeld & Nicolson, 1976), pp. 252–4.
38. Walter Scott, *The Fortunes of Nigel*, vol. 2 (Edinburgh: Archibald Constable, 1822), pp. 105, 110.
39. Cited in Porter, *Shakespeare's London*, pp. 50–1.
40. Quoted in Bucholz and Ward, *London*, p. 246.
41. Robert Copland, 'The Highway to the Spital-House', in A. V. Judges, ed., *The Elizabethan Underworld* (London: Routledge, 1930), p. 4.
42. Ibid., pp. 4–5.
43. Quoted in Beier, *Masterless Men*, p. 46.
44. Jacques Le Goff, *History and Memory*, trans. Steven Rendall and Elizabeth Claman (New York: Columbia University Press, 1992), p. 182.
45. See Beier, *Masterless Men*, p. 9.
46. Quoted in Arthur F. Kinney, ed., *Rogues, Vagabonds and Sturdy Beggars: A New Gallery of Tudor and Early Stuart Rogue Literature* (Amherst, MA: University of Massachusetts Press, 1973), p. 13.
47. Ibid., p. 13.
48. Manley, *London in the Age of Shakespeare*, p. 35.
49. Bucholz and Ward, *London*, p. 223.
50. Shakespeare, *Complete Works*, I. iii. 99–101.
51. See McMullan, *The Canting Crew*, p. 30. This appears to be roughly the number of apprentices in London at this time, which does not seem entirely plausible.
52. Christopher Hill, *The World Turned Upside Down: Radical Ideas During the English Revolution* (London: Penguin, 1975), p. 40.
53. Shakespeare, *Complete Works*, I. iii. 95.
54. Richard Younge, *The Poores Advocate: The Second Part* (London: Thomas Gataker, 1654), pp. 9–11.
55. George Herbert, *Jaculum Prudentium*, in *The Poetical Works of George Herbert* (Edinburgh: James Nichol, 1853), p. 319.
56. Jean Verdon, *Night and the Middle Ages*, trans. George Holoch (Notre Dame, IN: University of Notre Dame Press, 2002), p. 99.
57. Bucholz and Ward, *London*, p. 253.

58. See Thomas Dekker, *English Villanies Discovered by Lanthorne and Candle-light; or, The Bell-man's Second Nights walke*, in *Thomas Dekker* (The Stratford-Upon-Avon Library), ed. E. D. Pendry (Cambridge, MA: Harvard University Press, 1968), p. 173.
59. Manley, *London in the Age of Shakespeare*, p. 143.
60. Ekirch, *At Day's Close*, pp. 78–9.
61. Quoted in John Simpson, ed., *The First English Dictionary of Slang* (Oxford: Bodleian Library, 2010), p. xxiii.
62. Shakespeare, *Complete Works*, III. ii. 24–6.
63. Robert B. Shoemaker, *Petty Crime and the Law in London and Rural Middlesex, c. 1660–1725* (Cambridge: Cambridge University Press, 1991), p. 101.
64. It should not be forgotten, however, that, though Dogberry is the proverbial name of comically incompetent policemen, he and Verges nonetheless arrest Don John's villainous associates in *Much Ado About Nothing*.
65. Paul Griffiths, *Lost Londons: Change, Crime, and Control in the Capital City, 1550–1660* (Cambridge: Cambridge University Press, 2008), pp. 355, 359.
66. Ekirch, *At Day's Close*, p. 81.
67. Shakespeare, *Complete Works*, III. ii. 53–5.
68. Thomas Nabbes, *Microcosmus: A Morall Maske* (London: Richard Oulton, 1637), n.p.
69. See Jennine Hurl-Eamon, 'The Westminster Impostors: Impersonating Law Enforcement in Early Eighteenth-Century London', *Eighteenth-Century Studies* 38: 3 (2005), p. 464.
70. Samuel Rowl[e]y, *When You See Me, You Know Me; or the Famous Chronicle Historie of King Henry the Eight* (London: Nathaniell Butter, 1605), n.p.
71. James Howell, *Londinopolis: An Historicall Discourse or Perlustration of the City of London* (London: J. Streater, 1657), p. 77.
72. Marjorie Keniston McIntosh, *Controlling Misbehavior in England, 1370–1600* (Cambridge: Cambridge University Press, 1998), p. 66. Alison Shell confirms that, after the Middle Ages, 'bellmen regularly acted as a point of imaginative intersection between Christian moralism and sin'. See Alison Shell, *Shakespeare and Religion* (London: Methuen, 2010), p. 139.
73. Richard Huloet, *Huloet's Dictionarie Newly Corrected, Amended, Set in Order and Enlarged*, 2nd edn, ed. John Higgins (Londini: In ædibus I. Marshii, 1572), n.p.; Charles Hoole, *An Easie Entrance to the Latine Tongue* (London: William Du-gard, 1649), p. 228.

74. John Wilkes, John Jones and G. Jones, eds, *Encyclopaedia Londinensis; or, Universal Dictionary of Arts, Sciences, and Literature* (London: Encyclopaedia Office, 1820), p. 86.

Chapter 3: Affairs that Walk at Midnight

1. George Chapman, *The Shadow of Night*, in *The Poems of George Chapman*, in Arthur Acheson, *Shakespeare and the Rival Poet* (London: Bodley Head, 1903), p. 236.
2. Roland Barthes, *A Lover's Discourse: Fragments*, trans. Richard Howard (London: Penguin, 1990), p. 171.
3. Shakespeare, *Complete Works*, I. i. 172.
4. Ibid., V. vi. 17.
5. Quoted in Craig Koslofsky, *Evening's Empire: A History of the Night in Early Modern Europe* (Cambridge: Cambridge University Press, 2011), p. 41.
6. Shakespeare, *Complete Works*, V. v. 140.
7. Ibid., I. ii. 12–14.
8. Ibid., I. ii. 25–8.
9. Ibid., I. ii. 24.
10. Ibid., III. iii. 20, 44–5.
11. Ibid., V. v. 63.
12. Ibid., IV. Prologue.
13. Ibid., IV. i. 47.
14. William Shakespeare [*sic*], *The First Part of the True & Honorable Historie, of the Life of Sir John Old-castle, the Good Lord Cobham* (London: T. P., 1600), n.p.
15. Samuel Rowl[e]y, *When You See Me, You Know Me; or, the Famous Chronicle Historie of King Henry the Eight* (London: Nathaniell Butter, 1605), n.p.
16. Shakespeare, *Complete Works*, I. i. 72.
17. Ibid., V. iii. 181, 183.
18. See A. Roger Ekirch, *At Day's Close: A History of Nighttime* (London: Weidenfeld & Nicolson, 2005), pp. 300–4.
19. Shakespeare, *Complete Works*, IV. iii. 275.
20. Ibid., I. iii. 15–18.
21. Ibid., I. iii. 22–5.
22. Ibid., I. iii. 39–40.
23. Ibid., I. iii. 46–7.
24. Ibid., I. iii. 126–7.

25. Shakespeare had taken the idea of the assassin's insomnia from Thomas North's translation of Plutarch.
26. Shakespeare, *Complete Works*, II. i. 14–15.
27. Ibid., II. i. 63–5.
28. Ibid., II. i. 261–3.
29. Ibid., II. i. 268.
30. Ben Jonson, *Catiline, His Conspiracy: A Tragedy*, I. i. 12, 50, 62–3, 191, 193, in G. A. Wilkes, ed., *The Complete Plays of Ben Jonson*, vol. 3 (Oxford: Clarendon, 1982), pp. 363–5, 369.
31. See Georges Bataille, 'Rotten Sun', in Allan Stoekl, ed., *Visions of Excess: Selected Writings* (Minneapolis: University of Minnesota Press, 1985), pp. 57–8.
32. Jonson, *Catiline, His Conspiracy*, I. i. 194–7, in Wilkes, *Complete Plays of Ben Jonson*, p. 369.
33. Shakespeare, *Complete Works*, V. i. 2–4, V. i. 13–16..
34. Elizabeth Bronfen understates the matter when she observes that Shakespeare displays the night 'as the domain for encounters and insights that fall outside the business of the everyday'. See Elizabeth Bronfen, 'Shakespeare's Nocturnal World', in John Drakakis, ed., *Gothic Shakespeares* (London: Routledge, 2008), p. 21.
35. Shakespeare, *Complete Works*, I. iv. 16, 18.
36. Koslofsky, *Evening's Empire*, pp. 26, 27.
37. Thomas Nashe, *The Terrors of the Night; or, A Discourse of Apparitions*, in Ronald B. McKerrow, ed., *The Works of Thomas Nashe*, vol. 1 (London: A. H. Bullen, 1914), pp. 345, 349.
38. Stephen Greenblatt, *Hamlet in Purgatory* (Princeton: Princeton University Press, 2001), p. 45.
39. Shakespeare, *Complete Works*, I. i. 65–6.
40. Ibid., I. i. 69, 114–16.
41. Ibid., I. v. 9–10.
42. Ibid., I. v. 14.
43. Ibid., II. i. 49–51.
44. A. C. Bradley, *Shakespearean Tragedy: Lectures on Hamlet, Othello, King Lear, Macbeth* (London: Macmillan, 1985), p. 279.
45. Shakespeare, *Complete Works*, IV. i. 48.
46. Shakespeare, *Complete Works*, I. iii. 124. See Ann Pasternak Slater, 'Macbeth and the Terrors of the Night', *Essays in Criticism* 28: 2 (1978), pp. 112–28.
47. Shakespeare, *Complete Works*, III. i. 26.
48. Ibid., III. iii. 6. See John Milton, *Animadversions upon the Remonstrant's Defence Against Smectymnuus* (1641), in *The Prose Works of John*

Milton, ed. Charles Symmons (London: T. Bentley, 1806), p. 158.

49. Shakespeare, *Complete Works*, III. iii. 19.
50. Ibid., III. vi. 5.
51. Shakespeare, *Complete Works*, III. vi. 7. In a recent edition of *Macbeth*, A. R. Braunmuller notes that this line was excised in the Quarto edition of 1673, possibly because of the obscene associations of nightwalking. It 'may have become unacceptably comic by 1673', he comments, 'or the omission may arise from a desire to avoid even a hint of wrong-doing among the legendary ancestors (Banquo, Fleance) of James's grandson, Charles II.' I suspect that, if this is indeed the case, it is its gendered association with female prostitutes that rendered nightwalking potentially comic or inappropriate by the later seventeenth century. Note, though, that Braunmuller inaccurately claims that nightwalking 'had been a misdemeanour since 1331'. See William Shakespeare, *Macbeth*, ed. A. R. Braunmuller (Cambridge: Cambridge University Press, 1997), p. 243.
52. Thomas Kyd, *The Spanish Tragedy*, III. iii. 39–42, ed. J. R. Mulryne (London: A. & C. Black, 1989), p. 59.
53. Christopher Marlowe, *The Jew of Malta*, II. iii. 179–80, in J. B. Steane, ed., *The Complete Plays* (London: Penguin, 1986), p. 378.
54. Shakespeare, *Complete Works*, III. i. 110.
55. Ibid., I. v. 68.
56. Ibid., I. v. 47–51.
57. Ibid., III. ii. 46–7.
58. Ibid., I. v. 60–1.
59. Ibid., II. iv. 6–10.
60. Ibid., I. iv. 50–1.
61. Ibid., II. ii. 34, 38.
62. Ibid., II. i. 8–10.
63. Ibid., V. 1. 9–11.
64. Thomas Browne, *Religio Medici*, in John Addington Symonds, ed., *Sir Thomas Browne's Religio Medici, Urn Burial, Christian Morals, and Other Essays* (London: Walter Scott, 1886), p. 106.
65. Shakespeare, *Complete Works*, V. v. 24.
66. Ibid., III. iv. 125.
67. Ekirch, *At Day's Close*, p. 14.
68. Shakespeare, *Complete Works*, III. iv. 126.
69. Gérard Genette, discussing definitions of night and day, writes that the distinction between these categories operates at the level of language rather than reality, on the plane of the sign rather than the referent: 'cette opposition si forte n'est pas donnée dans les "choses", elle n'est pas entre les *référents*, car après tout aucun objet du monde ne peut être

réellement considéré comme la contraire d'un autre, elle est seulement entre les *signifiés*' ('This strong distinction isn't given in the "things", it isn't between the *referents*, for after all no object in the world can really be considered as the opposite of another, it is only between the *signifieds*'). See 'La Jour, la nuit', *Cahiers de l'Association internationale des études francaises* 20 (1968), p. 150.

70. Shakespeare, *Complete Works*, III. iii. 5.
71. Ibid., II. ii. 38.
72. John Webster, *The Duchess of Malfi*, II. iii. 23–5, ed. Elizabeth M. Brennan (London: A. & C. Black, 1993), p. 43.
73. Ibid., V. ii. 9–15, p. 108; and I. i. 29, p. 12.
74. Shakespeare, *Complete Works*, III. ii. 53.
75. G. B. Shand, 'Introduction', in Thomas Middleton, *The Black Book*, ed. G. B. Shand, in *The Collected Works* (Oxford: Clarendon Press, 2007), p. 204.
76. Middleton, *Black Book*, p. 208.
77. Ibid., p. 212.
78. Ibid., pp. 214, 218.
79. B. E., *A New Dictionary of the Terms Ancient and Modern of the Canting Crew, In its Several Tribes, of Gypsies, Beggers, Thieves, Cheats, &c.* (1699), reprinted as John Simpson, ed., *The First English Dictionary of Slang* (Oxford: Bodleian Library, 2010), p. 122.
80. Stanley Wells, *Shakespeare & Co.: Christopher Marlowe, Thomas Dekker, Ben Jonson, Thomas Middleton, John Fletcher, and Other Players in his Story* (London: Penguin, 2006), p. 107.
81. Thomas Dekker, *English Villanies Discovered by Lanthorne and Candle-light; or, The Bell-man's Second Nights walke*, in *Thomas Dekker* (Stratford-Upon-Avon Library), ed. E. D. Pendry (Cambridge, MA: Harvard University Press, 1968), pp. 177, 193, 228, 182.
82. William Chapman Sharpe, *New York Nocturne: The City after Dark in Literature, Painting, and Photography* (Princeton: Princeton University Press, 2008), p. 66.
83. Dekker, *Lanthorne and Candle-light*, pp. 223, 228, 250.
84. Ibid., pp. 249–50, 252.
85. Thomas Dekker, *O Per Se O; or, A New Cryer of Lanthorne and Candle-light, Being an Addition, or Lengthening, of the Bell-mans Second Night-Walke* (London: M. Parsons, 1638), n.p.
86. Thomas Dekker, *The Seven Deadly Sinnes of London: Drawn in Seven Severall Coaches Through the Seven Severall Gates of the Cittie, Bringing the Plague with Them* (London: E. A., 1606), p. 32.
87. Ibid., pp. 32–3.

88. Nahum Tate, *Brutus of Alba; or, The Enchanted Lovers: A Tragedy* (London: E. F., 1678), p. 24.
89. Dekker, *Seven Deadly Sinnes of London*, pp. 33, 37.
90. Karl Marx, *Capital: A Critique of Political Economy, Volume One*, trans. Ben Fowkes (London: Penguin/*New Left Review*, 1976), p. 230.
91. Dekker, *Seven Deadly Sinnes of London*, p. 33.
92. Thomas Dekker, *The Gull's Horn-Book; or, Fashions to Please All Sorts of Gulls* [1609], in *Thomas Dekker* (Stratford-Upon-Avon Library), ed. E. D. Pendry (Cambridge, MA: Harvard University Press, 1968), pp. 107–8.
93. Thomas Dekker, *Blurt, Master-Constable; or, The Spaniards Night-walke* (London: Henry Rockytt, 1602), n.p.
94. Thomas Dekker, *The Wonderful Year*, in Thomas Dekker, *The Wonderful Year and Other Writings*, ed. E. D. Pendry (Cambridge, MA: Harvard University Press, 1968), p. 42.
95. Ibid., pp. 43, 58.
96. Wells, *Shakespeare & Co.*, pp. 205–6.
97. Cyrus Hoy, 'Fletcherian Romantic Comedy', *Research Opportunities in Renaissance Drama* 27 (1984), p. 6.
98. John Fletcher (revised by James Shirley), *The Night-Walker; or, The Little Theife: A Comedy* (London: Andrew & William Cooke, 1640), n.p.
99. Andrew Gurr, *The Shakespearean Stage 1579–1642*, 3rd edn (Cambridge: Cambridge University Press, 1992), p. 186.
100. See Chris Fitter, 'The Poetic Nocturne: From Ancient Motif to Renaissance Genre', *Early Modern Literary Studies* 3: 2 (September 1997), p. 15.
101. Hoy, 'Fletcherian Romantic Comedy', p. 6.
102. These associations of nightwalking in the city with folkloric mischief are underlined in *Roome, for a Messe of Knaves* (1610), an anonymous imitation of Samuel Rowlands's *A Mery Meetinge* (1600), which includes a definition of a 'Diamond Knave': 'This fellow (for he hath many fellowes in these daies) predominats [*sic*] from midnight to morning, a night walker he is, and (as he saith) is neare of kin to *Oberon* the king of Fayries, and it should seems so, for all his exercise is the workes of darknesse.' *Roome, for a Messe of Knaves; or, a Selection, or a Detection, or, a Demonstration, or a Manifestation, of Foure Slaves* (London: N.F., 1610), n.p.
103. Shakespeare, *Complete Works*, III. iv. 113.
104. See Linda Woodbridge, *Vagrancy, Homelessness, and English Renaissance Literature* (Urbana, IL: University of Illinois Press, 2001), pp. 205–37.

105. Shakespeare, *Complete Works*, III. iv. 75, 262.
106. Ibid., III. iv. 28, 30.

Chapter 4: Darkness Visible

1. Jenny Uglow, *Hogarth: A Life and a World* (London: Faber & Faber, 1997), p. 309.
2. Jerry White, *London in the Eighteenth Century: A Great and Monstrous Thing* (London: Bodley Head, 2012), p. 329.
3. Henry Fielding, *An Enquiry into the Causes of the late Increase of Robbers, &c., With Some Proposals for Remedying this Growing Evil*, 2nd edn (London: A. Millar, 1751), pp. 27–8.
4. See John Gay, *Trivia*, III. 341–4, 375–6, in *Selected Poems*, ed. Marcus Walsh (Manchester: Fyfield Books, 2003), pp. 41–63. Hereafter citations from this poem are given in the form of the relevant line numbers.
5. John Keats, 'The Eve of St Agnes', l. 375, in *The Complete Poems*, 3rd edn, ed. John Barnard (London: Penguin, 1988), p. 324.
6. Gilles Deleuze and Félix Guattari, *Anti-Oedipus: Capitalism and Schizophrenia*, trans. Robert Hurley, Mark Seem and Helen R. Lane (London: Athlone, 1984), p. 112.
7. Anonymous, *Nocturnal Revels; or, A General History of Dreams* (London: Andrew Bell, 1707), p. 2.
8. See J. E. [John Evelyn], *Fumifugium; or, The Inconveniencie of the Aer and Smoak of London Dissipated* (London: W. Godbid, 1661), pp. [viii,] 14.
9. I have taken this phrase from the fictional philosopher de Selby's description of darkness in Flann O'Brien's comic masterpiece *The Third Policeman*, written in 1939 and 1940.
10. Michel Foucault, *The Order of Things: An Archaeology of the Human Sciences*, trans. anonymous (London: Routledge, 1989), p. 326.
11. See ibid., p. 326; and Michel Foucault, *Madness and Civilization: A History of Insanity in the Age of Reason*, trans. Richard Howard (London: Routledge, 1989), p. 103.
12. Richard Steele, 'Later Hours Kept Nowadays', from *The Tatler* 263 (14 December 1710), in *The Tatler*, ed. Lewis Gibbs (London: J. M. Dent, 1953), pp. 284–5.
13. J. M. Beattie, *Policing and Punishment in London, 1660–1750: Urban Crime and the Limits of Terror* (Oxford: Oxford University Press, 2001), p. 172.
14. Wolfgang Schivelbusch, *Disenchanted Night: The Industrialization*

of Light in the Nineteenth Century, trans. Angela Davies (Berkeley: University of California Press, 1995), p. 140.

15. Oliver Goldsmith, *The Citizen of the World; or, Letters from a Chinese Philosopher, Residing in London, to His Friends in the East* (London: R. Whiston et al., 1782), vol. 2, pp. 36–7.
16. See White, *London in the Eighteenth Century*, p. 322. Evoking the hundreds and even thousands of lights that illuminated the trees and colonnades of Vauxhall Gardens, Amanda Vickery has pointed out that 'we are so accustomed to electricity that it is difficult to imagine the thrill of these oil lamps in an era when most relied on the fire in the grate and a smelly tallow candle to hold back the night'. See Amanda Vickery, 'Venice-on-Thames', *London Review of Books* 35: 3 (7 February 2013), p. 31.
17. Robert B. Shoemaker, *The London Mob: Violence and Disorder in Eighteenth-Century England* (London: Hambledon & London, 2004), p. 10.
18. Ellen Wood, *The Pristine Culture of Capitalism: An Historical Essay on Old Regimes and Modern States* (London: Verso, 1991), p. 107.
19. Quoted in Roy Porter, *London: A Social History* (London: Penguin, 2000), p. 175.
20. Daniel Defoe, *The Complete English Tradesman* (Gloucester: Alan Sutton, 1987), p. 180.
21. Quoted in Porter, *London*, p. 174.
22. A. Roger Ekirch, *At Day's Close: A History of Nighttime* (London: Weidenfeld & Nicolson, 2005), p. 325.
23. John Milton, *Paradise Lost*, XI. 113–15, ed. Alastair Fowler (London: Longman, 1971), p. 570.
24. Quoted in Craig Koslofsky, *Evening's Empire: A History of the Night in Early Modern Europe* (Cambridge: Cambridge University Press, 2011), p. 233.
25. Malcolm Falkus, 'Lighting in the Dark Ages of English Economic History: Town Streets before the Industrial Revolution', in D. C. Coleman and A. H. John, eds, *Trade, Government and Economy in Pre-Industrial England: Essays Presented to F. J. Fisher* (London: Weidenfeld & Nicolson, 1976), pp. 254–6.
26. Quoted in Schivelbusch, *Disenchanted Night*, p. 88.
27. Stephen Inwood, *A History of London*, rev. edn (London: Papermac, 2000), p. 365.
28. Sophie von La Roche, *Sophie in London, 1786: Being the Diary of Sophie v. la Roche*, trans., Clare Williams (London: Jonathan Cape, 1933), pp. 141–2.

29. Louis-Sébastien Mercier, *Panorama of Paris: Selections from Le Tableau de Paris*, trans. Helen Simpson and Jeremy D. Popkin (Pennsylvania: Pennsylvania State University Press, 1999), pp. 41, 43.
30. Christopher Hill, *The World Turned Upside Down: Radical Ideas During the English Revolution* (Harmondsworth: Penguin, 1975), p. 40.
31. Fielding, *An Enquiry into the Causes of the Late Increase of Robbers*, pp. 116–17, 130, 144.
32. Quoted in Porter, *London*, p. 120.
33. Koslofsky, *Evening's Empire*, pp. 130, 136.
34. Beattie, *Policing and Punishment in London*, p. 170.
35. Anonymous, *The Oath of a Constable, So Far as it relates to his Apprehending Night-Walkers, and Idle Persons* (London: J. Downing, 1701), pp. 1–2.
36. For these comments and quotations, see Beattie, *Policing and Punishment in London*, pp. 174, 181.
37. Ibid., p. 188.
38. Ibid., pp. 188–9, 196–7.
39. On the terroristic system of criminal law in England, see Douglas Hay, 'Property, Authority and the Criminal Law', in *Albion's Fatal Tree: Crime and Society in Eighteenth-Century England*, rev. edn (London: Verso, 2011), pp. 17–63.
40. See George Rudé, *Hanoverian London 1714–1808* (London: Secker & Warburg, 1971), p. 96.
41. William Hawkins, *A Treatise of the Pleas of the Crown*, 5th edn (London, 1771), pp. 101–2.
42. Beattie, *Policing and Punishment in London*, p. 172.
43. Jonas Hanway, *The Defects of Police: The Cause of Immorality, and the Continual Robberies Committed, Particularly in and about the Metropolis* (London: J. Dodsley, 1775), p. 241.
44. Tim Hitchcock, *Down and Out in Eighteenth-Century London* (London: Hambledon & London, 2004), pp. 39–40.
45. Gregory Durst, *Victims and Viragoes: Metropolitan Women, Crime and the Eighteenth-Century Justice System* (Bury St Edmunds: Arima, 2007), p. 211.
46. Edward Hatton, *A New View of London; or, An Ample Account of That City* (London: John Nicholson, 1708), vol. 2, p. 734.
47. Tony Henderson, *Disorderly Women in Eighteenth-Century London: Prostitution and Control in the Metropolis 1730–1830* (London: Longman, 1999), pp. 108, 61.
48. Anonymous, *The Night-walkers Declaration; or, the Distressed Whores Advice to All their Sisters in City and Country* (London: D. M., 1676),

pp. 5, 8. On 'the elusive prostitute voice', see Laura J. Rosenthal, 'Introduction', in Laura J. Rosenthal, ed., *Nightwalkers: Prostitute Narratives from the Eighteenth Century* (Ontario: Broadview, 2008), pp. x–xiii.

49. Anonymous, *The Lady's Ramble; or, The Female Night-walker* (London: n.p., c. 1720), pp. 2, 4.
50. For these and subsequent quotations from the relevant articles, see Samuel Johnson, *The Rambler*, ed. Donald D. Eddy (New York: Garland, 1978), vol. 2, pp. 1,020–24.
51. James Boswell, *London Journal 1762–1763*, ed. Gordon Turnbull (London: Penguin, 2010), p. 223.
52. 'For the London Magazine: Rules of Behaviour, of General Use, though Much Disregarded in this Populous City', *The London Magazine or Gentlemen's Monthly Intelligencer* 49 (1780), p. 197.
53. Penelope J. Corfield, 'Walking the City Streets: The Urban Odyssey in Eighteenth-Century England', *Journal of Urban History* 16: 2 (February 1990), p. 154.
54. Koslofsky, *Evening's Empire*, p. 156.
55. Quoted in Miles Ogborn, *Spaces of Modernity: London's Cartographies 1680–1780* (New York: Guilford Press, 1998), p. 112.
56. Gay, *Trivia*, I. 29, 80.
57. Margaret R. Hunt, 'The Walker Beset: Gender in the Early Eighteenth-Century City', in Clare Brant and Susan E. Whyman, eds, *Walking the Streets of Eighteenth-Century London* (Oxford: Oxford University Press, 2007), p. 120.
58. I use the phrase 'man in the street' advisedly – Hunt is right to point to a misogynistic attitude in the poem, especially in the representation of prostitutes, who 'ooze disquietingly from every darkened alley, like a kind of evil sweat' (see 'The Walker Beset', p. 121).
59. Gay, *Trivia*, I. 1–10.
60. Ibid., III. 263.
61. Ross Chambers, *Loiterature* (Lincoln: University of Nebraska Press, 1999), pp. 7–8.
62. Gay, *Trivia*, III. 7–8.
63. Ibid., III. 10–11.
64. Ibid., III. 27–30.
65. Ibid., III. 42–4.
66. Walter Benjamin, 'On Some Motifs in Baudelaire', trans. Harry Zohn, in *Selected Writings*, vol. 4 (1938–1940), ed. Howard Eiland and Michael W. Jennings (Cambridge, MA: Harvard University Press, 2003), p. 328.
67. Gay, *Trivia*, III. 111–14.

68. Ibid., III. 53, 322.
69. Ibid., III. 101–2.
70. Ibid., II. 129.
71. Ibid., III. 267, 307–8.
72. Philip Carter, 'Faces and Crowds: Biography in the City', in Brant and Whyman, *Walking the Streets of Eighteenth-Century London*, p. 27.
73. Gay, *Trivia*, III. 260, 262.
74. Ibid., III. 127–8.
75. Ibid., III. 143–4.
76. Cited in Benjamin, 'On Some Motifs in Baudelaire', p. 328.
77. Gay, *Trivia*, III. 335–8.
78. Ibid., III. 406.
79. Bryan D. Palmer, *Cultures of Darkness: Night Travels in the History of Transgression* (New York: Monthly Review Press, 2000), p. 13.
80. White, *London in the Eighteenth Century*, p. 390.
81. *Spectator* 324, 12 March 1712, p. 1.
82. *Spectator* 8, 9 March 1711, p. 1.
83. Quoted in Max Byrd, *London Transformed: Images of the City in the Eighteenth Century* (New Haven, CT: Yale University Press, 1978), p. 91.
84. Rudé, *Hanoverian London 1714–1808*, p. 83. Rudé summarizes this layer of the population with reference to all those whom Patrick Colquhoun, the pioneer of police reform and author of *A Treatise on the Police of the Metropolis* (1796), 'tended to identify with London's "underworld" or "criminal classes", which he reckoned at 115,000 persons, or one-eighth of the city's population in 1797'.
85. See Karl Marx, *The Eighteenth Brumaire of Louis Bonaparte*, in *Surveys from Exile: Political Writings Volume 2*, ed. David Fernbach (London: Penguin, 1992), p. 197; and *The Class Struggles in France: 1848 to 1850*, in ibid., p. 52.
86. See Samuel Johnson, *A Dictionary of the English Language* (London: J. & P. Knapton et al., 1755), vol. 2.
87. Peter Linebaugh, *The London Hanged: Crime and Civil Society in the Eighteenth Century*, 2nd edn (London: Verso, 2006), p. 121.
88. Falkus, 'Lighting in the Dark Ages of English Economic History', p. 250.
89. Hitchcock, *Down and Out in Eighteenth-Century London*, pp. 152, 153.
90. Foucault, *Madness and Civilization*, p. 109.

Chapter 5: The Nocturnal Picaresque

1. See Samuel Johnson, *A Dictionary of the English Language* (London: J. & P. Knapton et al., 1755), vol. 2. The term 'noctuary', as Johnson indicates, seems to have been coined in the *Spectator* in 1714, where a correspondent named 'John Shadow' relates one of a 'parcel of visions' he has had in his sleep. See *Spectator* 586 (27 August 1714) and 587 (30 August 1714).
2. Leo Hollis, *The Phoenix: The Men Who Made Modern London* (London: Phoenix, 2009), p. 295.
3. Paul Zweig, *The Adventurer* (London: J. M. Dent, 1974), pp. 103–4.
4. On the ramble or spy narrative, see Alison F. O'Byrne's excellent PhD thesis, 'Walking, Rambling, and Promenading in Eighteenth-Century London: A Literary and Cultural History' (University of York, 2003), pp. 47–56.
5. Anonymous, *The Ambulator; or, The Stranger's Companion in a Tour Round London* (London: J. Bew, 1774), p. v. Vic Gattrell estimates that 'from west to east you could walk across the metropolis in a couple of hours or so, and from south to north in one'. See Vic Gattrell, *City of Laughter: Sex and Satire in Eighteenth-Century London* (London: Atlantic, 2006), p. 24.
6. Quoted in J. Paul Hunter, *Before Novels: The Cultural Contexts of Eighteenth-Century English Fiction* (New York: Norton, 1990), p. 102.
7. See Helen Berry, 'John Dunton (1659–1732), bookseller', in the *Oxford Dictionary of National Biography* (oxforddnb.com).
8. John Dunton, *The Night-Walker; or, Evening Rambles in Search after Lewd Women, with the Conferences Held with Them, &c.*, in *Marriage, Sex, and the Family in England 1660–1800*, ed. Randolph Trumbach (New York: Garland, 1985), n.p.
9. Ibid., n.p.
10. Joachim Schlör, *Nights in the Big City: Paris, Berlin, London, 1840–1930* (London: Reaktion, 1998), p. 260.
11. These quotations are taken from Howard William Troyer, *Ned Ward of Grub Street: A Study of Sub-Literary London in the Eighteenth Century* (London: Routledge, 1968), pp. 83, 204.
12. Ned Ward, *The London Spy*, ed. Paul Hyland (East Lansing: Colleagues Press, 1993), pp. 9–10.
13. Ibid., pp. 9, 11, 27–8, 29.
14. Robert Shiels, *The Lives of the Poets of Great Britain and Ireland*, ed. Theophilus Cibber et al. (London: R. Griffiths, 1753), vol. 4, p. 293.
15. Ward, *London Spy*, p. 29.
16. Ibid., pp. 30, 31, 33, 34.

17. Ibid., p. 67.
18. William Smith, *State of the Gaols in London, Westminster, and Borough of Southwark* (London: J. Bew, 1776), p. 33.
19. Ward, *London Spy*, p. 68.
20. Ibid., p. 35.
21. Ibid., p. 36.
22. Walter L. Woodfill, *Musicians in English Society from Elizabeth to Charles I* (Princeton, NJ: Princeton University Press, 1953), p. 76.
23. See Tim Hitchcock, *Down and Out in Eighteenth-Century London* (London: Hambledon & London, 2004), p. 40.
24. Daniel Defoe, *The History and Remarkable Life of the Truly Honourable Colonel Jaque, Vulgarly Call'd, Colonel Jack*, 3rd edn (London: J. Brotherton, 1724), p. 7.
25. Daniel Defoe, *Everybody's Business is Nobody's Business*, in *The History and Remarkable Life of the Truly Honourable Colonel Jaque, Commonly Called Colonel Jack*, ed. George A. Aitken (London: J. M. Dent, 1895), vol. 2, pp. 179, 181.
26. Ward, *London Spy*, p. 37.
27. Ibid., pp. 37–9.
28. Tobias Smollett, *The Expedition of Humphry Clinker*, ed. Lewis M. Knapp (Oxford: Oxford University Press, 1998), p. 120.
29. I cannot resist citing Ackroyd's evocative allusion to the occult qualities of this street in *London* (p. 109): 'There was once a Dark Lane, in the medieval city; a tavern was erected there, known as the Darkhouse. That narrow thoroughfare was then renamed Dark House Lane, and is to be seen on eighteenth-century maps of London. On the same site there now stands Dark House Wharf, which is dominated by the headquarters of the Bank of Hong Kong [HSBC]. This building is clad in dark blue steel and dark, tinted glass. So does the city maintain its secret life.'
30. Alexander Pope, 'The Alley', in *Poetical Works*, ed. Herbert Davis (Oxford: Oxford University Press, 1978), p. 230.
31. Ward, *London Spy*, pp. 39–40.
32. Ibid., pp. 41, 42, 44.
33. Mikhail Bakhtin, *Rabelais and His World*, trans. Helene Iswolsky (Bloomington: Indiana University Press, 1984), pp. 15–17.
34. Schlör, *Nights in the Big City*, p. 170.
35. Anonymous, *The Midnight-Ramble; or, The Adventures of Two Noble Females: Being a True and Impartial Account of their Late Excursion through the Streets of London and Westminster* (London: B. Dickinson, 1754), pp. 3, 8, 10.
36. Ibid., pp. 10–11, 12.

37. Vic Gatrell, *The First Bohemians: Life and Art in London's Global Age* (London: Allen Lane, 2013), p. xxii.
38. Anonymous, *Midnight-Ramble*, p. 18.
39. Ibid., pp. 19, 20, 23.
40. Ibid., pp. 26, 8.
41. 'Monthly Catalogue', *The Monthly Review, or, Literary Journal* (April 1754), vol. 10, p. 309.
42. Paul Griffiths, 'Meanings of Nightwalking in Early Modern England', *Seventeenth Century* 13: 2 (Autumn 1998), p. 212.
43. Anonymous, *A Catalogue of Jilts, Cracks, Prostitutes, Night-walkers, Whores, She-friends, Kind Women, and others of the Linnen-lifting Tribe Who are to Be Seen Every Night in the Cloysters in Smithfield, from the Hours of Eight to Eleven, during the Time of the Fair* (London: R. W., 1691), p. 1.
44. Anonymous, *Low-Life; or, One Half of the World, Knows Not How the Other Half Live. Being a Critical Account of What is Transacted by People of Almost All Religions, Nations, Circumstances, and Sizes of Understanding, in the Twenty-Four Hours between Saturday-Night and Monday-Morning. In a True Description of a Sunday, As it is Usually Spent within the Bills of Mortality, Calculated for the Twenty-first of June. With an Address to the Ingenious and Ingenuous Mr Hogarth*, 2nd rev. edn (London: T. Legg, 1750), pp. iii, 2–3, 4, 5, 7.
45. Charles Dickens, 'Night Walks', in *On London* (London: Hesperus Press, 2010), p. 76.
46. Henri Lefebvre, *The Production of Space*, trans. Donald Nicholson-Smith (Oxford: Blackwell, 1991), p. 86.
47. Hitchcock, *Down and Out in Eighteenth-Century London*, pp. 25, 30.
48. Anonymous, *Low-Life*, pp. 18, 24, 28, 98, 99, 102.
49. Anonymous, *The Midnight Rambler; or, New Nocturnal Spy, for the Present Year* (London: J. Cooke, 1770), p. 6.
50. Alain-René Le Sage, *Le Diable Boiteux; or, The Devil upon Two Sticks*, 2nd edn (London: Jacob Tonson, 1708), pp. 15–16.
51. See Alain-René Lesage, *The Devil on Two Sticks*, trans. Joseph Thomas (1841), p. 20.
52. Le Sage, *Le Diable Boiteux*, p. 16.
53. William Chapman Sharpe, *New York Nocturne: The City after Dark in Literature, Painting, and Photography* (Princeton, NJ: Princeton University Press, 2008), p. 66. Sharpe is discussing the publication of several novels about Asmodeus in the United States in the 1840s.
54. Anonymous, *Midnight Rambler*, p. 7.
55. Ibid., pp. 24, 30, 32.

56. Tom McDonough, 'Introduction', in *The Situationists and the City*, ed. Tom McDonough (London: Verso, 2009), p. 10.
57. Anonymous, *Midnight Rambler*, pp. 40, 41.
58. Ibid., pp. 43–4, 68–9, 91.
59. Ibid., pp. 134–5, 77.
60. Anonymous, *The Midnight Spy; or, A View of the Transactions of London and Westminster, From the Hours of Ten in the Evening, till Five in the Morning; Exhibiting a Great Variety of Scenes in High and Low Life, With the Characters of Some Well Known Nocturnal Adventurers of Both Sexes* (London: J. Cooke, 1766), pp. 143–4.
61. Boethius, *Of the Consolation of Philosophy*, trans. Richard Graham (London: A. & J. Churchill, 1695), vol. 2, p. 68.

Chapter 6: Grub Street at Night

1. See Thomas Dyche and William Pardon, *A New General English Dictionary* (London: Richard Ware, 1735).
2. Alexander Pope, *The Dunciad*, in *Poetical Works*, ed. Herbert Davis (Oxford: Oxford University Press, 1978), p. 476.
3. Pat Rogers, *Grub Street: Studies in a Subculture* (London: Methuen, 1972), p. 351.
4. Samuel Johnson, 'London: A Poem in Imitation of the Third Satire of Juvenal', l. 179, in *Selected Writings*, ed. Patrick Cruttwell (London: Penguin, 1986), p. 46.
5. John Gay, *Trivia*, I. 65–9, 117–18, in *Selected Poems*, ed. Marcus Walsh (Manchester: Fyfield Books, 2003), pp. 43, 45.
6. Quoted in Vic Gatrell, *The First Bohemians: Life and Art in London's Global Age* (London: Allen Lane, 2013), p. 121.
7. Walter Benjamin, 'The Paris of the Second Empire in Baudelaire', in Michael W. Jennings, ed., *The Writer of Modern Life: Essays on Charles Baudelaire* (Cambridge, MA: Harvard University Press, 2006), p. 54.
8. Ian Watt, *The Rise of the Novel: Studies in Defoe, Richardson and Fielding* (London: Pimlico, 2000), p. 53. The quotation from Defoe is also taken from Watt.
9. Samuel Johnson, 'Petty Writers Not to be Despised', *The Rambler* 145 (6 August 1751), in *The Rambler* (London: J. Payne, 1753), vol. 2, p. 866.
10. Benjamin, 'Paris of the Second Empire', p. 142. Benjamin is talking about the bourgeoisie in the later nineteenth century rather than the aristocracy in the earlier eighteenth century.
11. Karl Marx, *Capital: A Critique of Political Economy, Volume One*, trans.

Ben Fowkes (London: Penguin/New Left Review, 1976), pp. 272, 274; and Karl Marx, *The Communist Manifesto*, in *Selected Writings*, ed. David McLellan (Oxford: Oxford University Press, 1977), pp. 223–4.

12. Quoted in James Sambrook, *James Thomson (1700–1748): A Life* (Oxford: Clarendon Press, 1991), p. 27.
13. Jenny Uglow, 'Fielding, Grub Street, and Canary Wharf', in Jeremy Treglown and Bridget Bennett, eds, *Grub Street and the Ivory Tower: Literary Journalism and Literary Scholarship from Fielding to the Internet* (Oxford: Oxford University Press, 1998), p. 1.
14. Rogers, *Grub Street*, p. 284.
15. James Sambrook, 'Churchill, Charles (1732–1764)', *Oxford Dictionary of National Biography*. Sambrook quotes the description of Churchill's clothing from A. Kippis and others, *Biographia Britannia* (1784).
16. John Armstrong, 'A Day: An Epistle to John Wilkes, of Aylesbury, Esq.', in *The Works of the English Poets. With Prefaces, Biographical and Critical, by Samuel Johnson*, vol. 71, 'Armstrong and Langhorne' (London: H. Baldwin, 1790), p. 107.
17. Ibid., p. 110.
18. Charles Churchill, 'Night: An Epistle to Robert Lloyd', in *The Poetical Works*, ed. Douglas Grant (Oxford: Clarendon Press, 1956), pp. 51–3.
19. Ibid., pp. 54–5.
20. See Charles Cowden Clarke, 'Churchill – His Life and Writings', in *The Poetical Works of Charles Churchill*, ed. Charles Cowden Clarke (London: Cassell, Petter, Galpin, n.d.), p. x.
21. Joachim Schlör, *Nights in the Big City: Paris, Berlin, London, 1840–1930*, trans. Pierre Gottfried Imhof and Dafydd Rees Roberts (London: Reaktion, 1998), p. 288.
22. Edward Young, *The Complaint; or, Night-Thoughts on Life, Death, and Immortality* in *The Poetical Works* (London: n.p., 1755), vol. 3, pp. 97.
23. Raymond Williams, *The Country and the City* (London: Chatto & Windus, 1973), p. 233.
24. Oliver Goldsmith, 'A City Night-Piece', in *Collected Works of Oliver Goldsmith*, vol. 1, ed. Arthur Friedman (Oxford: Clarendon Press, 1966), p. 431.
25. Quoted in Watt, *Rise of the Novel*, pp. 53–4.
26. Oliver Goldsmith, *An Enquiry into the Present State of Polite Learning in Europe*, in *Collected Works*, vol. 1, p. 314.
27. Oliver Goldsmith, *She Stoops to Conquer; or, The Mistakes of a Night, A Comedy*, in *Collected Works of Oliver Goldsmith*, vol. 5, ed. Arthur Friedman (Oxford: Clarendon Press, 1966), p. 205.
28. Oliver Goldsmith, *The Life of Dr Parnell*, in *Collected Works of Oliver*

Goldsmith, vol. 3, ed. Arthur Friedman (Oxford: Clarendon Press, 1966), p. 426.

29. Thomas Parnell, 'A Night-Piece on Death', in *Poems on Several Occasions*, ed. Alexander Pope (London: B. Lintot, 1722), p. 152.
30. Richard C. Taylor, *Goldsmith as Journalist* (Rutherford, NJ: Fairleigh Dickinson University Press, 1993), pp. 83–4.
31. Anonymous, *The Midnight Spy; or, A View of the Transactions of London and Westminster, From the Hours of Ten in the Evening, till Five in the Morning* (London: J. Cooke, 1766), p. 144.
32. Oliver Goldsmith, *The Citizen of the World; or, Letters from a Chinese Philosopher, Residing in London, to His Friends in the East* (London: R. Whiston et al., 1782), vol. 2, p. 216.
33. Ibid., p. 216.
34. Young, *The Complaint*, p. 7.
35. Goldsmith, *Citizen of the World*, pp. 216, 217.
36. Daniel Defoe, *A Journal of the Plague Year*, ed. Anthony Burgess and Christopher Bristow (London: Penguin, 1986), p. 120.
37. Edward Gibbon, *The History of the Decline and Fall of the Roman Empire*, ed. J. B. Bury (London: Methuen, 1909), vol. 3, pp. 321–2.
38. Goldsmith, *Citizen of the World*, p. 217.
39. See Matthew Beaumont, *The Spectre of Utopia: Utopian and Science Fictions at the Fin de Siècle* (Oxford: Peter Lang, 2012), pp. 97–120.
40. Max Byrd, *London Transformed: Images of the City in the Eighteenth Century* (New Haven, CT: Yale University Press, 1978), p. 35.
41. Goldsmith, *Citizen of the World*, p. 217.
42. See Ernst Bloch, *The Principle of Hope*, trans. Neville Plaice, Stephen Plaice and Paul Knight (Cambridge, MA: MIT Press, 1986).
43. Terry Eagleton, 'The Good-Natured Gael', in *Crazy John and the Bishop and Other Essays on Irish Culture* (Cork: Cork University Press, 1998), p. 116.
44. Shakespeare, *Complete Works*, III. iv. 28–36.
45. Goldsmith, *Citizen of the World*, pp. 217–18.
46. Eagleton, 'Good-Natured Gael', pp. 120–1.
47. Goldsmith, *Citizen of the World*, p. 217.
48. Eagleton, 'Good-Natured Gael', p. 106.
49. Washington Irving, *Oliver Goldsmith: A Biography* (London: Library Press, n.d.), p. 46.
50. Quoted in John Ginger, *The Notable Man: The Life and Times of Oliver Goldsmith* (London: Hamish Hamilton, 1977), p. 85.
51. Oliver Goldsmith, *The Vicar of Wakefield*, ed. Arthur Friedman (Oxford: Oxford University Press, 2008), p. 92.

52. Francis Bacon, *The Essayes or Counsels, Civill and Morall*, ed. Michael Kiernan (Oxford: Clarendon Press, 1985), p. 58.
53. Richard Pyke, 'Round Italy', in R. S. Lambert, ed., *Grand Tour* (London: Faber & Faber, 1935), p. 97.
54. Oliver Goldsmith, 'The Traveller, or A Prospect of Society', in *The Poems of Thomas Gray, William Collins, Oliver Goldsmith*, ed. Roger Lonsdale (London: Longman, 1969), pp. 632, 633.
55. John Forster, *The Life and Adventures of Oliver Goldsmith* (London: Bradbury & Evans, 1848), pp. 57–8, 137.
56. Ibid., p. 201.
57. Laurence Sterne, *A Sentimental Journey*, ed. Ian Jack (Oxford: Oxford University Press, 1984), p. 107.
58. Oliver Goldsmith, 'National Prejudices', in *The Works of Oliver Goldsmith*, vol. 2 (London: Thomas Tegg, 1835), p. 215.
59. Oliver Goldsmith, 'The Adventures of a Strolling Player', in *Collected Works*, vol. 3, pp. 133, 138.
60. Quoted in Jerry White, *London in the Eighteenth Century: A Great and Monstrous Thing* (London: Bodley Head, 2012), p. 320.
61. Earl of Rochester, 'A Ramble in St James's Park', ll. 25–32, in *The Complete Poems of John Wilmot, Earl of Rochester*, ed. David M. Vieth (New Haven, CT: Yale University Press, 1968), p. 41.
62. Robert O. Bucholz and Joseph P. Ward, *London: A Social and Cultural History, 1550–1750* (Cambridge: Cambridge University Press, 2012), p. 358.
63. Anonymous, *Midnight Spy*, p. 14.
64. The biographical details in these paragraphs are derived from the 'Memoirs of the Author's Life', in William Pattison, *The Poetical Works of Mr William Pattison* (London: H. Curll, 1728), p. 8. See also Thomas Seccombe, 'Pattison, William (1706–1727), poet', rev. John Wyatt, in the *Oxford Dictionary of National Biography*.
65. The most authoritative account of this incident, and of Pattison's relations with Curll and Pope, is in Paul Baines and Pat Rogers, *Edmund Curll, Bookseller* (Oxford: Oxford University Press, 2007), pp. 183–6.
66. William Pattison, 'Effigies Authoris', *The Poetical Works of William Pattison, To which is Prefixed the Life of the Author* (Edinburgh: Mundell, 1794), in *A Complete Edition of the Poets of Great Britain*, vol. 8, p. 580.
67. Ibid., p. 580.
68. Ibid.
69. Ibid., p. 581.
70. Samuel Johnson, *An Account of the Life of Mr Richard Savage*, in *Selected Writings*, ed. Patrick Cruttwell (London: Penguin, 1986), p. 109.

71. Anonymous, 'Literary Adventurers', *All the Year Round* 233 (10 October 1863), p. 153. Vic Gatrell mistakenly ascribes this article to Dickens (*First Bohemians*, pp. 118–20).

Chapter 7: Midnight Rambles

1. See Richard Holmes, *Dr Johnson and Mr Savage* (London: Flamingo, 1993), p. xii.
2. See Samuel Johnson, *A Dictionary of the English Language* (London: J. & P. Knapton et al., 1755), vol. 2, n.p.
3. James Boswell, *Life of Johnson*, ed. R. W. Chapman (Oxford: Oxford University Press, 1998), p. 437.
4. Iain Sinclair, 'Diary', *London Review of Books*, 9 May 2013, p. 38.
5. William Hawkins, *A Treatise of the Pleas of the Crown*, 5th edn (London: n.p., 1771), vol. 2, p. 67.
6. Holmes, *Dr Johnson and Mr Savage*, pp. 166, 14.
7. Boswell, *Life of Johnson*, p. 127.
8. Holmes, *Dr Johnson and Mr Savage*, p. 235.
9. Samuel Johnson, *An Account of the Life of Mr Richard Savage*, in *Selected Writings*, ed. Patrick Cruttwell (London: Penguin, 1986), p. 55.
10. Ibid., pp. 69–70.
11. Ibid., p. 69.
12. Ibid., p. 64.
13. Ibid., pp. 64–5.
14. Anonymous [Thomas Cooke], *The Life of Mr Richard Savage* (London: J. Roberts, 1727), p. 21.
15. Johnson, *Life of Mr Richard Savage*, p. 65.
16. See *Select Trials, for Murders, Robberies, Rapes, Sodomy, Coining, Frauds, and Other Offences: At the Sessions-House in the Old Bailey*, vol. 2 (London: Wilford, 1735), p. 15.
17. Johnson, *Life of Mr Richard Savage*, p. 65.
18. Ibid., p. 73.
19. Henry Fielding, *'The Covent-Garden Journal' and 'A Plan of the Universal Register Office'*, ed. Bertrand A. Goldgar (Oxford: Clarendon Press, 1988), pp. 283–4.
20. Johnson, *Life of Mr Richard Savage*, p. 73.
21. Ibid., pp. 80–1.
22. Ibid., p. 86.
23. Ibid., p. 55.
24. Ibid., p. 61.

25. Pat Rogers, *Johnson* (Oxford: Oxford University Press, 1993), p. 15.
26. Iscariot Hackney [Richard Savage], *An Author to be Lett* (London: A. Moore, 1729), pp. 5, 3.
27. Richard Savage, 'The Bastard', ll. 3–4, 13–20, in *The Poetical Works of Richard Savage*, ed. Clarence Tracy (Cambridge: Cambridge University Press, 1962), pp. 87, 89.
28. Clarence Tracy, 'Introduction', in Savage, *The Poetical Works*, pp. 2–3.
29. Holmes, *Dr Johnson and Mr Savage*, p. 88.
30. Richard Savage, *The Wanderer: A Vision*, I. 100, in *The Poetical Works*, pp. 94–159.
31. Savage, *Poetical Works*, I. 176.
32. Ibid., I. 181–2.
33. Ibid., I. 215–16.
34. Ibid., II. 149–50.
35. Ibid., III. 34.
36. Ibid., III. 110.
37. Ibid., III. 123.
38. Ibid., III. 295–306.
39. Ibid., IV. 1–2.
40. Tracy, 'Introduction', pp. 3–4.
41. Savage, *Poetical Works*, V. 107.
42. Ibid., V. 621–2.
43. Holmes, *Dr Johnson and Mr Savage*, p. 150.
44. Boswell, *Life of Johnson*, p. 1,398.
45. Samuel Johnson, 'A Meditation on the Spring', *Rambler* 5 (3 April 1750), in *The Rambler*, vol. 1, p. 28. The claim that the *Rambler* was named after *The Wanderer* was first proposed by Johnson's friend the actor Arthur Murphy in *An Essay on the Life and Genius of Samuel Johnson* (1792).
46. Thomas Traherne, *Centuries, Poems, and Thanksgivings*, vol. 2, ed. H. M. Margoliouth (Oxford: Clarendon Press, 1958), p. 135.
47. Johnson, 'A Meditation on the Spring', p. 30.
48. See Peter Martin, *Samuel Johnson: A Biography* (London: Weidenfeld & Nicolson, 2008), pp. 71, 74.
49. Quoted in Walter Jackson Bate, *Samuel Johnson* (New York: Harcourt Brace, 1977), p. 180.
50. Boswell, *Life of Johnson*, pp. 47–8.
51. David Nokes, *Samuel Johnson: A Life* (London: Faber & Faber, 2009), p. 59.
52. For these and the following quotations, see Samuel Johnson, 'The Revolutions of a Garret', *The Rambler* 161 (1 October 1751), in *The Rambler*, vol. 2, pp. 960, 963, 964.

53. John Forster, *The Life and Adventures of Oliver Goldsmith* (London: Bradbury & Evans, 1848), p. 137.
54. Boswell, *Life of Johnson*, p. 118.
55. Ibid., p. 118.
56. Martin, *Samuel Johnson*, p. 140.
57. John Hawkins, *The Life of Samuel Johnson LL.D*, ed. Bertram H. Davis (London: Jonathan Cape, 1961), pp. 29–30.
58. Peter Linebaugh, *The London Hanged: Crime and Civil Society in the Eighteenth Century*, 2nd edn (London: Verso, 2006), p. 16.
59. Johnson, *Life of Mr Richard Savage*, p. 77.
60. Richard Savage, 'Of Public Spirit in Regard to Public Works: A Poem', ll. 301–4, in *The Poetical Works*, p. 233.
61. Johnson, *Life of Mr Richard Savage*, p. 101.
62. Bate, *Samuel Johnson*, p. 178.
63. Hawkins, *Life of Samuel Johnson*, pp. 48, 49.
64. Johnson, *Life of Mr Richard Savage*, p. 105. Note that, later in his life, Johnson too was guilty of keeping disruptive hours. 'Mrs Thrale wrote that his social habits were so sprawling that he upset family routines. His insomnia and fears of loneliness often forced her to stay up with him into the early morning hours.' See Martin, *Samuel Johnson*, p. 340.
65. Nokes, *Samuel Johnson*, p. 64.
66. Hawkins, *Life of Samuel Johnson*, pp. 48, 28–9.
67. Boswell, *Life of Johnson*, p. 119.
68. Thomas Kaminski, *The Early Career of Samuel Johnson* (New York: Oxford University Press, 1987), pp. 85, 89.
69. Boswell, *Life of Johnson*, p. 119.
70. Holmes, *Dr Johnson and Mr Savage*, p. 39. Holmes cites Murphy's account on p. 41.
71. Johnson, *Life of Mr Richard Savage*, pp. 103–4.
72. [Daniel Defoe], *The History and Remarkable Life of the Truly Honourable Colonel Jaque, Vulgarly Call'd, Colonel Jack*, 3rd edn (London: J. Brotherton, 1724), p. 19.
73. Johnson, *Life of Mr Richard Savage*, p. 104.
74. Raymond Williams, *The Country and the City* (London: Chatto & Windus, 1973), p. 233.
75. See Bate, *Samuel Johnson*, p. 172.
76. Samuel Johnson, 'London: A Poem in Imitation of the Third Satire of Juvenal', ll. 176–9, in *Selected Writings*, p. 46.
77. Johnson, *Life of Mr Richard Savage*, p. 107.
78. Johnson, 'London,' II. 222–3, II. 224–35, p. 47.
79. Note that, in a terrific attack on Lord Brougham's *Lives* of the

eighteenth-century men of letters printed in the *Leader* in 1855, George Eliot took him to task for 'his supposition, that because Johnson was sometimes wandering all night in the streets with Savage he must necessarily have indulged in certain vices "in their more crapulous form" (an unfortunate suggestion to come from the Brougham of Jeffrey's letters, who is described as "roaming the streets with the sons of Belial")'. See Rosemary Ashton, *George Eliot: A Life* (London: Allen Lane, 1996), pp. 142–3.

80. Johnson, 'London,' II. 238–41, p. 47.
81. Johnson, *Life of Mr Richard Savage*, p. 130.
82. Ibid., p. 109.
83. This is something that Boswell, in spite of his disapproval of Savage, might have understood: 'I must inform you, that there is a city called London, for which I have as violent an affection, as the most romantic lover ever had for his mistress', he wrote in a letter in to the Scottish poet Andrew Erskine in 1762; 'Every agreeable whim may be freely indulged without censure.' Quoted in Gordon Turnbull, 'Introduction', in James Boswell, *London Journal 1762–1763*, ed. Gordon Turnbull (London: Penguin, 2010), p. xxvi.
84. Christopher Hibbert, *Samuel Johnson: A Personal History* (New York: Palgrave Macmillan, 2009), p. 46.
85. Johnson, *Life of Mr Richard Savage*, pp. 116, 119, 121.
86. Holmes, *Dr Johnson and Mr Savage*, p. 217.
87. Walter Benjamin, 'The Paris of the Second Empire in Baudelaire', in Michael W. Jennings, ed., *The Writer of Modern Life: Essays on Charles Baudelaire* (Cambridge, MA: Harvard University Press, 2006), p. 57.
88. Johnson, *Life of Mr Richard Savage*, p. 101.
89. Richard Savage, 'A Poem, Sacred to the Glorious Memory of Our Late Most Gracious Sovereign Lord King George', ll. 11–12, in *Poetical Works*, p. 83.
90. Pat Rogers, *Grub Street: Studies in a Subculture* (London: Methuen, 1972), p. 368.

Chapter 8: Night on the Lengthening Road

1. C. P. Moritz, *Travels in England in 1782*, ed. Henry Morley (London: Cassell, 1886), p. 6.
2. Ibid., pp. 104, 92, 101, 126–7.
3. Quoted in Kenneth R. Johnston, *The Hidden Wordsworth: Poet, Lover, Rebel, Spy* (London: Pimlico, 2000), p. 189. In *The Excursion*, Wordsworth revisits this distinction between 'the Wealthy, the Luxurious', who 'roll in chariots', and those who pace on foot (II. 97, 99); but in this far more

conservative statement he affirms not so much a political difference as an aesthetic one – he emphasizes the pedestrians' superior sensitivity to the environment through which they travel. See William Wordsworth, *The Excursion*, ed. Sally Bushell, James A. Butler and Michael C. Jaye (Ithaca, NY: Cornell University Press, 2007), p. 79.

4. Rebecca Solnit, *Wanderlust: A History of Walking* (London: Verso, 2001), p. 107.
5. William Wordsworth, *The Prelude*, XII. 162–4, in *The Prelude: A Parallel Text*, ed. J. C. Maxwell (London: Penguin, 1986), p. 496.
6. Frédéric Gros, *A Philosophy of Walking*, trans. John Howe (London: Verso, 2014), p. 73.
7. Jean-Jacques Rousseau, *Reveries of the Solitary Walker*, trans. Peter France (London: Penguin, 1979), p. 35.
8. See Michel Foucault, *The History of Sexuality, Vol. 3: The Care of the Self*, trans. Robert Hurley (London: Vintage, 1988).
9. Jean-Jacques Rousseau, *Confessions*, ed. R. Niklaus (London: Everyman, 1931), vol. 1, p. 147.
10. Ibid., p. 153.
11. William Wordsworth, *The Prelude*, II. 321–2, in *Prelude*, p. 88.
12. Thomas De Quincey, 'William Wordsworth', in *Recollections of the Lakes and the Lake Poets*, ed. David Wright (London: Penguin, 1970), p. 135.
13. Solnit, *Wanderlust*, p. 104.
14. William Wordsworth, 'An Evening Walk', ll. 329–30, 334, 341–2, 345–7, in *William Wordsworth (The Oxford Authors)*, ed. Stephen Gill (Oxford: Oxford University Press, 1984), pp. 9–10. Wordsworth sketches another mysterious transition of the light in a later, shorter poem known as 'A Night-Piece' (1815), which he noted was composed in 1798 'on the road between Nether Stowey and Alfoxden, extempore'. Here, the sudden revelation of the moon driving along in its 'blue-black vault' interrupts the poet's thoughts as he pursues the road, before disappearing behind clouds again and leaving him 'to muse upon the solemn scene'. See Wordsworth, 'A Night-Piece', ll. 11, 23, in Gill, *William Wordsworth*, p. 45.
15. Wordsworth, *Prelude*, I. 305–6.
16. Ibid., I. 309–24.
17. Ibid., I. 336.
18. Ibid., I. 325–8.
19. Ibid., I. 329–32.
20. Ibid., IV. 169–70, 175–6.
21. Ibid., XIII. 27, 39–40.
22. Ibid., XIII. 41.
23. Ibid., XIII. 66, 105.

24. Ibid., XIII. 68–73.
25. Ibid., VI. 179–80.
26. William Hazlitt, 'On Going a Journey', in *Metropolitan Writings*, ed. Gregory Dart (Manchester: Carcanet, 2005), p. 29.
27. Ibid., p. 29.
28. P. B. Shelley, 'To a Skylark', ll. 1–2, in *Poetical Works*, 2nd edn, ed. Thomas Hutchinson (Oxford: Oxford University Press, 1970), p. 602.
29. Henri Lefebvre, *The Production of Space*, trans. Donald Nicholson-Smith (Oxford: Blackwell, 1991), p. 289.
30. Karl Marx, *Grundrisse: Foundations of the Critique of Political Economy (Rough Draft)*, trans. Martin Nicolaus (London: Penguin, 1993), p. 410.
31. Anne D. Wallace, *Walking, Literature, and English Culture* (Oxford: Clarendon Press, 1993), p. 10. It is difficult to resist retelling a delightful, perhaps apocryphal, story about Wordsworth defiantly 'unenclosing' a footpath in the Lake District when he was a curmudgeonly conservative in his mid sixties. The distinguished poet was due to attend a dinner in his honour at Lowther Castle, near Penrith, with Coleridge's nephew, Mr Justice Coleridge. (The Lowther family were the most powerful capitalists and landlords in the Lake District, and Wordsworth's father John had been steward to Sir James Lowther, the famously nasty and rapacious first Earl of Lonsdale.) When the two men got close to the house they decided to leave their chaise at the road and travel the remaining distance on foot. They took a path across the fields, but were abruptly forced to stop because it ended in a blind wall. 'The poet muttered something and attacked the wall as if it were a living entity, crying out, "This is the way, an ancient right of way too," and passed on.' That evening, after dinner, Coleridge remarked to Sir John Wallace, a neighbouring landowner, that he and Wordsworth might have committed trespass earlier in the day, since they had crossed a broken-down wall on his estate. Wallace was irate, and threatened to horsewhip the miscreant responsible for destroying the wall. But, leaping to his feet, Wordsworth supposedly responded: 'I broke down your wall, Sir John, it was obstructing an ancient right of way, and I will do it again.' It is as if, in this one important respect, the revolutionary embers of his youth still smouldered deep inside him. In spite of his reactionary politics, he was still prepared to fight in militant terms for freedom of movement on foot and the right to the countryside. See Howard Hill, *Freedom to Roam: The Struggle for Access to Britain's Moors and Mountains* (Ashbourne: Moorland Publishing, 1980), p. 40. The story is taken from the *Manchester Guardian*, 7 October 1887.
32. Quoted in Nicholas Roe, *The Politics of Nature: William Wordsworth and Some Contemporaries* (Basingstoke: Palgrave, 2002), p. 172.

33. Richard Holmes, *Coleridge: Early Visions* (London: Hodder & Stoughton, 1989), p. 61.
34. Quoted in ibid., p. 64.
35. John Thelwall, *The Peripatetic; or, The Sketches of the Heart, of Nature and Society* (London: The Author, 1793), vol. 2, p. 47. Arguing that 'the advanced reformers of the time found it more easy to advocate the political programme of equality – manhood suffrage – than they did to shed the cultural attitudes of superiority', E. P. Thompson quotes a passage from the *Tribune* in 1796 in which Thelwall boasts: 'I love to see the labourer in his ragged coat – that is I love the labourer: I am sorry his coat is obliged to be so ragged. I love the labourer then, in his ragged coat, as well as I love the Peer in his ermine; perhaps better …' Thompson emphasizes that Wordsworth was far more democratic than Thelwall in his attitude to 'common wayfarers on the road', and expresses admiration for the poet's condemnation of 'the levity and vulgarity of the polite'. See E. P. Thompson, 'Education and Experience', in *The Romantics: England in a Revolutionary Age* (London: Merlin Press, 1997), pp. 10–11.
36. Uvedale Price, *An Essay on the Picturesque, As Compared with the Sublime and Beautiful*, vol. 1, new edn (London: J. Robson, 1796), p. 76.
37. Arthur Redford, *Labour Migration in England 1800–1850*, 3rd edn, ed. W. H. Chaloner (Manchester: Manchester University Press, 1976), p. 138.
38. Wordsworth, 'An Evening Walk', ll. 245–6, 249–50, in Gill, *William Wordsworth*, p. 7.
39. See Mary Jacobus, *Tradition and Experiment in Wordsworth's* Lyrical Ballads *(1798)* (Oxford: Clarendon Press, 1976), p. 144.
40. William Wordsworth, 'The Female Vagrant', ll. 89, 124–6, in Wordsworth and Coleridge, *The Lyrical Ballads*, 2nd edition, ed. R. L. Brett and A. R. Jones (London: Routledge, 1991), pp. 47, 49.
41. William Wordsworth, 'Salisbury Plain', ll. 4, 1, in Gill, *William Wordsworth*, p. 13.
42. Wordsworth, *Prelude*, III. iv. 105–7.
43. Ibid., III. iv. 28, 30–1.
44. Ibid., III. iv. 33–6.
45. Ibid., III. iv. 144.
46. William Wordsworth, 'The Old Cumberland Beggar', ll. 1, 103, 115, in Gill, *William Wordsworth*, pp. 50, 52.
47. Jeffrey Robinson, *The Walk: Notes on a Romantic Image* (Norman: University of Oklahoma Press, 1989), p. 25.
48. William Wordsworth, *The Excursion*, I. 417, in *The Excursion*, ed. Sally Bushell, James A. Butler and Michael C. Jaye (Ithaca, NY: Cornell University Press, 2007), p. 59.

49. William Wordsworth, 'Fenwick Note to *The Excursion*', in *The Excursion*, ed. Bushell et al., pp. 1,215–6. Richard Savage's *The Wanderer* (1729) was an important precursor to *The Excursion*. Thelwall, who had become friends with Coleridge and Wordsworth in the course of a walking tour through the West Country in 1797, claimed, however, that *The Peripatetic* exercised the decisive influence on the shape of *The Excursion*.
50. [Walter Thom,] *Pedestrianism; or, An Account of the Performances of Celebrated Pedestrians during the Last and Present Century* (Aberdeen: Chalmers, 1813), pp. 40–1, iii–iv.
51. Quoted in Nicholas Roe, *John Keats: A New Life* (New Haven, CT: Yale University Press, 2012), pp. 125–6.
52. See C. J. Ribton-Turner, *A History of Vagrants and Vagrancy and Beggars and Begging* (London: Chapman & Hall, 1887), p. 235.
53. Jane Rendell's claim that this Act associated '"Night Walkers" with the term "Prostitutes" for the first time' is misleading. See Jane Rendell, *The Pursuit of Pleasure: Gender, Space and Architecture in Regency London* (London: Athlone, 2002), p. 57.
54. See Vagrancy Act 1824, at legislation.gov.uk.
55. A. L. Beier, *Masterless Men: The Vagrancy Problem in England 1560–1640* (London: Methuen, 1985), p. xxii. Note too that some early-nineteenth-century commentators realized with consternation that the Act was so sweeping that middle-class people also were at risk of prosecution. One anonymous barrister, in spite of his support for the new law, objected that the clause concerning people who refused to maintain their families could not necessarily be restricted to the labouring class, 'to which, of course, it is intended to apply'. Quoted in Audrey Eccles, *Vagrancy Law and Practice under the Old Poor Law* (Farnham: Ashgate, 2012), p. 55.
56. It remains true today. The stop-and-search provisions of the 1824 Act, which is still on the statute books, were used extensively to persecute black and ethnic minority communities prior to the riots that, in response to a police campaign of racist harassment, erupted throughout Britain in the early 1980s. This was the notorious 'sus law'. In licensing the authorities to detain individuals not because they had committed a crime but simply because they might do, it reproduced the logic of the medieval statutes against nightwalkers.
57. Wordsworth, *Prelude*, IV. 95, 104–5.
58. Ibid., IV. 102.
59. Ibid., IV. 109–11, 114.
60. Ibid., IV. 116–20.
61. Celeste Langan, *Romantic Vagrancy: Wordsworth and the Simulation*

of Freedom (Cambridge: Cambridge University Press, 1995), p. 17.

62. Wordsworth, *The Excursion*, I. 417–18, in *The Excursion*, ed. Bushell et al., p. 59.
63. Wordsworth, *Prelude*, XII. 145.
64. Ibid., XII. 158–9.
65. Ibid., XII. 161–2, 156.
66. Ibid., XII. 166–8.
67. Ibid., XII. 163–5.
68. M. M. Bakhtin, 'Forms of Time and of the Chronotope in the Novel', in *The Dialogic Imagination: Four Essays*, trans. Caryl Emerson and Michael Holquist (Austin: University of Texas Press, 1981), p. 84.
69. See ibid., pp. 120, 243.
70. Wordsworth, *Prelude*, IV. 360–2.
71. Ibid., IV. 363–8.
72. Ibid., IV. 371–2.
73. Ibid., IV. 386–8.
74. Ibid., IV. 393–9.
75. Ibid., IV. 385.
76. Ibid., IV. 401–2.
77. Ibid., IV. 403–4.
78. Ibid., IV. 405–19.
79. Ibid., IV. 420–1.
80. Ibid., IV. 446.
81. Ibid., IV. 449.
82. Ibid., IV. 451.
83. Ibid., IV. 466–8.
84. Ibid., IV. 470–1.
85. Ibid., IV. 473–5.
86. Ibid., IV. 481.
87. Ibid., IV. 490.
88. Ibid., IV. 503–4.
89. Jean-Paul Sartre, 'The Purposes of Writing', in *Between Existentialism and Marxism*, trans. John Matthews (London: Verso, 2008), p. 22.
90. Robin Jarvis, *Romantic Writing and Pedestrian Travel* (Basingstoke: Macmillan, 1997), p. 155.
91. John Clare, 'The Mores', ll. 7–8, 47–8, in *Major Works*, ed. Eric Robinson and David Powell (Oxford: Oxford University Press, 2004), pp. 167–8.
92. John Clare, *The Village Minstrel*, l. 47, in ibid., p. 50.
93. Clare, 'Evening', ll. 1–2, 19–20, in ibid., pp. 358–9.
94. Clare, 'Recollections after an Evening Walk', ll. 1–2, 10, 38, 36, in ibid., p. 41.

95. John Clare, 'Song', in *The Early Poems of John Clare*, ed. Eric Robinson and David Powell (Oxford: Clarendon Press, 1989), vol. 2, p. 197.
96. Jonathan Bate, *John Clare: A Biography* (London: Picador, 2003), pp. 93–4. John Goodridge and Kelsey Thornton claim that 'there is ample evidence in Clare's writings that being abroad at night is in itself a kind of trespass'. See 'John Clare: The Trespasser', in Hugh Haughton, Adam Phillips and Geoffrey Summerfield, eds, *John Clare in Context* (Cambridge: Cambridge University Press, 1994), pp. 109–10.
97. According to E. P. Thompson, the Black Act 'signalled the onset of the flood-tide of eighteenth-century retributive justice'. See *Whigs and Hunters: The Origin of the Black Act* (London: Penguin, 1990), esp. p. 23. Note that in 1828, five years after the effective repeal of the Black Act, the government introduced a Night Poaching Act, still on the statute books today, which condemned those convicted to up to three months hard labour for a first offence and transportation to the colonies for a third.
98. Iain Sinclair has traced the sinuous, tortuous arc of this flight on foot, and charted the topography of Clare's unconscious, in *Edge of the Orison* (London: Hamish Hamilton, 2005).
99. Clare, 'Journey out of Essex', in *Major Works*, p. 437.
100. Ibid., pp. 432–3.
101. Ibid., pp. 434–5.
102. Ibid., pp. 435–6.
103. Clare, 'Poems Written in Epping Forest and Northampton Asylum 1837–1864', ll. 241–3, 262–3, in *Major Works*, p. 286.
104. Ibid., ll. 266, 272, in *Major Works*, pp. 286–7.
105. Ibid., ll. 255–6, in *Major Works*, p. 286.
106. John Keats, 'Ode to a Nightingale', ll. 79–80, in *The Complete Poems*, 3rd edn, ed. John Barnard (London: Penguin, 1988), p. 348.

Chapter 9: London's Darkness

1. John Bunyan, *The Pilgrim's Progress*, ed. Roger Pooley (London: Penguin, 2008), p. 49.
2. William Blake, *XVII Designs to Thornton's Virgil, Reproduced from the Original Woodcuts* (Portland, ME: Thomas B. Mosher, 1899), p. 39.
3. Ibid., pp. 39–40, 41, 42.
4. Ibid., p. 43.
5. William Blake, letter to William Hayley, 28 May 1804, in *The Complete Poetry and Prose of William Blake*, rev. edn, ed. David V. Erdman (New York: Anchor Books, 1988), p. 751.

6. See Annabel Patterson, *Pastoral and Ideology: Virgil to Valéry* (Berkeley: University of California Press, 1987), p. 259.
7. See ibid., pp. 256–7.
8. Blake, 'Song', ll. 13–16, in *Complete Poetry and Prose of William Blake*, ed. Erdman, p. 415.
9. Peter Ackroyd, *Blake* (London: Vintage, 1999), p. 18.
10. Quoted in G. E. Bentley, *The Stranger from Paradise: A Biography of William Blake* (New Haven, CT: Yale University Press, 2001), p. 57.
11. Charles Dickens, *Barnaby Rudge*, ed. Clive Hurst (Oxford: Oxford University Press, 2003), p. 518.
12. *Complete Poetry and Prose of William Blake*, ed. Erdman, p. 24.
13. Ibid., p. 347.
14. See Tim Hitchcock, 'Re-negotiating the Bloody Code: The Gordon Riots and the Transformation of Popular Attitudes to the Criminal Justice System', in Ian Haywood and John Seed, eds, *The Gordon Riots: Politics, Culture and Insurrection in Late Eighteenth-Century Britain* (Cambridge: Cambridge University Press, 2012), pp. 187–8.
15. E. P. Thompson, *The Making of the English Working Class* (London: Penguin, 1968), p. 78.
16. D. V. Erdman, *Blake: Prophet Against Empire: A Poet's Interpretation of the History of His Own Times*, 3rd edn (Princeton, NJ: Princeton University Press, 1977), p. 9.
17. Ackroyd, *Blake*, p. 71.
18. Bentley, *Stranger from Paradise*, p. 57.
19. See Matthew White, '"For the Safety of the City": The Geography and Social Politics of Public Execution after the Gordon Riots', in Haywood and Seed, *Gordon Riots*, pp. 206–7.
20. Quoted in Vic Gatrell, *The Hanging Tree: Execution and the British People 1770–1868* (Oxford: Oxford University Press, 1994), pp. 10–11.
21. *Complete Poetry and Prose of William Blake*, ed. Erdman, p. 233.
22. Quoted in Peter Linebaugh, 'The Tyburn Riot against the Surgeons', in Douglas Hay, Peter Linebaugh and John G. Rule, *Albion's Fatal Tree: Crime and Society in Eighteenth-Century England*, rev. edn (London: Verso, 2011), p. 68. I have taken the details of my account of the Tyburn Tree from Linebaugh's article and from Andrea Mackenzie, *Tyburn's Martyrs: Execution in England, 1675–1775* (London: Continuum, 2007).
23. John Evelyn, *The Diary of John Evelyn*, ed. William Bray (London: George Newnes, 1903), p. 330.
24. Peter Linebaugh, *The London Hanged: Crime and Civil Society in the Eighteenth Century*, 2nd edn (London: Verso, 2006), p. 50.
25. Hitchcock, 'Re-negotiating the Bloody Code', p. 186.

26. Quoted in Bryan D. Palmer, *Cultures of Darkness: Night Travels in the History of Transgression* (New York: Monthly Review Press, 2000), p. 104.
27. Douglas Hay, 'Property, Authority and the Criminal Law', in Hay et al., *Albion's Fatal Tree*, p. 18.
28. Jerry White, *London in the Eighteenth Century: A Great and Monstrous Thing* (London: Bodley Head, 2012), pp. 383–4, 386.
29. Samuel Johnson, 'The Necessity of Proportioning Punishments to Crimes', *The Rambler* 114 (20 April 1751), in *The Rambler* (London: J. Payne, 1753), vol. 2, pp. 678–9.
30. Ibid., p. 678.
31. Roy Porter, *London: A Social History* (London: Penguin, 2000), p. 184.
32. See White, *London in the Eighteenth Century*, pp. 383–4, 386.
33. *Complete Poetry and Prose of William Blake*, ed. Erdman, p. 181.
34. Michel Foucault, *Discipline and Punish: The Birth of the Prison*, trans. Alan Sheridan (London: Penguin, 1991), p. 173.
35. Jeremy Tambling, *Blake's Night Thoughts* (Basingstoke: Palgrave Macmillan, 2005), p. 118.
36. See Bentley, *Stranger from Paradise*, p. 30.
37. *Complete Poetry and Prose of William Blake*, ed. Erdman, p. 217.
38. Ibid., p. 216.
39. Ibid., p. 219, 241.
40. Ibid., p. 213.
41. Ibid., p. 213.
42. Ibid., p. 174.
43. 'One must be prepared for seventeen types of ambiguity in Blake', cautions E. P. Thompson, in *Witness Against the Beast: William Blake and the Moral Law* (Cambridge: Cambridge University Press, 1993), p. 184.
44. *Complete Poetry and Prose of William Blake*, ed. Erdman, p. 253.
45. Ibid., p. 353.
46. Ibid., p. 564.
47. Karl Marx, *The Communist Manifesto*, in *Selected Writings*, ed. David McLellan (Oxford: Oxford University Press, 1977), p. 223.
48. *Complete Poetry and Prose of William Blake*, ed. Erdman, p. 254.
49. Rebuilt by Christopher Wren after the Great Fire of London, St Swithin's was demolished in 1962 after being bombed during the Blitz. It was subsequently replaced by 111 Cannon Street, which initially housed the Bank of China. Today, London Stone stands caged behind a grille in the façade of the same building (as if its dormant energies must be guarded against at all times). In a sinister elision, the current corporate tenants of this building style themselves the Stone's 'owner/custodian'.
50. Shakespeare, *Complete Works*, IV. vi. 2–4.

51. John Stow, *A Survey of London*, ed. Antonia Fraser (Stroud: Sutton, 2005), p. 201.
52. Ossulston appears to have remained in position until 1822, when it was earthed over. Then, after Marble Arch was built in 1851, it leaned up against this monument's impassive form for a number of years. It has not been seen since 1869, when it was presumably stolen. See A. S. Ellis, 'The Ossulstone', *Notes and Queries* 137 (12 August 1882), p. 125.
53. *Complete Poetry and Prose of William Blake*, ed. Erdman, p. 218.
54. Ibid., p. 221.
55. Ibid., p. 172.
56. Ibid., p. 155.
57. Quoted in M. Dorothy George, *London Life in the Eighteenth Century* (Harmondsworth: Penguin, 1966), p. 115.
58. Erdman, *Blake: Prophet Against Empire*, p. 474.
59. *Complete Poetry and Prose of William Blake*, ed. Erdman, p. 155.
60. Ibid., p. 157.
61. Ibid., p. 99.
62. Morton D. Paley, *The Continuing City: William Blake's* Jerusalem (Oxford: Clarendon Press, 1983), p. 136.
63. T. W. Adorno, *Minima Moralia: Reflections from Damaged Life*, trans. E. F. N. Jephcott (London: Verso, 1978), p. 247. Although Blake and Adorno make unlikely bedfellows, the passage from which this phrase is taken, in the book's 'Finale', does much to illuminate the former: 'The only philosophy which can be responsibly practiced in the face of despair is an attempt to contemplate all things as they would present themselves from the standpoint of redemption. Knowledge has no light but that shed on the world by redemption: all else is reconstruction, mere technique. Perspectives must be fashioned that displace and estrange the world, reveal it to be, with its rifts and crevices, as indigent and distorted as it will appear one day in the messianic light.'
64. *Complete Poetry and Prose of William Blake*, ed. Erdman, p. 53.
65. Ibid., p. 208.
66. Ibid., p. 195.
67. Ibid., p. 190.
68. For this definition, see Martin Jay, *Marxism and Totality: The Adventures of a Concept from Lukács to Habermas* (Berkeley: University of California Press, 1984), p. 351.
69. *Complete Poetry and Prose of William Blake*, ed. Erdman, p. 218.
70. Tambling, *Blake's Night Thoughts*, p. 97.
71. Theodor W. Adorno and Max Horkheimer, *Dialectic of Enlightenment*, trans. John Cumming (London: Verso, 1979), p. 3.

71. *Complete Poetry and Prose of William Blake*, ed. Erdman, p. 147.
72. Ibid., pp. 148, 147.
73. Ibid.
74. Ibid., p. 148.
75. Ibid., p. 142.
76. Ibid., p. 149.
77. Adorno and Horkheimer, *Dialectic of Enlightenment*, p. 3.
78. Michel Foucault, *Madness and Civilization: A History of Insanity in the Age of Reason*, trans. Richard Howard (London: Routledge, 1989), p. 108.
79. *Complete Poetry and Prose of William Blake*, ed. Erdman, pp. 168–9.
80. Ibid., p. 151.
81. Ibid., p. 193.
82. Ibid.
83. Ibid., p. 195.
84. Ibid., p. 194.
85. Ibid.
86. Ibid., p. 195.
87. Ibid., p. 99.
88. Perhaps the apotheosis of this idea, as *Jerusalem* approaches an apocalyptic climax, is the description of the Antichrist's 'dark, deadly' head, which 'in its Brain incloses a reflexion / Of Eden all perverted', for this seems to include the industrial building boom that occurred in the suburbs of London in the early nineteenth century: 'Minute Particulars in slavery I behold among the brick-kilns / Disorganized' (ibid., p. 248).
89. See Kathleen Raine, *Golgonooza, City of Imagination: Last Studies in William Blake* (Ipswich: Golgonooza Press, 1991), p. 103.
90. *Complete Poetry and Prose of William Blake*, ed. Erdman, p. 180.
91. Ibid., p. 243.
92. Ibid., p. 242.
93. Ibid., p. 243.
94. Ibid., p. 878.
95. Ibid., p. 243.
96. Ibid., p. 169.
97. Ibid., p. 212.
98. Ibid., pp. 104, 207.
99. Ibid., p. 331. Enion is a personification of bodily impulses, Ahania is an emanation of Urizen, the personification of the rationalistic intellect; so it is as if Freud were to have written, not 'Where Id was there Ego shall be', but 'Where Id had wandered there Ego wanders now' – a rather less rationalistic slogan.

100. Ibid., pp. 26–7.
101. Ibid., p. 325.
102. I do not agree with Thompson that, in the first three stanzas, Blake is evoking the 'street-cries' of the daytime city. See Thompson, *Witness Against the Beast*, pp. 187–8.
103. *Complete Poetry and Prose of William Blake*, ed. Erdman, p. 64.
104. Thompson, *Witness Against the Beast*, p. 177.
105. David Harvey, *The Right to the City* (London: Verso, 2012), p. 4.
106. *Complete Poetry and Prose of William Blake*, ed. Erdman, p. 38.
107. Michel de Certeau, *The Practice of Everyday Life*, trans. Steven Rendall (Berkeley: University of California Press, 1984), p. 96.
108. Michel Foucault, 'The Eye of Power', trans. Colin Gordon, in Michel Foucault, *Power/Knowledge: Selected Interviews and Other Writings, 1972–1977*, ed. Colin Gordon (New York: Pantheon, 1980), pp. 153–4.
109. See Palmer, *Cultures of Darkness*, pp. 93–116.
110. Linebaugh, *London Hanged*, p. 23.
111. See Jean-Paul Sartre, *Critique of Dialectical Reason, Volume 1: Theory of Practical Ensembles*, new edn, trans. Alan Sheridan (London: Verso, 2004).
112. *Complete Poetry and Prose of William Blake*, ed. Erdman, p. 295.
113. Ibid., p. 296.

Chapter 10: The Nocturnal Labyrinth

1. Grevel Lindop, *The Opium-Eater: A Life of Thomas De Quincey* (London: Weidenfeld, 1993), p. 81.
2. Thomas De Quincey, 'Walking Stewart', in *The Works of Thomas De Quincey: Protestantism and Other Essays* (Edinburgh: A. & C. Black, 1863), pp. 1, 13.
3. Thomas De Quincey, 'Autobiography of an English Opium-Eater: Literary Connexions or Acquaintances', in *The Works of Thomas De Quincey*, vol. 10, ed. Alina Clej (London: Pickering & Chatto, 2003), p. 209. See also Robert Morrison, *The English Opium Eater: A Biography of Thomas De Quincey* (London: Weidenfeld & Nicolson, 2009), p. 70.
4. Lindop, *Opium-Eater*, p. 81.
5. Thomas De Quincey, 'Sketches of *Life and Manners; from the Autobiography of an English Opium-Eater*', in *Works of Thomas De Quincey*', vol. 10, p. 143.
6. Thomas De Quincey, *Confessions of an English Opium-Eater and Other*

Writings, ed. Grevel Lindop (Oxford: Oxford University Press, 1985), pp. 16–17.
7. Ibid., pp. 16, 35.
8. Ibid., p. 16.
9. Ibid., pp. 16–19.
10. Ibid., pp. 19–20.
11. See Thomas De Quincey, *The Works of Thomas De Quincey*, vol. 1, ed. Barry Symonds (London: Pickering & Chatto, 2000), p. 22
12. De Quincey, *Confessions*, p. 20.
13. Francis Place, *The Autobiography of Francis Place*, ed. Mary Thale (Cambridge: Cambridge University Press, 1972), p. 229.
14. De Quincey, *Confessions*, p. 20.
15. Morrison, *English Opium Eater*, p. 77.
16. De Quincey, *Confessions*, pp. 20–1.
17. Ibid., p. 21.
18. Ibid., p. 20.
19. Ibid., pp. 21–2.
20. Ibid., p. 26.
21. Thomas Shepherd and James Elmes, *Metropolitan Improvements; or, London in the Nineteenth Century, Being a Series of Views of the New and Most Interesting Objects in the British Metropolis and its Vicinity* (London: Jones, 1827), p. 7.
22. Jerry White, *London in the Nineteenth Century: 'A Human Awful Wonder of God'* (London: Vintage, 2008), p. 24.
23. Walter Benjamin, *The Arcades Project*, trans. Howard Eiland and Kevin McLaughlin (Cambridge, MA: Harvard University Press, 1999), p. 88.
24. De Quincey, *Confessions*, p. 27.
25. Ibid., p. 33.
26. Morrison, *English Opium Eater*, p. 82.
27. De Quincey, *Confessions*, pp. 32, 34.
28. Lindop, *Opium-Eater*, p. 85.
29. De Quincey, *Confessions*, pp. 29, 30.
30. Ibid., p. 29
31. Andrew Knapp and William Baldwin, *Newgate Calendar* (London: Robins, 1825), vol. 3, p. 437. For the trial proceedings, see Old Bailey Proceedings Online (oldbaileyonline.org, version 7.0, 8 April 2014), February 1807, trial of John Holloway, alias Oliver Owen Haggerty, alias Eggerty (t18070218-1).
32. V. A. C. Gatrell, *The Hanging Tree: Execution and the English People, 1770–1868* (Oxford: Oxford University Press, 1994), p. 57.

33. Thomas De Quincey, 'Suspiria de Profundis: Being a Sequel to the Confessions of an English Opium-Eater', in *Confessions*, p. 153.
34. John Barrell, *The Infection of Thomas De Quincey: A Psychopathology of Imperialism* (New Haven, CT: Yale University Press, 1991), p. 29.
35. De Quincey, *Confessions*, pp. 37, 48.
36. Ibid., p. 46.
37. Ibid., p. 47.
38. Barrell, *Infection of Thomas De Quincey*, pp. 2–3.
39. De Quincey, *Confessions*, p. 47.
40. Charles Baudelaire, *On Wine and Hashish*, ed. Andrew Brown (London: Hesperus Press, 2002), p. 22.
41. De Quincey, *Confessions*, pp. 47, 68.
42. Ibid., pp. 47–8.
43. Morrison, *English Opium Eater*, p. 205.
44. De Quincey, *Confessions*, p. 19.
45. Ibid., p. 23.
46. Ibid., pp. 34–5.
47. Ibid., pp. 34, 36.
48. Thomas De Quincey, 'William Wordsworth and Robert Southey', in *Recollections of the Lakes and the Lake Poets*, ed. David Wright (London: Penguin, 1970), pp. 228–9.
49. Walter Benjamin, 'Surrealism', in *One-Way Street and Other Writings*, trans. Edmund Jephcott and Kingsley Shorter (London: Verso, 1997), p. 237.
50. Morrison, *English Opium Eater*, p. 252.
51. Arnold Hauser, *The Social History of Art*, 3rd edn, vol. 3 (London: Routledge, 1999), pp. 169–70.
52. De Quincey, *Works*, vol. 1, p. 22.

Chapter 11: Crowded Streets, Empty Streets

1. Charles Lamb, *The Letters of Charles Lamb, with a Sketch of his Life*, ed. Thomas Noon Talfourd, vol. 1 (London: Edward Moxon, 1838), pp. 212–13.
2. William Wordsworth, 'Composed Upon Westminster Bridge, September 2, 1802', l. 14, in *William Wordsworth (The Oxford Authors)*, ed. Stephen Gill (Oxford: Oxford University Press, 1984), p. 285.
3. 'Common Sense' [Richard Phillips], 'Causes of the Increase of London', *Monthly Magazine* 209 (1 February 1811), p. 4.
4. For some of the details of this sketch of the city, and for a panorama, see

Jerry White, *London in the Nineteenth Century: 'A Human Awful Wonder of God'* (London: Jonathan Cape, 2007), pp. 9–28.

5. Walter Benjamin, 'The Paris of the Second Empire in Baudelaire', in Michael W. Jennings, ed., *The Writer of Modern Life: Essays on Charles Baudelaire* (Cambridge, MA: Harvard University Press, 2006), p. 114.
6. William Wordsworth, *The Prelude*, VIII. 465, in *The Prelude: A Parallel Text*, ed. J. C. Maxwell (London: Penguin, 1986), p. 322.
7. Ibid., VII. 571–6.
8. 'The city tormented him', comments Iain Sinclair, in *Edge of the Orison: In the Traces of John Clare's 'Journey out of Essex'* (London: Hamish Hamilton, 2005), p. 108.
9. Raymond Williams, *The Country and the City* (London: Hogarth Press, 1993), p. 150.
10. Wordsworth, *Prelude*, VII. 626, 628–9.
11. Georg Simmel, 'The Metropolis and Mental Life', in *Simmel on Culture: Selected Writings*, ed. David Frisby and Mike Featherstone (London: Sage, 1997), pp. 183–4.
12. Theodor W. Adorno, *Aesthetic Theory*, trans. Robert Hullot-Kentor (London: Athlone Press, 1997), p. 32.
13. Wordsworth, *Prelude*, VII. 695, 701–4.
14. Ibid., VII. 627–35.
15. William Wordsworth, 'St Paul's', ll. 24, 4–5, in *William Wordsworth: The Oxford Authors*, ed. Stephen Gill (Oxford: Oxford University Press, 1984), pp. 332–3.
16. John Bunyan, *The Pilgrim's Progress*, ed. Roger Pooley (London: Penguin, 2008), p. 49.
17. On the social identity, and sexual politics, of Cyprians as 'female ramblers', see Jane Rendell, *The Pursuit of Pleasure: Gender, Space and Architecture in Regency London* (London: Athlone, 2002), pp. 54–62.
18. Pierce Egan, *Life in London; or, The Day and Night Scenes of Jeremy Hawthorn, Esq. and his Elegant Friend Corinthian Tom; Accompanied by Bob Logic, the Oxonian, in their Rambles and Sprees through the Metropolis* (London: Sherwood, Neely & Jones, 1821), pp. 170, 184, 189.
19. Ibid., p. 232.
20. Ibid., p. 181.
21. See Gregory Dart, *Metropolitan Art and Literature, 1810–1840: Cockney Adventures* (Cambridge: Cambridge University Press, 2012), p. 116.
22. Fredric Jameson, *Postmodernism: Or, the Cultural Logic of Late Capitalism* (London: Verso, 1991), p. 17.
23. Dart, *Metropolitan Art and Literature*, pp. 39–40.
24. These and the succeeding quotations are taken from [James Henry]

Leigh Hunt, 'Walks Home by Night in Bad Weather. Watchmen', in *The Companion* (London: Hunt & Clarke, 1828), pp. 40–6.

25. Quoted in Anthony Holden, *The Wit in the Dungeon: A Life of Leigh Hunt* (London: Little, Brown, 2005), p. 205.
26. See Nicholas Roe, *Fiery Heart: The First Life of Leigh Hunt* (London: Pimlico, 2005), p. 305.
27. Percy Bysshe Shelley, 'The Devil's Walk: A Ballad', ll. 97–9, in *Poetical Works*, ed. Thomas Hutchinson (Oxford: Oxford University Press, 1971), p. 879.
28. Quoted in Philip John Stead, 'The New Police', in David H. Bayley, ed., *Police and Society* (London: Sage, 1977), p. 73.
29. Quoted in ibid.
30. See White, *London in the Nineteenth Century*, pp. 389–92.
31. For this petition, see the 'Rolls Governors' Minutes' transcribed on behalf of the International Centre for the History of Crime, Policing and Justice, the Open University, at open.ac.uk.
32. See Clive Emsley, *The English Police: A Political and Social History*, 2nd edn (London: Longman, 1996), p. 20.
33. See White, *London in the Nineteenth Century*, pp. 385–6.
34. 10 Geo.4, C. 44.
35. 2 & 3 Vict C. 47.
36. See Wolfgang Schivelbusch, *Disenchanted Night: The Industrialization of Light in the Nineteenth Century*, trans. Angela Davies (Berkeley: University of California Press, 1988), p. 31.
37. See Anonymous, 'Account of the First Experiment of the Public Use of Gas Lights', *Monthly Magazine* 23 (July 1807), p. 520; and 'Varieties, Literary and Philosophical', *Monthly Magazine* 24 (January 1808), p. 581.
38. See Leslie Tomory, *Progressive Enlightenment: The Origins of the Gaslight Industry, 1780–1820* (Cambridge, MA: MIT Press, 2012), p. 239.
39. See A. Roger Ekirch, *At Day's Close: A History of Nighttime* (London: Weidenfeld & Nicolson, 2005), p. 331.
40. Schivelbusch, *Disenchanted Night*, pp. 40–4.
41. John Keats, 'The Cap and Bells; or, The Jealousies', ll. 208–16, in *The Complete Poems*, 3rd edn, ed. John Barnard (London: Penguin, 1988), p. 466.
42. Nicholas Roe, *John Keats: A New Life* (New Haven, CT: Yale University Press, 2012), p. 324.
43. John Keats, 'Ode to a Nightingale', ll. 41–5, 56, in *Complete Poems*, p. 347.
44. Quoted by Anthony Vidler, 'Dark Space', in *The Architectural Uncanny:*

Essays in the Modern Unhomely (Cambridge, MA: MIT Press, 1992), p. 175.

45. Michael Löwy, 'The Current of Critical Irrealism', in Matthew Beaumont, ed., *Adventures in Realism* (Oxford: Blackwell, 2007), p. 198.
46. Quoted in Roe, *John Keats*, p. 200.
47. Ibid., p. xx.
48. Novalis, *Christianity or Europe: A Fragment*, in Frederick C. Beiser, ed., *The Early Political Writings of the German Romantics* (Cambridge: Cambridge University Press, 1996), p. 70; and *Hymns to Night*, trans. James Thomson, in Simon Reynolds, ed., *Novalis and the Poets of Pessimism* (Norwich: Michael Russell, 1995), p. 33.
49. Lynda Nead, *Victorian Babylon: People, Streets and Images in Nineteenth-Century London* (New Haven, CT: Yale University Press, 2000), p. 103.
50. A. Alvarez, *Night: An Exploration of Night Life, Night Language, Sleep and Dreams* (London: Vintage, 1996), p. 194.
51. Michel Foucault, 'The Eye of Power', in *Power/Knowledge: Selected Interviews and Other Writings, 1972–1977*, ed. Colin Gordon (New York: Pantheon, 1980), pp. 153–4.

Chapter 12: The Dead Night

1. Charles Dickens, *Great Expectations*, ed. Charlotte Mitchell (London: Penguin, 1996), p. 359.
2. Ibid., pp. 365, 367.
3. Charles Dickens, 'The Streets – Night', in *Dickens' Journalism: Sketches by Boz and Other Early Papers, 1833–39*, ed. Michael Slater (London: Phoenix, 1996), p. 54.
4. Lynda Nead, *Victorian Babylon: People, Streets and Images in Nineteenth-Century London* (New Haven, CT: Yale University Press, 2000), p. 103.
5. George Augustus Sala, *Gaslight and Daylight, with Some London Scenes They Shine Upon* (London: Chapman & Hall, 1859), p. 159. For an excellent discussion of Sala and what Nead calls the poetics of gas, see Nead, *Victorian Babylon*, pp. 101–8.
6. 'He was making clear to his wife – and inevitably to the rest of the household – that he was rejecting the proximity of her body in the marriage bed.' See Claire Tomalin, *Charles Dickens: A Life* (London: Viking, 2011), p. 292.
7. Charles Dickens, *The Pilgrim Edition of the Letters of Charles Dickens*, vol. 7, ed. Graham Storey, Kathleen Tillotson and Angus Easson (Oxford: Clarendon Press, 1993), p. 545.

8. Tomalin, *Charles Dickens*, p. 45.
9. Edgar Johnson, *Charles Dickens: His Tragedy and Triumph*, rev. and abridged edn (London: Penguin, 1986), p. 517.
10. Charles Dickens, 'Shy Neighbourhoods', in *Selected Journalism, 1850–1870*, ed. David Pasco (London: Penguin, 1997), p. 204.
11. Tomalin, *Charles Dickens*, pp. 291, 464n.
12. G. K. Chesterton, *Charles Dickens* (Ware: Wordsworth, 2007), p. 16.
13. John Hollingshead, *My Lifetime* (London: Sampson Low, Marston, 1895), vol. 1, pp. 101–2.
14. Dickens, *Letters of Charles Dickens*, vol. 7, p. 429.
15. Charles Dickens, *The Pilgrim Edition of the Letters of Charles Dickens*, vol. 8, ed. Graham Storey and Kathleen Tillotson (Oxford: Clarendon Press, 1995), p. 489.
16. Shakespeare, *Complete Works*, I. ii. 198.
17. Dickens, 'Shy Neighbourhoods', p. 204.
18. Thomas De Quincey, *Suspiria de Profundis*, in *Confessions of an English Opium-Eater and Other Writings*, ed. Grevel Lindop (Oxford: Oxford University Press, 1985), p. 156.
19. Dickens, 'Shy Neighbourhoods', p. 204.
20. Ian Hacking, *Mad Travelers: Reflections on the Reality of Transient Mental Illnesses* (Cambridge, MA: Harvard University Press, 1998), p. 62.
21. Charles Dickens, 'Gone Astray', in *Selected Journalism*, pp. 35, 44.
22. Chesterton, *Charles Dickens*, pp. 23–4.
23. See Joachim Schlör, *Nights in the Big City: Paris, Berlin, London, 1840–1930* (London: Reaktion, 1998), pp. 55–6.
24. Fred Kaplan, *Dickens: A Biography* (Baltimore, MD: Johns Hopkins, 1998), pp. 112–13.
25. John Forster, *The Life of Charles Dickens*, vol. 1, 5th edn (London: Chapman & Hall, 1872), pp. 50, 33.
26. Charles Dickens, *The Pilgrim Edition of the Letters of Charles Dickens*, vol. 4, ed. Kathleen Tillotson (Oxford: Clarendon Press, 1977), p. 2.
27. Ibid., pp. 199–200.
28. Ibid., pp. 612–13.
29. Ibid., p. 627.
30. Ibid., p. 622.
31. Forster, *The Life of Charles Dickens*, vol. 2, p. 289.
32. Peter Ackroyd, *Dickens* (London: Minerva, 1991), p. 548.
33. Charles Dickens, *Bleak House*, ed. Stephen Gill (Oxford: Oxford University Press, 1998), p. 752.
34. Emmanuel Levinas, *Existence and Existents*, trans. Alphonso Lingis (Pittsburgh, PA: Duquesne University Press, 2001), pp. 64, 62.

35. Charles Dickens, 'Lying Awake', *Selected Journalism*, p. 25.
36. Ibid., pp. 25–6.
37. Ibid., pp. 26, 27.
38. Ibid., p. 27.
39. Ibid., p. 28.
40. Ibid., p. 29.
41. For the references in these paragraphs, see Charles Dickens, 'Night Walks', in *On London* (London: Hesperus, 2010), p. 71.
42. Rachel Bowlby, 'Commuting', in *Restless Cities*, ed. Matthew Beaumont and Gregory Dart (London: Verso, 2010), pp. 47, 45.
43. Dickens, 'Night Walks', pp. 71, 72.
44. Ibid., pp. 71–3, 80.
45. Ibid., p. 77.
46. Ibid., p. 75.
47. Ibid., p. 71.
48. George Augustus Sala, *Twice Round the Clock; or, The Hours of the Day and Night in London* (London: J. & R. Maxwell, 1859), p. 318.
49. Sala, *Gaslight and Daylight*, p. 1.
50. Charles Dickens, 'On Duty with Inspector Field', in *Selected Journalism*, p. 309.
51. Charles Dickens, 'A Sleep to Startle Us', in *Selected Journalism*, pp. 328, 332.
52. Charles Dickens, 'A Nightly Scene in London', in *Selected Journalism*, pp. 361, 365.
53. Forster, *Life of Charles Dickens*, vol. 1, pp. 35–7.
54. Charles Dickens, *Little Dorrit*, ed. Harvey Peter Sucksmith (Oxford: Oxford University Press, 1982), pp. 146–7.
55. Ibid., p. 147.
56. Ibid., p. 148.
57. J. Ewing Ritchie, *The Night Side of London*, rev. edn (London: William Tweedie, 1858), pp. 65–6.
58. Dickens, *Little Dorrit*, p. 150.
59. Schlör, *Nights in the Big City*, pp. 51–2.
60. Dickens, 'Night Walks', pp. 72, 78.
61. Ibid., pp. 77–8. The reference to the New Testament is to Mark 14: 51–2.
62. Shakespeare, *Complete Works*, III. iv. 105–6.
63. See Leo Rauch, *Hegel and the Human Spirit: A Translation of the Jena Lectures on the Philosophy of Spirit (1805–6) with Commentary* (Detroit: Wayne State University Press, 1983), p. 87. See also Elizabeth Bronfen, *Night Passages: Philosophy, Literature, Film*, trans. Elizabeth Bronfen, with David Brenner (New York: Columbia University Press, 2013), p. 69.

64. Shakespeare, *Complete Works*, III. iv. 28, 30–2.
65. See Slavoj Žižek, *Less than Nothing: Hegel and the Shadow of Dialectical Materialism* (London: Verso, 2012), p. 166.
66. Fyodor Dostoevsky, *Winter Notes on Summer Impressions*, trans. David Patterson (Evanston, IL: Northwestern University Press, 1997), p. 39.
67. Lieut. John Blackmore, *The London by Moonlight Mission: Being an Account of Midnight Cruises on the Streets of London during the Last Thirteen Years* (London: Robson and Avery, 1860), p. 94. On the 'midnight missions' of the mid nineteenth century, see Schlör, *Nights in the Big City*, pp. 217–24.
68. Jacques Lacan, 'The Mirror Stage as Formative of the I as Revealed in Psychoanalytic Experience', in *Écrits: A Selection*, trans. Alan Sheridan (London: Routledge, 1977), p. 7.
69. Charles Dickens, 'On an Amateur Beat', in *Selected Journalism*, pp. 386–7.

Chapter 13: A Darkened Walk

1. Charles Dickens, 'Night Walks', in *On London* (London: Hesperus, 2010), pp. 71, 80.
2. In the previous chapter, Eliot informs the reader that Tito Melema, the novel's villain, 'came as a wanderer to Florence' in 1492. George Eliot, *Romola*, ed. Andrew Brown (Oxford: Oxford University Press, 1998), pp. 202–3, 198.
3. Walter Benjamin, *Charles Baudelaire: A Lyric Poet in the Era of High Capitalism*, trans. Harry Zohn (London: Verso, 1983), p. 54.
4. Adam Smith, *An Inquiry into the Nature and Causes of the Wealth of Nations*, ed. Edwin Cannan (Chicago: Chicago University Press, 1976), pp. 12–13.
5. Cited in Norman Feltes, 'To Saunter, to Hurry: Dickens, Time, and Industrial Capitalism', *Victorian Studies* 20 (1977), pp. 251–2. I have relied extensively on pp. 150–2 of Feltes's excellent article in this paragraph, though it should be pointed out that he is interested in time-discipline as opposed to walking per se.
6. Theodor W. Adorno, 'Trying to Understand *Endgame*', in *Notes to Literature*, vol. 2, ed. Rolf Tiedemann, trans. Shierry Weber Nicholsen (New York: Columbia University Press, 1991), p. 255.
7. Quoted in Joseph A. Amato, *On Foot: A History of Walking* (New York: New York University Press, 2004), p. 1.
8. See E. P. Thompson, 'Time, Work-Discipline and Industrial Capitalism', *Past and Present* 38 (1967), pp. 56–97.

9. Charles Dickens, 'The Street – Morning', in *Dickens's Journalism: Sketches by Boz and Other Early Papers 1833–39*, ed. Michael Slater (London: Phoenix, 1996), p. 54.
10. Quoted in Michael Slater, 'Introduction', in Dickens, *Dickens's Journalism*, p. xvi. These sentences were subsequently omitted from collected editions of the *Sketches*.
11. Karl Marx, *Capital: A Critique of Political Economy, Volume One*, trans. Ben Fowkes (London: Penguin/New Left Review, 1976), p. 486.
12. Charles Dickens, 'Shy Neighbourhoods', in *The Uncommercial Traveller and Reprinted Pieces*, ed. Leslie C. Staples (Oxford: Oxford University Press, 1958), p. 95.
13. Charles Dickens, *A Tale of Two Cities*, ed. Andrew Sanders (Oxford: Oxford University Press, 1998), p. 21.
14. Charles Dickens, *The Old Curiosity Shop*, ed. Elizabeth M. Brennan (Oxford: Oxford University Press, 1998), pp. 5, 33.
15. Dickens, *Old Curiosity Shop*, pp. 119, 120, 122.
16. Peter Ackroyd, *Dickens* (London: Minerva, 1991), p. 335.
17. John Forster, *The Life of Charles Dickens*, vol. 1, 5th edn (London: Chapman & Hall, 1872), pp. 184–5.
18. For example, Michael Hollington does not mention him in his discussion of *The Old Curiosity Shop* in *Dickens and the Grotesque* (Croom Helm: Harvester Press, 1984), pp. 79–95.
19. John Bowen, *Other Dickens: Pickwick to Chuzzlewit* (Oxford: Oxford University Press, 2000), p. 141.
20. James Joyce, *Finnegans Wake*, ed. Seamus Deane (London: Penguin, 2000), p. 434.
21. Dickens, *Old Curiosity Shop*, p. 9.
22. Alfred Tennyson, 'Maud', ll. 249–50, in *Tennyson: A Selected Edition*, ed. Christopher Ricks (London: Longman, 1989), p. 575.
23. Charles Dickens, *Master Humphrey's Clock*, ed. Derek Hudson (Oxford: Oxford University Press, 1958), p. 5.
24. Charles Baudelaire, 'The Painter of Modern Life', in *The Painter of Modern Life and Other Essays*, trans. Jonathan Mayne (London: Phaidon Press, 1995), p. 7. See also Matthew Beaumont, 'Convalescing', in Matthew Beaumont and Gregory Dart, eds, *Restless Cities* (London: Verso, 2010), pp. 59–77.
25. Dickens, *Master Humphrey's Clock*, pp. 9–10.
26. Baudelaire, 'The Painter of Modern Life', p. 9.
27. Dickens, *Master Humphrey's Clock*, pp. 6–7.
28. Charles Dickens, *The Mystery of Edwin Drood*, ed. Arthur J. Cox (London: Penguin, 1985), p. 213.

29. Joachim Schlör, *Nights in the Big City: Paris, Berlin, London, 1840–1930* (London: Reaktion, 1998), p. 273.
30. Dickens, *Old Curiosity Shop*, p. 7.
31. Ibid., pp. 7–8.
32. Ibid., p. 9.
33. Catherine Robson, *Men in Wonderland: The Lost Girlhood of the Victorian Gentleman* (Princeton, NJ: Princeton University Press, 2001), p. 87.
34. Judith R. Walkowitz, *City of Dreadful Delight: Narratives of Sexual Danger in Late-Victorian London* (Chicago, IL: Chicago University Press, 1992), p. 22.
35. Fyodor Dostoevsky, *Winter Notes on Summer Impressions*, trans. David Patterson (Evanston, IL: Northwestern University Press, 1997), p. 40.
36. See Elizabeth M. Brennan, 'Introduction', in Dickens, *Old Curiosity Shop*, p. xxviii.
37. Henry Mayhew, *London Labour and the London Poor*, ed. Victor Neuberg (London: Penguin, 1985), p. 475.
38. Dickens, 'The Prisoner's Van', in *Dickens's Journalism*, p. 272.
39. Dickens, *Old Curiosity Shop*, p. 10.
40. Charles Dickens, *The Pilgrim Edition of the Letters of Charles Dickens*, vol. 8, ed. Graham Storey and Kathleen Tillotson (Oxford: Clarendon Press, 1995), p. 96.
41. Walter Benjamin, 'The Paris of the Second Empire in Baudelaire', in Michael W. Jennings, ed., *The Writer of Modern Life: Essays on Charles Baudelaire* (Cambridge, MA: Harvard University Press, 2006), p. 77.
42. Charles Dickens, ed., *The Pilgrim Edition of the Letters of Charles Dickens*, vol. 2, Madeline House and Graham Storey (Oxford: Oxford University Press, 1969), p. 4.
43. Charles Dickens, *Oliver Twist*, ed. Stephen Gill and Kathleen Tillotson (Oxford: Oxford University Press, 1999), pp. 3, 54–5.
44. Ibid., p. 388.
45. Charles Dickens, *Barnaby Rudge*, ed. Clive Hurst (Oxford: Oxford University Press, 2003), pp. 134–5, 143.
46. Ibid., pp. 293, 134, 526.
47. Ibid., p. 136.
48. Ibid., pp. 137–8, 141.
49. Ibid., p. 149.
50. Ibid., p. 150.
51. Charles Dickens, *The Pilgrim Edition of the Letters of Charles Dickens*, vol. 9, ed. Graham Storey (Oxford: Clarendon Press, 1997), p. 177.
52. Dickens, *A Tale of Two Cities*, pp. 179, xxvii.
53. Ibid., pp. 384, 386, 387.

54. Ibid., pp. 387–9, 464.
55. Quoted in Craig Koslofsky, *Evening's Empire: A History of the Night in Early Modern Europe* (Cambridge: Cambridge University Press, 2011), p. 84.
56. Benjamin, *Charles Baudelaire*, p. 55.
57. Dickens, 'Night Walks', pp. 76, 80.
58. Jeremy Tambling, *Going Astray: Dickens and London* (London: Longman, 2009), p. 232.
59. Charles Dickens, 'The Heart of London', in *On London*, pp. 5–6.
60. Dickens, *Great Expectations*, p. 185
61. George Augustus Sala, *Twice Round the Clock; or, The Hours of the Day and Night in London* (London: J. & R. Maxwell, 1859), p. 373.
62. Dickens, *Barnaby Rudge*, p. 613.
63. Ibid., pp. 613, 615.
64. Thomas De Quincey, *Confessions of an English Opium-Eater and Other Writings*, ed. Grevel Lindop (Oxford: Oxford University Press, 1985), p. 71.
65. Walter Benjamin, 'A Berlin Chronicle', in *One-Way Street and Other Writings*, trans. Edmund Jephcott and Kingsley Shorter (London: Verso, 1997), p. 301.
66. Leo Rauch, *Hegel and the Human Spirit: A Translation of the Jena Lectures on the Philosophy of Spirit (1805–6) with Commentary* (Detroit: Wayne State University Press, 1983), p. 87.

Chapter 14: Conclusion

1. Quoted in Peter Ackroyd, *Poe: A Life Cut Short* (London: Chatto & Windus), p. 33.
2. Edgar Allan Poe, 'The Murders in the Rue Morgue', in *Selected Tales*, ed. David Van Leer (Oxford: Oxford University Press, 1998), pp. 95–6.
3. Ibid., p. 96.
4. Ned Lukacher, *Primal Scenes: Literature, Philosophy, Psychoanalysis* (Ithaca, NY: Cornell University Press, 1986), pp. 294–5. Note too that the nocturnal chases conducted by Bradley Headstone and Eugene Wrayburn in *Our Mutual Friend* comprise Dickens's reinscription of 'The Man of the Crowd'.
5. Edgar Allan Poe, 'The Man of the Crowd', in *Selected Tales*, pp. 84–5.
6. Charles Baudelaire, 'The Painter of Modern Life', in *The Painter of Modern Life and Other Essays*, trans. Jonathan Mayne (London: Phaidon, 1995), p. 7. See also Matthew Beaumont, 'Convalescing', in Matthew

Beaumont and Gregory Dart, eds, *Restless Cities* (London: Verso, 2010), pp. 59–77.

7. Friedrich Engels, *The Condition of the Working Class in England* (London: Lawrence & Wishart, 1973), p. 60.
8. Poe, 'Man of the Crowd', pp. 85–7.
9. William Wordsworth, *The Prelude*, VII. 596–7, in *The Prelude: A Parallel Text*, ed. J. C. Maxwell (London: Penguin, 1986), p. 286.
10. Poe, 'Man of the Crowd', pp. 87–8.
11. Charles Baudelaire, *Les Fleurs du Mal*, trans. Richard Howard (London: Picador, 1987), p. 277.
12. Poe, 'Man of the Crowd', p. 88.
13. Lynda Nead, *Victorian Babylon: People, Streets and Images in Nineteenth-Century London* (New Haven, CT: Yale University Press, 2000), p. 103.
14. Poe, 'Man of the Crowd', pp. 87–8.
15. Benjamin, 'The Paris of the Second Empire in Baudelaire', p. 132.
16. Poe, 'Man of the Crowd', p. 88.
17. Ibid., pp. 89–90.
18. Ibid., p. 90.
19. Ibid., pp. 90–1.
20. For this formulation, see Charles Dickens, 'On an Amateur Beat', in *Selected Journalism, 1850–1870*, ed. David Pasco (London: Penguin, 1997), pp. 386–7.
21. Poe, 'Man of the Crowd', p. 91.
22. Walter Benjamin, 'On Some Motifs in Baudelaire', in *The Writer of Modern Life: Essays on Charles Baudelaire*, ed. Michael W. Jennings (Cambridge, MA: Harvard University Press, 2006), p. 188.
23. William Chapman Sharpe, *New York Nocturne: The City after Dark in Literature, Painting, and Photography, 1850–1950* (Princeton, NY: Princeton University Press, 2008), p. 72.

Index